MAKERS OF MODERN INDIA

MAKERS OF MODERN INDIA

EDITED BY

RAMACHANDRA GUHA

THE BELKNAP PRESS OF HARVARD UNIVERSITY PRESS

Cambridge, Massachusetts   London, England

2011

LIBRARY OF CONGRESS CATALOGING-IN-PUBLICATION DATA

Makers of modern India / edited by Ramachandra Guha.

p.   cm.

Includes bibliographical references and index.

ISBN 978-0-674-05246-8 (alk. paper)

1. India—Politics and government—18th century—Sources.

2. India—Politics and government—19th century—Sources.

3. India—Politics and government—20th century—Sources.

4. Political culture—India—History—18th century—Sources.

5. Political culture—India—History—19th century—Sources.

6. Political culture—India—History—20th century—Sources.

7. Politicians—India—Biography.   I. Guha, Ramachandra.

DS446.3.M36   2011

954.009'9—dc22   2010034625

To the selfless tribe of librarians and archivists—
and in particular for Dr. N. Balakrishnan of the
Nehru Memorial Museum and Library

CONTENTS

PROLOGUE

Thinking through India

I

THE STRIKING THING ABOUT MODERN INDIA is that the men and women who made its history also wrote most authoritatively about it. The country's leading politicians were its leading political thinkers. This is especially true of the trinity of Mohandas K. Gandhi, Jawaharlal Nehru, and B. R. Ambedkar. Gandhi was the father of Indian nationalism who, between the 1920s and 1940s, forged a popular countrywide movement against British colonial rule. Nehru was the architect of the modern Indian nation-state, serving as prime minister from the nation's birth in August 1947 until his death in May 1964. Ambedkar was the great leader of the country's oppressed castes who also oversaw, as the country's first law minister, the drafting of the Indian constitution, which came into effect on 26 January 1950. But even as they fought and struggled, led and governed, Gandhi, Nehru, and Ambedkar wrote at great length about the world they saw and shaped.

Gandhi's *Collected Works,* published by the Government of India between 1958 and 1994, run to more than ninety volumes. More than fifty volumes of Nehru's *Selected Works* have so far been published by a trust created in his name. In the 1980s the government of Ambedkar's home state, Maharashtra, published sixteen volumes of his writings, some of them exceeding a thousand pages. Although many of the entries in these collected or selected works are routine letters or speeches, others represent extended essays on subjects such as national identity, democracy, religious culture, and social justice. Indians in general (and Indian writers in particular) tend to be verbose, but in these instances at least quantity has not necessarily been at odds with quality.

This combination of political activism and theoretical reflection was not peculiar to these three men. Other Indian politicians and reformers were also serious writers, articulating, in their own more restricted spheres, ideas that had a powerful resonance in their own day and continue to do so in ours.

Modern India is unusual in having had so many politicians who were also original political thinkers. However, it is not unique. In the making of some other nations, activists and campaigners have likewise doubled up as authors and polemicists. The first generation of American nationalists—Madison, Hamilton, Jefferson, and Franklin—were certainly men of action and of thought. This was also true of José Martí of Cuba, Leopold Senghor of Senegal, and Kwame Nkrumah of Ghana, who participated in movements to free their countries from foreign rule while writing important works of propaganda and/or scholarship.

Nations tend to produce thinker-activists at their birth and in moments of crisis. When, in the middle decades of the last century, England and France found their national sovereignty threatened by Nazi Germany, the patriots who led the resistance also wrote most evocatively about it. The books written by Winston Churchill before and after World War II were to win him the Nobel Prize for Literature. Likewise, Charles de Gaulle produced a series of stirring works in the 1940s and 1950s that defined anew the meanings of France and of being French.

A third conjuncture that produces the politician-as-writer is a revolutionary change in the system of government. Paradigmatic here are Lenin and Mao, the acknowledged leaders of the Russian and Chinese revolutions, respectively. Pre-eminently men of action, both also wrote influential works of political and economic analysis. Their essays and books were required reading in their own homelands, while they also attracted considerable attention in other countries.

This wider history notwithstanding, I believe India still constitutes a special case. Its distinctiveness is threefold. First, the tradition of the thinker-activist persisted far longer in India than elsewhere. Although the men who founded the United States in the late eighteenth century had fascinating ideas about democracy and nationhood, thereafter American politicians have merely governed and ruled, or sometimes misgoverned and misruled.[1] Their ideas, such as these have been put forth, have come from professional ideologues or intellectuals. On the other hand, from the first decades of the nineteenth century until the last decades of the twentieth century, the most influential political thinkers in India were, as often as not, its most influential political actors. Long before India was conceived of as a nation, in the extended run-up to Indian independence, and in the first few decades of freedom, the most interesting reflections on society and politics were offered by men (and women) who were in the thick of political action.

This tradition of the thinker-activist has been more enduring in India than elsewhere. The relevance of individual thinkers has lasted longer as well. For instance, Lenin's ideas were influential for about seventy years, that is to say, from the time the Soviet state was founded to the time it disappeared. Mao's heyday was even shorter—roughly three decades, from the victory of the Chinese Revolution in 1949 to the repudiation by Deng Xiaoping of his mentor's ideas in the late 1970s. When we turn to politicians in Western Europe, Churchill's impassioned defense of the British Empire would find no takers after the 1950s. De Gaulle was famous for his invocation of 'grandeur de la France', but those sentiments have now been (fortunately?) diluted and domesticated by the consolidation of the European Union. On the other hand, as this book will demonstrate, Indian thinkers of the nineteenth and early twentieth centuries still speak in many ways to the concerns of the present.

---

1. One should perhaps make a distinction here between the 'thinking politician' and the 'thinker-politician'. Of the leaders who came after the Founders, at least four American presidents have reflected deeply on questions of political and social reform—and then sought to act on their reflections. These are Abraham Lincoln, Woodrow Wilson, Franklin Delano Roosevelt, and, most recently, Barack Obama. However, the first three did not leave behind a body of writing that has stood the test of time. The jury is still out on Obama: on the evidence of his two memoirs, he might yet, once he leaves office as president, give us an original and insightful work on how democracy functions—or malfunctions.

A third difference has to do with the greater diversity of thinkers within the Indian political tradition. Even Gandhi and Nehru never held the kind of canonical status within their country as Mao or Lenin did in theirs. At any given moment, there were as many Indians who were opposed to their ideas as were guided by them. Moreover, the range of issues debated and acted upon by politicians and social reformers appears to have been far greater in India than in other countries. This depth and diversity of thought were, as I argue below, in good part the products of the depth and diversity of the society itself.

II

I have long believed India to be the most interesting country in the world. This is the impartial judgement of a historian, not the partisan claim of a citizen. India may also be the most exasperating and the most hierarchical as well as the most degrading country in the world. But whatever qualifier or adjective one uses or prefers, it remains the most interesting, too. For one thing, India is very large and contains one-sixth of humankind. For another, its territory is astonishingly diverse, with its peoples differentiated by religion, language, caste, and ethnicity, as well as by ecology, technology, dress, and cuisine.

Beyond the size and the diversity, what truly makes India interesting is that it is simultaneously undergoing five dramatic transformations. The Indian economy was once very largely based on agriculture; now, it increasingly depends upon industry and services. An overwhelming majority of Indians once lived in the villages; now, hundreds of millions of Indians live in cities and towns. India was once a territory ruled over by Europeans; now, it is an independent nation-state. The political culture of India was once feudal and deferential; now, it is combative and participatory. The social system of India was once governed by community and patriarchy; now, it has had increasingly to make space for the assertion of individual rights as well as the rights of previously subordinated groups such as women and members of the lower castes.

As stated above, there were, and are, five revolutions simultaneously occurring in India: the urban revolution, the industrial revolution, the national revolution, the democratic revolution, and the social revolution. The key word here is *simultaneously*. In Europe and North America these revolutions were staggered. Thus, the United States proclaimed its national independence in the eighteenth century; urbanized and industrialized in the nineteenth century; and became fully democratic in the twentieth century, after both freed African Americans and women were granted the vote. In Europe, which was a continent broken up into many different nationalities, the pace of these different revolutions varied greatly across countries. Crucially, in every country the national revolution preceded the democratic revolution by several decades or more. That is to say, the residents of a certain, circumscribed territory came together under a single flag and single currency well before they were allowed to choose the leaders who would govern them.

India has three times as many people as the United States. It has as many major languages as Europe, with this significant difference—each of these languages has its own, distinctive script. It has far greater religious diversity than either the United States or Europe. And it became a democracy at the same time as it became a nation, this in contrast to the countries of Western Europe and North America, where nationhood came long before democracy; and in contrast also to its great Asian neighbour, China, where nationhood has been sustained only by the repressive regime of a one-party state. In any event, the industrial and national revolutions would have produced major conflicts and upheavals—as they have elsewhere in the world. Notably, in India these conflicts have been articulated on the one hand through armed insurgencies or secessionist movements, and on the other hand through street protests, legal challenges, press campaigns, and parliamentary debates: that is to say, through the processes of political mobilization and rhetorical expression that a democracy permits and even encourages.

The size of India's territory, plus the diversity of its people, plus the simultaneity of these five great revolutions—these, taken together, are what make India the most interesting country in the world.

The individuals featured in *Makers of Modern India* lived through these revolutions, struggled to facilitate or reshape them, and—the aspect of their careers that is of most interest to us here—wrote about the impact of these events on themselves and their compatriots. Their writings probed deeply into each of these five revolutions. They explored, for example, how to harmonize the interests of city and countryside in the transformation of the national economy; how to promote national unity amidst religious diversity and discord; how to advance the rights of women and people of low castes; how to reconcile the sometimes competing claims of individual freedom and social equality. The orientation of some of these thinker-activists was outward as well as inward; in seeking to unite their country and to make it more democratic, they also looked at the most productive ways in which India could engage with other nations in an increasingly inter-connected world.

The men and women featured in this book did not speak in one voice. Their perspectives were sometimes complementary and more often competitive. But they were always instructive. Their writings were (and are) not merely of academic interest; rather, they had a defining impact on the formation and evolution of the Indian Republic. The essays and speeches excerpted here take us from the sub-continent's first (and unasked for) engagement with modernity through the successive phases of the Indian freedom struggle, on through the now six-decades-old career of the world's largest democracy. Through them, we can track the course of two centuries of Indian history, as seen and interpreted by the men and women who themselves helped to shape and define these most interesting times in the world's most interesting country.

III

This book features the writings of nineteen individuals in all. It begins with Rammohan Roy, who was perhaps the first Indian thinker to seriously engage with the challenge of the West. Born in Bengal, the first province to come under British rule, Roy saw in the presence of the foreigner an invitation to re-examine the pre-suppositions of his own society. On the one hand, he sought to reform his native faith of its ugly and exploitative aspects; on the other, he demanded of the white-dominated East India Company those democratic rights that were granted at home yet denied in the colonies. In both respects, Roy set the tone for the reformers and activists who were to follow.

From Roy we move on to a quintet of thinkers active in the last part of the nineteenth century and the first part of the twentieth. In 1857 there was a major uprising against colonial rule, led by disaffected soldiers who drew many peasants and preachers into their fold. After suppressing the revolt, the British Crown assumed direct responsibility for the Government of India from the East India Company. In 1885, as the new regime was consolidating itself, a group of city-based and well-educated colonial subjects came together to found the Indian National Congress.

In mediating between the rulers and the ruled, the Congress sought (in Mukul Kesavan's felicitous phrase) to serve as a 'Noah's Ark of nationalism'.[2] As its name implied, the party made room for all kinds of Indians, regardless of language, religion, region, race, or gender. In this effort it was substantially but not entirely successful. Although many intelligent and ambitious Indians joined its ranks, others stayed away, claiming that the Congress represented a sectional, elite interest that was inimical to other (and often less advantaged) kinds of Indians.

Of the five thinkers profiled in Part II of the book, two were long-standing members of the Congress, whereas two others were opposed to it. (The fifth was agnostic.) All, however, articulated original and distinctive arguments on how India might best obtain its freedom from colonial rule, or on how it might most effectively deal with the divisions and schisms within.

Part III of the book is oriented around the debates inspired by the life and work of Mahatma Gandhi. In 1915 Gandhi returned to British India after two decades in South Africa. By 1920 or thereabouts he had become the acknowledged leader of the Indian National Congress. In subsequent decades he organized three major campaigns against colonial rule, initiated various social reform measures, and wrote ceaselessly on the problems and prospects of the nation-in-the-making.

Even in his lifetime, Gandhi was hailed as the Father of the Nation; but he was equally the mother of all battles concerning its future. No modern politician was as ready to be criticized as Gandhi. His daily activities were open to public scrutiny, while his campaigns were always intimated in advance to his adversaries. Nor were the latter always (or even principally) British. Among the Indian critics of Gandhi were

2. See Mukul Kesavan, *Secular Common Sense* (New Delhi: Penguin India, 2001), p. 31 and passim.

colleagues who worked alongside him but could not follow him in all respects, as well as rivals who set themselves up in political opposition to him.

All his life, Gandhi engaged in argument with friends and rivals. These debates are presented here, in Gandhi's words and those of his principal interlocutors. Of the five other 'Makers' included in Part III, two were critical admirers of Gandhi; the three others, hostile adversaries.

Part IV is oriented around the statecraft of Jawaharlal Nehru, who, as prime minister for the first, formative years of Independence, had an influence on modern India that was arguably as great as Gandhi's. In 1957 a Canadian scholar and diplomat wrote of Nehru that 'there is no one since Napoleon who has played both so large a role in the history of his country and has also held the sort of place which Nehru holds in the hearts and minds of his countrymen. For the people of India, he is George Washington, Lincoln, Roosevelt and Eisenhower rolled into one'.[3]

No modern statesman, not even Winston Churchill, was as much of a thinking politician as Nehru. Like Churchill, Nehru had a deep interest in history; unlike him, he also had an interest in political ideas and ideologies (and hence also a special fondness for intellectuals). In 1958 the British writer E. M. Forster imagined Voltaire being reborn and composing a letter on the fate of humankind. However, the philosopher did not know whom to address, since there was now 'not a single crowned head who would wish to receive a letter from him'. Forster, and Voltaire, scanned the world to see only amiable but poorly read monarchs (such as Queen Elizabeth II who was 'so charming, so estimable, but no philosopher'; so unlike Frederick of Prussia or even Catherine of Russia, 'both Greats'). The rulers in uniform were as philistine as those who sat on thrones; Voltaire could scarcely bring himself to write to living Generals such as Ayub Khan of Pakistan or Tito of Yugoslavia. Forster, speaking through Voltaire, quickly reached the conclusion that 'only one head of a state would welcome a letter from him, and that was President [sic] Nehru of India. With an exclamation of delight he took up his pen'.[4]

---

3. Escott Reid, *Envoy to Nehru* (Delhi: Oxford University Press, 1981), p. 227.

4. 'Fog over Ferney' (1958), reproduced in E. M. Forster, *The Prince's Tale and Other Uncollected Writings,* ed. P. N. Furbank (London: Penguin Books, 1999), pp. 149–154.

Like Gandhi, Nehru's ideas were controversial, not least among his countrymen. Of the five other 'Makers' featured in Part IV, one was a lifelong opponent of the prime minister. A second was an admirer. The remaining were sometime colleagues and friends. Before Independence, as fellow congressmen they had been incarcerated in the same jails and for the same cause; now, with freedom finally won, they parted ways on how best to serve the interests of the Indian people.

Of these three friends-turned-rivals of Nehru and the Congress, one was the main ideologue of the socialist Left; a second the founder of the party of the libertarian or free-market Right. The third critic chose to reject the party system altogether, offering instead a model of grass-roots democracy based on village councils. Like Nehru, all were *thinker*-politicians, with the sophistication of their arguments and the depth of their beliefs manifest in their writings.

The last part of the book, like the first, foregrounds one individual alone. Unlike Rammohan Roy, however, he is quite obscure, his name wholly unknown outside India and unrecognizable even to most educated Indians. But, as I hope the excerpts chosen from his work shall show, as the 'last modernist' of Indian politics he remains a figure of much interest and relevance.

IV

Why were these nineteen thinkers chosen?[5] And who or what got left out?

One important strand that is not represented here is Marxism. In 1920 a few radical exiles in Moscow proclaimed the formation of a Communist Party of India (CPI), although the party actually started operating

---

As prime minister, Nehru was actually head of government rather than head of state, the latter being the president of the Indian Republic.

5. The nineteen are Rammohan Roy (Part I); Syed Ahmad Khan, Jotirao Phule, G. K. Gokhale, Bal Gangadhar Tilak, and Tarabai Shinde (Part II); M. K. Gandhi, Rabindranath Tagore, B. R. Ambedkar, Muhammad Ali Jinnah, E. V. Ramaswamy, and Kamaladevi Chattopadhyay (Part III); B. R. Ambedkar, Jawaharlal Nehru, M. S. Golwalkar, Rammanohar Lohia, Jayaprakash Narayan, C. Rajagopalachari, and Verrier Elwin (Part IV); and Hamid Dalwai (Part V).

in India only in 1925. Ever since, Marxism in one form or another has had a substantial presence in Indian politics. Through the inter-war years, Communists were among the sharpest critics of the Indian National Congress. The achievement of political Independence in August 1947 was dismissed by them as a sham, a mere transfer of power between elites, with a brown comprador bourgeoisie said to have replaced a white metropolitan bourgeoisie as the ruling class of India.

In February 1948 the CPI launched an armed insurrection against the infant Indian state. It took the better part of three years for the insurrection to be contained. Finally, and in part because of the influence of the Soviet dictator Joseph Stalin (then keen for the Soviet Union to befriend former Western colonies such as India), the revolutionaries came overground and swore allegiance to the Indian Constitution.

Through the 1950s the CPI fought (and even occasionally won) elections. Then, in the early 1960s, the party split into two. The breakaway group, called the Communist Party of India (Marxist), wished to cultivate close ties with both Russia and China, whereas the parent body identified with Russia alone. Toward the end of the decade the CPI(M) itself broke up into two distinct entities. While one group stayed (for the moment) within the system, the other sought to overthrow the Indian state by armed struggle. The latter group's model was Maoist China, as indicated in one of their chosen slogans, 'China's Chairman is our Chairman!'

The Indian Maoists are commonly known as 'Naxalites', after the north Bengal village of Naxalbari, where their struggle began. From the late 1960s, they have been active in central and eastern India. In the past decade they have greatly expanded their reach and influence. Attacking police stations, beheading public officials, the Naxalites remain committed to an armed revolution resulting in the eventual capture of state power in New Delhi. Meanwhile, the CPI and the CPI(M) live on in an uneasy compact with bourgeois democracy. Although they participate in elections, and even run provincial governments, in theory they still subscribe to an ideology that promises India an authoritarian political system to be run by a single party, their own.[6]

6. For the history and politics of the Communist movement in India, see, among other works, John H. Kautsky, *Moscow and the Communist Party of India* (New York:

Aside from its not inconsiderable presence in politics, Marxism in its various forms has had a major impact on intellectual life in India. This impact persisted through the last century and promises to continue well into this one. The appeal of Marxism has much to do with the pervasive inequalities in Indian society. Admittedly, there is also a lack of knowledge of, or a wilful shutting of one's eyes to, the horrors and errors of Communist states themselves.

I have not included any Indian Marxists in this book because their work has been mostly derivative. As Anthony Parel has remarked, Indian Marxists 'were and are bent on changing India on Marx's terms; they simply refuse to change Marxism on India's terms'.[7] That is to say, they have hoped to create on the sub-continent's soil a system closely modelled on the Russian or Chinese experience. As a consequence, there have been no novel contributions by Indian thinkers, no expanding or deepening of the ideas of Marx, Engels, Lenin, and Mao.

Despite their formal absence, Marxists and Marxism remain an 'absent presence' in this book. Their work and legacy have powerfully influenced the ideas of many of the thinkers featured here, who have sought, in more democratic and incremental ways, to contain or transcend the divisions within Indian society.

I should also explain a few other omissions. At least two great, iconic leaders of the Indian national movement are not included here. These are Subhas Chandra Bose and Vallabhbhai Patel. In the crucial decades of the 1930s and 1940s, Bose inspired many young men and women to join the opposition to foreign rule. As for Patel, he both built the Congress

---

John Wiley & Sons, 1956); Gene D. Overstreeet and Marshall Windmiller, *Communism in India* (Berkeley: University of California Press, 1959); T. J. Nossiter, *Communism in Kerala: A Study in Political Adaptation* (Delhi: Oxford University Press, 1982); Nossiter, *Marxist State Governments in India: Politics, Economics, and Society* (London: Pinter, 1988); Marcus F. Franda, *Radical Politics in West Bengal* (Cambridge, Mass.: MIT Press, 1971); Sumanta Banerjee, *In the Wake of Naxalbari: A History of the Naxalite Movement in India* (Calcutta: Subarnarekha, 1980); Sudeep Chakravarti, *Red Sun: Travels in Naxalite Country* (New Delhi: Penguin India, 2008).

7. Anthony J. Parel, 'Gandhi and the Emergence of the Modern Indian Political Canon', *The Review of Politics* 70, no. 1 (2008): 62.

party machine before 1947 and secured the unity of the Indian state in the early years of Independence. They were both considerable figures, Patel especially. In each case, the decision to leave them out was taken only because of the paucity of *original* ideas contained in their published work. Both were out-and-out 'doers', whose writings were either insubstantial or merely humdrum.[8]

Like Bose and Patel, Indira Gandhi was also known principally by her actions. As prime minister of India between 1966 and 1977 and again between 1980 and 1984, she had a profound impact on the history of her country. Her legacy remains controversial—whereas some venerate her for her qualities as a war leader and her concern for the poor, others criticize her authoritarian tendencies and her populism. At any rate, the speeches and writings that carried her name were written by her staff. In this (and perhaps other respects) she differed from her father, Jawaharlal Nehru, who was a widely published author before he became prime minister and whose speeches and writings as prime minister were almost always drafted by himself.[9]

Some other individuals not included here were known principally for their writings. These include the revolutionary-turned-spiritualist Aurobindo Ghose and the philosopher-turned-public-figure Sarvepalli Radhakrishnan. Both wrote prodigiously; whereas Radhakrishnan wished to make Hinduism compatible with the modern world, Aurobindo sought to spiritualize literature and politics on the basis of classical Indian ideals and traditions. In their lifetime, both had a considerable following among English-speaking Indians. However, that influence never really extended beyond the middle class; nor did it last much beyond their deaths.[10]

8. Cf. Leonard Gordon, *Brothers against the Raj: A Biography of Sarat and Subhas Chandra Bose* (New York: Columbia University Press, 1990); Rajmohan Gandhi, *Patel: A Life* (Ahmedabad: Navajivan Press, 1991).

9. Katherine Frank, *Indira: A Life of Indira Nehru Gandhi* (London: HarperCollins, 2001); Inder Malhotra, *Indira Gandhi: A Personal and Political Biography* (London: Hodder & Stoughton, 1989).

10. Peter Heehs, *The Lives of Sri Aurobindo* (New York: Columbia University Press, 2008); Sarvepalli Gopal, *Radhakrishnan: A Biography* (New Delhi: Oxford University Press, 1989).

I have also not included spiritualists such as Swami Vivekananda and Dayanand Saraswati, who represented a muscular brand of Hinduism that sought to meet the challenge of the West by breaking down caste barriers and consolidating the community as one. Both were, in their own day, quite influential; yet (as with Radhakrishnan and Aurobindo) their influence has passed. It could also be said that they were superseded by Gandhi, who took on (and deepened) their reformist impulses while practicing a more catholic and dialogic form of Hinduism.[11]

Vivekananda and Gandhi sought to save Hinduism while reforming the caste system. Other reformers more directly challenged the principle of caste itself. The most famous of these radicals, B. R. Ambedkar, is represented in this book. But two other fascinating and intriguing figures are not. One was Iyothee Thass, a gifted Tamil activist of low-caste, or "Untouchable" origins who later embraced Buddhism; the other was Narayana Guru, a charismatic preacher whose mobilization of the low-castes in Kerala lies behind that state'e widely praised work in bringing education and health care to the rural poor.[12]

I was particularly sorry not to have found space for one of my favourite Indians. This is Dadabhai Naoroji, the businessman, social reformer, author, and activist who helped found the Indian National Congress, who became the first Asian ever to become a Member of the British Parliament (in the 1890s), who lobbied for decades for the rights of Indians with the British Government, and who was an early influence on Gandhi. Naoroji also wrote several books, at least one of which was widely read by nationalists. The book was called *Poverty and Un-British Rule in India;* it chastised the rulers for focusing on draining wealth out of the sub-continent rather than on fostering economic development

11. Cf. Kenneth W. Jones, *Socio-Religious Reform Movements in British India* (Cambridge: Cambridge University Press, 1990).

12. On Iyothee Thass, see G. Aloysius, *Nationalism without a Nation in India* (New Delhi: Oxford University Press, 1998); V. Geetha and S. V. Rajadurai, *Towards a Non-Brahmin Millenium: From Iyothee Thass to Periyar* (Calcutta: Samya, 1998). On the enduring legacies of Narayana Guru, see Robin Jeffrey, *Politics, Women and Wellbeing: How Kerala Became a 'Model'* (New Delhi: Oxford University Press, 1992); Dilip M. Menon, *Caste, Nationalism and Communism in South India: Malabar, 1900–1948* (Cambridge: Cambridge University Press, 1994).

within it. The book and its themes are somewhat dated in this postcolonial age, but in his day Naoroji was a fascinating and important figure.[13]

The churning provided by the colonial encounter led to a range of rich and fascinating writings in the various Indian languages. Some of these are represented here, in translation; but a great deal could not be. One reason, of course, is space; another is my focus on politics and social reform. Contemporaneous with the individuals featured in this book were a set of creative writers, operating in the various Indian languages, who used poetry and fiction to articulate and nurture new ways of thinking and feeling. These writers cultivated a distinctively modern sensibility, which paid greater attention to the individual self and to inter-personal relations. The changes they collectively wrought in the domain of culture were profound and long-lasting ones. Regrettably, the work and influence of these writers lie beyond the scope of this book.

The Republic of India has twenty-eight states, each of which had its own set of radicals and reformers who have written insightfully on politics, society, or culture. The present selection cannot ever hope to satisfy the strong linguistic and regional sentiments prevalent in India. About the reception of this volume I am certain of only one thing: that each region and language will have its own special grouse about people I have left out. That being the case, perhaps this book can provoke a series of volumes (by other hands) on the 'Makers of Modern Bengal', the 'Makers of Modern Tamil Nadu', and so on.[14]

Despite the omissions, acknowledged and unacknowledged, we have here a very diverse body of work indeed. The individuals represented here come from all parts of India. Born in north, south, east, and west, many also travelled extensively in parts of the country that were not originally their own. They wrote in various languages, among them

---

13. Cf. R. P. Masani, *Dadabhai Naoroji: The Grand Old Man of India* (London: George Allen and Unwin, 1939). The Harvard historian Dinyar Patel is currently working on a new life of Naoroji.

14. Among these 'Makers' would be some outstanding novelists who also happened to be political essayists, such as Bankim Chandra Chatterjee and Mahasweta Devi (Bengali), Subramania Bharati (Tamil), Fakirmohan Senapati (Oriya), and Shivarama Karanth and U. R. Anantha Murty (Kannada).

Gujarati, Hindi, Bengali, Urdu, Tamil, Marathi, and English. They were born into different castes and display a wide variety of religious and political orientations. Three are Muslims, and among the Hindus there are Brahmins, Banias, Sudras, and former Untouchables. At least four of these thinkers were as much shaped by Christianity as by Hinduism. One was born a Hindu but died a Buddhist. Another was ordained as a Christian priest but later left the church, being attracted, successively, to tribal faiths and to Buddhism. Several were anti-religious atheists who never said a prayer or entered a temple (nor a church or mosque). There are only two women, but at least six of the men campaigned energetically for gender equality.[15]

In terms of conventional political categories, we have here two conservative or right-wing thinkers, about a half-dozen liberals, and as many socialists. Then there is Gandhi, who cannot be categorized according to convention at all, unless one sees him as being at once socialist, liberal, and conservative.

The diversity of individuals and ideologies is matched by a suitable diversity of themes. The topics explored and analysed in these pages include race, religion, caste, gender, tribe, language, nationalism, colonialism, democracy, economic development, violence, and non-violence—that is to say, all that is significant and important in the human condition.

In this respect, it is tempting to compare this volume to Richard Hofstadter's magisterial book on the American political tradition. The politicians whose legacies Hofstadter so skillfully analysed were all male, all Christian, and all English-speaking.[16] The far greater diversity on offer here is in part a product of the distinctive and different experiences of my thinker-activists and in part a product of the heterogeneity of their homeland. Sociologically speaking, one might view India as having three principal *axes of diversity,* representing religion, language, and region, respectively; and as simultaneously having three principal

15. Brief biographical portraits of these individuals are provided at appropriate places in the book.

16. Richard Hofstadter, *The American Political Tradition: And the Men Who Made It* (New York: Alfred Knopf, 1948).

axes of disparity, representing caste, gender, and class. In terms of these six categories, these thinkers had widely varying backgrounds and life experiences, which were reflected in their writings (as well as in their political choices).

The Indians featured in this book all led very unusual and exciting lives. They travelled overseas and lost caste identification by doing so. They opposed the British rulers and so found themselves in jail. Later, they fought among themselves and thus found themselves out of favour or out of office. They lived in tumultuous times, which they helped sometimes to tame and, at other times, to make even more tumultuous.

As I worked through the collected writings of these thinker-activists, reading standard works still sold in bookshops as well as fugitive pamphlets that are unavailable even in the best libraries, I was struck by the congruence of substance with style. The nineteen individuals included here all wrote very fluently in their own languages, and at least a half-dozen were fluent in English as well. One was a Nobel-prize-winning author; others were educated in the great universities of Oxford, Cambridge, Columbia, London, Wisconsin, and Berlin. Most of them could, if they had so chosen, have made a living from journalism—indeed, many ran their own journals to further their social and political campaigns.

What these nineteen Indians saw and experienced was exciting and important enough. We are exceptionally fortunate that they presented what they saw and experienced in such compelling prose. While their language was sometimes idiosyncratic, it was always expressive. The eccentricities of syntax and grammar notwithstanding, their arguments were made with clarity and directness.

Political partisans, past and present, would tend to foreground the work and contribution of their particular hero (or heroine). I have chosen instead to view each thinker and life as nesting within a wider and longer tradition of democratic debate and dispute. Viewed individually, in isolation, they may provide consolation to this or another sect or party; taken together, they provide proof of the depth and robustness of the Indian political tradition.

V

After the fall of the Berlin Wall in 1989, there was an outpouring of books reflecting on the rivalry between totalitarian and democratic political systems. Some were triumphalist, seeing the victory of the West as inevitable and owing to the superiority of its institutions and values. Others were more introspective, recognizing that the two major forms of totalitarianism, fascism and Marxism-Leninism, were themselves invented in the West and that they had, for large swathes of the twentieth century, a profound appeal for some Western intellectuals and opinion makers.[17]

More recently, the market for serious political writing has been invaded by books opposing Western ideals to Islamic fundamentalism, since the latter now appears to have replaced secular totalitarianism as the major threat to the democratic way of life. Once more, the mood varies: where some books are apocalyptic and even hysterical, viewing Islam as in every way irreconcilable to modernity, others are more sober and accommodative, seeking to wean ordinary Muslims away from the grip of fanatics and into the home camp of liberal democrats.[18]

These books, published in the wake of the lifting of the Iron Curtain, have sought to defend Western democracy against its enemies at

17. A sample of these works would include Robert Conquest, *Reflections on a Ravaged Century* (New York: W. W. Norton, 2000); Francis Fukuyama, *The End of History and the Last Man* (New York: Free Press, 1992); Timothy Garton Ash, *Free World: America, Europe, and the Surprising Future of the West* (New York: Random House, 2004); and François Furet, *The Passing of an Illusion: The Idea of Communism in the Twentieth Century,* trans. from the French by Deborah Furet (Chicago: University of Chicago Press, 1999)—the last being perhaps the most wide ranging and thoughtful of them all.

18. Again, a representative sample might include Samuel Huntington, *The Clash of Civilization and the Remaking of World Order* (New York: Simon & Schuster, 1996); Bernard Lewis, *What Went Wrong? Western Impact and Middle Eastern Response* (New York: Oxford University Press, 2001); Paul Berman, *Terror and Liberalism* (New York: W. W. Norton, 2003); Christopher Caldwell, *Reflections on the Revolution in Europe: Immigration, Islam, and the West* (New York: Doubleday, 2009).

home and abroad. From this perspective, Soviet Russia stood menacingly against the West during the Cold War, its work aided by malign or misguided fellow travellers living within democratic capitalist countries. With Islamism the threat is likewise internal as well as external. On the one hand, there are *jihadi* terrorists waiting to attack Westerners and Western institutions everywhere as part of a global campaign for dominance; on the other hand, there are the growing numbers of Muslim immigrants in Western Europe and North America, who tend to live in enclosed ghettos rather than integrate with the host society.

To this writer, what is remarkable about this substantial (and still growing literature) is that it largely ignores India. Some books may have a passing reference or two to this country; others do not even grant it that favour. Yet one would think that given its size, diversity, and institutional history, the Republic of India would provide a reservoir of political experience with which to refine or rethink theories being articulated in the West. For six decades now, democratic India has lived next to, and somehow coped with, an even larger and more populous nation run as a single-party state. Its other neighbours have included military dictatorships and absolutist monarchies. For the same period of time, India, a dominantly Hindu country, has had as equal citizens of the nation a substantial Muslim minority. As the historian W. C. Smith wrote more than fifty years ago, it was only in modern, postcolonial India that Muslims lived in very large numbers without being the ruling power. Here they shared their citizenship 'with an immense number of other people. They constitute the only sizable body of Muslims in the world of which this is, or ever has been true'.[19]

That was certainly the case in 1957, but now some Western nations also have large Muslim minorities of their own. Thus, India provides a test case of the challenges to democracy from its critics on both the left and the right and a test case of the challenge to social harmony posed by a multi-religious citizenry. This makes its currently being disregarded in modern debates on politics and citizenship all the more surprising.

The absence of a substantial literature on Indian political ideas may be one reason why the country is rarely invoked in wider discussions

---

19. W. C. Smith, *Islam in Modern History* (1957; reprint, New York: Mentor Books, 1959), pp. 263–264.

on democracy and its rivals. Responding to this neglect, the economist Amartya Sen has published a book drawing our attention to the long history of intellectual debate in South Asia. Sen argues that there existed, among scientists and philosophers of the sub-continent, a rational and critical tradition of enquiry that was often as vital and influential as rival traditions based on faith and mysticism. He further claims that ideas of democracy and secularism associated with modern India were anticipated by kings who ruled in the ancient and medieval periods.[20]

In speaking of India, or indeed of any other country or civilization, one must distinguish between two argumentative traditions—the *distant* and the *proximate*. By the first I mean traditions of debate that were distinctive of long-dead states and kingdoms; by the second, those traditions which actually shaped the political and social institutions of the present. With one exception (the poet Rabindranath Tagore), Sen's own focus is on thinkers of the remote past. This is fair enough—except that Sen then claims, on the basis of little evidence, that these distant arguments shaped the ideals of the Indian Constitution and the practices of the Indian nation-state.[21]

Makers of Modern India deals centrally with the arguments and arguers of the past two centuries. The choice is dictated in part by the fact that I am myself a historian of the modern period and, in part, by the fact that the India we know today has been shaped far more by plebeians who lived closer to our time than by ancient monarchs. This is a book aimed in the first instance at those interested in Indian history, who might wish to acquire a fuller understanding of how this unnatural nation and unlikely democracy was argued into existence. However, given India's size and representativeness, I hope that the materials it contains may yet help make the country somewhat less marginal to global debates on the political system(s) most appropriate to the twenty-first century.

20. Amartya Sen, *The Argumentative Indian: Reflections on Indian History, Culture and Identity* (London: Allen Lane, 2005).

21. These paragraphs carry on a conversation that began in the pages of the *Economic and Political Weekly (EPW)*. See Ramachandra Guha, 'Arguments with Sen, Arguments about India', *EPW*, 20 October 2005; Amartya Sen, 'Our Past and Our Present', *EPW*, 25 November 2006; Jaithirth Rao, 'Harking Back to the Past', *EPW*, 14 April 2007.

PART ONE

THE OPENING OF THE INDIAN MIND

INTRODUCTION TO PART I

WRITING OF BRITISH RULE IN INDIA, Karl Marx remarked that 'England, it is true, in causing a social revolution in Hindustan, was actuated only by the vilest interests, and was stupid in her manner of enforcing them. But that is not the question. The question is, can mankind fulfil its destiny without a fundamental revolution in the social state of Asia? If not, whatever may have been the crimes of England she was the unconscious tool of history in bringing about that revolution'.

Those 'vile interests' that brought the British to India were the search for gold, spices, and textiles. Other European powers had the same motives—although some were also searching for Christian converts. The Portuguese arrived on the west coast of the sub-continent at the end of the fifteenth century, with the Dutch, the French, and the British following soon afterward. In the eighteenth century the focus of the European traders shifted to the east coast, and in particular to the province of Bengal, which had a flourishing textile industry and was also the source of rich supplies of rice, sugar, and saltpetre.

Bengal was at the time under the control of a Muslim prince, who owed allegiance to the Mughals in Delhi. In 1757 the forces of the British East India Company defeated the army of this prince in battle. Eight years later, the Mughals transferred economic and political control of the province of Bengal to the Company. They were now responsible for collecting land revenue, for controlling the trade, for framing the laws, and for running the civil and military administration.

Bengal provided a base from which the British slowly expanded to other parts of India. At the end of the eighteenth century the British defeated Tipu Sultan of Mysore to make their presence felt in the south. The defeat of the Peshwas in 1818 extended their reach to the west; the defeat of the Sikhs of the Punjab in the 1840s made them sovereign through much of the north. By the middle of the nineteenth century the East India Company thus controlled virtually all of the sub-continent, either directly or through alliances with subordinate—and subservient—Maharajas and Nawabs.

British rule was enforced and consolidated by a network of native collaborators. Themselves a minuscule minority, the Europeans relied on Indian merchants to help organise their trade, Indian soldiers to staff their armies, Indian clerks to keep accounts, and Indian officials and village headmen to collect taxes.

In 1793 the British instituted a 'Permanent Settlement' in eastern India where, following what they had done in Ireland, they promoted a class of large landlords responsible for collecting revenue. The impact of the Permanent Settlement has been much debated by historians. The general view is that it created a class of indolent and self-satisfied exploiters and left the real tillers of the land with no incentive to improve it. Agricultural productivity stagnated in Bengal and its neighbouring provinces. On the other hand, in the west and south, where the East India Company chose to deal more directly with peasant proprietors, there was far more energy in the rural economy.

British rule also changed the urban landscape of Bengal. The old capital, Murshidabad, declined, while the newer settlement of Calcutta prospered. Located on the Hooghly, this emerged as an active port and administrative centre. The rural gentry who were the beneficiaries of the Permanent Settlement flocked here to make their homes, visiting their estates at erratic intervals.

By the 1820s Calcutta had a permanent population of at least 250,000. There was a white town and a black town, each characterised by spacious and well-staffed houses where the European and Indian elite resided. In between the two, and on the margins, were a 'scattered and confused chaos of houses, huts, sheds, streets and lanes, alleys, windings, gutters, sinks and tanks' occupied by the workers and artisans who serviced the elite.

The printing press, another British import into Bengal, was arguably as consequential as the Permanent Settlement. According to the historian B. S. Kesavan, the first book printed in the province was Nathaniel Halhed's *Grammar of the Bengali Language,* which appeared in 1778. Twenty years later the Baptist minister William Carey transported a printing press to his mission in Serampore. The Serampore Press now issued a steady stream of books in many European and Indian languages. According to one source it printed more than 200,000 items in the first thirty years of its existence, and in as many as forty different languages. Serampore quickly found its imitators, with other presses being established to print religious texts, philosophical works, grammars, and dictionaries.

The consumers of this growing literature were Bengali as well as British. They read books, as well as newspapers, which by the early nineteenth century had become a part of the public sphere in Bengal. Through their reading, educated Indians became acquainted with their own sacred texts as well as with the most recent trends in Western science and philosophy. They now sought to take this knowledge to the next generation. In 1817 a Calcutta School-Book Society was established, whose members included Bengali Hindus and Muslims as well as Europeans. In its first four years the Society had printed and distributed some 125,000 copies of books published in a half-dozen languages.

The book society was but one sign of a growing associational culture in colonial Bengal. Some members of the Hindu and Muslim middle class poured their collective energies into faith—establishing or refurbishing temples and mosques and vigorously celebrating community festivals. Others took a more secular turn, starting schools, newspapers, and discussion societies. This latter group had been given a wake-up call by the new rulers. They were challenged by Western missionaries, who poured contempt on their idolatry and practice of caste, as well as by French Enlightenment thought, which asked why Hindu and Muslim tradition paid such little attention to the rights of individuals.

Our first maker of modern India exemplified both kinds of responses to the West. In seeking to reform and reinvigorate his society, he was, *pace* Karl Marx, a very conscious tool of history indeed.

1

THE FIRST LIBERAL

RAMMOHAN ROY

A RECENT BIOGRAPHY OF RAMMOHAN ROY is sub-titled 'The Father of Modern India'. The hyperbole may be excused. Roy was unques-
tionably the first person on the sub-continent to seriously engage
with the challenges posed by modernity to traditional social structures
and ways of being. He was also one of the first Indians whose thought
and practice were not circumscribed by the constraints of kin, caste, and
religion.

Rammohan Roy[1] was born in the village of Radhanagar in Bengal in
1772. His family were of the Vaishnava sect of Hindus. Moderately prosperous landowners, they had served for several generations as revenue
officials under the Mughals. Rammohan was married twice before he
entered his teens; this was customary among high-caste families, among
whom child marriage and polygamy were both very common. According
to his early biographers, Rammohan studied Bengali and Persian as a

1. Roy's first name is sometimes rendered as 'Rammohun'. However, 'Rammohan'
is more accurate, phonetically speaking. I have also not used his title 'Raja' (awarded
by the Mughals)—this can perhaps be dispensed with in this republican age.

boy; he was then sent to Patna to learn Arabic, where his teachers made him read Euclid and Aristotle in translation. The last stop on this mobile college was Benares, where he studied Sanskrit with traditional *pandits*.

This version of Rammohan Roy's peripatetic education has been challenged by later scholars. What they do not dispute, however, is that he was formidably multi-lingual. It may be that he learnt these languages in Bengal itself, rather than being sent to distant towns to be educated. What seems clear is that through his studies—wherever these may have been—Roy became less willing to accept the claims and prejudices of orthodox Hinduism. The disenchantment was confirmed by what he saw around him. His elder brother died, and the wife, to Rammohan's dismay, was forced to commit *sati*.[2]

After he had finished with his studies, Rammohan Roy worked with the East India Company at various places in Bengal, before settling in Calcutta in the year of the Battle of Waterloo, 1815. By this time he had already published several books. His first book, written in Persian with a preface in Arabic, was an attack on idol worship.

After he moved to Calcutta, Roy became increasingly involved in literary and social work. He translated the Upanishads from Sanskrit into Bengali. He published a tract in English against *sati*. He debated orthodox scholars on the rights of Hindu women. He also contested the claim of Christian missionaries that their religion was superior to all others. In 1815 he founded an *Atmiya Sabha* or 'friendship association', which, among other things, searched for elements common to different religious traditions.

Roy himself had now come to believe that the 'omnipresent God, who is the only proper object of religious veneration, is one and undivided in person'. He claimed this was the message of the Vedas, and of the Bible and the Quran as well. Seeking to promote inter-religious understanding, Roy wrote a book on the precepts of Jesus and began work on a life of Muhammad.

Roy and his circle were roundly abused by orthodox Hindus, who derided them as sinful atheists and 'moderns blinded by passion'.

---

2. The practice, prevalent among some upper-caste families, of a wife immolating herself on her husband's funeral pyre.

However, the European Christians in India did not warm to him either. They complained that he opposed conversion and that his admiration for Jesus did not extend to acknowledging his divinity.

In 1816 Roy opened a school for boys whose medium of instruction was English. In 1821 he started a weekly newspaper in Bengali—one of the first such in any Indian language. Then he started a paper in Persian (of which, as with its Bengali predecessor, he wrote the contents). In 1828 he founded the Brahmo Samaj (the Society of God), which preached the worship of the One God on the basis of what its founder claimed were the original teachings of the Vedas.

When the practice of *sati* was legally abolished in 1829, the credit for its abolition was given to the governor general, Willian Bentinck. However, as a contemporary English observer—herself a woman—pointed out, the legislation could not have been brought about 'but for the powerful though unacknowledged aid of the great Hindu philosopher Rammohun Roy'. Roy's great contribution toward this reform was to demonstrate that *sati* was not a religious duty sanctioned or upheld by Hindu scriptural tradition.

Through the 1820s, Roy's ideas were being propagated through his Bengali newspaper, which was called the *Sangbad Kaumudi* or the 'Moon of Intelligence'. The historian A. F. Salahuddin Ahmed quotes two remarkable contemporary testimonies to this paper's influence. In December 1821 the *Calcutta Journal,* a periodical of (and for) the English in India, wrote of Roy's newspaper that 'she will be the means of the moral and intellectual renovation of India'. Nine years later, a London magazine described the *Sangbad Kaumudi* as 'the *Morning Chronicle* of India, advocating freedom, civil and religious, opposed to corruption and tyranny, and labouring, we are happy to say effectively and extensively, to eradicate the idolatrous rites of the Brahmins, and awaken the Hindoos to a sense of the degradation and misery into which they have been plunged.'

Notably, Rammohan Roy had a keen interest in politics outside India as well. He welcomed the movements that delivered the countries of South America from Spanish colonial rule. Within Spain, he supported the liberal opposition to an autocratic monarchy. He championed the emancipation of Catholics within the United Kingdom. This internationalist orientation set him apart from moralists and thinkers of the past—thus, as C. A. Bayly has recently pointed out, Roy 'was the first Indian to represent the growth of freedom in India as an essential part of a wider trans-national quest of humanity for self-realization'.

In 1830 Rammohan Roy was sent by the now much weakened Mughal Emperor to England to petition the King to increase his allowance and perquisites. Arriving in London in April 1831, Roy spent the next two years in the city. He met with officials of the East India Company, lobbied with members of Parliament, was granted an audience with the king, and wrote and published books on Indian economics and law. He exchanged views with British Utilitarians and English socialists, and also travelled to Paris. His biographer Sophia Dobson Collet remarks that 'as he had interpreted England to India, so now he interpreted India to England'. In London he watched with interest from the side-lines as Parliament passed the Reform Bill of 1831, which extended the franchise to a greater number of British men.

After many months of patient lobbying, Roy was able to persuade the British government to increase the stipend of the Mughal Emperor by £30,000 a year. However, he never saw the Emperor again, nor his native Bengal. On a visit to English friends in Bristol, Roy took ill and died on 27 September 1833. He is buried there, with a tombstone whose inscription notes his scholarship and mastery of languages, and his belief in the unity of the godhead, before summarising his life's work as follows:

> HIS UNW[E]ARIED LABOURS TO PROMOTE THE SOCIAL, MORAL AND PHYSICAL CONDITION OF THE PEOPLE OF INDIA, HIS EARNEST ENDEAVOURS TO SUPPRESS IDOLATRY AND THE RITE OF SUTTEE, AND HIS CONSTANT ZEALOUS ADVOCACY OF WHATEVER TENDED TO ADVANCE THE GLORY OF GOD AND THE WELFARE OF MAN, LIVE IN THE GRATEFUL RE-MEMBRANCE OF HIS COUNTRYMEN.

And so they should. For, as the excerpts below demonstrate, although it is perhaps too much to claim that Rammohan Roy was the 'Father of Modern India', he was nonetheless its first liberal thinker of con-sequence, without whose work and writings India's encounter with modernity would have been even more conflicted and painful than it has been.

RELATIONS BETWEEN MEN AND WOMEN

In 1818 Rammohan Roy wrote a pamphlet in his native Bengali opposing the practice of asking Hindu widows to immolate themselves on their husband's funeral pyre. In the same year he published an English version, entitled 'A Conference between an Advocate for, and an Opponent of, the Practice of Burning Widows Alive'. The excerpts below are from this work. The 'you' in the text is the advocate of widow-burning, but Rammohan is also addressing the Hindu patriarch more generally.[3]

✦ ✦ ✦

... Women are in general inferior to men on bodily strength and energy; consequently the male part of the community, taking advantage of their corporeal weakness, have denied to them those excellent merits that they are entitled to by nature, and afterwards they are apt to say that women are naturally incapable of acquiring those merits. But if we give the subject consideration, we may easily ascertain whether or not your accusation against them is consistent with justice. As to their inferiority in point of understanding, when did you ever afford them a fair opportunity of exhibiting their natural capacity? How then can you accuse them of want of understanding? If, after instruction in knowledge and wisdom, a person cannot comprehend or retain what has been taught him, we may consider him as deficient; but as you keep women, generally void of education and acquirements, you cannot therefore, in justice pronounce on their inferiority. ...

Secondly. You charge them with want of resolution, at which I feel exceedingly surprised: for we constantly perceive, in a country where the name of death makes the male shudder, that the female, from her firmness of mind,

3. From Sophia Dobson Collet, *The Life and Letters of Raja Rammohun Roy*, ed. Dilip Kumar Biswas and Prabhat Chandra Ganguli, 4th ed. (Calcutta: Sadharan Brahmo Samaj, 1988 [originally published in 1900]), pp. 94–96.

offers to burn with the corpse of her deceased husband; and yet you accuse those women of deficiency of resolution.

Thirdly. With regard to their trustworthiness, let us look minutely into the conduct of both sexes, and we may be enabled to ascertain which of them is the most frequently guilty of betraying friends. If we enumerate such women in each village or town as have been deceived by men, and such men as have been betrayed by women, I presume that the numbers of the deceived women would be found ten times greater than that of the betrayed men. Men are, in general, able to read, write, and manage public affairs, by which means they easily promulgate such faults as women occasionally commit, but never consider as criminal the misconduct of men towards women. One fault they have, it must be acknowledged, which is, by considering others equally void of duplicity as themselves, to give their confidence too readily, from which they suffer much misery, even so far that some of them are misled to suffer themselves to be burnt to death.

In the fourth place, with respect to their subjection to the passions, this may be judged of by the custom of marriage as to the respective sexes; for one man may marry two or three, sometimes even ten wives and upwards; while a woman, who marries but one husband, desires at his death to follow him forsaking all worldly enjoyments, or to remain leading the austere life of an ascetic.

Fifthly. The accusation of their want of virtuous knowledge is an injustice. Observe what pain, what slighting, what contempt, and what afflictions their value enables them to support! How many Kulin Brahmins[4] are there who marry ten or fifteen wives for the sake of money, that never see the greater number of them after the day of marriage, and visit others only three or four times in the course of their life. Still amongst those women, most, even without seeing or receiving any support from their husbands, living dependent on their fathers or brothers, and suffering much distress, continue to preserve their virtue; and when Brahmins, or those of other tribes, bring their wives to live with them, what misery do the women not suffer? At marriage the wife is recognized as half of her husband, but [after marriage] they are treated worse than inferior animals. For the woman is employed to do the work of a slave in the house, such as, in her turn, to clean the place very early in the morning,

4. A Brahmin sub-caste in Bengal.

whether cold or wet, to scour the dishes, to wash the floor, to cook night and day, to prepare and serve food for her husband, father and mother-in-law, brothers-in-law, and friends and connections! (For amongst Hindus more than in other tribes relations long reside together, and on this account quarrels are more common amongst brothers respecting their worldly affairs). If in the preparation or serving up of the victuals they commit the smallest fault, what insult do they not receive from their husband, their mother-in-law, and the younger brothers of their husband! After all the male part of the family have satisfied themselves the women content themselves with what may be left, whether sufficient in quantity or not. . . . In the afternoon they fetch water from the river or tank; and at night perform the office of menial servants in making the beds. In case of any fault or omission in the performance of those labours, they receive injurious treatment. Should the husband acquire wealth, he indulges in criminal amours to her perfect knowledge, and almost under her eyes, and does not see her, perhaps once a month. As long as the husband is poor she suffers every kind of trouble and when he becomes rich she is altogether heart-broken. All this pain and affliction their virtue alone enables them to support. Where a husband takes two or three wives to live with him, they are subjected to mental miseries and constant quarrels. Even this distressed situation they virtuously endure. Sometimes it happens that the husband, from a preference for one of his wives, behaves cruelly to another. Amongst the lower classes, and those even of the better class who have not associated with good company, the wife on the slightest fault, or even on bare suspicion of her misconduct, is chastised as a thief. Respect to virtue and their reputation generally makes them forgive even this treatment. If, unable to bear such cruel usage, a wife leaves her husband's house to live separately from him, then the influence of the husband with the magisterial authority is generally sufficient to place her again in his hands; when, in revenge for her quitting him, he seizes every pretext to torment her in various ways, and sometimes even puts her privately to death. These are facts occurring every day, and not to be denied. What I lament is, that seeing the women thus dependent and exposed to every misery, you feel for them no compassion that might exempt them from being tied down and burnt to death.

✦   ✦   ✦

THE FREEDOM OF THE PRESS

In 1824 the government of Bengal (which was in the hands of the East India Company) issued an ordinance placing strict restrictions on the press. Newspapers and journals had to obtain a license that could be granted or withdrawn at the Government's discretion. A memorial protesting this move was drafted by Rammohan Roy and, with the signatures of several other prominent Bengalis, sent to the government. Note the deferential tone of the memorial, which masks its challenging and combative contents.[5]

❖   ❖   ❖

. . . Your Lordship may have learned from the works of the Christian Missionaries, and also from other sources, that ever since the art of printing has become generally known among the Natives of Calcutta, numerous Publications have been circulated in the Bengalee Language, which by introducing free discussion among the Natives and inducing them to reflect and inquire after knowledge, have already served greatly to improve their minds and ameliorate their condition. This desirable object has been chiefly promoted by the establishment of four Native Newspapers, two in the Bengalee and two in the Persian Languages, published for the purpose of communicating to those residing in the interior of the country, accounts of whatever occurs worthy of notice at the Presidency or in the country, and also the interesting and valuable intelligence of what is passing in England and in other parts of the world, conveyed through the English Newspapers or other channels. . . .

While your Memorialists were indulging the hope that Government, from a conviction of the manifold advantages of being put in possession of full and impartial information regarding what is passing in all parts of the Country, would encourage the establishment of Newspapers in the cities and districts under the special patronage and protection of Government, that they might furnish the Supreme Authorities in Calcutta with an accurate account of local occurrences and reports of Judicial proceedings,—they have the misfortune

5. The excerpts that follow are from Collet, *The Life and Letters of Raja Rammohun Roy*, pp. 390–393, 406–419.

to observe, that on the contrary, his Excellency the Governor General in Council has lately promulgated a Rule and Ordinance imposing severe restraints on the Press and prohibiting all Periodical Publications even at the Presidency and in the Native Languages, unless sanctioned by a License from Government, which is to be revocable at pleasure whenever it shall appear to Government that a publication has contained anything of an unsuitable character.

Those Natives who are in more favourable circumstances and of respectable character, have such an invincible prejudice against making a voluntary affidavit, or undergoing the solemnities of an oath, that they will never think of establishing a publication which can only be supported by a series of oaths and affidavits, abhorrent to their feelings and derogatory to their reputation amongst their countrymen.

After this Rule and Ordinance shall have been carried into execution, your Memorialists are therefore extremely sorry to observe, that a complete stop will be put to the diffusion of knowledge and the consequent mental improvement now going on, either by translations into the popular dialect of this country from the learned languages of the East, or by the circulation of literary intelligence drawn from foreign publications. And the same cause will also prevent those Natives who are better versed in the laws and customs of the British Nation, from communicating to their fellow subjects a knowledge of the admirable system of Government established by the British, and the peculiar excellencies of the means they have adopted for the strict and impartial administration of justice. Another evil of equal importance in the eyes of a just Ruler, is, that it will also preclude the Natives from making the Government readily acquainted with the errors and injustice that may be committed by its executive officers in the various parts of this extensive country; and it will also preclude the Natives from communicating frankly and honestly to their Gracious Sovereign in England and his Council, the real condition of his Majesty's faithful subjects in this distant part of his dominions and the treatment they experience from the local Government; since information cannot in future be conveyed to England, as it has heretofore been, either by the translations from the Native publications inserted in the English Newspapers printed here and sent to Europe, or by the English publications which the Natives themselves had in contemplation to establish, before this Rule and Ordinance was proposed.

After this sudden deprivation of one of the most precious of their rights, which has been freely allowed them since the Establishment of the British Power, a right which they are not, and cannot be charged with having ever abused, the inhabitants of Calcutta would be no longer justified in boasting, that they are fortunately placed by Providence under the protection of the whole British Nation or that the King of England and Lords and Commons are their Legislators, and that they are secured in the enjoyment of the same civil and religious privileges that every Briton is entitled to in England.

Your Memorialists are persuaded that the British Government is not disposed to adopt the political maxim so often acted upon by Asiatic Princes, that the more a people are kept in darkness, their Rulers will derive the greater advantages from them; since, by reference to History, it is found that this was but a short-sighted policy which did not ultimately answer the purpose of its authors. On the contrary, it rather proved disadvantageous to them; for we find that as often as an ignorant people, when an opportunity offered, have revolted against their Rulers, all sorts of barbarous excesses and cruelties have been the consequence; whereas a people naturally disposed to peace and ease, when placed under a good Government from which they experience just and liberal treatment, must become the more attached to it, in proportion as they become enlightened and the great body of the people are taught to appreciate the value of the blessings they enjoy under its Rule.

Every good Ruler, who is convinced of the imperfection of human nature, and reverences the Eternal Governor of the world, must be conscious of the great liability to error in managing the affairs of a vast empire; and therefore he will be anxious to afford every individual the readiest means of bringing to his notice whatever may require his interference. To secure this important object, the unrestrained Liberty of Publication, is the only effectual means that can be employed. And should it ever be abused, the established Law of the Land is very properly armed with efficient powers to punish those who may be found guilty of misrepresenting the conduct or character of Government, which are effectually guarded by the same Laws to which individuals must look for protection of their reputation and good name.

Your Memorialists conclude by humbly entreating your Lordship to take this Memorial into your gracious consideration; and that you will be pleased by not registering the above Rule and Ordinance, to permit the Natives of this country to continue in possession of the civil rights and privileges which they and their fathers have so long enjoyed under the auspices of the British nation, whose kindness, and confidence, they are not aware of having done anything, to forfeit.

Chunder Coomar Tagore
Dwarka Nauth Tagore
Rammohan Roy
Hurchunder Ghosh
Gowree Churn Bonnergee
Prosunno Commar Tagore

✦   ✦   ✦

When the Governor-General refused to heed the protest, Rammohan chose to appeal directly to the King of England. This second memorial, as the excerpts below show, was more analytical in tone, outlining moral and political reasons why the freedom of the press had to be safeguarded. This may very well have been the first communication ever addressed to a British monarch by an Indian.

✦   ✦   ✦

... Asia unfortunately affords few instances of Princes who have submitted their actions to the judgement of their subjects, but those who have done so, instead of falling into hatred and contempt, were the more loved and respected, while they lived, and their memory is still cherished by posterity; whereas more despotic Monarchs, pursued by hatred in their life time, could with difficulty escape the attempts of the rebel or the assassin, and their names are either detested or forgotten. . . .

Men in power hostile to the Liberty of the Press, which is a disagreeable check upon their conduct, when unable to discover any real evil arising from its existence, have attempted to make the world imagine, that it might, in some possible contingency, afford the means of combination against the Government, but not to mention that extraordinary emergencies would warrant measures which in ordinary times are totally unjustifiable, your Majesty is well aware, that a Free Press has never yet caused a revolution in any part of the world because, while men can easily represent the grievances arising from the conduct of the local authorities to the supreme Government, and thus get them redressed, the grounds of discontent that excite revolution are removed; whereas, where no freedom of the Press existed, and grievances consequently remained unrepresented and unredressed, innumerable revolutions have taken place in all parts of the globe, or if prevented by the armed force of the Government, the people continued ready for insurrection. . . .

It is well known that despotic Governments naturally desire the suppression of any freedom of expression which might tend to expose their acts to the obloquy which ever attends the exercise of tyranny or oppression, and the argument they constantly resort to, is, that the spread of knowledge is dangerous to the existence of all legitimate authority, since, as a people become enlightened, they will discover that by a unity of effort, the many may easily shake off the yoke of the few, and thus become emancipated from the restraints of power altogether, forgetting the lesson derived from history, that in countries which have made the smallest advance in civilization, anarchy and revolution are most prevalent—while on the other hand, in nations the most enlightened, any revolt against governments which have guarded inviolate the rights of the governed, is most rare, and that the resistance of a people advanced in knowledge, has ever been—not against the existence,—but against the abuses of the Governing power. Canada, during the late war with America, afforded a memorable instance of the truth of this argument. The enlightened inhabitants of that colony, finding that their rights and privileges had been secured to them, their complaints listened to, and their grievances redressed by the British Government, resisted every attempt of the United States to seduce them from their allegiance to it. In fact, it may be fearlessly averred, that the more enlightened a people become, the less likely are they to revolt against the governing power, as long as it is exercised with justice tempered with mercy, and the rights and privileges of the governed are held sacred from any invasion. . . .

While therefore the existence of a free Press is equally necessary for the sake of the Governors and the governed, it is possible a national feeling may lead the British people to suppose, that in two points, the peculiar situation of this country requires a modification of the laws enacted for the control of the Press in England. First, that for the sake of greater security and to preserve the union existing between England and this country, it might be necessary to enact a penalty to be inflicted on such persons as might endeavour to excite hatred in the minds of the Natives of India against the English nation. Secondly, that a penalty should be inflicted on such as might seditiously attempt to excite hostilities with neighbouring or friendly states. Although your Majesty's faithful subjects are not aware that anything has yet occurred to call for the precautions thus anticipated, yet should such or any other limitations of the liberty of the Press be deemed necessary, they are perfectly willing to submit to additional penalties to be legally inflicted. But they must humbly enter their protest against the injustice of robbing them of their long standing privileges, by the introduction of numerous arbitrary restrictions, totally uncalled for by the circumstances of the country—and whatever may be their intention, calculated to suppress truth, protect abuses—and encourage oppression. . . .

The publication of truth and the natural expression of men's sentiments through the medium of the Press, entail no burden on the State, & should it appear to your Majesty and the enlightened men placed about your throne, that this precious privilege which is so essential to the well-being of your faithful subjects, could not safely be entrusted to the Natives of India, although they have given such unquestionable proofs of their loyalty and attachment, subject only to the restraints wisely imposed upon the Press by the laws of England, your faithful subjects entreat on behalf of their countrymen, that your Majesty will be graciously pleased to grant it, subject to such severer restraints and heavier penalties as may be deemed necessary; but legal restraints, not those of arbitrary power—and penalties to be inflicted after trial and conviction according to the forms of the Laws of England,—not at the will and pleasure of one or two individuals without investigation or without hearing any defence or going through any of the forms prescribed by law, to ensure the equitable administration of justice.

Notwithstanding the despotic power of the Mogul Princes who formerly ruled over this country, and that their conduct was often cruel and arbitrary, yet the wise and virtuous among them, always employed two intelligencers at the residence of their Nawabs or Lord Lieutenants, *Akhbar-navees,* or newswriter who published an account of whatever happened, and a *Khoofea-navees,* or confidential correspondent who sent a private and particular account of every occurrence worthy of notice; and although these Lord Lieutenants were often particular friends or near relations to the Prince, he did not trust entirely to themselves for a faithful and impartial report of their administration, and degraded them when they appeared to deserve it, either for their own faults or for their negligence in not checking the delinquencies of their subordinate officers; which shows that even the Mogul Princes, although their form of Government admitted of nothing better, were convinced, that in a country so rich and so replete with temptations, a restraint of some kind was absolutely necessary, to prevent the abuses that are so liable to flow from the possession of power.

The country still abounds in wealth, and its inhabitants are still addicted to the same corrupt means of compassing their ends, to which from having long lived under arbitrary Government, they have become naturally habituated; and if its present Rulers have brought with them purer principles from the land of their birth which may better withstand the influence of long residence amid the numerous temptations to which they are exposed;—on the other hand, from the seat of the Supreme government being placed at an immense distance and the channel of communication entirely in their own hands, they are left more at liberty to follow their own interests, and looking forward to the quiet and secure enjoyment of their wealth in their native land, they may care little for the character they leave behind them in a remote country, among a people for whose opinion they have no regard. Your Majesty's faithful subjects, therefore, humbly presume, that the existence of a restraint of some kind, is absolutely necessary to preserve your faithful subjects from the abuses of uncontrolled power. . . .

It might be urged on the other hand, that persons who feel aggrieved, may transmit representations to the Court of Directors [of the East India Company], and thus obtain redress; but the natives of this country are generally ignorant of this mode of proceeding; and with neither friends in England nor knowledge of the country, they could entertain no hope of success, since they know that the transmission of their representations, depends in point of time, upon the pleasure of the local Government, which will probably, in order to counteract their influence, accompany them with observations, the nature of which would be totally unknown to the complainants,—discouragements which in fact have operated as complete preventives, so that no instance of such a representation from the Natives of Bengal, has ever been known.

In conclusion, your Majesty's faithful subjects humbly beseech your Majesty, first, to cause the Rule and Ordinance and Regulation before mentioned, which has been registered by the Judge of your Majesty's Court, to be rescinded; and prohibit any authority in this country, from assuming the leg-islative power, or prerogatives of your Majesty and the High Council of the Realm, to narrow the privileges and destroy the rights of your Majesty's faith-ful subjects, who claim your protection, and are willing to submit to such laws, as your Majesty with the advice of your Council, shall be graciously pleased to enact.

Secondly, your Majesty's faithful subjects humbly pray, that your Majesty will be pleased to confirm to them the privilege, they have so long enjoyed, of expressing their sentiments through the medium of the Press, subject to such legal restraints as may be thought necessary or that your Majesty will be gra-ciously pleased to appoint a commission of intelligent and independent Gen-tlemen, to inquire into the real condition of the millions Providence has placed under your high protection.

Your Majesty's faithful subjects from the distance of almost half the globe, appeal to your Majesty's heart by the sympathy which forms a paternal tie between you and the lowest of your subjects, not to overlook their condition; they appeal to you by the honour of that great nation which under your Royal auspices has obtained the glorious title of Liberator of Europe, not to permit the possibility of millions of your subjects being wantonly trampled on and oppressed; they lastly appeal to you by the glory of your Crown on which the eyes of the world are fixed, not to consign the natives of India, to perpetual oppression and degradation.

✦   ✦   ✦

THE NEED FOR MODERN EDUCATION

Our final selection, written in December 1823, makes an urgent plea for the introduction of modern education in India. It is addressed to the Governor-General. I have retained the sometimes archaic spellings of Indian words, such as 'Sangscrit' for 'Sanskrit'.[6]

✦   ✦   ✦

6. From Collet, *The Life and Letters of Raja Rammohun Roy,* pp. 420–424.

To

His Excellency the Right Hon'ble William Pitt,

Lord Amherst.

My Lord,

Humbly reluctant as the natives of India are to obtrude upon the notice of Government the sentiments they entertain on any public measure, there are circumstances when silence would be carrying this respectful feeling to culpable excess. The present Rulers of India, coming from a distance of many thousand miles to govern a people whose language, literature, manners, customs, and ideas are almost entirely new and strange to them, cannot easily become so intimately acquainted with their real circumstances, as the natives of the country are themselves. We should therefore be guilty of a gross dereliction of duty to ourselves, and afford our Rulers just ground of complaint at our apathy, did we omit on occasions of importance like the present to supply them with such accurate information as might enable them to devise and adopt measures calculated to be beneficial to the country, and thus second by our local knowledge and experience their declared benevolent intentions for its improvement.

The establishment of a new Sangscrit School in Calcutta evinces the laudable desire of Government to improve the Natives of India by Education. . . .

When this Seminary of learning was proposed, we understood that the Government in England had ordered a considerable sum of money to be annually devoted to the instruction of its Indian Subjects. We were filled with sanguine hopes that this sum would be laid out in employing European Gentlemen of talents and education to instruct the natives of India in Mathematics, Natural Philosophy, Chemistry, Anatomy and other useful Sciences, which the Nations of Europe have carried to a degree of perfection that has raised them above the inhabitants of other parts of the world.

While we looked forward with pleasing hope to the dawn of knowledge thus promised to the rising generation, our hearts were filled with mingled feelings of delight and gratitude; we already offered up thanks to Providence for inspiring the most generous and enlightened of the Nations of the West with the glorious ambitions of planting in Asia the Arts and Sciences of modern Europe.

We now find that the Government are establishing a Sangscrit school under Hindoo pundits to impart such knowledge as is already current in India. This seminary (similar in character to those which existed in Europe before the time of Lord Bacon) can only be expected to load the minds of youth with grammatical niceties and metaphysical distinctions of little or no practicable use to the possessors or to society. The pupils will there acquire what was known two thousand years ago, with the addition of vain and empty subtleties since produced by speculative men, such as is already commonly taught in all parts of India.

The Sangscrit language so difficult that almost a life time is necessary for its perfect acquisition, is well known to have been for ages a lamentable check on the diffusion of knowledge; and the learning concealed under the almost impervious veil is far from sufficient to reward the labour of acquiring it. But if it were thought necessary to perpetuate this language for the sake of the portion of the valuable information it contains, this might be much more easily accomplished by other means than the establishment of a new Sangscrit College; for there have been always and are now numerous professors of Sangscrit in the different parts of the country, engaged in teaching this language as well as the other branches of literature which are to be the object of the new Seminary. Therefore their more diligent cultivation, if desirable, would be effectually promoted by holding out premiums and granting certain allowances to those most eminent Professors, who have already undertaken on their own account to teach them, and would by such rewards be stimulated to still greater exertions.

From these considerations, as the sum set apart for the instruction of the Natives of India was intended by the Government in England, for the improvement of its Indian subjects, I beg leave to state, with due deference to your Lordship's exalted situation, that if the plan now adopted be followed, it will, completely defeat the object proposed; since no improvement can be expected from inducing young men to consume a dozen of years of the most valuable period of their lives in acquiring the niceties of the Byakurun or Sangscrit Grammar. For instance, in learning to discuss such points as the following: *Khad* signifying to eat, *khaduty,* he or she or it eats. Query, whether does the word *khaduti* taken as a whole, convey the meaning *he, she,* or *it eats,* or are separate parts of this meaning conveyed by distinct portions of the word? As if in the English language it were asked, how much meaning is there in the *eat,* how much in the *s?* and is the whole meaning of the word conveyed by those two portions of it distinctly, or by them taken jointly?

Neither can such improvement arise from such speculations as the following, which are the themes suggested by the Vedant:- In that manner is the soul absorbed into the deity? What relation does it bear to the divine essence? Nor will youths be fitted to be better members of society by the Vedantic doctrines, which teach them to believe that all visible things have no real existence; that as father, brother, etc., have no actual entity, they consequently deserve no real affection, and therefore the sooner we escape from them and leave the world the better. Again, no essential benefit can be derived by the student . . . from knowing what it is that makes the killer of a goat sinless on pronouncing certain passages of the Veds and what is the real nature and operative influence of passages of Ved, etc.

Again the student . . . cannot be said to have improved his mind after he has learned it into how many ideal classes the objects in the Universe are divided, and what speculative relation the soul bears to the body, the body to the soul, the eye to the ear, etc.

In order to enable your Lordship to appreciate the utility of encouraging such imaginary learning as above characterized, I beg your Lordship will be pleased to compare the state of science and literature in Europe before the time of Lord Bacon, with the progress of knowledge made since he wrote.

If it had been intended to keep the British nation in ignorance of real knowledge the Baconian philosophy would not have been allowed to displace the system of the schoolmen, which was the best calculated to perpetuate ignorance. In the same manner, the Sangscrit system of education would be best calculated to keep this country in darkness, if such had been the policy of the British Legislature. But as the improvement of the native population is the object of the Government, it will consequently promote a more liberal and enlightened system of instruction, embracing mathematics, natural philosophy, chemistry and anatomy, with other useful science[s] which may be accomplished with the sum proposed by employing a few gentlemen of talents and learning educated in Europe, and providing a college furnished with the necessary books, instruments and other apparatus.

In representing this subject to your Lordship I conceive myself discharging a solemn duty which I owe to my countrymen and also to that enlightened Sovereign and Legislature which have extended their benevolent cares to this distant land actuated by a desire to improve its inhabitants and I therefore humbly trust you will excuse the liberty I have taken in thus expressing my sentiments to your Lordship.

Calcutta,
I have etc.,
RAMMOHUN ROY

✦   ✦   ✦

PART TWO

REFORMERS AND RADICALS

INTRODUCTION TO PART II

BRITISH RULE IN THE SUB-CONTINENT was by no means uncontested. Indian chiefs and armies had to be subdued and conquered through a series of military offensives, extending over the better part of a century. Between the 1770s and the 1850s, there were also many small-scale rebellions, where peasants, tribals, and preachers protested against colonial policies as these related especially to land and natural resources on the one hand and to religious practices on the other.

These localised protests had no real chance of overthrowing the British. A rebellion which carried this potential began in the early months of 1857. This is referred to by some (usually British) writers as the 'Sepoy Mutiny' and by other (always Indian) writers as the 'First War of Independence'. In fact, it was much more than the former, yet somewhat short of the latter. Its origins lay in the disaffection of soldiers in the employ of the East India Company. The mutinies in the barracks soon merged with the continuing discontent of the peasantry with regard to colonial agrarian policies. The arrogance of Christian missionaries and the fear that the state was promoting conversion also contributed to the disaffection. Stoking the fires further were princes and nobles who had been dispossessed or rendered impotent by the new order.

This uprising was underpinned neither by a sense of a common nationality nor by a modern idea of freedom. Had it succeeded, it would not have created a new Indian nation-state. Rather, it would have led to the restoration of a pre-colonial political order, with a Mughal Emperor in Delhi exercising uncertain control over regional satraps and chiefs. Victory for the rebels was likely to have led to low-level conflict and economic statis rather than to peace and economic development.

That said, the rebellion had a genuinely popular base as well as a very wide reach. Beginning in army camps near Calcutta and Delhi, it soon spread into the countryside, gathering support as it went along. There were bitter and continuing clashes between the rebels and troops who had stayed loyal to the British. Large parts of north, east, and central India were caught up in the conflict. There were horrible atrocities by both sides. The death toll ran into the hundreds of thousands. Many more perished through starvation and disease.

It was only towards the middle of 1858 that the East India Company was able to restore some semblance of order. The old, weak, and some-what decadent Mughal Emperor in London, Bahadur Shah Zafar, was found guilty of aiding the rebels and exiled to Rangoon. The government of the middle-aged and rather more authoritative Queen in London, Victoria, now assumed responsibility for the affairs of the sub-continent. Indians were henceforth to be subjects of the British Empire, rather than of the East India Company. A major reorganisation of the Government of India took place, with the creation of a professional civil service whose members would serve as magistrates and tax collectors in the districts and oversee the departments of finance, home, education, and public works in the provincial and central secretariats. The organisation of the colonial army was also streamlined, and a massive expansion of the railway network was set in motion, to facilitate speedy troop movements in case of a future uprising against British rule.

The rebellion of 1857 is a topic of continuing interest, not to say enchantment, to historians as well as the lay public. One hundred and fifty years later, a steady stream of books continues to appear, which memorialise afresh the victories and defeats, the heroes and the villains, of both sides. However, less remembered now is an event of perhaps even greater significance in Indian history, which likewise took place in 1857. This was the establishment of the first universities in India.

Founded in the same year as the Mutiny/War of Independence, the universities of Calcutta, Bombay, and Madras were the crucibles of modernity in India. As the sociologist André Béteille has pointed out, these universities 'opened new horizons both intellectually and institutionally in a society that had stood still in a conservative and hierarchical mould for centuries'. These universities were 'among the first open and secular institutions in a society that was governed largely by the rules of kinship, caste and religion'. Thus 'the age-old restrictions of gender and caste did not disappear in the universities, but they came to be questioned there'.

The Bengal, Bombay, and Madras presidencies were the three main territories under British control. Each was the size of a large European country, and each was home to a diverse as well as divided population. The first universities were located in the capitals of these three presidencies. These were soon followed by the Allahabad University, in the United Province; and the Punjab University, located in that province's capital and main city, Lahore. Dozens of colleges were also founded in the smaller towns; these were affiliated to the new universities, which set their curricula and certified their degrees.

Although open to all castes and communities, at least in the first decades of their existence, Indian universities were patronised most actively by Brahmins. Scribes, scholars, and advisers to pre-colonial regimes, this highest caste of Hindus now sought to serve in the same capacity under the new rulers. In a study of Western India, the social historian Ravinder Kumar observes that although Brahmins were merely 5 percent of the population, in the 1880s they constituted 80 percent of all university students and graduates. This turn to modern education was partly disinterested—a genuine search for knowledge—but mostly instrumental, namely, a means to employment in the colonial administration as clerks, teachers, tax and revenue officials, and subordinate judges. Brahmin dominance in the academy quickly translated into Brahmin preponderance in the middle rungs of the colonial administration. For example, of 384 Indian officials in the Bombay civil services in the year 1886–1887, 328 were Hindus, of which as many as 211 were

Brahmins. The bulk of these belonged to the sub-caste of Chitpavan Brahmins from the west coast.

Whereas some Brahmins were content with loyal service to the Raj, others had higher ambitions. They were reading Burke, Mill, Bentham, and other European thinkers as part of their university education; this inculcated the desire to work for an India whose leaders and lawmakers would be Indians, rather than Englishmen. The historian B. R. Nanda thus remarks that 'thanks to western education, the thoughts of the Chitpavan Brahmans were turning not towards a violent upheaval, but towards greater participation in the government of their own country through representative institutions'. Contemporary British historians put it less dispassionately, the Governor of Bombay, Richard Temple, writing in 1879 that 'never have I known in India a national and political ambition so continuous, so enduring, so far reaching, and so utterly impossible for us to satisfy, as that of the Brahmins of Western India'.

These reform-minded, Western-educated Indians formed clubs and associations in their respective towns and provinces. It was a far-sighted Englishman, Allan Octavian Hume, who first suggested that these associations be brought together in an all-India body with a representative character. In December 1885, some eighty educated men from all over the country met to form what was at first called the 'Indian National Union', but which was soon renamed the 'Indian National Congress'. One speaker said that with this gathering 'we now begin to perceive that notwithstanding the existing differences in our mother tongue, social habits and manners, we possess the true elements of nationality about us'. Another said that from this meeting onwards, 'we can with greater propensity than heretofore speak of an Indian nation, of national opinion and national aspirations'.

These aims might have been sincere, but in actual fact the new body was less than representative of the nation-in-the-making. The historian of that first Congress, Briton Martin Jr., points out that only two of its delegates were Muslims. Not unexpectedly, there were far more Brahmins than their proportion in the Indian population would warrant. There was a sprinkling of participants from other high castes such as Rajputs, Banias, and Kayasths, four representatives of farming castes, and apparently no Untouchables. However, 'this religious and caste distribution did not mean necessarily that specific religious and caste interests were given political representation or expression'. Rather, the speeches and debates at the Congress stressed the non-parochial and inclusive aims of the new organisation.

The Indian National Congress was to meet every year hereafter, the meetings circulating among the major cities of the sub-continent. The rebellion of 1857, the establishment of the universities in the same year, and the formation of the Congress, are the three framing events of Part II of this book. The five makers featured here all lived and wrote against the background of these events.

Four of these individuals came from a single region, western India. All had Marathi as their mother tongue. Two were Brahmins, two were not. There had been a long history of contestation among different castes in western India. Local Brahmins had refused to officiate at the coronation of the warrior-chief Shivaji (1630–1680), on the grounds that the caste of Marathas, to which the king belonged, were not really Kshatriyas, but Sudras, that is to say, from the fourth (or peasant) rather than the second (or warrior) strata of the Hindu hierarchy. Brahmins from the north came to legitimise the ruler—at a price—but the slight was not forgotten by Shivaji's kinsmen. The Peshwas, who ruled Maharashtra after Shivaji but before the British, were Brahmins, and tended to favour their kinsmen in matters of politics and economics.

Despite these divisions by caste, there remained a strong sense of regional identity in Maharashtra. From Shivaji onwards there was a tradition of local resistance to the Mughals in Delhi. Through the medieval period the region had given birth to many fine poets in the *bhakti* tradition, who sought to finesse caste hierarchies by suggesting that all were equal before God. In the absence of a Bengal-style Permanent Settlement, there was a thriving agrarian economy, with enterprising and outward-looking peasant-cultivators. Finally, the emergence of Bombay as a major centre of commerce and culture promoted a growing and increasingly self-aware middle class. Nor was Bombay the only urban centre of consequence—there was also Puné, the old capital of the Peshwas, where some of the best modern colleges were situated and where the most active Marathi newspapers were based.

In sum, Maharashtra was to the late nineteenth century what Bengal had been to the early nineteenth century—the epicentre of critical thinking and social reform among Indians coming to terms with modernity and alien rule.

2

THE MUSLIM MODERNIST

SYED AHMAD KHAN

AN EARLY BIOGRAPHER of Syed Ahmad Khan claimed that as a young boy, Khan had several times seen Rammohan Roy in the court of the Mughal Emperor. This is not altogether implausible—for Khan's family was closely associated with the ruling family of Delhi, in whose service Roy had also been. Could this sighting have been in 1828 or 1829, when Roy called on the Emperor en route to London to plead his case? And would this (admittedly tenuous) acquaintance with the moderniser of the Hindus have been a precocious influence on the first modernizer of Indian Islam? It is an intriguing thought.

Syed Ahmad Khan[1] was born in Delhi in 1817. His grandfather had served briefly as prime minister to one of the Mughal Emperors. The family was not orthodox—they patronized musicians and mystics and may also have allowed the consumption of wine. There was a tradition of scholarship: among Syed Ahmad's forebears were some keen mathematicians.

1. As with Rammohan Roy, I have used what I consider to be the most accurate of several variant spellings. Likewise, I have dispensed with Khan's title, which in this case came from the British having awarded him a knighthood.

Syed Ahmad was educated at home by his mother and later sent to a traditional school. The language he grew up with was Urdu, the lingua franca of the court and of the city beyond. In his studies he learnt Arabic and Persian. At the age of twenty he departed from tradition by joining the service of the East India Company. His family of Mughal loyalists were not best pleased, but, by identifying with the rulers-to-be, the young man had accurately read the future. He served as a clerk and then a judge in various towns in north India, rising steadily up the Company's hierarchy.

Like Rammohan Roy, Khan's facility in English was acquired through keeping company with Englishmen. Like Roy again, he wrote prolifically in more than one language. His first book, in Urdu, was an archaeological history of Delhi. Another early book examined doctrinal disputes in early Islam. He also published an edition of the *Ain-i-Akbari,* the great work by the scholar Abu Fazl on the reign of the Mughal Emperor Akbar.

During the uprising of 1857 Syed Ahmad Khan was posted in the town of Bijnor, in the western part of the United Provinces. In a quiet but determined way, he took the side of his masters and helped shepherd several English families to safety. However, he was deeply affected by the revolt and worried about its consequences for his fellow Muslims in particular. A book he wrote shortly afterwards challenged the theory that the uprising was planned by disaffected Muslims who opposed British rule. He pointed out that as many Hindus as Muslims had taken part in the revolt; and that more Muslims had stayed loyal to the British. He rejected the theories that the rebels were egged on by Russia or Persia. In his view, the protests were neither a conspiracy nor a crusade. Rather, they were a response to the arrogance of Christian preachers and to the failure of the Company to admit Indian members into the Legislative Council.

Khan's book on the 1857 uprising was followed by another whose title gave a clue to its contents, *The Loyal Mohammedans of India.* This documented the various acts of loyalty by Muslim officials and subjects during the uprising. Its author was convinced that the way forward for the Muslims now was to embrace modern education, which would serve to dispel the idea that they were inherently nostalgic or disloyal, while bringing them on par with the Hindus who were taking advantage of the opportunities afforded by British rule. In 1864, he started a Scientific Society for Muslims, whose members would study modern works of history, science, and political economy, in English and in translation. Two years later the Society started a journal edited and largely written by Khan himself.

The parallels with the endeavours of Rammohan Roy are quite striking. These may not have been entirely accidental. The biographer who claimed Khan had seen Roy as a young boy was the Urdu poet and writer Altaf Husain Hali. Hali writes that after the 1857 uprising, Khan 'realized that the future well-being of his fellow Muslims depended on two major factors—western education and an ability to understand and mix freely with the British; otherwise it seemed to him that the Muslims stood little chance of making progress or of retaining a place of honour and respect in India'. Compare this with what Rammohan Roy wrote in December 1829: 'From personal experience, I am impressed with the conviction that the greater our intercourse with European gentlemen, the greater will be our improvement in literary, social and political affairs; a fact which can be easily proved by comparing the condition of those of my countrymen who have enjoyed this advantage with that of those who unfortunately have not had that opportunity'.

In April 1869 Khan travelled to England himself. He was then almost exactly the same age (fifty-seven) as Rammohan Roy had been when he made *his* journey to the centre of imperial power. Like Roy, he met with British notables; like him, he published books in English for an English audience (in his case, a book of essays on Muhammad, which sought to refute the belief that Islam was a religion of the sword). Like his great predecessor, Khan travelled to England to learn more about the land of the conqueror, and to place before that conqueror the problems and aspirations of his people, who were the Muslims of the sub-continent.

It was while he was in England that Khan decided that he must start a college for Muslim young men desirous of modern education. On his return to India in October 1870, he set about raising funds for the enterprise. He visited the towns he knew in the United Provinces, but he also ventured further afield: to the capital of the Punjab, Lahore, and to the great principality in the Deccan, Hyderabad, whose ruler, the Nizam, was reputed to be one of the richest men in the world. After making dozens of speeches and travelling thousands of miles, he had finally collected enough money to formally inaugurate his project. The Mohammadan Anglo-Oriental College (as it was at first called) was founded on 24 May 1875. Classes commenced three years later.

In later years Khan continued to travel across India to raise funds for his college and to encourage Muslim families to send their children there. In a speech of 1893 he warned that the gap between Hindus and Muslims on this, the educational front, was very wide indeed. For example, in Bengal, where Muslims constituted 45.9 percent of the population, only one graduate in thirty was Muslim; in Madras, where Muslims constituted some 7 percent of the population, they had less than 1 percent of the graduates. The one province that countered the trend was his own, and largely because of his own efforts. Thus in the United Provinces, where Muslims were 11.2 percent of the population, they supplied 17.25 percent of the graduates.

Khan died in the year of Queen Victoria's Diamond Jubilee, 1897. In 1920 the Mohammadan Anglo-Oriental College was renamed the Aligarh Muslim University (AMU). Ninety years later it remains the university of choice for many young Muslims in India—with schools of medicine, law, and engineering, it has (and Khan would have approved) an especially well-regarded department of history. The AMU, now well into its second century, is the chief institutional legacy of Syed Ahmad Khan. A flavour of his intellectual and political legacy is captured in the excerpts that follow.

EDUCATING THE MUSLIMS

In 1882, the Viceroy, Lord Ripon, appointed a commission to review the state of primary and secondary education in British India. This commission was chaired by the civil servant and scholar W. W. Hunter. Excerpts from the testimony of Syed Ahmad Khan to the Education Commission follow. Here, the phrase 'our nation' refers to the Muslims of India. Note also the now somewhat archaic preference for 'Muhammadans' over 'Muslims'.[2]

◆ ◆ ◆

QUESTION: With reference to English schools for primary, middle, high and collegiate education, do you consider that English education is essentially requisite for the interests of the country, and for the people in their daily affairs of life? If so, to what standard?

ANSWER: About thirty years have now elapsed since the dispatch of 1854.[3] During this period the condition of India has undergone a considerable change. Railways have united distant provinces, and have facilitated intercourse to a great extent. Telegraphic lines have been extended all over the country, and have provided facilities for distant persons to talk with one another as if they were in the same room. These very things have [infused] a new life into commercial business, and have given a fresh impulse to every sort of enterprise.

In 1854, when the above named dispatch was written, India was certainly in a condition which might justify our thinking that the acquisition of knowledge through the medium of the vernaculars of the country would be enough to meet our immediate wants. But now such is not the case. Vernacular education is no more regarded as sufficient for our daily affairs of life. It is only of use to us in our private and domestic affairs, and no higher degree of proficiency than what is acquired in primary and middle vernacular schools is requisite for that purpose; nor is more wanted by the country. It is English education which is urgently needed by the country and by the people in their daily life. It will be useless to realize the truth of what I have said by any theoretical argument when we practically find so many proofs of it every day. We see that an ordinary shopkeeper, who is neither himself acquainted with English nor has any English knowing persons in his employment, feels it is [a] serious hindrance in the progress of his business. Even the itinerant pedlars and

2. From Shan Mohammad, ed., *Writings and Speeches of Syed Ahmad Khan* (Bombay: Nachiketa Publications, 1972), pp. 82–96.

3. That dispatch for the first time accepted the responsibility of the state for providing education to its subjects in India.

boxwalas, who go from door to door selling their articles, keenly feel the necessity of knowing at least the English names of their commodities, and of being able to tell their prices in English. A gentleman who visits a merchant's or a chemist's shop to make necessary purchases, but is neither himself acquainted with English nor is accompanied by a person knowing that language, feels his position as one of real perplexity. In consequence of the facilities afforded for travelling, respectable men are often under the necessity of sending and receiving telegraphic messages, and their ignorance of English proves a serious hardship to them. A few months ago a respectable Native gentleman sent his wife by railway from one station to another, telegraphing to a relation of his at the latter station to be present at the railway station with a conveyance for the lady, who was of course a pardahnashin.[4] The message reached him in time, but he was unhappily not acquainted with English. He was yet in search of an English-knowing person who might explain to him the import of the communication, when the train reached the station and the lady was necessarily compelled to leave the carriage and to wait outside. The state of affairs has therefore been so altered during the last thirty years that a necessity for English education is as much felt as that for a Vernacular one. . . .

QUESTION: Have all classes of the people benefited from the study of Western sciences and literature in Government or other institutions, and have the Muhammadans also derived this benefit as readily as the communities? If not, to what causes may their forbearance be attributed?

ANSWER: Of all the sections of the Indian community the Muhammadans have derived the least benefit from European sciences and literature. It is evident from the annual reports on public instruction that in Government and missionary schools and colleges, which may be regarded as the only means of disseminating Western science and literature in this country, the number of Muhammadans is extremely limited. . . .

I have myself earnestly endeavoured for years to trace the causes to which this shortcoming of the Muhammadans[5] may be ascribed. And in 1871 my

---

4. That is, she was in purdah.

5. At that time, 'Mahomedan' or 'Muhammadan' was the preferred alternative to the now common 'Muslim'.

humble endeavours resulted in the formation of a committee the object of which was to investigate the causes which prevented our community from taking advantage of the system established by Government, and to suggest means by which education could be spread amongst them. As a means of receiving aid in their enquiries the committee offered three prizes for the best essays by educated Muhammadan gentlemen on the subject of Muhammadan education, and no less than thirty-two essays were sent in. The views expressed in these essays were fully discussed at a large meeting of respectable and educated Musalmans, and the committee arrived at the conclusion that Muhammadans had strong feelings of dislike to modern education, and that their antagonism to the Government educational system was not a mere matter of chance.

This aversion of the Musalman community is due to the fact that when in the reigns of the Caliphs of Baghdad the Greek sciences of logic, philosophy, astronomy, and geography, were translated into Arabic, they were accepted by the whole Muhammadan world without hesitation, and, with slight modification and alterations, they gradually found their way into the religious books of the Muhammadans, so that in course of time these sciences were identified with their very religion, and acquired a position by no means inferior to that of the sacred traditions of the faith. A few spurious but well-known foreign as well as indigenous traditions which referred to remote historical events, and to which time had lent a charm, were likewise adopted and accepted like other religious doctrines.

European learning, which was founded on the results of modern investigations differed widely in principle from these Asiaticised Greek dogmas, and the Muhammadans certainly believed that the philosophy and logic taught in the English language were at variance with the tenets of Islam, while the modern sciences of geography and astronomy were universally regarded, and are still regarded by many, as altogether incompatible with the Muhammadan religion. History was viewed in no better light, inasmuch as it differed from their adopted traditions. As regards literature, it must be admitted that it is a subject which is always more or less connected with the religion of the nation to which it belongs: as such being the case, the Muhammadans, as a matter of course, viewed this branch of knowledge, too, in anything but a favourable light. Their antipathy was carried so far indeed that they began to look upon the study of English by a Musalman as a little less than the embracing of

Christianity, and the result was that Muhammadans generally kept aloof from the advantages offered by Government institutions. There are still some Musalmans who denounce the study of English in the severest terms, and those who pursue or endeavour to promote that study are positively pronounced to be Christians. But this prejudice has of late decreased to a great extent, and is not entertained by so large a portion of the Muhammadan community as formerly. This may be said to be the main cause of the abstention of the Muhammadans from the study of European science and literature.

QUESTION: Can you suggest how the causes, which may have hitherto operated in excluding the Muhammadans from this benefit, might be removed?

ANSWER: The very nature of the causes which have operated in excluding the Muhammadans from the benefit of English education, makes it impossible for Government to bring about their removal. Government could in no way interfere with or make an attempt to expose the fallacy of those views which the Muhammadans had rightly or wrongly believed to be their religious doctrines. There was no remedy but that some members of their own community might undertake the arduous task of impressing on the Muhammadans the advantages accruing from English education, and of proving by argument and reason that such education was in no way inconsistent with the tenets of their religion, and that the fanciful theories of Arabicised Greek science and philosophy which the advance of modern science and enlightenment tended to subvert, had no connection with the doctrines of Islam. Numerous discouraging circumstances and serious social dangers lay in the path of those advanced Muhammadans who undertook the task, odious as it seemed to the detractors of modern civilization among Muhammadans. The advocates of reform and enlightenment were sure to be made the object of furious and frantic abuse, and to be denounced as atheists, apostates, and Nazarenes [i.e., Christians]. But they were fully convinced that the Muhammadan nation could never be able to get rid of those illusive ideas and prejudices, until some members of their community prepared themselves to incur the odium which fanaticism and bigotry are always ready to offer to the advocates at enlightened reform. I was an humble participator in the endeavours of those who determined to devote themselves to this unpleasant task for the well-being of their co-religionists. With this object a periodical, named the *Muhammadan*

Social Reformer, was issued, in which the more advanced Muhammadans from time to time wrote articles on the subject of education and social reform, and, in spite of the vigorous opposition from the bigoted and conservative Muhammadans, made public speeches in various parts of Upper India to rouse the Muhammadans to make exertions to educate themselves and to realize their duties as citizens. The advocates of the cause of reform and enlightenment had, of course, anticipated the opposition with which they had to contend before undertaking so momentous a task and had prepared themselves for the worst consequences to their personal popularity among the common people. They did not mind the difficulties and obstacles which bigotry and ignorance placed in their way, but preserved in their endeavours; and I am glad to notice that my co-religionists have now begun to yield to reason and to acknowledge and amend their errors. The number of Muhammadan students in English-teaching institutions is now much greater than what it was ten years ago. The Muhammadan Anglo-Oriental College at Aligarh has some two hundred and twenty-five Muhammadan pupils at present, most of whom belong to good families, and have travelled from various parts of India to study European science and literature along with their own religion, languages, and literature. The Musalmans are now everywhere relaxing their undue prejudices, and reconciling themselves to modern thoughts and conditions of life. Time is no doubt a great reformer, but I think the endeavours above alluded to, which have been going on for the last twelve years, have in no small degree contributed to the present state of things. The remedy therefore lies in no hands but those of the Muhammadans themselves, and the evils can be removed by their efforts alone. . . .

✦ ✦ ✦

A MODERN CURRICULUM

Continuing on the theme of education, Khan now offers an up-to-date reading list for his fellow Muslims. These paragraphs are from a talk delivered to the Mohammedan Literary Society, Calcutta, in 1884.[6]

6. From G. F. I. Graham, *The Life and Work of Syed Ahmad Khan* (Delhi: Idrah-i Adabiyat-i Delli, 1974 [originally published in 1885]), pp. 76–81.

✦   ✦   ✦

I have now a few words to offer in connection with the business to be entered upon from to-day—the business of the Society. The most important and the most difficult subject which you gentlemen of the Directing Council will be requested to deliver your opinions on, is the selection of books to be trans-lated and published as a commencement. Looking at the state of my fellow-countrymen's minds, I find that, from their ignorance of the past history of the world at large, they have nothing to guide them in their future career. From their ignorance of the events of the past, and also of the events of the present,—from their not being acquainted with the manner and means by which infant nations have grown into powerful and flourishing ones, and by which the present most advanced ones have beaten their competitors in the race for position among the magnates of the world,—they are unable to take lessons, and profit by their experiences. Through this ignorance, also, they are not aware of the causes which have undermined the foundations of those nations once the most wealthy, the most civilized, and the most powerful in the history of their time, and which have since gradually gone to decay or re-mained stationary instead of advancing with the age. If, in 1856, the natives of India had known anything of the mighty power which England possesses,—a power which would have impressed the misguided men of the Bengal army with the knowledge how futile their efforts to subvert the empire of her Maj-esty in the East would be,—there is little doubt but that the unhappy events of 1857 would never have occurred. For the above reasons, I am strongly in favour of disseminating a knowledge of history, ancient and modern, for the improvement of my fellow-countrymen. There are certainly several works on history extant, written by our own authors; but they do not contain that infor-mation which is necessary to improve the civilization and morality of men. Their views of the age in which they wrote were entirely those of their rulers; and their works abounded in flattery of those same rulers, as writing the truth, in many cases, would have doomed them to death or torture. Thus, much that was evil and tyrannical in the governors of our country has never been transmitted to us. They never enlightened the people of this continent on those subjects of which, as I have stated above, they were ignorant. Sir Charles Trevelyan[7] has offered a prize of 500 rupees for the best essay on a

7. A former governor of Madras and member of the Viceroy's Executive Council.

comparison of the influence of the Greek literature on the Arabs under the Abbaside Caliphs of Bagdad, and the Ommizade Caliphs of Cordova, with the subsequent influence of Arabic literature on Europe. This is a step in the right direction, and this country ought to be very grateful to Sir Charles Trevelyan for his liberality. Various small editions of works on history have been translated by the Department of Public Instruction for the use of schools; but these do not contain that copiousness of detail, that full description of the morals, virtues, and vices of nations, which, in my opinion, are necessary in order to confer any real benefit on the native mind. The book which, I think, would be very suitable for our Society to commence with, is one written by M. Rollin on the ancient races, in which are admirably described their discovery of, and improvements on, the arts and sciences; as also their lives and systems of government, together with their virtues and vices. This book is equally adapted to old and young, and is, I think, admirably adapted for the training of the native mind. This history is that of the ancient nations. At present the natives of India firmly believe that the arts and sciences were perfected by the Greeks. Now I do not mean to deny that nation's ability. I quite agree with M. Rollin that, whether we regard their splendid army, their wise laws, or their introduction of, and improvements on, various arts and science, we must allow that they brought all these to a very high pitch of perfection. We may with truth designate the Greeks as the schoolmasters of the world in their own and also in succeeding ages. But we in India know nothing of their former state of barbarism, of the means by which they raised themselves to the position which we know they attained, and we are also utterly ignorant of what conduced to bringing about the prosperity of Europe, which now so far excels the Greece of ancient days. . . .

Again, gentlemen, with regard to works on natural philosophy. All those who have anything to do with the internal management of districts are well aware how the producing capabilities of the soil are gradually decreasing. One great reason for this evil, which, if not remedied, will some day seriously affect the finances of India, is that the natives have never even heard of the principles on which the cultivation of the soil ought to be conducted, or of the many new inventions for improving their acres. The basis of these principles is natural philosophy, by the study of which we acquire a knowledge of the various properties of bodies, and by which we learn how to make use of the same. Steam, which we thought of no use whatever, is revealed to us in all its usefulness by the above science. Those among us who have been to

Roorkee[8] will have observed how wonderful are the uses to which a solitary shaft set in motion by steam is turned—how by it many works are set in motion, and many and varied articles turned out; and at first you have doubtless thought that all this was done by something more than human. The works at Roorkee, great as they are, are small compared with the many wonderful ones in England. I would therefore strongly advocate the translation of small works on natural philosophy in separate series. We might, for example, translate a small one on steam, one on the properties of water, or one on electricity.

Another work which is most necessary for India to read is one on political economy. Political economy was formerly known to us, but none of the works on it of our ancient authors are now extant. . . . Besides, even if they were [available], Europe has so perfected this science as to have made them comparatively useless. From a want of knowledge of it, the natives of India are utterly in the dark as to the principles on which the government of their country is carried on. They do not know that the revenue is collected for their own benefit, and not for that of Government. Millions are under the idea that the rupees, as fast as they are collected, are hurried on board ship, and carried off to England! Why is this? Only through their ignorance of political economy. Their own immediate prosperity is also seriously impaired by this ignorance. They do not know how to manage their affairs, how to so apply their present wealth that it may increase tenfold, and at the same time relieve other countries by letting loose their capital, and not burying it in their houses. I would therefore recommend the translating little by little, so as not to interfere with smaller works, of Mill's 'Political Economy'. There is this to be said against it, that it is very voluminous; but, gentlemen, this is also an argument in its favour, as unless a work be voluminous, this important science cannot be treated of as it deserves. Again, against it might be advanced that there are certain portions of it which are not applicable to this country, but only to England or Europe. But this is exactly what ought to be put clearly before us natives, in order that we may comprehend what Europe is doing. . . .

+ + +

8. The town of Roorkee, in the northern part of the United Provinces, had extensive canals around it—it was also home to one of India's oldest engineering colleges.

THE TWO EYES OF INDIA

In January 1883 Syed Ahmad Khan delivered a speech in Patna empha-sising the need for cordial relations between Hindus and Muslims. Ex-cerpts from this speech follow.[9]

✦ ✦ ✦

Friends, in India there live two prominent nations which are distinguished by the names of Hindus and Mussulmans. Just as a man has some principal or-gans, similarly these two nations are like the principal limbs of India. To be a Hindu or a Muslim is a matter of internal faith which has nothing to do with mutual relationship and external conditions. How good is the saying, who-ever may be its author, that a human being is composed of two elements—his faith which he owes to God and his moral sympathy which he owes to his fellow-being. Hence leave God's share to God and concern yourself with the share that is yours.

Gentlemen, just as many reputed people professing Hindu faith came to this country, so we also came here. The Hindus forgot the country from which they had come; they could not remember their migration from one land to another and came to consider India as their homeland, believing that their country lies between the Himalayas and the Vindhiyachal.[10] Hundreds of years have lapsed since we, in our turn, left the lands of our origin. We remember neither the climate nor the natural beauty of those lands, neither the fresh-ness of the harvests nor the deliciousness of the fruits, nor even do we re-member the blessings of the holy deserts. We also come to consider India as our homeland and we settled down here like the earlier immigrants. Thus In-dia is the home of both of us. We both breathe the air of India and take the water of the holy Ganges and the Jamuna. We both consume the products of

9. From Mohamed, *Writings and Speeches of Syed Ahmad Khan,* pp. 159–160.

10. The Vindhya mountains, running east to west in the middle of the peninsula, are generally said to divide north from south India. It is interesting that Syed Ahmad Khan leaves the area south of the Vindhyas out of his purview, this despite the fact that it was home to millions of Hindus as well as Muslims. This may have been be-cause the Mughals (his frame of reference) had never really penetrated into this region.

the Indian soil. We are living and dying together. By living so long in India, the blood of both have changed. The colour of both have become similar. The faces of both, having changed, have become similar. The Muslims have acquired hundreds of customs from the Hindus and the Hindus have also learned hundreds of things from the Mussulmans. We mixed with each other so much that we produced a new language—Urdu, which was neither our language nor theirs. Thus if we ignore that aspect of ours which we owe to God, both of us, on the basis of being common inhabitants of India, actually constitute one nation; and the progress of this country and that of both of us is possible through mutual cooperation, sympathy and love. We shall only destroy ourselves by mutual disunity and animosity and ill-will to each other. It is pitiable to see those who do not understand this point and create feeling of disunity among these two nations and fail to see that they themselves will be the victims of such a situation, and inflict injury to themselves. My friends, I have repeatedly said and say it again that India is like a bride which has got two beautiful and lustrous eyes—Hindus and Mussulmans. If they quarrel against each other that beautiful bride will become ugly and if one destroys the other, she will lose one eye. Therefore, people of Hindustan you have now the right to make this bride either squint eyed or one eyed.

Undoubtedly, what to say of Hindus and Mussulmans, a quarrel among human beings is a natural phenomenon. Within the ranks of the Hindus or Mussulmans themselves, or even between brothers as also between fathers and sons, mothers and daughters there are dissensions. But to make it perennial is a symptom of decay of the family, the country, and of the nation. How blessed are those who repent, and step forward to unite the knot which has by chance, marred their mutual relations and do not allow it to get disrupted. O! God, let the people of India change to this way of thinking.

✦   ✦   ✦

POLITICS AND DISCORD

Two years after the above speech, the Indian National Congress was founded. Syed Ahmad Khan was from the first suspicious of the Congress, which he thought would promote rivalry between communities while alienating Indians from the British. The activities of the Congress were to radically alter his views of Hindu-Muslim relations, as witness the next excerpt, from a speech delivered to a Muslim audience in Meerut in March 1888. Provincial rivalries were also at work here—as a native of Delhi, and a resident of the United Provinces, Khan had reservations about the Bengalis who then dominated the Congress.[11]

✦ ✦ ✦

I think it expedient that I should first of all tell you the reason why I am about to address you on the subject of to-night's discourse. You know, gentlemen, that, from a long time, our friends the Bengalis have shown very warm feelings on political matters. Three years ago they founded a very big assembly, which holds its sittings in various places, and they have given it the name 'National Congress'. We and our nation[12] gave no thought to the matter. And we should be very glad for our friends the Bengalis to be successful if we were of opinion that they had by their education and ability made such progress as rendered them fit for the claims they put forward. But although they are superior to us in education, yet we have never admitted that they have reached that level to which they lay claim to have attained. Nevertheless, I have never, in any article, or in any speech, or even in conversation in any place, put difficulties or desired to put difficulties in the way of any of their undertakings. It has never been my wish to oppose any people or any nation who wish to make progress, and who have raised themselves up to that rank to which they wish to attain and for which they are qualified. But my friends the Bengalis have made a most unfair and unwarrantable interference with my nation, and therefore it is my duty to show clearly what this unwarrantable interference has been, and to protect my nation from the evils that may arise from it. It is quite wrong to suppose that I have girded up my loins for the purpose of fighting my friends the Bengalis: my object is only to make my nation understand what I consider conducive to its prosperity. It is incumbent on me to show

11. From Mohamed, *Writings and Speeches of Syed Ahmad Khan*, pp. 181–186.

12. By our 'nation', Khan means the Muslims of India. The speech would originally have been in Urdu—where he most likely would have used the word 'qaum', which would more precisely translate as 'community of believers' rather than 'nation'.

what evils would befall my nation from joining in the opinions of the Bengalis: I have no other purpose in view. . . .

Gentlemen, what I am about to say is not only useful for my own nation, but also for my Hindu brothers of these [United] Provinces, who from some wrong notions have taken part in this Congress. At last they also will be sorry for it, although perhaps they will never have occasion to be sorry; for it is beyond the region of possibility that the proposals of the Congress should be carried out fully. These wrong notions which have grown up in our Hindu fellow-countrymen, and on account of which they think it expedient to join the Congress, depend upon two things. The first thing is this: that they think that as both they themselves and the Bengalis are Hindus, they have nothing to fear from the growth of their influence. The second thing is this: that some Hindus—I do not speak of all the Hindus but only of some—think that by joining the Congress and by increasing the power of the Hindus they will perhaps be able to suppress those Mohammedan religious rites which are opposed to their own, and, by all uniting, annihilate them. But I frankly advise my Hindu friends that if they wish to cherish their religious rites they can never be successful in this way. If they are to be successful, it can only be by friendship and agreement. The business cannot be done by force; and the greater the enmity and animosity the greater will be their loss. I will take Aligarh as an example. There Mohammedans and Hindus are in agreement. The Dasehra and Moharrum fell together for three years, and no one knows what took place. It is worth notice how, when an agitation was started against cow-killing, the sacrifice of cows increased enormously, and religious animosity grew on both sides, as all who live in India well know. They should understand that those things which can be done by friendship and affection cannot be done by any pressure or force. If these ideas which I have expressed about the Hindus of these Provinces be correct and their condition be similar to that of the Mohammedans, then they ought to continue to cultivate friendship with us. Let those who live in Bengal eat up their own heads. What they want to do, let them do it. What they don't want to do, let them not do it. Neither their disposition nor their general condition resembles that of the people of this country. Then what connection have the people of this country with them? As regards Bengal, there is, as far as I am aware in Lower Bengal, a much larger proportion of Mohammedans than Bengalis. . . . Those Mohammedans are quite unaware of what sort of thing the National Congress is. No Mohammedan Rais[13] of Bengal took part in it; and the ordinary Bengalis who live in the district are also as ignorant of it as the Mohammedans. In Bengal the Mohammedan population is so great that if the aspirations of those Bengalis who are making so loud an agitation be fulfilled, it will be extremely difficult for the Bengalis to remain in peace even in Bengal. These proposals of the Congress are extremely inexpedient for the country which is inhabited by two different nations, who drink from the same well, breathe the air of the same city, and depend on each other for its life. To create animosity between them is good neither for peace, nor for the country, nor for the town.

After this long preface, I wish to explain what method my nation, nay, rather the whole people of this country, ought to pursue in political matters. I will treat in regular sequence of the political questions of India, in order that you may have full opportunity of giving your attention to them. The first of all is this—In whose hands shall the Administration and the Empire of India rest? Now, suppose that all the English and the whole English army were to leave India, taking with them all their cannon and their splendid weapons and everything, then who would be rulers of India? Is it possible that under these circumstances two nations—the Mohammedans and the Hindus—could sit on the same throne and remain equal in power? Most certainly not. It is necessary that one of them should conquer the other and thrust it down. To hope that both could remain equal is to desire the impossible and the inconceivable. At the same time you must remember that although the number of Mohammedans is less than that of the Hindus, and although they contain far fewer people who have received a high English education, yet they must not be thought insignificant or weak. Probably they would be by themselves enough to maintain their own position. But suppose they were not. Then our Mussalman brothers, the Pathans, would come out as a swarm of locusts from their mountain valleys, and make rivers of blood to flow from their frontier on the north to the extreme end of Bengal. This thing—who after the departure of the English would be conquerors—would rest on the will of God. But until one nation had conquered the other and made it obedient, peace cannot reign in the land. This conclusion is based on proofs so absolute that no one can deny it. Now, suppose that the English are not in India and that

---

13. 'Rais' may be roughly translated as landlord. It refers to a class of Muslim gentry who were wealthy as well as cultured.

one of the nations of India has conquered the other, whether the Hindus the Mohammedans, or the Mohammedans the Hindus. At once some other nation of Europe, such as the French, the Germans, the Portuguese, or the Russians, will attack India. Their ships of war, covered with iron and loaded with flashing cannon and weapons, will surround her on all sides. At that time who will protect India? Neither Hindus can save [India] nor Mohammedans; neither the Rajputs nor my brave brothers the Pathans. And what will be the result? The result will be this—that foreigners will rule India, because the state of India is such that if foreign powers attack her, no one has the power to oppose them. From this reasoning it follows of necessity that an empire, not of any Indian race, but of foreigners, will be established in India. Now, will you please decide which of the nations of Europe you would like to rule over India? I ask if you would like Germany, whose subjects weep for heavy taxation and the stringency of their military service? Would you like the rule of France? Stop! I fancy you would, perhaps, like the rule of the Russians, who are very great friends of India and of Mohammedans, and under whom the Hindus will live in great comfort, and who will protect with the tenderest care the wealth and property which they have acquired under English rule? (Laughter). Everybody knows something or other about these powerful kingdoms of Europe. Everyone will admit that their governments are far worse, nay, beyond comparison worse, than the British Government. It is, therefore, necessary that for the peace of India and for the progress of everything in India the English Government should remain for many years—in fact for ever! . . .

✦   ✦   ✦

3

THE AGRARIAN RADICAL

JOTIRAO PHULE

RUNNING THROUGH SYED AHAMD KHAN'S WORK to modernise Muslims was an undercurrent of rivalry with the Hindus, who had taken earlier and in larger numbers to Western education and to employment in the schools, colleges, offices, law courts, and factories that had been established under colonial rule. The point of departure for our next maker of modern India was not so much the advance, under the Raj, of Hindus in general, but of upper-caste Hindus in particular. Jotirao Phule[1] was born in 1827, less than a decade after the advent of the East India Company in his native Maharashtra. He belonged to the caste of Malis, who had traditionally cultivated fruits and vegetables. Phule's family had supplied flowers to the court of the Peshwas, these grown on a holding of thirty-five acres granted them by the rulers. They were thus not poor, but not really affluent either.

Jotirao studied in a school in the town of Puné that was run by Scottish missionaries. Here he mixed with boys of other castes, including some Untouchables. As a young man he visited and was powerfully

---

1. Phule's first name is sometimes rendered as 'Jotiba'.

impressed by a school for girls run by American missionaries in the town of Ahmednagar. These experiences inspired him, then still in his twenties, to start a school for girls of low castes himself. He also opened several other schools, which admitted children from the Untouchable castes of Mangs and Mahars.

An autodidact, Phule seems to have been influenced by Thomas Paine as a young man. In 1855 he wrote a play against the iniquities of the caste system. (In view of the dominance of Brahmins over book production and publishing in western India, the play was published only after the playwright's death.) By now Phule was convinced that Western education, with its rationalist outlook, could play a key role in the emancipation of the low castes and the concomitant undermining of Brahmin power.

Although his teachers seem to have seen a potential convert, Phule resisted the pressure to become a Christian. As with Rammohan Roy, the encounter with missionaries helped him fashion a critique of orthodox Hinduism. Like Roy, again, he came to profess a deism which held that there was a single Creator who provided the moral touchstone for society as a whole.

From the 1860s, Phule's interest shifted from managing his schools to wider programmes of social reform, such as widow re-marriage. Meanwhile, he was also active in business, selling hardware to factories in and around Puné. He was also successful as a contractor for road-works and bridges. The money he made from these enterprises was ploughed back into his social activities.

By the 1870s, Phule was a figure of some influence and importance in Maharashtra. His profile was enhanced by a series of powerful tracts that he published, which spoke out against the stranglehold of Brahmins over the social, economic, political, and spiritual life of western India. These were sometimes written in the form of a dialogue between the reformer and one of his adversaries. Through innovative readings of Hindu legends, he presented the Brahmin as a wily and unscrupulous operator who acted always to exploit and suppress the peasant and the labourer. Likewise, in a reinterpretation of the career of the warrior-king Shivaji, he represented the warrior as relying, in his campaigns and for his victories, on his peasant armies rather than (as the conventional historiography had it) on his Brahmin ministers and advisers.

In 1873 Phule helped found the Satyashodak Samaj, the Society of Truth-Seekers. To qualify as a member, an individual had to get fifty letters of support and nomination. Some of the rules of the society were typical of reformers of the time—the vow not to consume alcohol, for example. Others were daringly precocious, such as the obligation to spread education among women and the low castes. The Samaj also promoted marriages that would take place without the involvement of Brahmin priests.

Phule's status and achievements were recognised by his nomination to the Municipal Council of Puné in 1876. He, in turn, looked with favour upon the British Raj, which held the balance of power between the different communities, and which—so he thought—could be persuaded to recognise that it was not the Brahmins but the members of more numerous, cultivating castes who were the real representatives of Indian society and the real carriers of its history.

Under Phule's direction, the Satyashodak Samaj lobbied Government to promote policies that would benefit the farmers and labourers who came under the caste category of 'Shudras'. As the Samaj's first published report put it, the organisation was founded 'in order to free the Shudra people from slavery to Brahmans, *Bhats*, Joshis, priests, and others. For thousands of years, these people have heedlessly despised and exploited the Shudras, with the aid of their cunningly devised books. This action was taken, therefore, so that through good advice and the spread of education, the Shudras might be got to understand their real rights, and freed both in religious and more general matters from the false and self-interested books of the Brahmans'. The British, believed Phule, had a historic mission 'to liberate the disabled Shudras from the slavery of the crafty Aryas' [i.e., the upper castes].

Jotirao Phule was a remarkable social activist as well as a gifted writer. By the time of his death in 1890, he had published polemics, plays, songs, and ballads. Of the two excerpts from his oeuvre below, the first was written in the language of the rulers; the second in his mother tongue. The editor of the latter work, G. P. Deshpande, writes that 'it is impossible to translate the vigour and ruggedness of his Marathi'. This seems unduly modest; for, as our reproduction of the translation by Desh-pande and his collaborators demonstrates, the power and intensity of Phule's ideas are by no means entirely lost when rendered into English.

EDUCATING THE MASSES

Our first excerpt from Jotirao Phule is from his evidence to the same Education Commission of 1882 to which Syed Ahmad Khan also testi-fied. Like Khan, he saw access to modern education as crucial to the advancement of his people, who were the peasant masses of western India. Khan, in turn, had been provoked and inspired by the work of Rammohan Roy. Roy thought that by means of modern education Hin-dus would come to be on a par with the British; Khan hoped the same instrument would bring Muslims on a par with Hindus; Phule hoped that it would bring non-Brahmins on a par with Brahmins. The paral-lels are striking.[2]

✦ ✦ ✦

. . . I wrote some years ago a Marathi pamphlet exposing the religious prac-tices of the Brahmins, and incidentally among other matters, adverted therein to the present system of education, which, by providing ampler funds for higher education, tended to educate Brahmins and the higher classes only, and to leave the masses wallowing in ignorance and poverty. I summarized the views expressed in the book in an English preface attached thereto, por-tions of which I reproduce here so far as they relate to the present enquiry—

Perhaps a part of the blame in bringing matters to this crisis may be justly laid to the credit of the Government. Whatever may have been their motives in providing ampler funds and greater facilities for higher education, and ne-glecting that of the masses, it will be acknowledged by all that in justice to the latter, this is not as it should be. It is an admitted fact that the greater portion of the revenues of the Indian Empire are derived from the ryot [peasant]'s labour—from the sweat of his brow. The higher and richer classes contribute

2. From G. P. Deshpande, ed., *Selected Writings of Jotirao Phule* (New Delhi: Left-Word Books, 2002), pp. 103–112.

little or nothing to the state exchequer. A well-informed English writer states that our income is derived, not from surplus profits, but from capital; not from luxuries, but from the poorest necessaries. It is the product of sin and tears.

That Government should expend profusely a large portion of revenue thus raised, on the education of the higher classes, for it is these only who take advantage of it, is anything but just or equitable. Their object in patronizing this virtual high class education appears to be to prepare scholars who, it is thought, would in time vend learning without money and without price. If we can inspire, say they, the love of knowledge in the minds of the superior classes, the result will be a higher standard, of morals in the cases of the individuals, a large amount of affection for the British Government, and unconquerable desire to spread among their own countrymen the intellectual blessings which they have received. . . .

It is proposed by men who witness the wondrous changes brought about in the Western world, purely by the agency of popular knowledge, to redress the defects of the two hundred millions of India, by giving superior education to the superior classes and to them only. We ask the friends of Indian Universities to favour us with a single example of the truth of their theory from the instances which have already fallen within the scope of their experience. They have educated many children of wealthy men and have been the means of advancing very materially the worldly prospects of some of their pupils. But what contribution have these made to [the] great work of regenerating their fellowmen? How have they begun to act upon the masses? Have any of them formed classes at their own homes or elsewhere, for the instruction of their less fortunate or less wise countrymen? Or have they kept their knowledge to themselves, as a personal gift, not to be soiled by contact with the ignorant [and] vulgar? Have they in any way shown themselves anxious to advance the general interests and repay the philanthropy with patriotism? Upon what grounds is it asserted that the best way to advance the moral and intellectual welfare of the people is to raise the standard of instruction among the higher classes? . . .

One of the most glaring tendencies of [the] Government system of high class education has been the virtual monopoly of all the higher offices under them by Brahmins. If the welfare of the ryot [peasant] is at heart, if it is the duty of Government to check a host of abuses, it behoves them to narrow this monopoly day by day so as to allow a sprinkling of the other castes to get into the public services. Perhaps some might be inclined to say that it is that if

Government looks a little less after higher education which is able to take care of itself and more towards the education of the masses there would be no difficulty in training up a body of men every way qualified and perhaps far better in morals and manners.

My object in writing the present volume is not only to tell my Shudra brethren how they have been duped by the Brahmins,[3] but also to open the eyes of Government to that pernicious system of high class education, which has hitherto been so persistently followed. . . . I sincerely hope that [the] Government will ere long see the error of their ways, trust less to writers or men who look through high-class spectacles, and take the glory into their own hands of emancipating my Shudra brethren from the trammels of bondage which the Brahmins have woven around them like the coils of a serpent. It is no less the duty of each of my Shudra brethren as have received any education, to place before Government the true state of their fellowmen and endeavour to the best of their power to emancipate themselves from Brahmin thralldom. Let there be schools for the Shudras in every village; but away with all Brahmin school-masters! The Shudras are the life and sinews of the country, and it is to them alone, and not to the Brahmins, that Government must ever look to tide over their difficulties, financial as well as political. If the hearts and minds of the Shudras are made happy and contented, the British Government need have no fear for their loyalty in the future.

✦   ✦   ✦

Phule now turns to what the state must do to improve education at different levels.

✦   ✦   ✦

Primary Education

. . . With regard to the few Government primary schools that exist in the Presidency, I beg to observe that the primary education imparted in them is not at

3. Brahmins or priests were the highest caste, Sudras the caste of peasants and laborers at the bottom of the Hindu social hierarchy (but above the Untouchables). After the Brahmins in rank were the Kshatriyas or warriors, and then came the Vaishyas or merchants.

all placed on a satisfactory or sound basis. The system is imperfect in so far as it does not prove practical and useful in the future career of the pupils. The system is capable of being developed up to the requirement of the community, if improvements that will result in its future usefulness be effected in it. Both the teaching machinery employed and the course of instruction now followed, require a thorough remodelling.

(a) The teachers now employed in the primary schools are almost all Brahmins; a few of them are from the normal training college, the rest being all untrained men. Their salaries are very low, seldom exceeding Rs. 10, and their attainments also very meager. But as a rule they are all unpractical men, and the boys who learn under them generally imbibe inactive habits and try to obtain [government] service, to the avoidance of their hereditary or other hardy or independent professions. I think teachers for primary schools should be trained, as far as possible, out of the cultivating classes, who will be able to mix freely with them and understand their wants and wishes much better than a Brahmin teacher, who generally holds himself aloof under religious prejudices. These would, moreover, exercise a more beneficial influence over the masses than teachers of other classes, and who will not feel ashamed to hold the handle of a plough or the carpenter's adze when required, and who will be able to mix themselves readily with the lower orders of society. The course of training for them ought to include, besides the ordinary subjects, an elementary knowledge of agriculture and sanitation. The untrained teachers should, except when thoroughly efficient, be replaced by efficient trained teachers. To secure a better class of teachers and to improve their position, better salaries should be given. Their salaries should not be less than Rs. 12 and in larger villages should be at least Rs. 15 or 20. Associating them in the village polity as auditors of village accounts or registrars of deeds, or village postmasters or stamp vendors, would improve their status, and thus exert a beneficial influence over the people among whom they live. The schoolmasters of village schools who pass a large number of boys should also get some special allowance other than their pay, as an encouragement to them.

(b) The course of instruction should consist of reading, writing . . . , and accounts, and a rudimentary knowledge of general history, general geography, and grammar, also an elementary knowledge of agriculture and a few lessons on moral duties and sanitation. The studies in the village schools might be fewer than those in larger villages and towns, but not the less practical. In connection with lessons in agriculture, a small model farm, where practical instruction to the pupils can be given, would be a decided advantage and, if really efficiently managed, would be productive of the greatest good to the country. The text-books in use ... require revision and recasting as much as they are not practical or progressive in their scope. Lessons on technical education and morality, sanitation and agriculture, and some useful arts, should be interspersed among them in progressive series. . . .

(c) The supervising agency over these primary schools is also very defective and insufficient. The Deputy Inspector's visit once a year can hardly be of any appreciable benefit. All these schools ought at least to be inspected quarterly if not oftener. I would also suggest the advisability of visiting these schools at other times and without any intimation being given. No reliance can be placed on the district or village officers owing to the multifarious duties devolving on them, as they seldom find time to visit them, and when they do, their examination is necessarily very superficial and imperfect. [A] European Inspector's supervision is also occasionally very desirable, as it will tend to exercise a very efficient control over the teachers generally.

(d) The number of primary schools should be increased—

1) By utilizing such of the indigenous schools as shall be or are conducted by trained and certificated teachers, by giving them liberal grants-in-aid.

2) By making over one half of the local cess fund for primary education alone.

3) By compelling, under a statutory enactment, municipalities to maintain all the primary schools within their respective limits.

4) By an adequate grant from the provincial or imperial funds. . . .

Higher Education

The cry over the whole country has been for some time past that Government have amply provided for higher education, whereas that of the masses has been neglected. To some extent this cry is justified, although the classes directly benefited by the higher education may not readily admit it. But for all this no well-wisher of his country would desire that Government should, at the present time, withdraw its aid from higher education. All that they would wish is, that as one class of the body politic has been neglected, its advancement should form as anxious a concern as that of the other. Education in India is still in its infancy. Any withdrawal of State aid from higher education cannot but be injurious to the spread of education generally.

A taste of education among the higher and wealthy classes, such as the Brahmins and Purbhoos, especially those classes who live by the pen, has been created, and a gradual withdrawal of State aid may be possible so far as these classes are concerned; but in the middle and lower classes, among whom higher education has made no perceptible progress, such a withdrawal would be a great hardship. In the event of such withdrawal, boys will be obliged to have recourse to inefficient and sectarian schools, much against their wish, and the cause of education cannot but suffer. Nor could any part of such education be entrusted to private agency. For a long time to come the entire educational machinery, both ministerial and executive, must be in the hands of Government. Both the higher and primary education require all the fostering care and attention which Government can bestow on it.

The withdrawal of Government from schools or colleges would not only tend to check the spread of education, but would seriously endanger that spirit of neutrality which has all along been the aim of Government to foster, owing to the different nationalities and religious creeds prevalent in India. This withdrawal may, to a certain extent, create a spirit of self-reliance for local purposes in the higher and wealthy classes, but the cause of education would be so far injured that the spirit of self-reliance would take years to remedy that evil. . . .

With regard to the question as to educated natives finding remunerative employments, it will be remembered that the educated natives who mostly belong to the Brahminical and other higher classes are mostly fond of service. But as the public service can afford no field for all the educated natives who come out from schools and colleges, and moreover the course of training they receive being not of a technical or practical nature, they find great difficulty in breaking themselves to other manual or remunerative employments. Hence the cry that the market is overstocked with educated natives who do not find any remunerative employment. It may, to a certain extent, be true that some of the professions are overstocked, but this does not show that there is not other remunerative employment to which they can betake themselves. The present number of educated men is very small in relation to the country at large, and we trust that the day may not be far distant when we shall have the present number multiplied a hundred-fold, and all betaking themselves to useful and remunerative occupations and not be looking after [government] service.

In conclusion, I beg to request the Education Commission to be kind enough to sanction measure for the spread of female primary education on a more liberal scale.

Poona
Joteerao Govindrao Phooley,
19th October 1882
Merchant and Cultivator and Municipal Commissioner,
Peth Joona Ganja

✦　✦　✦

THE CONDITION OF THE PEASANTRY

In 1883 Phule wrote *Shetkaryacha Asud* (The Cultivator's Whipcord), a powerful and still resonant description of the plight and poverty of the majority of Indians who were agriculturists. This is a continuous saga of woe, the stream of consciousness style and the lack of paragraphs heightening the intensity and impact. I present three excerpts from a recent translation of the book. The first excerpt is an account of the daily life and troubles of the peasant.[4]

✦　✦　✦

One day a farmer was walking towards his village from the Collector's[5] tent in the breezy mangrove beside the river, striding in anger and grinding his teeth.

4. From Deshpande, *Selected Writings of Jotiba Phule*, pp. 157–163, 167–169, 179–182. Translated by Aniket Jaaware. Note that for 'Brahmin' this translation uses the equally acceptable 'Brahman'.

5. The Collector was the most powerful state official in a district.

He seemed about forty and a little demoralized. He had a white twisted turban on his head, which was tied down with a cloth, he was wearing a double
half-shirt made of khadi [home-spun cloth] and old curled Satara boots. . . .
The boot heels were strong and thick, but he was walking a little oddly because they had developed cracks in a few places. He had a beard and mous-
tache, which were hiding his front teeth. The forehead and eyes were large
and the pupils were grey. He was fair and reasonably pleasant to look at. The
face was a little rounded though. After reaching home around two in the afternoon, he went to the kitchen and taking a sheet off the peg, he spread it on
the ground and with a rolled up blanket under his head, lay down to sleep,
covering his face with a handkerchief. But he could not sleep, thinking of his
meeting with the Collector—'He was still busy with his breakfast and tea, and
he did not listen to the truth that I was telling him, and did not allow me to pay
my instalment later.' He could not sleep, and putting his hands on his chest,
as if a little crazy, he started talking to himself thus:

> Unlike other villagers, I have not warmed the hands of the *bhat*
> [upper-caste] servants and so they have spoken to the white offi-
> cer and doubled my tax, and in the same year the rain was indif-
> ferent and my fields and gardens were burnt out, and then sud-
> denly Father died. There were a lot of expenses for the rituals. So
> in the first year, I assured the garden-plot to the Brahman money-
> lender, registered it in his name as well, for the money to pay the
> taxes with. Later he calculated the interest, doubling and tripling
> it, and took over my garden-plot. The moneylender's uncle is a
> clerk in the revenue office, his cousin is the Collector's secretary,
> his brother-in-law is the munsif and his father-in-law the taluk's[6]
> police officer, and moreover, most of the people in the govern-
> ment offices are his caste relations, so if I had argued with him,
> they would have troubled me no end and reduced me to a dry
> summer, on the smallest excuses. Thus in the second year, I sold
> off the few ornaments women of my house had on their bodies
> and put all that money into paying the taxes and later borrowed

6. A munsif is a village headman; a taluk is a territorial sub-division of a district.

money every year from Gujar[ati] and Marwadi[7] moneylenders to pay for that. Now they have filed suits against me, which have been lying in the court for so many years. I have paid so much in bribes to the court officers, peons, scribes, lawyers and all, that I am at the end of my tether. Now sometimes one finds government servants who do not take bribes, but they are even more useless than those who do, because they are nonchalant and do not care about the poor farmer at all, and the clever lawyers take money from us, in the name of these servants and put the bite on us regularly. And if we do not do that then we have to accept the orders secured by the moneylenders. Now no moneylender lets me stand at his door! I paid off the tax instalments last year with my newly-married elder daughter's ornaments and now her father-in-law does not let her live in his house. Oh, how unfortunate I am that I sold off her ornaments to avoid a calamity and ruined her marriage in the process! And now, how do I pay this year's tax? There is no money to buy new *mot*[8], the old ones are torn and the sugarcane is drying up. The corn has also gone to waste. The cattle-feed is about to finish, as is all the dried grass and fodder. The bullocks are weak because they do not get enough to eat. The women's clothes are in tatters and they are forced to wear ancient bedsheets bought for marriage. The children have to go about half-naked and feel ashamed of meeting people. Because the grain in the house is nearly over, we are surviving on sweet radishes. I do not have enough money to feed our mother with good food as she prepares to die. What shall I do? How will I be able to till the land if I sell the bullock? I cannot think of starting a business because I cannot read or write at all. If I leave my province and go to alien places, I have no skill which will help me fill my belly. If I swallow a potion made of roots, the able children might be able to survive somehow, but who will look after the old woman and along with my little ones, look after my wife?

7. Maharashtra, Phule's homeland, had no indigenous trading caste, so the merchants and moneylenders were mostly migrants from Gujarat and from Marwar in present-day Rajasthan.

8. Containers to draw water from the well.

At whose doors can they know if they need help? Where will
they beg?

Thus finally sighing, he fell asleep weeping. Later when I come out, wiping
my tears and look around, I see that his house is single storied and tile-
roofed. Beside the house, there is a covered shed for cattle. There are two or
three bullocks, old and ruminating and a few large empty containers are
pushed into a corner and outside, in the courtyard, there stands an old cart
for eight bullocks. On it, there is a broken basket. On the left, a square platform is made . . . and beside it, there is place for storing water and on that
there are a few clay pots filled with water and beside it, there is a crudely tiled
bathing place, with a half-wall on three sides. Outside it, water has collected
in a small ditch and it is filled with insects and worms. Beyond, under the
white *chafa* tree, there are a few children dancing, half-naked, with all manner
of stains on their bodies, noses running, sweating and stinking, playing with
lumps of mud. One of them is playing at being a shop-keeper, with anklets of
seeds on her feet, pretending to sell arrack [country liquor]. Many of the children giving her pebbles and seeds as coins . . . are shuffling about, falling on
each other, pretending to be drunk. Behind the house stands a cattle shed
made with wooden beams and pillars. In it lies a buffalo who has just calved
and a wretched mare. There are all manner of insects sticking to the walls. In
the cracks of the roof knots of hair are stuck all over, collected from the head
while combing. Beside this, is a chicken-run. . . . There is a waste-heap beyond and large green flies are buzzing over it because little children have
been shitting there. Beside that, because the heaps of grass and fodder are
finished, lie small heaps of leaves. In the other corner cow-pats are stacked,
beside it, under the tree, there are broken implements lying about and a
vilayati dhattura[9] grows under them, and a mangy bitch who's just littered
lies there, growling at passers-by. Beside it lies a heap of waste fodder, and in
the remaining area sits a youngish woman, with her back to the house, ar-
ranging cow-pats. She is up to her knees in the dung, pounding it with her
feet. In the kitchen itself there is uneven flooring and one sees the waste from
grinding and cleaning and cleaned vegetables lying about here and there.
Here is a heap of pith thrown about, and there a heap of rotting onions. A
stale stink rises from them. In the middle, an ancient woman is lying on a sheet,

9. A shrub that is not indigenous to India.

groaning. Beside her head lies a plate of food—a bowl of crushed *bhakri* [coarse grain] softened in the liquid of the dal, and [a] jug of water. In the cradle a little baby is weeping loudly. Besides all this, at places one finds a line of a child's piss, at some other place a patch of white ash where a child's turd has been cleaned up. Several corners of the house are red and dark from tobacco spit. In one corner sits a large grinder, to be drawn by three or four women, in another there is a large mortar and pestle and in the corner near the door under the broom, all the dirt pushed there after sweeping the floor, and on top, a rag which was used to clean a baby's arse. There beside the cooking fire stands a dirty frying pan and the milk pot. Beside it, the cat has covered up its shit with ash. The walls are covered with stains left from squishing bugs and insects on them, and fingers wiping off snot. In a small cabinet is the oil pot, tooth powder, a horn comb, a rickety mirror, and on a ledge three or four stone lamps are stacked for the night. An oil stain spreads from them onto the ground. Maybe once in a year all the grease is scraped away. In another cabinet beside the flour basket are placed pieces of stale *bhakri,* in a third cabinet there are green chillies, garlic, coriander, and baskets of mangoes, on which flies eat from one side and excrete from the other. And in the fourth stands a heap of old and torn footwear. A flintstone lies beside them. Old and worn bedsheets hang from one peg, and on another, bedcovers. . . . If you look up you can see that the tiles of the roof have not been changed for three or four years, and with grass ropes rats have made holes in it. There are no windows or ventilators of any kind anywhere in the whole house to let in fresh air. The beams and corners and supports and pillars are tarred with black smoke, and in most empty spaces spiders have [woven] most artistic and delicate webs, like mosquito nets, on which a thousand baby spiders are playing. On the undergird of the roof, on the beams, on pillars the poisonous shells of insects and spiders are sticking, and especially on wooden spaces there are heaps of dust mixed with rat shit and cockroach shit and for years a broom has not touched them for lack of time. Suddenly, the kind of dust storm which rises because of the heat before the summer rains, swept through the house, and as the dust rose and filled the house with the wind streaming in through the gaps in the roof tiles, the poisonous dust filled the snoring farmer's open mouth, and he woke up coughing. The poisonous cough so troubled him that he nearly fainted and he started moaning and thrashing about. His sick old mother somehow managed to stumble up to him, and putting a blanket roll under his head, cupping his chin, staring into his eyes, said, 'Oh lord!, please open your eyes. So many times have I given money to [God] so that [the Devil] should not harm you, and that too sometimes without your knowledge, selling off grain, and have made the Brahman sit with his rosary in front of [the deity] and fed so many brahman women!! Dear child, so many times have I spent money without telling you so that the gods will be pleased with you. Why did not that god speak through the Collector's mouth today, and allow you to pay the taxes in instalments? . . . O you cunning brahmans, from the very birth of my dear child you have threatened me with ill-favoured stars and taken money from me, where is all the virtue that you collected? O, you have cheated me so much in the name of *dharma* that with that money I could have saved my child's neck! . . .'

+ + +

Phule now turns from ethnography to social critique, from describing the plight of the farmer to analysing its causes.

+ + +

Now let us turn to the present condition of the farmer. Since our generous and kind government began to rule in this brahmanic nation, they have started killing bullocks and cows and calves, without any proper ritual, and have started eating them. . . . One of the important resources of the farmer is diminishing. On top of that, because of the lack of rain there was a drought, and the cattle were destroyed by lack of fodder. Secondly, because of the rules of the Forest Department and the inadequacy of pastures, the cattle could not be fed, their off-spring became weak and cattle [were] seized by diseases, and thousands died, and the farmers had to uproot their pegs. Next, because there [were] not enough cattle to labour on their farms, the farmer could not take proper care of his fields, and the yield has decreased. Moreover, our cunning government, through its brahman employees, has carried out surveys every thirty years and have established levies and taxes as they willed, and the farmer, losing his courage, has not properly tilled his lands, and therefore millions of farmers have not been able to feed themselves or cover themselves. As the farmers weakened further because of this, they started dying by the thousands in epidemics. There was drought to add to the misery, and thousands of farmers died of starvation, but in spite of all this, their numbers did increase, and that led to the tilling of the same lands in increasing proportion, and the lands could not be rested. So the yield of the lands decreased. Moreover, every year vast amounts of grain, cotton, leather, wool were being exported to alien countries, and because of the inadequate information or because of their own rough nature itself, the white engineers and doctors and employees wasted large amounts of manure into the sea, and now most of the lands are close to being fallow. O, these foreign white engineers, in cahoots with white doctors devise schemes to make money, and sell the goods manufactured by craftsmen from their own countries, waste unlimited amounts of local people's money, and then make sure that there are buildings named after them. Later if all the local citizens are ruined along with these buildings, why should they care? Having made money and acquired fame, they are done. Sometimes it does not rain one year and there is not enough crop. Sometimes because there are not enough bullocks, the crop suffers. Sometimes because the moneylender does not lend money in time to buy fresh seeds or sometimes because the farmer uses seeds bought last year, the crop suffers. If for these heavenly or earthly reasons, the farmer does not get a sufficient yield, and goes alone to the brahman employee's house to tell him of his condition and of his crops, he finds the brahman, newly bathed, sitting with stripes of holy ash on his body, enveloped in incense-smoke, engrossed in worship, some other [Brahman] sitting with an old and dirty book, reading it, and someone else counting the beads, while thinking of women. Hearing his footsteps, without opening his eyes the brahman asks, 'Who is it?' Farmer: 'My lord it's me, a farmer.' Brahman: 'Why have you come at this holy hour? If you have brought vegetables and stuff, hand it in inside, without touching the children. Come to the office in the afternoon and make an application in your name, then I will talk to the officer myself. Now go.' Then the farmer turns and walks straight to the Collector's tent in the mangrove, and saluting the butlers, the jamadar [sergeant] and the sepoy, and standing at a distance from the tent-door, what he sees is that some white officer dressed in a Mughal manner, with a velvet carpet under his feet, bathed in lavender perfume, is busy eating, some other is lying face down on a couch and is busy reading rosy descriptions in a book and is therefore disinterested, so the sepoys rudely turn the farmer back and he cannot even tell his woes and plaints to the white officers. Therefore there is not any manner in which the farmer can convey his condition to the white officers, who are inured in their customary luxury, status, attendants; or to black officers who are engrossed in their wealth, their higher caste and colour, and their rituals of purity (neither is there any interaction between the women and children of white and black officers and the ignorant women and children of the farmers' houses to establish a communication). Both these officers are so completely different from the farmer, and such alien people will survey the farmer's lands, and give him relief? Or how else? . . . Let that be. But when the ignorant farmer borrows money to pay the taxes, these brahmans dress up as *bhats* [priests] and blocking his path, give him all manner of blessings and surely extract some money from him. If there is timely rainfall, and the farmer gets a reasonable crop, since the cowardly employees of our brave government have disallowed use of firearms and other weapons to the farmer, he cannot protect his crop from wild boar and pigs. Of the remaining crop, the brahman, the Marwadi moneylenders, Gujarati traders and brokers from other castes keep an eye on the crop and grab whatever they can of it. Not only this, but even the Gujarati brahman cooks in traders' households have started claiming some amount of jiggery. Let that be. Eventually when the farmer returns from the market and enters the town gate, a few hoodlums and the patil [headman] demand to be given drink, and if he does not, then we can be sure that after a few days, he will receive a summons of some kind or other. What a just kingdom this is, wealthy in knowledge! But in this just kingdom, there was a time when it was possible to travel from the southern most point to the northern most, carrying gold, without being challenged. But at present, the goddess of wealth cannot find food and clothes in the houses of the farmer, deprived of education and clothes, and has therefore gone away to her father, the ocean, and beyond the seas, the English people have shed laziness, following her wishes, and have become industrious and hard working, and have started treating all women young and old with equality, so she has not become a domestic servant in their houses. And now even though they speak sweetly to all the farmers, and collect money as they will, they avoid educating the farmer. The main reason behind this must be that they realize that the moment the farmer educates himself and acquires knowledge, he will carry his whip on his shoulder, and he will bring the goddess of wealth back to his own home, and make her stay there happily. Because if this ever happens, the English will have to scream and yell, and travel to America, and somehow manage to fill their bellies by working hard day and night. . . .

+   +   +

Phule ends his tract with a positive agenda for agrarian reform, addressed to the highest officials of the British Raj.

+   +   +

Now I will go to the cool mountains of [the imperial summer capital] Simla, and resting there for some time, I will call upon our government beyond the seas, and in the presence of our supremely kind Governor, suggest measures for improving the farmers' condition:

Now our good and law-abiding government should keep aside the greed of money and appoint detective doctors to keep an eye on the farmer's behaviour, and if the farmer misbehaves and loses his health, or begins to steal and do other sinful things, then arrangements must be made for proper punishment, without that they will not become moral. Unless laws are passed forbidding the farmer from marrying more than one woman and forbidding him from marrying his children at an early age, their off-spring will not turn out strong. Because the white employees are ill informed there is a disproportionate number of *bhat* brahmans appointed, and therefore they do not have to slave in the farms, and their women do not have to fill their bellies by frequenting the market with produce. Moreover, because the farmer is ignorant, the *bhat* brahmans benefit immensely from caste distinctions and hierarchies. Thus the brahmans, employed in government jobs, and the mythologists, storytellers, teachers in schools strive day and night, using all their cunning, to prevent the breakdown of these distinctions and hierarchies. Therefore until the farmers' children become able enough to manage positions in government, not more than the proportionate number of brahmans should be employed in government jobs, and the remaining posts should be given to Mussalman or [non-Brahman] Hindu or Britons. It is only then that they (the brahmans) will stop obstructing the education of the farmer. This, their artifice has become invisible to white eyes because in most government departments, it is the brahmans who are employed. Thus the brahman caste becomes more and more educated, and wealthy, whereas the farmer becomes poorer and eventually pauperized, and sometimes takes part in the brahman's rebellions and loses his life. Moreover the brahmans have so impressed their cunning religion on the minds of the farmers that they think it virtuous to plead guilty for murders that they have committed on the say of the brahmans. This wastes the energies and labour of the police and the Justice Department. Therefore in order to educate the farmers' children, there should be teachers from their own castes, who can hold the plough properly, weed the farm and do other things as well. A law should be made which will ensure that children are sent to the schools run by such teachers, and for the first few years, some lower and easier divisions should be created, enticing them with degrees equal to those of brahmans, and unless other castes are prevented from forcing the farmer to perform rituals in their marriages, the farmers' children will not be interested in education. . . . And when there are such educated and qualified patils [headmen] in all villages, the cunning *bhat* kulkarnis [Brahmin accountants] will not be able to make the farmers fight amongst themselves and file cases against each other, and that will benefit our government immensely, since in a short time the farmer will be able to pay more tax than now, and the unjustifiable swellings in the police and justice departments can then be reduced. Also, the government should for a time believe that there are no *bhat* brahmans to be employed, and as capable people come up from amongst the farmers, they should be employed . . . in other government offices in big and small positions, and are trained to do these jobs. Until this happens, the farmers' feet will not find the ground, and the government's revenue will never increase. . . .

Let that be. Now I will suggest measures for improving the lands of the farmer, which are increasingly become fallow—

The benevolent government should educate all the farmers, and until they become mature enough to use machines to do the usual things on the farms like European farmers, all the white people and the Mussalmans should slaughter goats and sheep instead of slaughtering cows and oxen; or they should import cattle and slaughter and eat them here, because otherwise there will not be sufficient supply of cattle for the farms, and there will not be enough compost and other fertilizer as well, and so neither the farmer, nor the government will benefit. The essences of leaf, grass, flower, dead insects and animals, [are] washed away by summer rain, therefore our industrious government should, as and when convenient, use the white and black soldiers and the extra manpower in the police department to construct small dams and bunds [embankments] in such a way that this water would seep into the ground, and only later go and meet streams and rivers. This would make the land very fertile, and the soldiers in general, having got used to working in [the] open air, will also improve their health and become strong. Even if they labour to the value of one anna every day, this will mean an increase in the government's earnings to the tune of twenty-five lakh[10] [rupees] per year, because our careful government has, including the police department, at least two lakh sepoys. Similarly the government should, in all the hills and valleys, build lakes wherever possible, so that the small dams in the lower areas will fill with water, and the wells too will have a supply of water and the land for fruit and flower and vegetables will be used, and the government too will benefit along with the farmer. Therefore the government should maintain these bunds in good condition, especially in the backwaters. The government should conduct surveys of all the lands in its territory, employing water specialists, and wherever it is found that there is enough water to be drawn from more than one source, these places should be clearly marked in the maps of the towns, and the government should give some awards to farmers who dig wells without its assistance. Also, the government should allow the farmer to collect all the silt and other things extracted from rivers and lakes, as in the olden times, and it should also return all the cow pastures to the villages, which it has included in its 'forest'; it should, however, make sure that no firewood is collected, or land tilled in the areas that belong to it, and it should also forbid the cutting of wood for selling as wood for construction and destroy the oppressive Forest Department. Our own government should, spending money from its own coffers, purchase breeds of good sheep from several countries, bring them here, and when they are bred here, their droppings will make for a good supply of fertilizer and their wool will benefit the shudra farmer. If the government does not have the courage to allow the farmer to possess old guns in order to protect his farms from wild beasts, then the government should assign that job to our clean black police department, and if a farmer's crop is devastated by wild boar, then the loss should be made up from the salaries of the senior officers or from the government's coffers—and until such a law is passed, the farmer will not be able to sleep peacefully at night and he will not be able to labour fully on his farm during the day. If the

10. Sixteen annas then made a rupee. A lakh is one hundred thousand.

government sincerely wishes to improve the condition of the ignorant shudra farmer, and increase its own yield, it should hold annual tests and competitions of greatest yield and greatest skill, and give awards to the best farmers. Calculating the yield average every three years, the best farmers should be given titles, and if the educated children of the farmer, along with good maintenance of their own farms, also learn some iron-work and carpentry and give exams in those subjects, the government should take them abroad, for them to see the agricultural schools there, so that the farmer will immediately improve his farming and be happy. . . . In general, the shudra and atishudra [Untouchable] farmer is slaving on his farms, along with women and children, day and night, until he is exhausted, and paying the various taxes, funds, etc., but our charitable government does not even think of educating the farmers' children enough to enable them to read a book on farming or relevant notices in newspapers, and while lakhs of farmers do not have enough cloth and enough food, our government spends inordinate amounts of money on the salaries and pensions of people in the army, the police, the justice departments, who are employed to protect and ensure the farmer's happiness and security. What should we say to this!!! Our government gives pensions worth hundreds of rupees per month to many of these apples of their eyes, white and black employees having worked on a fat per month salary of thirty or thirty-five [rupees]. Many of the black and white employees become too weak and blind to work for the government, and cheating even some very good European doctors, manage to get pensions, the white employees escape to England, and from amongst the black employees, many become suddenly young, as if Jesus Christ himself has roused them from the dead, and polishing their moustaches with wax and blacking, find employment in municipalities or in offices of big traders and earn thousands of rupees. Our watchful government should, without changing the salaries of any of the army carriage bearers, or construction workers, iron-workers, carpenters, the casual employee etc., slowly reduce all the inordinately increased salaries of all the black and white employees and slowly reduce the pensions as well. Unless the things written above are thought of, the foundations of the government will not be strengthened, and the farmers' fated penury will not change, and the days of his starvation will never end. . . .

◆   ◆   ◆

4

THE LIBERAL REFORMER

G. K. GOKHALE

Jotirao Phule's Satyashodkak Samaj was in part a reaction to the founding of the Poona Sarvajanik Sabha in 1870. Founded by the scholar, jurist, and reformer Mahadev Govind Ranade, this organisation stood, as its name implied, for the interests of all people, *'sarvajan'*. However, its leadership was almost exclusively from the Brahmin caste. Ranade was a Brahmin, as was his remarkable protégé, Gopal Krishna Gokhale.

Gokhale was born in 1866 in a village in coastal Maharashtra, the son of a police sub-inspector. He learnt his letters in a rural school before proceeding to the inland town of Kolhapur, where he completed his matriculation. He was then admitted to the Deccan College in Puné, from where he transferred to Bombay's Elphinstone College. On being awarded his B.A., he began to coach students, to pay back the loans his family had incurred to send him to college.

In 1884 two brilliant young Brahmin reformers, Gopal Ganesh Agarkar and Bal Gangadhar Tilak, founded the Deccan Education Society. The following year, Gokhale joined one of the Society's schools as a teacher. In 1889 Ranade appointed him editor of the quarterly journal of the Poona Sarvajanik Sabha. In the same year he attended his first session of the Indian National Congress. The next year Gokhale joined the faculty of Ferguson College in Puné, where he worked for the next two decades, teaching English literature, mathematics, and political economy. By now, he had acquired a taste for British writers and thinkers, among them Edmund Burke and John Stuart Mill.

By the time he was in his mid-twenties, Gokhale was a regular fixture at the annual meetings of the Congress. At the Calcutta session in 1890, for example, he spoke on the inequities of the salt tax. In 1897, having just turned thirty, Gokhale made the first of several trips to London, where he usually stayed at the National Liberal Club. On this visit he testified to a Royal Commission on poverty and famines in his homeland. Meanwhile, in a speech in the seaside town of Hastings, he compared the relationship between Britain and India to that between a giant and a dwarf, where 'everything went to the giant and what was left went to the dwarf'.

Gokhale was now a rising star in Indian politics. He was elected to the Bombay Legislative Council in 1899 and to its all-India counterpart, the Imperial Council, two years later. Between 1902 and 1906 he also served as the president of the Poona municipality, all while he continued taking classes in Ferguson College.

As befitting a teacher, Gokhale's speeches were rich in facts and subtle in argument. Favourite subjects included the excessive tax burden on the peasantry and the need for more and better schools to provide free and compulsory education for all regardless of caste, religion, or gender. He demanded more seats for Indians in the Imperial Council and asked also that the annual budget of the Government of India be open for scrutiny and amendment in the light of criticism.

Meanwhile, through his work for the Congress, Gokhale had acquainted himself with different parts of India. His outlook was further broadened by a visit to South Africa to study the condition of the Indian diaspora in that country.

In 1905 Gokhale founded the Servants of India Society, whose members dedicated themselves to serving the nation-in-the-making. These 'Servants of India' were required to 'work for the advancement of all [Indians], regardless of caste or creed'. He visited the United Kingdom again the same year. When he spoke at Cambridge, a young John Maynard Keynes told an Indian friend that Gokhale 'has feeling, but feeling guided and controlled by thought, and there is nothing in him which reminds us of the usual type of political agitators'. Indeed, 1905 ended for Gokhale with him presiding in December over the Congress meeting in Benares.

As a leader of the Congress, Gokhale tried hard to reach out to the Muslims. He was wholly free of sectarian prejudice himself. However, he was regarded as excessively pro-British by militants such as Bal Gangadhar Tilak. His was the classical liberal dilemma—too moderate for the radicals, yet too extreme for the Establishment. One Viceroy, Lord Hardinge, called Gokhale 'the most dangerous enemy of British rule in this country'.

In 1914 Gokhale turned down the offer of a knighthood. He died the following year, not yet fifty. He had already done a great deal for his country, then still a colony, and shown his compatriots many new directions. Summing up his life's work, his biographer B. R. Nanda remarks that Gokhale 'hated foreign rule, but he did not blame all the ills from which India suffered on the British. He wanted her to shake off the shackles of social and economic backwardness as well as of political subjection. He wanted to turn the encounter with the Raj into an opportunity for building a secular, modern and democratic society'.

ELEVATING THE DEPRESSED CLASSES

Our first excerpt is from a speech made by Gokhale to a meeting of the Social Conference in Dharwad in 1903, where he focused on the plight of the lowest castes, also known as the Depressed Classes.[1]

✦   ✦   ✦

Mr. President and Gentlemen,—the proposition which has been entrusted to me runs thus:-

1. From *Speeches of Gopal Krishna Gokhale,* 2nd ed. (Madras: G. A. Natesan, 1916), pp. 1054–1059.

That this Conference hold that the present degraded condition of the low castes is in itself and from the national point of view unsatisfactory, and is of opinion that every well-wisher of the country should consider it his duty to do all he can to raise their moral and social condition by trying to rouse self-respect in these classes and placing facilities for education and employment within their reach.

Gentlemen, I hope I am not given to the use of unnecessarily strong language and yet I must say that this resolution is not as strongly worded as it should have been. The condition of the low castes—it is painful to call them low castes—is not only unsatisfactory as this resolution says—it is so deeply deplorable that it constitutes a grave blot on our social arrangements; and, further, the attitude of our educated men towards this class is profoundly painful and humiliating. I do not propose to deal with this subject as an antiquarian; I only want to make a few general observations from the standpoint of justice, humanity, and national self-interest. I think all fair-minded persons will have to admit that it is absolutely monstrous that a class of human beings, with bodies similar to our own, with brains that can think and with hearts that can feel, should be perpetually condemned to a low life of utter wretchedness, servitude and mental and moral degradation, and that permanent barriers should be placed in their way so that it should be impossible for them ever to overcome them and improve their lot. This is deeply revolting to our sense of justice. I believe one has only to put oneself mentally into their place to realize how grievous this injustice is. We may touch a cat, we may touch a dog, we may touch any other animal, but the touch of these human beings is pollution! And so complete is now the mental degradation of these people that they themselves see nothing in such treatment to resent, that they acquiesce in it as though nothing better than that was their due.

I remember a speech delivered seven or eight years ago by the late Mr. Ranade in Bombay, under the auspices of the Hindu Union Club. That was a time when public feeling ran high in India on the subject of the treatment which our people were receiving in South Africa. Our friend, Mr. Gandhi, had come here on a brief visit from South Africa and he was telling us how our people were treated in Natal and Cape Colony and the Transvaal—how they were not allowed to walk on foot-paths or travel in first-class carriages on the railway, how they were not admitted into hotels and so forth. Public feeling, in consequence, was deeply stirred, and we all felt that it was a mockery that we should be called British subjects, when we were treated like this in Great Britain's colonies. Mr. Ranade felt this just as keenly as any one else. He had been a never-failing adviser of Mr. Gandhi, and had carried on a regular correspondence with him. But it was Mr. Ranade's peculiar greatness that he always utilized occasions of excitement to give a proper turn to the national mind and cultivate its sense of proportion. And so, when every one was expressing himself in indignant terms about the treatment which our countrymen were receiving in South Africa, Mr. Ranade came forward to ask if we had no sins of our own to answer for in that direction. I do not exactly remember the title of his address. I think it was 'Turn the searchlight inwards,' or some such thing. But I remember that it was a great speech—one of the greatest that I have ever been privileged to hear. He began in characteristic fashion, expressing deep sympathy with the Indians in South Africa in the struggle they were manfully carrying on. He rejoiced that the people of India had awakened to a sense of the position of their countrymen abroad, and he felt convinced that this awakening was a sign of the fact that the dead bones in the valley were once again becoming instinct with life. But he proceeded to ask:- Was this sympathy with the oppressed and down-trodden Indians to be confined to those of our countrymen only who had gone out of India? Or was it to be general and to be extended to all cases where there was oppression and injustice? It was easy, he said, to denounce foreigners, but those who did so were bound in common fairness to look into themselves and see if they were absolutely blameless in the matter. He then described the manner in which members of low caste were treated by our own community in different parts of India. It was a description, which filled the audience with feelings of deep shame and pain and indignation. And Mr. Ranade very justly asked whether it was for those who tolerated such disgraceful oppression and injustice in their own country to indulge in all that denunciation of the people of South Africa. This question, therefore, is in the first place a question of sheer justice.

Next, as I have already said, it is a question of humanity. It is sometimes urged that if we have our castes, the people in the West have their classes, and after all, there is not much difference between the two. A little reflection will, however, show that the analogy is quite fallacious. The classes of the West are a perfectly elastic institution, and not rigid or cast-iron like our castes. Mr. Chamberlain, who is the most masterful personage in the British Empire to-day,[2] was

2. Joseph Chamberlain was then Secretary of State for Colonies in the British Government.

at one time a shoemaker and then a screw-maker. Of course, he did not make shoes himself, but that was the trade by which he made money. Mr. Chamberlain to-day dines with Royalty, and mixes with the highest in the land on terms of absolute equality. Will a shoemaker ever be able to rise in India in the social scale in a similar fashion, no matter how gifted by nature he might be? A great writer has said that castes are eminently useful for the preservation of society, but that they are utterly unsuited for purposes of progress. And this I think is perfectly true. If you want to stand where you were a thousand years ago, the system of castes need not be modified in any material degree. If, however, you want to emerge out of the slough in which you have long remained sunk, it will not do for you to insist on a rigid adherence to caste. Modern civilization has accepted greater equality for all as its watchword, as against privilege and exclusiveness, which were the root-ideas of the old world. And the larger humanity of these days requires that we should acknowledge its claims by seeking the amelioration of the helpless condition of our down-trodden countrymen.

Finally, gentlemen, this is a question of National Self-interest. How can we possibly realize our national aspirations, how can our country ever hope to take her place among the nations of the world, if we allow large number[s] of our countrymen to remain sunk in ignorance, barbarism, and degradation? Unless these men are gradually raised to a higher level, morally and intellectually, how can they possibly understand our thoughts or share our hopes or co-operate with us in our efforts? Can you not realize that so far as the work of national elevation is concerned, the energy, which these classes might be expected to represent, is simply unavailable to us? I understand that that great thinker and observer—Swami Vivekananda—held this view very strongly. I think that there is not much hope for us as a nation unless the help of all classes, including those that are known as low castes, is forthcoming for the work that lies before us. Moreover, is it, I may ask, consistent with our own self-respect that these men should be kept out of our houses and shut out from all social intercourse as long as they remain within the pale of Hinduism, whereas the moment they put on a coat and a hat and a pair of trousers and call themselves Christians, we are prepared to shake hands with them and look upon them as quite respectable? No sensible man will say that this is a satisfactory state of things. Of course, no one expects that these classes will be lifted up at once morally and intellectually to a position of equality with their more-favoured countrymen.

This work is bound to be slow and can only be achieved by strenuous exertions for giving them education and finding for them honourable employment in life. And, gentlemen, it seems to me that, in the present state of India, no work can be higher or holier than this. I think if there is one question of social reform more than another that should stir the enthusiasm of our educated young men and inspire them with an unselfish purpose, it is this question of the degraded condition of our low castes. Cannot a few men—five per cent., four per cent., three, two, even one per cent.—of the hundreds and hundreds of graduates that the University turns out every year, take it upon themselves to dedicate their lives to this sacred work of the elevation of low castes? My appeal is not to the old or the middle-aged—the grooves of their lives are fixed—but I think I may well address such an appeal to the young members of our community—to those who have not yet decided upon their future course and who entertain the noble aspiration of devoting to a worthy cause the education which they have received. What the country needs most at the present moment is a spirit of self-sacrifice on the part of our educated young men, and they may take it from me that they cannot spend their lives in a better cause than raising the moral and intellectual level of these unhappy low castes and promoting their general well-being.

✦   ✦   ✦

ON HINDU-MUSLIM CO-OPERATION

In 1906 the Muslim League was formed as a party independent of the Indian National Congress. Three years later the principle of separate electorates was conceded, whereby a proportion of seats in the legislative council were set aside for Muslims elected by other Muslims. In the background of these potentially polarising events Gokhale urged for better relations between Hindus and Muslims. The excerpts that follow are from a speech originally delivered in Marathi in July 1909.[3]

✦   ✦   ✦

3. From *Speeches of Gopal Krishna Gokhale*, pp. 1134–1142.

. . . After glancing briefly at the past history of the two communities and the contributions made by them to the progress of the world, Mr. Gokhale proceeded to consider their respective positions at the present day in India. The Mahomedan minority, who were a little over one-fifth of the whole population, was very unequally divided among the different Provinces. In the Punjab and East Bengal they actually formed a majority of the population, being a little over one-half in the Punjab and about three-fifths in East Bengal. In Bombay, on the other hand, they were only one-fifth, in West Bengal between one-fifth and one-sixth, in the United Provinces one-seventh, in Madras about one-sixteenth, and in the Central Provinces less than one-twentieth. The bulk of the Mahomedans did not differ from the Hindus in race, but they had to remember that religion was a most powerful factor in life and it modified and sometimes profoundly modified race characteristics. In numbers, in wealth, in education and public spirit, the advantage at present lay with the Hindus. They had also so far contributed far more than the other community to the present national awakening in India. But they were greatly hampered by caste, and by temperament they were mild and passive. On the other hand, the Mahomedans were burdened with fewer divisions, their social structure rested on a more democratic basis, they had more cohesion among them, and they were more easily roused to action. The worst of the situation was that over the greater part of India the two communities had inherited a tradition of antagonism, which, though it might ordinarily lie dormant, broke forth into activity at the smallest provocation. It was that tradition that had to be overcome. And though there were certain special difficulties in their way and the task at times appeared well-nigh impossible, it was no more impossible than what Europe had to face for more than two centuries in the fierce antagonism between Protestants and Catholics. Spread of education, a wide and efficient performance of civic duties, growth of national aspirations and a quickening of national self-respect in both communities were among the forces which would ultimately overcome the tradition. The progress in that direction was bound to be slow and there were sure to be repeated set-backs. But they must believe in final success with all their will and persevere ceaselessly against all odds. It was a common-place of Indian politics that there could be no future for India as a nation, unless a spirit of co-operation of a sufficiently durable character was developed and established between the two great communities in all public matters. They could not get over that, no matter how angry they might be at times with one another. And those among them who wished to devote themselves to the promotion of such co-operation had no choices but to refrain as far as possible from joining in controversies likely to embitter the relations between the two sides, and exercising forbearance and self-restraint themselves to counsel it in others. The speaker was of opinion that a special responsibility lay in the matter with the Hindus, who had an advantage over the other community in regard to the spread of education and who were therefore in a better position to appreciate the needs of a growing nationality. They could also do a great deal towards the establishment of better relations if some of them devoted themselves to educational and other useful work among Mahomedans for the special benefit of that community. Such work could not in course of time fail to be appreciated, and it would powerfully help in gradually substituting confidence and goodwill and co-operation in place of the present distrust and suspicion and aloofness.

Having thus dealt with the general position Mr. Gokhale proceeded to express his view of the controversy that had agitated the country during the last six months. Much of the excitement, he said, had been due to a misapprehension of the character and scope of the new reforms. Mr. Gokhale stated his own position in [the] matter quite frankly. He had all along been in favour of special separate electorates for important minorities but he wanted such electorates to provide not the whole of the representation to which the communities were entitled but only so much of it as was necessary to redress the deficiencies and inequalities of general elections; and he wanted the same treatment to be extended to other important minorities than Mahomedans where necessary. Mr. Gokhale held strongly that in the best interests of their public life and for the future of their land they must first have elections on a territorial basis in which all communities without distinction of race or creed should participate and then special separate supplementary elections should be held to secure the fair and adequate representation of such important minorities as had received less than their full share in the general elections. . . .

When any one said that his community was important and should receive fair and adequate representation, the claim was entitled to the sympathetic consideration of all. But when any one urged that his community was specially important and should therefore receive representation in excess of its fair share, the undoubted and irresistible implication was that the other communities were comparatively inferior and should receive less than their fair share. That was a position to which naturally the other communities could not assent. British rule was based on equal treatment for all communities, and the speaker trusted that the Government would never be so weak as to lean for support on any one community in particular. It was urged that the Mahomedans had ruled in India for five centuries. It must not however be forgotten that the Hindus had ruled for countless centuries before them and even afterwards, before the British came on the scene, the Mahomedan power had been broken and displaced over nearly the whole country by a revival of Hindu rule. Then it was said that there were large Mahomedan populations in other countries—some of them self-governing countries—and that invested the Mahomedans of India with special importance. Mr. Gokhale could not see how that mattered in determining the extent of the representation which the Government of India should grant to its own subjects, unless it was on the assumption that in the administration of this country, those whose heart was not with India were to have preference over those whose was. Moreover the same ground could with equal reason be urged by Indian Christians and by Buddhists. Lastly, as regards the higher traditional loyalty of Mahomedans to British rule, the claim was not historically tenable. And even during the last two or three years Mahomedan names had not been altogether absent from the lists of those speakers and writers against whom the Government had though[t] it necessary to proceed, though it must be admitted that the number of such names had been extremely small. Before concluding Mr. Gokhale referred to the speech recently made by His Highness the Aga Khan. He said that he read portions of that speech with considerable astonishment, and he could not help regretting that so well informed and broad-minded a gentleman as His Highness should have been labouring under so much misapprehension. His Highness had said that unless larger concessions were made to the Mahomedans, the Hindus would be exultant and triumphant. All that Mr. Gokhale could say about this was that His Highness was evidently not in touch with Hindu feeling in the matter. Not only was there no disposition among the Hindus to exult or to feel triumphant but there was actually a sullen feeling of resentment throughout the country, a feeling daily growing deeper and stronger that the Government had not held the balance even and that it had already leaned too much on the Mahomedan side. His Highness had further said that unless additional concessions were made to Mahomedans, it would mean a monopoly of political power to the Hindus. Mr. Gokhale said that he rubbed his eyes as he read that statement. Surely the Aga Khan could not be under the impression that what the Government proposed to do was to hand over the administration of the country to elected Councils with Hindu majority in them. No, even with the Councils reconstituted as proposed the last word would still be with the officials. The enlargements of the Councils and the increase in the proportion of elected members were no doubt important matters, but they were not so important as to afford to any community a shadow of an opportunity to obtain a monopoly of political power in the country. As the speaker had often pointed out, the most important and the valuable part of the reform, of Legislative Councils was the power proposed to be conferred on members to raise discussions on administrative matters. This power, if wisely exercised, would gradually give the country an administration conducted in the light of day and under the scrutiny of public discussion in place of the present administration carried on in the dark and behind the backs of the people. For this purpose what really mattered was the capacity, the public spirit, and the sense of responsibility of the members. How many members were returned by any particular community was not of much consequence, and a member or two more or less on this side or that would not make the smallest difference in practice. Mr. Gokhale earnestly trusted that [the] Government would soon close the question in a definite manner and he was confident that before long the present soreness of feeling would disappear and normal relations again return between the two communities. When once the new Councils commenced to work it would be realized that there was no demand or scope there for work on sectarian lines and the man who worked for all would find his service appreciated by all communities. Controversies like the present were occasionally inevitable, but if they took care not to employ words or express sentiments which would leave soreness behind, they might succeed in averting the injury which otherwise was likely to result to the best interests of their growing nationality. They were all of them trustees of those interests, and the world and their own posterity would judge them by the manner in which they discharged that trust.

✦   ✦   ✦

A CALL TO SERVICE

This last excerpt comes from a speech delivered by Gokhale at Pachai-yappa's College, Madras, in 1904, where he urged the young men in the audience to devote themselves to some form of national service. Typically, he asks them to serve their countrymen in general rather than enrol specifically in his own Servants of India Society.[4]

✦   ✦   ✦

. . . Gentlemen, it is now nearly 20 years since I first enrolled myself as a member of a body of men at Poona who had come forward to undertake the responsibility of spreading higher education among our countrymen. They had come forward to take up this work, because they felt convinced that the future of this country was bound up with the spread of higher education in the land, and that the resources of no Government, however liberally disposed, could cope single-handed with the problem of public education. Well, I threw in my lot with these men, 20 years ago, and although my active participation in that work has now come to an end, my interest in the welfare of students, in all that concerns their present and future, is as warm as ever. During these 20 years of my life, the greater part of my time has been spent in the society of students. With them some of my happiest hours have been spent. To them my best work, such as it was, was given, and on them my dearest hopes for the future of this land are based. It is, therefore, natural that I should rejoice whenever there is an opportunity for me to meet students, and I am sincerely pleased that the students of this College should have given me this opportunity to meet them. . . .

Gentlemen, I hope that the students of this College realize adequately the character of the work in which they are engaged within the walls of this College. It is true that our Colleges and Universities, even the oldest of them, are comparatively of recent growth, and so that venerable tradition which surrounds the ancient seats of learning in the West and which exercises so powerful a hold on the minds and imagination of the students there—that venerable

4. Reproduced in D. G. Karve and D. V. Ambekar, eds., *Speeches and Writings of Gopal Krishna Gokhale*, vol. 3: *Educational* (Bombay: Asia Publishing House, 1967), pp. 187–191.

tradition has yet to grow round our institutions. But in one sense the very newness of this College learning you seek, marks you off from the rest of the people of this land, marks you off, I hope not in sympathies and interests—that would be a misfortune—but marks you off as men to whom a special trust is given, marks you off as persons who have entered a new brotherhood with special aims and aspirations in life. I want you to see that in proportion as you realize this, in that proportion the purpose which those great persons who introduced Western education in this country had in view, would be accomplished.

In one respect I think it is best to make an admission at once. One of the first objects of the Universities all over the world is to produce a class of men who would devote themselves to research and scholarship on the highest plane. I fear this is not possible in this country, at any rate not possible on a large scale for some time to come. In the first place the atmosphere must come into existence only slowly. Then our men do not enjoy those opportunities of learned leisure which are necessary for such work to be done. Further, those material equipments that are essential in the shape of libraries and laboratories are here of the poorest. You cannot, therefore, expect much work on this highest plane in this country for some time to come, and that should be admitted at once.

There is, however, other work perhaps not so dignified in appearance, but not less useful for the immediate welfare of the country, that can be done by our educated men. You can recognize this education as a new factor in your life, as an ennobling influence under which you have now placed yourself. And that means that your studies should not end when your College career is over. For if this influence is recognized by you as an ennobling influence, you can never have too much of it. It is a reproach that is sometimes justly urged against you that your studies end with your College career, and this reproach you must try to wipe away. And if you do that, you will attain a higher measure of culture, a higher degree of refinement and you will have qualified yourselves better even for the ordinary duties of life than if you give up your studies the moment you leave your College. This is one of the directions in which all can take advantage of facilities that are placed at their disposal though you may not be able to do much work on the highest plane.

In other directions too you may make yourselves useful. There is the call of duty on all sides, whichever way we turn. There is a great deal of work to be done in this ancient land. I do not stand here to preach one set of views in preference to another, but I simply point out the responsibilities that lie on you. You will soon be surrounded by duties of a pressing character. There is work to be done for the mass of your countrymen who are plunged in ignorance and superstition. This mass has been kept at a lower level of existence from which level it has got to be raised. Then there is work to be done for the elevation of the status of the womankind of the land. A whole sex shut out from the intellectual life of a people—this is not good for any country. In religion many of the old institutions are existing only in form and the spirit seems to have fled from them. You have got to recognize that there is work to be done in that direction as well. Further, the whole country is on a low level in regard to political existence and that means arduous work for those who interest themselves in that question. Lastly, the industrial development of the country needs to be urgently attended to. In all these directions there is work to be done. It is true that it is not everyone who can undertake such work, but a fair proportion might be reasonably expected to take some interest in this work in one or another of the various fields that I have mentioned. This is the call of the duty which you will have to recognize when you leave College and take your place in life.

Even if you are unable to do anything distinctive in this connection, there is one other direction in which you can all show yourselves worthy of the education you have received. Each one of you can do your duty all the better for the education you have received, can show that you recognize the responsibilities that devolve upon you better on account of the education that you have received. Many of us are apt to imagine that those who loom largely in the eyes of the public are the only ones that lead really useful lives. We sometimes talk and write as though only one or two individuals were really doing useful work and the rest only vegetating. It is, however, a mistake to think so. A nation's true greatness depends upon its average man and woman.

Seven years ago I was privileged to go to England. There were, of course, great statesmen, great generals and men of great learning, men of great wealth but what struck me most was that the greatness of England was due to the fact that the average men and women there led more earnest lives, recognized their responsibilities better than we do, endeavoured to prove more serviceable to society than is the case here. It is in the life, thoughts and actions of the average man and woman that the solid strength of a nation really lies. You may not be privileged to make any large contribution to the world's knowledge by research and scholarship, but every one of you can lead better, more earnest lives on account of the education you have received. If you do that in your own persons, you will have set a high example to those who come after you, and you will also have largely added to the moral energy of the nation. I therefore ask you to realize this, that it is in the power of every educated man to show that he is worthy of the education he has received, first by continuing his interest in his studies, secondly, by trying to be of service to his countrymen in any of the five fields I have just referred to, and thirdly, by leading in his own particular sphere a better, a more earnest, and a more dutiful life. . . .

✦ ✦ ✦

5

THE MILITANT NATIONALIST

BAL GANGADHAR TILAK

IN THE FIRST DECADE of the twentieth century, the Indian National Congress was divided into two camps, referred to as 'Moderates' and 'Extremists' respectively. Gopal Krishna Gokhale was the pre-eminent spokesman for the first camp. The second camp was most eloquenty represented by Gokhale's fellow Chitpavan Brahmin, fellow native of Ratnagiri, and fellow resident of Puné city, Bal Gangadhar Tilak.

Tilak was born in July 1856, the son of a schoolteacher and petty landowner. The family moved to Puné when he was ten. He completed high school and then graduated from Deccan College with first-class honours. Apart from his native Marathi, he was formidably fluent in Sanskrit and English. In 1880 he started teaching in a school. The next year he began publishing two newspapers with his friend Gopal Ganesh Agarkar, one in English, the other in Marathi. The polemical tone of their articles attracted much comment as well as several libel suits. In 1882 both Tilak and Agarkar were sentenced to four months in prison for defaming the *diwan* (chief minister) of the princely state of Kolhapur.

Agarkar and Tilak founded the Deccan Education Society in 1884. Six years later Tilak left the society for more openly political work. The rift between Agarkar and Tilak was also related to their different attitudes to gender relations—whereas Agarkar (and Gokhale) thought that Hindu women should get a modern education, Tilak had a more conservative view, believing that they were homemakers who had to subordinate themselves to the needs of their husbands and children. By the late 1880s, Tilak was also involved in the cow-protection movement, which sought to ban the eating of beef by Muslims on the grounds that it offended Hindu sentiments.

Tilak's first major work was an attempt to establish the antiquity of the Rig Veda, to demonstrate that the Hindus were civilised and sophisticated while the rest of humanity, and especially the Europeans, were still illiterate barbarians. In 1893 his revivalism took a more formal shape, through his promotion of a festival devoted to the worship of Ganapati or Ganesh, the elephant-headed son of Shiva. Previously a private domestic affair, observed in homes and temples, Tilak turned the festival into a mass celebration on the streets of the towns and cities of western India, featuring processions where the deity was led along by young men. Tilak also began another festival, to celebrate the memory and achievements of the medieval warrior-chieftain Shivaji.

Tilak was much more hostile to British rule than Gokhale. He saw it as leading to the decline and emasculation of India and Indians. He rejected the idea that 'the people of Asia will always remain slaves of the foreigners'. In 1897 Tilak was sentenced to eighteen months in prison for preaching disaffection against the Raj. After his release he travelled through South India, Ceylon, and Burma. From these journeys he concluded that there was a common Hindu core to social practice and customs throughout the sub-continent and that (as he put in a speech at the Ganapati festival in 1900) 'Hinduism is of higher worth than other religions'.

In the same year, 1900, the Viceroy, Lord Curzon, noted with satisfaction that the Congress had settled into a placid annual routine of earnest and dull speeches by well-meaning but ineffectual people. 'One of my ardent desires', remarked Curzon, 'is to assist it [the Congress] to a peaceful demise'. Tilak played a crucial role in invalidating this prophecy. He was helped by Curzon himself, in particular by the Viceroy's decision to partition the province of Bengal in 1905, with a view to weaning the Muslims of the eastern part of the province away from the Congress cause. The opposition to the partition was combined with the Swadeshi movement, which opposed the import of foreign goods into India. In these struggles Tilak played a leading part. He demanded a tariff of 10 percent on imports to promote Indian enterprise and called for a common language to promote national unity.

Where moderates like Gokhale asked young men to serve, Tilak asked them to protest and, if necessary, go to prison. In this respect the sarcasm and sharpness of Tilak's writings are in contrast to the understated reasonableness of Gokhale. As the Puné militant put it in a speech of 1897, 'God has not conferred upon foreigners the grant inscribed on a copper plate to the kingdom of India'. In a speech in Calcutta in 1906, Tilak insisted that 'love of nation is one's first duty. Next comes religion'. Claiming that 'no nation can equal India' in the antiquity of its history and the depth of its cultural traditions, he tended to believe that India was (as his biographer Stanley Wolpert puts it) 'God's chosen nation'.

In 1908 Tilak was charged again with sedition and with intensifying racial animosity between Indians and the British. He was defended by the brilliant Bombay lawyer Muhammad Ali Jinnah. The defence could not completely annul the evidence contained in Tilak's polemical articles. In the event, he was sentenced to six years in prison and deported to Burma. When they heard of the sentence, the textile workers of Bombay downed tools in a spontaneous strike that shut down seventy mills. While in Mandalay prison, Tilak wrote a major and still influential work on the meanings of the Bhagavad Gita.

Tilak came out of jail in 1914, run down in health and in spirit. The fire of his early years was now much attenuated. He was more accommodative of British rule: where he had once thundered that 'swaraj [freedom] is my birthright and I shall have it', he was willing to settle for Dominion status within the British Empire rather than full Independence. However, he continued to be active in politics, forming a Home Rule League in 1916. The same year he was charged once more with sedition. He was defended once again by Jinnah, this time successfully, and acquitted of the charges.

Tilak was a militant, populist leader who did a great deal to encourage young Indians to join the national movement. (On the negative side, the Hindu tenor of his speeches and writings may have alienated Indian Muslims.) For much of his career, he insisted that political freedom must take precedence over all else, including or even especially social reform. This credo is manifest in an excerpt from a speech of 1916, which carries on a long-running debate with the recently deceased Gokhale: 'If there is no svarajya there is no use labouring for the spread of female education, there is no use trying to secure industrial development and social reform also can avail but little. . . . Power is the primary necessity and where there is power, there alone resides wisdom; wisdom never resides apart from power'.

Bal Gangadhar Tilak died in Bombay in August 1920.

THE NEED FOR A NATIONAL HERO

In this essay, written as the Swadeshi movement was gathering momentum, Tilak writes of how the Maratha warrior Shivaji could serve as an exemplar and model for the Indian patriot opposing British rule.[1]

✦ ✦ ✦

Hero-worship is a feeling deeply implanted in human nature; and our political aspirations need all the strength which the worship of a Swadeshi [indigenous] hero is likely to inspire into our minds. For this purpose Shivaji is the only hero to be found in Indian history. He was born at a time when the whole nation required relief from misrule; and by his self-sacrifice and courage he proved to the world that India was not a country forsaken by Providence. It is true that the Mahomedans and the Hindus were then divided; and Shivaji who respected the religious scruples of the Mahomedans, had to fight against the Mogul rule that had become unbearable to the people. But it does not follow from this that, now that the Mahomedans and the Hindus are equally shorn of the power they once possessed and are governed by the same laws and rules, they should not agree to accept as a hero one who in his own days

1. From an article published in *The Mahratta*, 24 June 1906, reproduced in *Bal Gangadhar Tilak: His Writings and Speeches* (Madras: Ganesh and Co., 1918), pp. 28–33.

took a bold stand against the tyranny of his time. It is not preached nor is it to be at all expected that the methods adopted by Shivaji should be adopted by the present generation. . . . No one ever dreams that every incident in Shivaji's life is to be copied by any one at present. It is the *spirit* which actuated Shivaji in his doings that is held forth as the proper ideal to be kept constantly in view by the rising generation. No amount of misrepresentation can succeed in shutting out this view of the question from our vision; and we hope and trust that our Mahomedan friends will not be misled by such wily methods. We do not think that the Anglo-Indian[2] writers will object to England worshipping Nelson or France worshipping the great Napoleon on the ground that such national festivals would alienate the sympathies of either nation from the other, or would make the existence of amicable relations between the two nations an impossibility in future. And yet the same advice is administered to us in a patronizing tone by these Anglo-Indian critics, being unmindful of the fact that we have now become sufficiently acquainted with their tactics to take their word for gospel truth. The Shivaji festival is not celebrated to alienate or even to irritate the Mahomedans. Times are changed, and, as observed above, the Mahomedans and the Hindus stand in the same boat or on the same platform so far as the political condition of the people is concerned. Can we not both of us derive some inspiration from the life of Shivaji under these circumstances? That is the real question at issue; and if this can be answered in the affirmative it matters little that Shivaji was born in Maharashtra. . . . We are not against a festival being started in honour of Akbar or any other hero from old Indian history. Such festivals will have their own worth; but that of Shivaji has a peculiar value of its own for the whole country, and it is the duty of every one to see that this characteristic of the festival is not ignored or misrepresented. Every hero, be he Indian or European, acts according to the spirit of his times; and we must therefore judge of his individual acts by the standard prevalent in his time. If this principle be accepted we can find nothing in Shivaji's life to which one can take exception. But as stated above we need not go so far. What makes Shivaji a national hero for the present is the spirit which actuated him throughout and not his deeds as such. His life clearly shows that Indian races do not so soon lose the vitality which [has] given them able leaders at critical times. That is the lesson which

2. 'Anglo-Indian' then meant Englishmen resident in India.

the Mahomedans and the Hindus have to learn from the history of the great Mahratta Chief; and the Shivaji festival is intended to emphasize the same lesson. It is a sheer misrepresentation to suppose that the worship of Shivaji includes invocations to fight either with the Mahomedans or with the Government. It was only in conformity with the political circumstances of the country at the time that Shivaji was born in Maharashtra. But a future leader may be born anywhere in India and who knows, may even be a Mahomedan. That is the right view of the question, and we do not think that the Anglo-Indian writers can succeed in diverting our attention from it.

+ + +

THE NECESSITY FOR A MILITANT NATIONALISM

The Swadeshi movement of 1905–1907 brought to the fore a split between two tendencies within the Indian National Congress—known as the Moderates and the Extremists. In this speech delivered in Calcutta in January 1907, Tilak makes an eloquent case for the extremist tendency. Note that the speech singles out, for special and sarcastic attention, Tilak's rival and fellow townsman, Gopal Krishna Gokhale.[3]

+ + +

Two new words have recently come into existence with regard to our politics, and they are *Moderates* and *Extremists*. These words have a specific relation to time, and they, therefore, will change with time. The Extremists of to-day will be Moderates to-morrow, just as the Moderates of to-day were Extremists yesterday. When the National Congress was first started and Mr. Dadabhai [Naoroji]'s views, which now go for Moderates, were given to the public, he was styled an Extremist, so that you will see that the term Extremist is an expression of progress. We are Extremists to-day and our sons will call themselves Extremists and us Moderates. Every new party begins as Extremists and ends as Moderates. The sphere of practical politics is not unlimited. We

3. From a speech made in Calcutta on 2 January 1907, reproducd in *Bal Gangadhar Tilak: His Writings and Speeches*, pp. 37–52.

cannot say what will or will not happen 1,000 years hence—perhaps during the long period, the whole of the white race will be swept away in another glacial period. We must, therefore, study the present and work out a programme to meet the present condition.

It is impossible to go into details within the time at my disposal. One thing is granted, viz., that this Government does not suit us. As has been said by an eminent statesman—the Government of one country by another can never be a successful, and therefore, a permanent Government. There is no difference of opinion about this fundamental proposition between the Old and New schools. One fact is that this alien Government has ruined the country. In the beginning, all of us were taken by surprise. We were almost dazed. We thought that everything that the rulers did was for our good and that this English Government has descended from the clouds to save us from the invasion of Tamerlane and Chengis Khan, and, as they say, not only from foreign invasions but from internecine warfare, or the internal or external invasions, as they call it. We felt happy for a time, but it soon came to light that the peace which was established in this country did this as Mr. Dadabhai [Naoroji] has said in one place—that we were prevented from going at each other's throats, so that a foreigner might go at the throats of us all. Pax Britannica has been established in this country in order that a foreign Government may exploit the country. That this is the effect of this Pax Britannica is being gradually realized in these days. It was an unhappy circumstance that it was not realized sooner. We believed in the benevolent intentions of the Government, but in politics there is no benevolence. Benevolence is used to sugar-coat the declarations of self-interest, and we were in those days deceived by the apparent benevolent intentions under which rampant self-interest was concealed. That was our state then. But soon a change came over us. English education, growing poverty, and better familiarity with our rulers, opened our eyes and our leaders; especially, the venerable leader who presided over the recent Congress[4] was the first to tell us that the drain from the country was ruining it, and if the drain was to continue, there was some great disaster awaiting us. So terribly convinced was he of this that he went over from here to England and spent twenty five years of his life in trying to convince the English people of the injustice that is being done to us. He worked very hard. He had conversations

---

4. Namely, Dadabhai Naoroji.

and interviews with Secretaries of State, with Members of Parliament—and with what result?

He has come here at the age of eighty-two to tell us that he is bitterly disappointed. Mr. Gokhale, I know, is not disappointed. He is a friend of mine and I believe that this is his honest conviction. Mr. Gokhale is not disappointed but is ready to wait another eighty years till he is disappointed like Mr. Dadabhai.

He is young, younger than myself, and I can very well see that disappointment cannot come in a single interview, from interviews which have lasted only for a year or so. If Mr. Dadabhai is disappointed, what reason is there that Mr. Gokhale shall not [be], after twenty years? It is said there is a revival of Liberalism, but how long will it last? Next year it might be, they are out of power, and are we to wait till there is another revival of Liberalism,[5] and then again if that goes down and [a] third revival of Liberalism takes place; and after all what can a liberal Government do? I will quote the observation of the father of the Congress, Mr. A. O. Hume. This was made in 1893. Let the Government be Liberal or Conservative, rest sure that they will not yield to you willingly anything. A Liberal Government means that the Government or the members of the Government are imbued with liberal principles because they want to have the administration of their country conducted on those principles. They are Liberals in England, but I have seen Liberals in England come out to India to get into conservative ways. Many of the civilian officers from schools and colleges, when they come out are very good Liberals. Coming in contact with Anglo-Indian women, they change their views, and by the time they leave India they are conservatives. This has been the experience all over. So liberal or conservative, the point is, is any one prepared to give you those rights and concessions which intellectually a philosopher may admit to be fit to be conceded or granted to a subject nation in course of time? It is [an] intellectual perception. A philosopher and statesman cannot be forced to do it. I laughed when I read the proceedings of the meeting in Calcutta, congratulating people on the appointment of Mr. [John] Morley to the Secretaryship of State for India. Passages were read from Mr. Morley's books. Mr. Morley had

5. The Liberal Party had just come into power in Great Britain, raising the hopes of the Indian Moderates that their concerns would be more sympathetically addressed.

said so and so in Mr. Gladstone's life[6]; Mr. Morley had said this and had said that; he was the editor of a certain paper thirty years ago, and he said so and so. I asked myself if it would not have been better that some of the passages from the *Bhagavad Gita* were so quoted. The persons to whom I refer are gentlemen for whom I have the highest respect. But what I say is, that they utterly misunderstood the position or absolutely ignored the distinction between a philosopher and a statesman. A statesman is bound to look to the present circumstances and see what particular concessions are absolutely necessary, and what is theoretically true or wrong. He has to take into consideration both the sides. There are the interested Anglo-Indians and the Secretary of State is the head of the Anglo-Indian bureaucracy whose mouth-piece he is. Do you mean to say that when the whole bureaucracy, the whole body of Anglo-Indians, is against you, the Secretary of State will set aside the whole bureaucracy and give you rights? Has he the power? If he does, will he not be asked to walk away? So then it comes to this that the whole British electorate must be converted. So you are going to convert all persons who [have] a right to vote in England, so as to get the majority on your side, and when this is done and when by that majority the [L]iberal [P]arty is returned to Parliament bent upon doing good to India and it appoints a Secretary of State as good as Mr. Morley, then you hope to get something by the old methods. The new Party has realized this position. The whole electorate of Great Britain must be converted by lectures. You cannot touch their pocket or interest, and that man must be a fool indeed who would sacrifice his own interest on hearing a philosophical lecture! He will say, 'It is a very good lecture; but I am not going to sacrifice my interest.' I will tell you a story. One of my friends who had been lecturing in England delivered a lecture on the grievances of India. A man from the audience came and asked him how many of them there were. The lecturer replied, 'thirty crores'.[7] The inquirer replied, 'Then you do not deserve anything.' That is the attitude with which an English workman looks at the question. You now depend on the Labour Party. Labourers have their own grievances, but they won't treat you any better. On the contrary they will treat you worse, because British labourers obtain their livelihood by sending

6. John Morley had written a celebrated life of the great Liberal leader W. E. Gladstone.

7. A crore is 10 million.

us their goods. This is the real position. This position is gradually recognized. Younger people who have gone to England like Mr. Gokhale are not so disappointed though those who went with him were, like Mr. Lala Lajpat Rai.[8] I am entering into personalities but I cannot place these facts in an intelligent manner, if I do not give the names, although all of them are my friends. This is then the state of things. The new party perceives that this is futile. To convert the whole electorate of England to your opinion and then to get indirect pressure to bear upon the members of Parliament, they in their turn to return a cabinet favourable to India and the whole Parliament, the [L]iberal [P]arty and the cabinet to bring pressure on the bureaucracy to yield—we say this is hopeless. You can now understand the difference between the old and the new parties. Appeals to the bureaucracy are hopeless. On this point both the new and old parties are agreed. The old party believes in appealing to the British nation and we do not. That being our position, it logically follows we must have some other method. There is another alternative. We are not going to sit down quiet. We shall have some other method by which to achieve what we want. We are not disappointed, we are not pessimists. It is the hope of achieving the goal by our own efforts that has brought into existence this new party.

There is no empire lost by a free grant of concessions by the rulers to the ruled. History does not record any such event. Empires are lost by luxury, by being too much bureaucratic or over-confident or from other reasons. But an empire has never come to an end by the rulers conceding power to the ruled.

You got the Queen's proclamation.[9] But it was obtained without a Congress. They wanted to pacify you, as you had grown too turbulent, and you got that proclamation without a demand, without Congress and without constitutional agitation. That is a very good and generous declaration indeed. The Queen was very anxious that it should be couched in such terms as would create hopes in you. Now, all that anxiety did not proceed from constitutional agitation. It was after 1858, that constitutional agitation began. The result was, the proclamation remained a dead letter, because you could not get it enforced, the conditions under which it was made having disappeared. A

8. A well-known nationalist leader from the Punjab.

9. In 1858, following the rebellion of the previous year, Queen Victoria had issued a proclamation promising her Indian subjects good governance and respect for all faiths.

promise was made but you proved too weak to have it enforced. That is the reason why it was not enforced. The bureaucracy got the upper hand and they established a system of administration in which it made it impossible for the proclamation to be acted upto. . . . Is Mr. Morley going to fulfil it? The explanation of the proclamation is not the question. The question is what will compel him to fulfil it. This is the point at issue. I admit that we must ask; but we must ask with the consciousness that the demand cannot be refused. There is great difference between asking and petitioning. . . . Your industries are ruined utterly, ruined by foreign rule; your wealth is going out of the country and you are reduced to the lowest level which no human being can occupy. In this state of things, is there any other remedy by which you can help yourself? The remedy is not petitioning but boycott. We say prepare your forces, organise your power, and then go to work so that they cannot refuse you what you demand. A story in *Mahabharata* tells that Sri Krishna was sent to effect a compromise, but the Pandavas and Kauravas were both organising their forces to meet the contingency of failure of a compromise. This is politics. Are you prepared in this way to fight if your demand is refused? If you are, be sure you will not be refused; but if you are not, nothing can be more certain than that your demand will be refused, and perhaps, for ever. We are not armed, and there is no necessity for arms either. We have a stronger weapon, a political weapon, in boycott. We have perceived one fact, that the whole of this administration, which is carried on by a handful of Englishmen, is carried on with our assistance. We are all in subordinate service. The whole Government is carried on with our assistance and they try to keep us in ignorance of our power of co-operation between ourselves by which that which is in our own hands at present can be claimed by us and administered by us. The point is to have the entire control in our hands. I want to have the key of my house, and not merely one stranger turned out of it. Self-Government is our goal; we want a control over our administrative machinery. We don't want to become clerks and willing instruments of our own oppression in the hands of an alien Government, and that Government is ruling over us not by its innate strength but by keeping us in ignorance and blindness to the perception of this fact. . . . Every Englishman knows that they are a mere handful in this country and it is the business of every one of them to befool you in believing that you are weak and they are strong. This is politics. We have been deceived by such policy so long. What the new party wants you to do is to realize the fact that your future rests entirely in your own hands. If you mean to be free, you can be free; if you do not mean to be free, you will fall and be for ever fallen. So many of you need not like arms; but if you have not the power of active resistance, have you not the power of self-denial and self-abstinence in such a way as not to assist this foreign Government to rule over you? This is boycott and this is what is meant when we say, boycott is a political weapon. We shall not give them assistance to collect revenue and keep [the] peace. We shall not assist them in carrying on the administration of justice. We shall have our own courts, and when time comes we shall not pay taxes. Can you do that by your united efforts? If you can, you are free from to-morrow. Some gentlemen who spoke this evening referred to half bread as against the whole bread. I say I want the whole bread and that immediately. But if I cannot get the whole, don't think that I have no patience.

I will take the half they give me and then try for the remainder. This is the line of thought and action in which you must train yourself. We have not raised this cry from a mere impulse. It is a reasoned impulse. Try to understand that reason and try to strengthen that impulse by your logical convictions. I do not ask you to blindly follow us. Think over the whole problem for yourselves. If you accept our advice, we feel sure, we can achieve our salvation thereby. This is the advice of the new party. Perhaps we have not obtained a full recognition of our principles. Old prejudices die very hard. Neither of us wanted to wreck the Congress, so we compromised, and were satisfied that our principles were recognised, though only to a certain extent. That does not mean that we have accepted the whole situation. We may have a step in advance next year, so that within a few years our principles will be recognised, and recognised to such an extent that the generations who come after us may consider us Moderates. This is the way in which a nation progresses. This is the way national sentiment progresses, and this is the lesson you have to learn from the struggle now going on. This is a lesson of progress, a lesson of helping yourself as much as possible, and if you really perceive the force of it, if you are convinced by these arguments, then and then only is it possible for you to effect your salvation from the alien rule under which you labour at this moment. . . .

+ + +

6

THE SUBALTERN FEMINIST

TARABAI SHINDE

IN THE PROLOGUE TO THIS BOOK I observed that it would attract complaints from admirers of those I had left out. Some of the exclusions will be controversial; so, perhaps, shall be some inclusions. This chapter features an individual who was obscure in her time and remains so in ours. But her writing, if not her life, compels our serious attention. Her claim to be a 'maker of modern India' rests on the literary quality and political resonance of the only book she published. This speaks across the decades and centuries, and it remains one of the most powerful pieces of social criticism ever written by an Indian.

We know little about the life and upbringing of Tarabai Shinde. Born in the 1830s, she lived into the early years of the twentieth century. She is known principally through a tract she published in 1882 comparing the situation of men and women in the Maharashtra, and India, of her time. The pamphlet may have been provoked by the case of a young brahmin widow who became pregnant, and then killed—or was forced to kill—the baby. The widow was arrested and sentenced to be hanged for the crime (on appeal, the sentence was modified to transportation for life).

Tarabai was born in a fairly wealthy Maratha family in the town of Buldana, in the Berar region of the present-day state of Maharashtra. Her family owned some land, and her father worked as a senior clerk in the office of the Deputy Commissioner of Buldana. He was also apparently a member, although one does not know how active a member, in Jotirao Phule's Satyashodak Samaj. With no girls' schools in the area, Tarabai would have learnt her letters at home. She read and wrote in Marathi, but she may also have known some English. She was married when quite young; however, since her husband moved into her parents' home, Tarabai was perhaps less confined than she might otherwise have been.

Unlike some other parts of India, Maharashtra had a long tradition of women who were active in public life. As princesses and queens, women had advised their royal kinsmen and sometimes even ruled in place of a male king who was not yet an adult. Among the leading *bhakti* poets of the medieval period were some women. The daughters of Brahmins were often learned and literate. By the late nineteenth century, a handful of Brahmin women had become doctors and teachers in Maharashtra. These pioneers called for the emancipation of women from oppression within the household.

In 1877 a Marathi periodical for women had been started, catering chiefly to wives and daughters of Brahmin families. To find learning among a Maratha girl was less common. Even more unusual was the direct language in which Tarabai Shinde questioned the presumed superiority of men. Through the nineteenth century, men and women had called for widow remarriage, for the education of young girls, and for the abolition of practices such as *sati*. These efforts, sincere and well-intentioned though they undoubtedly were, could all be categorised under the label of 'women's uplift'. What Tarabai Shinde called for, however, was altogether different and more radical—namely, for equality or parity between men and women. No one before her had so directly challenged the social arrangements and cultural prejudices which underpinned patriarchy and male domination.

The translator of Tarabai's text, the British historian Rosalind O'Hanlon, also happens to be the foremost authority on the life and work of Jotirao Phule. O'Hanlon notes that although the two may or may not have met, Phule certainly knew and admired Tarabai's writings. Their approaches were complementary: For Phule, brahmanic religion oppressed lower-caste people, because it had been devised by brahmans; for Tarabai, it oppressed women because it had been devised by men. Phule referred to Tarabai as *chiranjivini,* or dear daughter, and commended her tract to his colleagues so that they could understand and suitably respond to her charges of the systematic ill-treatment of women by men.

Like Phule, Tarabai was a brilliant stylist in Marathi, using sarcasm and satire to puncture the pretensions of the powerful. Her book is compellingly readable in English; one wonders how much better it is in the original.

A COMPARISON OF MEN AND WOMEN

The one work that Tarabai Shinde published was fifty-two pages. It was printed in Puné in 1882 and priced at nine annas, or a little over half a rupee. The excerpts below speak for themselves. But we must at least flag the feminist interpretation of the Hindu epics, whereby renouncers and gods are seen as lustful predators always in search of pretty women.[1]

✦ ✦ ✦

. . . A father and mother make you the gift of their daughter once and for all, they pour the water over your hands and that's the end of it. Then she leaves and she's lost to them. Oh, the pity of it—from the day of her birth, the father and mother have followed their natural feelings and raised her up from child to adult with praise and love, each as best they could. See how hard they've worked to get her a place that's good and happy, to please her new family of in-laws in the hope they'll love her and treat her kindly. If good luck's on her side, everything's fine. But what if it isn't? All her life long, her mother and father have cherished her, dear as life itself. What must it be like for her,

1. From Rosalind O'Hanlon, ed. and trans., *A Comparison between Women and Men: Tarabai Shinde and the Critique of Gender Relations in Colonial India* (New Delhi: Oxford University Press, 1994), pp. 97–111.

whose father and mother never gave her the lightest slap, when she feels the sharp blows of your fist on her back? What must her parents feel? If I wrote down the raw truth it would fill up a book as big as the Ramayana. And when you do treat a woman well, it's usually only just for show. You're like someone who wears a wonderful bit of red and gold silk brocade on his top half, and a tattered old blanket below. You can even cover her with gold ornaments and put her in a house set with jewels. But if you're not kind and loving, she'll still feel nothing but misery—which you can't just describe, you have to experience it.

Women in this world are forever putting up with all sorts of hard toil, difficulty, hunger and thirst, harassment and beatings—and all they ask is a kindly word from you. It's true, you go out and earn the money. But she has to see to the running of the house, has to do exactly as you tell her, perpetually obedient, kept in ignorance, toiling at the most exhausting work till her body's pleasure breaks into little pieces, her bones waste away and her blood turns to water—her eyes always on your face. You've only got to glance at her approvingly and flash your teeth in a smile, and she feels it's a joy divine! This encourages her to take up the burden of labour again, to learn and do even more kinds of work. Look at it from what you know already. There's a saying of yours, 'A husband's praise is like nectar and ambrosia'. Let's say she brings some beautiful piece of sewing to show you, or serves up a nicely prepared little delicacy, and you tell her 'Well now, look at this! Did you really make it yourself? Look now, don't work so hard! You'll give yourself [a] backache; you might hurt your eyes. We don't want the children to suffer for it, and we must keep you out of the hands of the doctor! You just take it easy now'. Or if you're with your friends and you say, 'You know, I'm so lucky, I don't have to worry about anything at home. Let's just go off to my place and do something there. It'd be hard to find a home as good as ours'. As soon as she hears these words of love and praise, she forgets all the pain she's suffered since childhood, all the times that you've kicked and punched and sworn at her. With this praise from her lord and master, she tells herself she's the luckiest person on earth. Her heart overflows with affection. So there she is, eagerly looking to you for the smallest sign of love—and you still go on calling her all sorts of insulting names. There's no denying it—this is what her fate really is. . . .

So the first point . . . , you're stronger than her when it comes to brains. Is there anything you haven't done with those great brains of yours, a single monstrous deed in the world you haven't committed? What strength have women got next to you and your huge power? They've got nothing at all.

In the second place, it's true women are whirled about by many whims! But it's because they're uneducated that every kind of whim makes its home in their minds. Even so, theirs only go as far as their own families. But if we look at your minds, all the whims there go round so fast we can hardly see them. Your minds are constantly churned up with all sorts of cunning schemes, to do with things native and foreign, imaginary and practical. Today you might say, perhaps we should trick some moneylender and fleece him of a thousand rupees. We could pass information to a particular jagirdar [landlord] and take him for four or five hundred. I know, you'll say, 'Today let's tell the sahib [i.e., Englishman] such and such', and get that case decided on some chap's be-half. Another day, and it's 'Maybe we should bring along that false title-deed for copying and entry'. But do you ever find women scheming, 'That woman, you know, she acts so superior—you'd think she had to peel onions with her nose! We ought to set a trap for the little snob and get rid of her for good!' Whims like this never even come into women's minds. All women on this earth don't shine as brightly as the light of the sun, of course not. Nor are they all purer than Ganges water inside and out. But if you added up all the women in the world, you'd find only ten in a hundred with minds going round and round like yours, when there isn't a single one of you that's free from it.

Thirdly, then: that women are the very abode of debauchery. You think your kind are better, do you? If you weighed it up, the scales would sink down a hundred, a hundred and a half times heavier on your side.

In the fourth place, the idea that women are a very city of thoughtlessness. But does thoughtlessness only come from women's hands? And you, who are mean and faithless, who make promises to others then cut their throats be-hind a mask of kindness—are you never thoughtless? Oh yes, you're absolute temples of thought, let's congratulate you! You're meant to be so wonderfully learned and thoughtful, but you've actually committed acts of thoughtless-ness like we've never seen before, and so you carry on every day. Yet you call yourselves such great thinkers—so I wonder what we should call you?

Women are ignorant, just like female buffaloes in a pen. They may not be able to read or write, but does that mean God never gave them any intelli-gence at all? They may be thoughtless, but they're still much better than you. You men are all very clever, it's true. But you just go and look in one of our prisons—you'll find it so stuffed full of your countrymen you hardly put your foot on the ground. Oh yes, they're all very clever there, aren't they? One's there for making counterfeit notes, another for taking bribes. Another for running off with someone else's wife, another for taking part in a rebellion, another for poisoning, another for treason, another for giving false evidence, another for setting up as a raja and destroying the people, yet another for doing a murder. Of course, it's these great works of thought that make the government offer you a room so reverently in its palatial prisons! What women do things like these? How many prisons are filled with women? For every two or three thousands of you, you won't find even a hundred women. If we ask ourselves what's the worst thoughtlessness women can be guilty of, it would be adultery. . . . But whoever caused it should get the blame. When a woman gets into adultery, who is it who takes the first steps by planting bad desires in her mind? Her or you? However shameless a woman might be, she'll never force her arms round a man's neck, that's for certain. Because what's the greatest happiness in the world for a woman? In the first place, it's a husband who suits her and really loves her. If he and she are of one mind, she can be ever so poor, live in a hut short of food and clothes, put up with all sorts of suffering and trouble, go off and live in the jungle—but she'll still only have eyes for one man and regard all her trials as happiness. Left to herself a woman would never turn to adultery. . . .

The fifth point, then—that women are the storehouse of all guilt. In fact, it's the other way round—when women go wrong it's always because of you. See now. Many fathers marry off their daughters of ten or eleven, girls who shine like little stars, they marry them for a fat wad of rupees to some rich old man of eighty or ninety. They eye the old man's wealth and say, 'Well—it won't really matter if he does die, will it? She'll never want for money, after all. In a couple of days, she'll be back to eating and drinking, putting on ornaments, dressing as usual and so on. What does it matter if there's no husband? With words like that they hand her over shamelessly, like a goat to the tiger. Oh, but the husband has gone who would have been her real happiness and love, who would have taken pleasure in her ornamenting and dressing up, who would have praised her and cherished her more than life itself. With him gone, the whole world is just a wilderness to her. What's the point of this empty ceremony for her? In the old days, a woman used to go as sati—that was good. She could turn herself to ashes along with him, and it was all over with.

Apart from her mother, no one will ever love her as much as a husband, that's certain. When she's lost both, where's she going to get strength to pull on through her days, with the flaming coals of youth burning in her breast? This is the position of girls given away just for money.

Some people give away their daughters as second wives. But there's no weapon that pierces a woman so painfully as the thorn of being given as second wife. A wife's blood boils if her husband just looks a bit closely at another woman. And that's just looking. So how can she bear it if he goes and marries someone else, or takes another woman on the side, whether it happens inside the house or not? You'll never ever find two women living happily in the same house. You can treat them as equally as you like in things like jewellery and clothes. But how can you love two in the same way as one? Love isn't like a mango or a guava—you can't cut it up and share it out. Love is like milk. Once it's gone sour, you can't make it good again, no matter how much you stir it about. Once it's separated, you can't put it back together. Yes, it's only natural for people to prefer new things over the old, it doesn't matter who it is. But a man's wife has only to look at someone else with a bit of interest and he'll work himself up into the most furious rage. Then her family has to suffer in disgrace and she gets beaten, locked up and harassed. Why doesn't any of this apply to you?

If you can't bear her just looking, will she stand it when it feels like a burning pan right on her chest? Why do people give their girls away as second wives? If someone has lots of daughters, often they'll just give them to any husband that comes along. It doesn't matter what he's like—some push their daughters off onto a man who'll quite plainly destroy his family. A man can be as ugly as you like, full of vices, pitiless and cruel, fond of beating and harassing, who'll even keep his family short of food and drink. But people still give their girls to such bringers of misery, handing them over like cows to a butcher. A whole cartload of paper wouldn't be enough if I tried to describe it all here. So whose fault is it then, if women run away because of it? The father's or the daughter's? . . .

Now for the sixth point. Which of us is really soaked a hundred times over in deceit? You're number one here. How can we describe your deceit? Every step and there's an example. Look at all the disguises you get yourself up in—you could even paint your body black and yellow striped and change into a tiger. You turn yourselves into gosavis, fakirs, haridasas, brahmacharis, sadhus, dudharais, giripuris, bharatis, nanaks, kanphotas, jogis, jatadharis, nanges,[2] you pretend you've renounced the whole world, smear ashes on your bodies, grow your hair matted and go off to live in the jungle—you go round deceiving all the world with your tricks. Who's that, it's a ramgiribuva, that one a shastribuva, another parades as Ganpatibuva Phaltankar the great sadu [saint], another as a nanakpanthi. What qualities they all have! What can we say? They've got all the proper merits, they're so detached, they hand out holy mantras. They only have to tell us and we believe them. As the buva's fame spreads he takes to stuffing himself with rich delicacies and grows sleek and shiny like a tomcat, then somehow his religious duties get forgotten. He sits there as the women come to take his darshan [blessing] and prays on very different beads. He picks out some specially who are young and freshly nubile, and there he sits, meditating and repeating to himself, this one's nice, that one's pretty! Not a word about your Shiva or Hari, they're all forgotten! The only name on his lips is that girl's who looks just like the milkmaid Radha. The only thing he's got eyes for is that fresh young flower's pretty laughing face, and inside it's Mr. Money he's meditating on! He might look as though he's crazy—but it's crazy like a fox! . . .

Oh yes, you put strings of sacred tulsi beads around your necks, you go round reciting the virtues of Viththal, posing as servants of Hari, famous beggars, you take yourselves off to Kashi.[3] But do you think you can wipe it all clean by going off there and shaving your beard and moustaches as penance?

You can offer up your moustaches and throw them on the waters of the [Ganga], but do you think you can bundle up your vices and do the same with them? Of course you can't—that way you only get more pride and bad desires. Outside you make as if you're the holiest of holy men—but can even [the Ganga's] waters put out the flaming torch of deceit inside you?

So, you take the sanyasi [renouncer's] vow, do you? Then you should give up all your hopes and desires. There you are, with your saffron robes, your staff and water-pot in your hand, honouring all the world and its creatures like Narayan [God] himself. But let's look at what happens on the banks of the Ganges, when you're washing and purifying yourself on the beautiful stone steps, smearing pound after pound of ashes on your body, sitting there re-

2. These are all names of Hindu religious sects, open only to men.
3. Kashi is another name for [the holy city of] Banaras.

peating the name, Paramatma Sheshashayi Shrinarayan,[4] and telling prayer beads with the gomukhi on your hand. When your ears catch the sound of feet on the first step of the ghat, your eyes dart up, the glove falls from your hand, our buva's thrown into confusion and Narayan runs right out of his mouth. What sort of a Narayan is it coming now? It's one in the form of a woman, and now it's she who goes and sits in the buva's gomukhi. 'Outside they parade in saffron robes; inside the ulcer of evil thoughts'. Who really sees what's going on? It's collect money from alms and off to a whore with it—that's what abandoning the world means here!

The gods themselves bring destruction on women, so is it any wonder you do the same? When Krishna got Arjuna to disguise himself as a big holy man and steal Subhadra away, the Yadavas' sons said to each other 'A holy man's carried Aunty off!' But do you ever hear of the aunt carrying off the holy man? There was the time when no one could stand up against Ravana and he went about harassing all the three worlds. Everywhere people were crying and groaning, Indraput was deserted and the gods and rishis went running to Sheshashayi Bhagavan at Kshirasagar, shouting for pity, 'Stop that devil tormenting us and making us his slaves'. That all-powerful god could raise the whole world or destroy it in an instant, just as he wished. What was Ravana worth against that infinite power? But that isn't how people interpret it now. Ravana stole Sita away, so the monkey army had to go after them to his kingdom in the south and destroy it—that was what really happened. But now people say, 'Oh, never mind all that other stuff; it was that whore who really ruined Ravana. See what these wretched women get up to, destroying homes and kingdoms'.

What have we got, then? It's all women's fault again. Sita even took the fire ordeal, but people still went on blaming her. Did that make Ramchandra all the greater or something? What wonderful gods you've got! You're the shadows of them: they show up once, but you really show up double. How can we tell about this deceit of yours? There's one of you pretending to be just like a brother to someone, and all the time secretly hoping something bad will happen to him; another who pretends to be like a father, and really hopes his friend will suffer a loss; and another of you who makes as if he's a true friend, and all the while his eye's on everything from his friend's wife to his dog.

4. These are names of Hindu deities.

Hardly any men are pure outside as well as in. Five or six of you characters get together and then what? 'That chap, you know, he really flashes his money around, it'd be good to see his nose pulled down for once!' Or: 'That fellow's done all right for himself, what a marvel! He never even used to get enough to eat, but now that son of a whore rides round in a two horse buggy!' That's work to you—you're like a lot of crows, heads full of dirty tricks and you're pecking holes in other people for their secret follies. Tell us then, go on—do women ever do that? Has a woman ever dressed up as a gosavi or sadhu and got a man to run away with her? Show us, then, if you can find even one single example? . . .

Now for the seventh point, that women are the beginning of all wickedness. No—wickedness starts off with you and you alone. You desert your own dharma and carry on just as you please, getting drunk and rolling in the road, going round looking at young boys in tamashas, gambling, smoking ganja, keeping whores, all sorts of badness and filth. Tell me this now, what is a whore? Do you think she's some form of life that wasn't made in the same way as the rest of creation? Was it some other God who made her? In fact, whores are just some of those women you've seduced and lured away from their homes. Take any woman you like. Her home can be an agony, a danger to her very life, she can be trapped, one well in front of her and another behind, she can lose her life. But she can't survive without someone to lean on—no matter how brave she is, she can't stand on her own legs even in her own house's courtyard. The reason is she's always been locked up, strictly confined to the same house, never able to put even a foot outside. So however bold and shameless she may be, she'd never go chasing another man on her own. It's you that starts it off, giving her little hints of your own bad desires, and once she's tasted them it's enough. After that, she doesn't need a teacher to show her what wickedness is. . . .

✦   ✦   ✦

PART THREE

NURTURING A NATION

INTRODUCTION TO PART III

THE NINETEENTH CENTURY IN EUROPE WAS a century of national-isms large and small, defensive as well as assertive. Countries such as France, Italy, Germany, and Great Britain consolidated their boundar-ies, standardised their official languages, and modernised their politi-cal systems and their armies. Among less populous peoples such as the Poles and Czechs, there arose a similar desire to create a nation of their own, whose citizens would adhere to a common flag and a common cur-rency. In pursuit of this aim they fought valiantly, if not always success-fully, against the empires that ruled over them.

The 'national' in the Indian National Congress was clearly inspired by these European precedents. But it was inspired also by the develop-ment of self-governing institutions in British colonies such as Australia and Canada. These were not full-fledged nations but British 'Domin-ions'. A formal connection with the Mother Country remained—the British monarch was still head of state, and his (or her) representative served as Governor General. However, in day-to-day matters of gover-nance and administration the British Government rarely interfered. Australia and Canada were administered by Australians and Canadi-ans, not by Englishmen.

With regard to the white Dominions, Indian aspirations presented a problem—that Indians were not white. Racial prejudice was rarely ex-pressed openly, but it was nonetheless believed by a majority of the British in India that brown (and black) men could not be trusted to take care of their own affairs. Dominion status was all right for the whites in Canada and Australia, but not here. Or at least not yet. The more broad-minded colonial administrators of the nineteenth century were prepared to allow that, perhaps in a few hundred years, the Indians would have sufficiently matured under British tutelage to be trusted to run their own government.

With regard to the European nations, Indian aspirations presented an even greater problem—that Indians were very diverse and divided. The nations of the West had been forged—or sought to be forged—on the basis of a common language and a shared faith. A tongue other than the national language was permitted in the home and in private conversations but could not intrude into the public domain, and certainly not in the business of the state. Minority religions were likewise permitted in small doses and behind closed doors. Thus, Britain was united on the basis that its citizens all spoke English, while the marriage between faith and state was made formal by the monarch also acting as the head of the Church of England. Likewise, to be a citizen of the existing or putative nation of Poland you had to speak Polish. It also helped enormously if you were simultaneously a member of the Catholic Church. France and Germany were equally insistent on linguistic uniformity, if somewhat more lax on the question of religion.

In this respect, the representativeness of the Indian National Congress was challenged very early in its existence. As we have seen, Syed Ahmad Khan did not believe that the Congress could or should speak for Muslims. Although every Congress meeting had a sprinkling of Muslims attending, on the whole the Muslim elite followed Syed Ahmad's advice and stayed away from it. But among the Hindus the organisation continued to gain ground. Its leaders were intelligent and articulate, and they had a programme. The status of the Congress grew as a result of the Swadeshi movement of 1905 onwards. The boycott of foreign cloth was seen, by the young especially, as a prelude to the attainment of self-government itself.

The rise of the Congress was not welcomed by the British rulers. Their misgivings were shared by Muslim notables, a group of whom met the Viceroy, Lord Minto, in October 1906, to ask for greater representation for their co-religionists in government, and for separate electorates as well. The Viceroy and his advisers viewed these demands with sympathy, seeing them as a means of stemming the advance of the Congress. In December 1906 an All-India Muslim League was formed, to provide a separate and distinct platform for Muslim interests and aspirations.

Religious divisions existed in Europe as well. Germany had both Protestants and Catholics, but by the late nineteenth century, reconciling the two seemed within the bounds of possibility. Hindu-Muslim unity in India was a greater challenge. Adding to the difficulty was the existence of other robust religious communities in British India, such as the Sikhs, the Christians, the Parsis, and the Jains.

An equally great challenge to a single Indian nationality was presented by divisions of language. The English had, within their national borders, successfully promoted their own language at the expense of Welsh and Celtic. But the major Indian languages were spoken by tens of millions of people. Each was written in a different script; each had a very old and very rich literary tradition. How could a single common language be made acceptable to all?

Adding to the diversities of faith and language were the divisions of caste, class, and gender. And yet the movement for a common nation persisted. By the time of World War I, there had been thirty annual meetings of the Indian National Congress. The organisation remained largely male, largely Hindu, and largely upper-caste. On the other hand, it had some exceptional individuals, as well as institutional staying power. And it was active in most cities and towns of British India.

Three events outside India helped to energise the Congress further— the Irish Home Rule Bill of 1914, the Bolshevik Revolution in Russia in 1917, and the Versailles Conference of 1919. Since the Irish were conceded self-government by the British, the Indians demanded the same from the British. (Unsurprisingly, various Home Rule Leagues sprung up in the sub-continent soon afterwards.) The victory of the Bolsheviks was widely seen as a victory for the underdog, which naturally included subject peoples. And in Versailles in 1919 the American president, Woodrow Wilson, had spoken sympathetically of the rights of those who lived in colonies, even if he used the euphemism 'autonomous development' rather than 'independence' or 'national sovereignty'.

By the end of World War I, the Indian National Congress was no longer a gentleman's debating club but a genuine mass movement. Fewer than 100 delegates had attended the first Congress in Bombay in 1885; over 7,000 attended the Amritsar Congress of 1919; whereas more than 14,000 came to the Nagpur Congress the next year. Each delegate represented or spoke for thousands of ordinary party workers. The historian Gopal Krishna has estimated that by 1921, the Congress had more than 1.5 million members, who came from all parts of India.

The Congress had reached beyond the Anglicised elite to the vernacular middle class; and it was soon to penetrate even deeper. The popular campaigns it organized in the 1920s and 1930s resonated deeply with peasants across the country, who participated in large numbers in these movements. (Admittedly, they were attracted not so much by abstract ideals such as 'nationalism' and 'freedom' but by the opportunity to demand concrete concessions from the rulers, such as lower taxes and the freedom of the forest.)

The British now realised that they had to progressively devolve power to Indians. The more die-hard imperialists (such as Winston Churchill), who thought that the sun would never set on the British Empire, found themselves in a minority. The climate of the time, within and outside India, was in favour of self-government. To be sure, the rulers could still delay and dilute the process. Thus, Indian representation in government bodies was increased in small doses, and with special provisions for minorities. The intention was to maintain British control at the higher levels of government for as long as possible. Through a series of reforms in the 1920s and 1930s, Indians were elected to legislative councils and allowed to form ministries in the provinces, these working under the close supervision of British Governors, and with the implementation of their policies in the hands of British civil servants.

Meanwhile, the political awareness of Indians was being intensified by the growth of tertiary education and by a very active press. New colleges and universities were established, whose products compared and contrasted European ideals of liberty with conditions in the colonies. The inter-war period also witnessed a massive expansion in the publication of newspapers and magazines. There were daily newspapers published in every city, and in every language. These were read by the ever growing numbers of literate Indians. The better journals were very good indeed. Apart from on-the-ground reportage, they carried analytical editorials, and they paid close attention to popular culture.

I have called this part of the book 'Nurturing a Nation'. From 1917, when he organised his first campaign, to 1947, when his country finally became independent, one man was at the centre of debates about the nation-in-the-making, namely, Mohandas K. Gandhi. Naturally, he dominates the pages that follow, which juxtapose Gandhi's writings on major questions of politics and social reform with the writings of his critics and contemporaries.

7

THE MULTIPLE AGENDAS OF

M. K. GANDHI

IN JANUARY 1915 MOHANDAS K. GANDHI returned to his homeland after two decades in South Africa. Born on the west coast of India in 1869, Gandhi studied law in London and briefly practiced as a lawyer in Bombay and Rajkot before leaving for Durban in 1893. He lived in that city and in Johannesburg, fighting cases for his Indian clients, and increasingly being drawn into social activism. In 1896 he published a long pamphlet on the condition of Indian immigrants in South Africa. This was the first of many interventions against laws that restricted the freedom of movement and the freedom to trade for those who were not whites. Gandhi's protests against racial discrimination took the form of newspaper articles and editorials, petitions to government, cases in court, and mass campaigns of non-violent protest or *satyagraha.*

In South Africa Gandhi was a diasporic leader whose reach and influence was restricted to the one hundred thousand or so Indians who lived there. Within four years of his return, however, Gandhi had become the most famous—as well as most controversial—person in a sub-continent whose population was in the region of 300 million. In 1917 and 1918 he led localised protests against specific grievances of peasants and workers; in 1919 he organised *satyagrahas* in the major cities of British India against a restrictive new legislation known as the Rowlatt Act; and in 1920 he launched a countrywide campaign of 'non-co-operation' against British colonial rule.

Gandhi liked to refer to Gopal Krishna Gokhale as his 'guru'. He had certainly been influenced by the Puné reformer, whose pro-grammes of Hindu-Muslim unity and the uplift of the depressed castes he also made his own. Gokhale had taken a keen interest in Gandhi's work in South Africa and even visited him in that country. Gandhi was suitably grateful; at the same time, he was keenly aware of the potential of the approach of Gokhale's main rival, Bal Gangadhar Tilak. Fortu-itously, Gandhi was in Bombay when Tilak died in 1920 and able to ac-company the body to the cremation. This was seen by some, not un-reasonably, as a passing of the baton. For his penchant for mass action was not unlike Tilak's; and he was likewise a militant opponent of colo-nial rule.

Gandhi was influenced, and possibly inspired, by both Gokhale and Tilak. Like them, he owed a close allegiance to the Indian National Con-gress. He borrowed from each, yet his own programme was by no means a mere mixture of Tilak's and Gokhale's. The theory and practice of *satya-graha* he developed wholly on his own. Again, where Gokhale and Tilak were essentially urban leaders from western India, Gandhi's appeal cut across boundaries of caste, class, region, and language. His adoption of a garment made of homespun cotton and his generally frugal lifestyle allowed him to come much closer to the peasants who formed the bulk of India's population. At the same time, Gandhi also did far more than his predecessors to deepen the organisational base of the Congress, drawing in many new members, among them young men and women, and extending the party's reach to virtually all parts of the country, the princely states not excluded. The democratisation of the Congress was facilitated by a key innovation of Gandhi's, which was to encourage regional committees based on language, such that the proceedings at the provincial level were conducted not in English but in the mother tongue.

Gandhi led and organised three major campaigns against colonial rule. These were the non-co-operation movement of the 1920s, the civil disobedience movement of the 1930s (whose highlight was his march to the sea to make salt, then a state monopoly), and the 'Quit India' movement of the 1940s. Through these campaigns, Gandhi came to spend extended periods in jail, the suffering and sacrifice further increasing his popularity. The movements were important, but not necessarily more so than Gandhi's programmes of social reform and economic renewal. Among his abiding concerns were the abolition of Untouchability; the promotion of Hindu-Muslim harmony; the uplift of women; and the revival of the village and artisanal economy. In his *ashrams* in Ahmedabad (where he was based between 1915 and 1930) and near Wardha (where he moved in 1934), he trained hundreds of men and women to take these programmes further.

The anthologist of Gandhi's writings is spoilt for choice. The *Collected Works of Mahatma Gandhi* run to more than ninety volumes, in a well-annotated series edited by a team of scholars headed by a former professor of English literature, K. Swaminathan. All his life, while he was thinking and acting, Gandhi was also writing. His first appearance in print was in the journal of the Vegetarian Society of London, which in 1890 published a six-part series by him on Indian food habits. In 1903 he founded his own journal, *Indian Opinion,* much of which he wrote himself. On his return to India he edited a journal called *Young India* (published between 1919 and 1932), and then another called *Harijan,* which he ran from 1933 until his death. Gandhi also wrote extensively in his mother tongue, Gujarati, and published several books, among them two volumes of autobiography. He replied to every letter he received, often at length. His speeches were transcribed *verbatim,* and of course, the older and more famous he became, the more interviews he gave to the press.

In both Gujarati and English, Gandhi wrote a clear, direct, unadorned prose. As his editor, K. Swaminathan, points out,

> Gandhi's literary style is a natural expression of his democratic
> temper. There is no conscious ornamentation, no obstrusive
> trick of style calling attention to itself. The style is a blend of
> the modern manner of an individual sharing his ideas and experiences with his readers and the impersonal manner of the
> Indian tradition in which the thought is more important than

the person expounding it. The sense of equality with the common man is the mark of Gandhi's style and the burden of his teaching. To feel and appreciate this essence of Gandhi the man, in his writings and speeches, is the best education for true democracy.

Mohandas K. Gandhi was murdered by a Hindu fanatic on 30 January 1948.

THE POWER OF NON-VIOLENCE

In 1909 Gandhi wrote a critique of colonialism and Western civilisation called *Hind Swaraj* (Indian Home Rule). Perhaps the most valuable and enduring parts of this polemic relate to the theory and practice of non-violence. In the excerpt that follows, Gandhi is the editor, who answers the queries and doubts of a reader.[1]

✦   ✦   ✦

READER: Is there any historical evidence as to the success of what you have called soul-force or truth-force? No instance seems to have happened of any nation having risen through soul-force. I still think that the evil-doers will not cease doing evil without physical punishment.

EDITOR: . . . The force of love is the same as the force of the soul or truth. We have evidence of its working at every step. The universe would disappear without the existence of that force. But you ask for historical evidence. It is, therefore, necessary to know what history means. The Gujarati equivalent [of the English word 'history'] means: 'It so happened'. If that is the meaning of history, it is possible to give copious evidence. But, if it means the doings

---

1. From M. K. Gandhi, *Hind Swaraj*, in K. Swaminathan, ed., *The Collected Works of Mahatma Gandhi* (New Delhi: Publications Division, 1958 [hereafter *CWMG*]), vol. 10, pp. 47–53. Throughout this chapter I have used the standard edition of the *CWMG*. There was a later, error-ridden edition (since withdrawn), and there are also versions on the Internet—these follow a different pagination.

of kings and emperors, there can be no evidence of soul-force or passive re-sistance in such history. You cannot expect silver-ore in a tin-mine. History, as we know it, is a record of the wars of the world, and so there is a proverb among Englishmen that a nation which has no history, that is, no wars, is a happy nation. How kings played, how they became enemies of one another, and how they murdered one another is found accurately recorded in history, and, if this were all that had happened in the world, it would have been ended long ago. If the story of the universe had commenced with wars, not a man would have been found alive today. Those people who have been warred against have disappeared, as, for instance, the natives of Australia, of whom hardly a man was left alive by the intruders. Mark, please, that these natives did not use soul-force in self-defence, and it does not require much foresight to know that the Australians will share the same fate as their victims. Those that wield the sword shall perish by the sword. With us, the proverb is that professional swimmers will find a watery grave.

The fact that there are so many men still alive in the world shows that it is based not on the force of arms but on the force of truth or love. There-fore, the greatest and most unimpeachable evidence of the success of this force is to be found in the fact that, in spite of the wars of the world, it still lives on.

Thousands, indeed tens of thousands, depend for their existence on a very active working of this force. Little quarrels of millions of families in their daily lives disappear before the exercise of this force. Hundreds of na-tions live in peace. History does not, and cannot, take note of this fact. His-tory is really a record of every interruption of the even working of the force of love or of the soul. Two brothers quarrel; one of them repents and re-awakens the love that was lying dormant in him; the two again begin to live in peace; nobody takes note of this. But, if the two brothers, through the intervention of solicitors or some other reason, take up arms or go to law—which is another form of the exhibition of brute force—their doings would be immediately noticed in the press, they would be the talk of their neigh-bours, and would probably go down to [sic] history. And what is true of fami-lies and communities is true of nations. There is no reason to believe that there is one law for families and another for nations. History, then, is a re-cord of an interruption of the course of nature. Soul-force, being natural, is not noted in history.

READER: According to what you say, it is plain that instances of this kind of passive resistance are not to be found in history. It is necessary to understand this passive resistance more fully. It will be better, therefore, if you enlarge upon it.

EDITOR: Passive resistance is a method of securing rights by personal suffering; it is the reverse of resistance by arms. When I refuse to do a thing that is repugnant to my conscience, I use soul-force. For instance, the government of the day has passed a law which is applicable to me. I do not like it. If, by using violence, I force the government to repeal the law, I am employing what may be termed body-force. If I do not obey the law, and accept the penalty for its breach, I use soul-force. It involves sacrifice of self. . . .

READER: You would then disregard laws—this is rank disloyalty. We have always been considered a law-abiding nation. . . .

EDITOR: . . . A man who realized his manhood, who fears only God, will fear no one else. Man-made laws are not necessarily binding on him. Even the government do[es] not expect any such thing from us. They do not say: 'You must do such and such a thing' but they say: 'If you do not do it, we will punish you.' We are sunk so low, that we fancy that it is our duty and our religion to do what the law lays down. If man will only realize that it is unmanly to obey laws that are unjust, no man's tyranny will enslave him. This is the key to self-rule or home-rule. . . .

READER: From what you say, I deduce that passive resistance is a splendid weapon of the weak, but that, when they are strong, they may take up arms.

EDITOR: This is gross ignorance. Passive resistance, that is, soul-force, is matchless. It is superior to the force of arms. How, then, can it be considered only a weapon of the weak? Physical-force men are strangers to the courage that is [required] in a passive resister. . . . What do you think? Wherein is courage required—in blowing others to pieces from behind a cannon or with a smiling face to approach a cannon and to be blown to pieces? Who is the true warrior—he who keeps death always as a bosom-friend or he who controls the death of others? Believe me that a man devoid of courage and manhood can never be a passive resister.

This, however, I will admit: that even a man weak in body is capable of offering this resistance. One man can offer it just as well as millions. Both men and women can indulge in it. It does not require the training of an army; it needs no Jiu-jitsu. Control over the mind is alone necessary, and, when that is attained, man is free like the king of the forest, and his very glance withers the enemy.

Passive resistance is an all-sided sword; it can be used anyhow; it blesses him who uses it and him against whom it is used. Without drawing a drop of blood, it produces far-reaching results. . . . It is strange indeed that you should consider such a weapon to be a weapon merely of the weak.

READER: You have said that passive resistance is a speciality of India. Have cannons never been used in India?

EDITOR: Evidently, in your opinion, India means its few princes. To me, it means its teeming millions, on whom depends the existence of its princes and our own.

Kings will always use their kingly weapons. To use force is bred in them. They want to command, but those who have to obey commands, do not want guns; and these are in a majority throughout the world. They have to learn either body-force or soul-force. Where they learn the former, both the rulers and the ruled become like so many mad men, but, where they learn soul-force, the commands of the rulers do not go beyond the point of their swords, for true men disregard unjust commands. Peasants have never been subdued by the sword, and never will be. They do not know the use of the sword, and they are not frightened by the use of it by others. That nation is great which rests its head upon death as its pillow. Those who defy death are free from all fear. For those who are laboring under the delusive charms of brute force, this picture is not over-drawn. The fact is that, in India, the nation at large has generally used passive resistance in all departments of life. We cease to cooperate with our rulers when they displease us. This is passive resistance.

I remember an instance when, in a small principality, the villagers were offended by some command issued by the prince. The former immediately began vacating the village. The prince became nervous, apologized to his subjects and withdrew his command. Many such instances can be found in India. Real home rule is possible only where passive resistance is the guiding force of the people. Any other rule is foreign rule.

READER: From what you say, then, it would appear that it is not a small thing to become a passive resister, and, if that is so, I would like you to explain how a man may become a passive resister.

EDITOR: To become a passive resister is easy enough, but it is also equally difficult. I have known a lad of fourteen years become a passive resister; I have known also sick people doing likewise; and I have also known physically strong and otherwise happy people being unable to take up passive resistance. After a great deal of experience, it seems to me that those who want to become passive resisters for the service of the country have to observe perfect chastity, adopt poverty, follow truth, and cultivate fearlessness.

Chastity is one of the greatest disciplines without which the mind cannot attain requisite firmness. A man who is unchaste loses stamina, becomes emasculated and cowardly. He whose mind is given over to animal passions is not capable of any great effort. This can be proved by innumerable instances. What, then, is a married person to do, is the question that arises naturally; and yet it need not. When a husband and wife gratify the passions, it is no less an animal indulgence on that account. Such an indulgence, except for perpetuating the race, is strictly prohibited. But a passive resister has to avoid even that very limited indulgence, because he can have no desire for progeny. A married man, therefore, can observe perfect chastity. . . . Several questions arise: How is one to carry one's wife with one? What are her rights, and other such questions? Yet those who wish to take part in a great work are bound to solve these puzzles.

Just as there is necessity for chastity, so is there for poverty. Pecuniary ambition and passive resistance cannot well go together. Those who have money are not expected to throw it away, but they are expected to be indifferent about it. They must be prepared to lose every penny rather than give up passive resistance.

Passive resistance has been described in the course of our discussion as truth-force. Truth, therefore, has necessarily to be followed, and that at any cost. In this connection, academic questions such as whether a man may not lie in order to save a life, etc., arise, but these questions occur only to those who wish to justify lying. Those who want to follow truth every time are not placed in such a quandary, and, if they are, they are still saved from a false position.

Passive resistance cannot proceed a step without fearlessness. Those alone can follow the path of passive resistance who are free from fear, whether as to their possessions, false honour, their relatives, the government, bodily injuries, death. . . .

✦   ✦   ✦

'NON-CO-OPERATION' WITH THE BRITISH RAJ

In 1919 a British General ordered his troops to fire on a group of unarmed protesters in the Punjab town of Amritsar. More than four hundred people were killed. This massacre lent great momentum to Gandhi's campaign against colonial rule. By this time he had made common cause with Muslims upset over the abolition under British direction of the Islamic Caliphate (or Khilafat). Gandhi now called for the restoration of the Khilafat and for 'non-co-operation' with the rulers. The next excerpt, from a speech on the beach in Madras in August 1920, outlines this new political credo. A crowd of 50,000 heard this speech—many more would have heard of it through word of mouth or read about it in the newspapers.[2]

✦   ✦   ✦

. . . What is this non-co-operation about which you have heard much, and why do we want to offer this non-co-operation? I wish to go for the time being into the why. There are two things before this country. The first and the foremost is the Khilafat question. On this the heart of the Mussulmans of India has become lacerated. British pledges, given after the greatest deliberation by the Prime Minister of England in the name of the English nation, have been dragged into the mire. The promises given to Moslem India, on the strength of which the consideration that was accepted by the British nation was exacted,

2. From *The Hindu*, 13 August 1920, as reproduced in *CWMG*, vol. 18, pp. 144–154.

have been broken and the great religion of Islam has been placed in danger. The Mussulmans hold—and I venture to think they rightly hold—that so long as British promises remain unfulfilled so long is it impossible for them to tender whole-hearted fealty and loyalty to the British connection; and, if it is to be a choice for a devout Mussulman between loyalty to the British connection and loyalty to his Code and Prophet, he will not require a second to make his choice and he has declared his choice. . . .

It is a question, then, for the rest of the Indian population to consider whether they want to perform a neighbourly duty by their Mussulman countrymen and, if they do, they have an opportunity of a lifetime which will not occur for another hundred years, to show their goodwill, fellowship and friendship and to prove what they have been saying for all these long years that the Mussulman is the brother of the Hindu. If the Hindu regards that before the connection with the British nation comes his natural connection with his Moslem brother, then I say to you that if you find that the Moslem claim is just, that it is based upon real sentiment, and that at its background is this great religious feeling, you cannot do otherwise than help the Mussulmans through and through so long as their cause remains just and the means for attaining the end remains equally just, honourable and free from harm to India. . . . It is then for Hindus and Mussulmans to offer a united front to the whole of the Christian powers of Europe and tell them that weak as India is, India has still got the capacity of preserving her self-respect, she still knows how to die for her religion and for her self-respect.

That is the Khilafat in a nutshell; but you have also got the Punjab. The Punjab has wounded the heart of India as no other question has for the past century. I do not exclude from my calculation the Mutiny of 1857. Whatever hardships India had to suffer during the Mutiny, the insult that was attempted to be offered to her during the passage of the Rowlatt legislation, and that which was offered after its passage, were unparalleled in Indian history. It is because you want justice from the British nation in connection with the Punjab atrocities, you have to devise ways and means as to how you can get this justice. The House of Commons, the House of Lords, Mr. Montagu,[3] the Viceroy of India, every one of them knows what the feeling of India is on this Khilafat question and on that of the Punjab; the debates in both the Houses of

3. E. S. Montagu, at the time Secretary of State for India in the British Government.

Parliament, the action of Mr. Montagu and that of the Viceroy have demonstrated to you completely that they are not willing to give the justice which is India's due and which she demands. I suggest that our leaders have got to find a way out of this great difficulty and unless we have made ourselves even with the British rulers in India, and unless we have gained a measure of self-respect at the hands of the British rulers in India, no connection and no friendly intercourse is possible between them and ourselves. I, therefore, venture to suggest this beautiful unanswerable method of non-co-operation.

I have been told that non-co-operation is unconstitutional. I venture to deny that it is unconstitutional. On the contrary, I hold that non-co-operation is a just and religious doctrine; it is the inherent right of every human being and it is perfectly constitutional. A great lover of the British Empire has said that under the British Constitution, even a successful rebellion is perfectly constitutional and he quotes historical instances which I cannot deny in support of his claim. I do not claim any constitutionality for a rebellion successful or otherwise so long as that rebellion means in the ordinary sense of the term what it does mean, namely, wresting justice by violent means. On the contrary, I have said it repeatedly to my countrymen that violence, whatever end it may serve in Europe, will never serve us in India. . . .

As soon as India accepts the doctrine of the sword, my life as an Indian is finished. It is because I believe in a mission special to India, and it is because I believe that the ancients of India, after centuries of experience, have found out that the true thing for any human being on earth is not justice based on violence but justice based on sacrifice of self, justice based on *yajna* and *kurbani*[4]—I cling to that doctrine and I shall cling to it for ever. . . . I believe that a man is the strongest soldier for daring to die unarmed with his breast bare before the enemy. So much for the non-violent part of non-co-operation. I, therefore, venture to suggest to my learned countrymen that so long as the doctrine of non-co-operation remains non-violent so long there is nothing unconstitutional in the doctrine.

I ask further, is it unconstitutional for me to say to the British Government, 'I refuse to serve you'? . . . Is it unconstitutional for any parent to withdraw

---

4. *Yajna* and *kurbani* both more or less mean the same thing, namely, sacrifice. The fact that one word is Sanskrit and the other Urdu is significant, in that by using them both in one breath Gandhi was symbolically signalling the imperative of Hindu-Muslim unity.

his children from a Government or aided school? Is it unconstitutional for a lawyer to say, 'I shall no longer support the arm of the law so long as that arm of law is used not to raise me but to debase me? Is it unconstitutional for a civil servant or for a judge to say, 'I refuse to serve a Government which does not wish to respect the wishes of the whole people'? I ask, is it unconstitutional for a policeman or for a soldier to tender his resignation when he knows that he is called to serve a Government which traduces its own countrymen? Is it unconstitutional for me to go to the *krishak,* to the agriculturist, and say to him, 'It is not wise for you to pay any taxes, if these taxes are used by the Government not to raise you but to weaken you'? I hold and I venture to submit that there is nothing unconstitutional in it. . . .

I submit that in the whole plan of non-co-operation there is nothing unconstitutional. But I do venture to suggest that it will be highly unconstitutional . . . for the people of India to become weak and to crawl on their belly—it will be highly unconstitutional for the people of India to pocket every insult that is offered to them; it is highly unconstitutional for the 70 millions of Mohammedans of India to submit to a violent wrong done to their religion; it is highly unconstitutional for the whole of India to sit still and co-operate with an unjust Government which has trodden under its feet the honour of the Punjab; I say to my countrymen: 'So long as you have a sense of honour and so long as you wish to remain the descendants and defenders of the noble traditions that have been handed to you for generations after generations, it is unconstitutional for you not to non-co-operate and unconstitutional for you to co-operate with a government which has become so unjust as our Government has become.'

I am not anti-English; I am not anti-British; I am not anti-any government; but I am anti-untruth—anti-humbug and anti-injustice. . . . So long as the Government spells injustice, it may regard me as its enemy, implacable enemy. . . . You may consider that I have spoken these words in anger because I have considered the ways of this Government immoral, unjust, debasing and untruthful. I use these adjectives with the greatest deliberation. I have used them for my own true brother with whom I was engaged in a battle of non-co-operation for full 13 years, and although the ashes cover the remains of my brother, I tell you that I used to tell him that he was unjust when his plans were based upon immoral foundation. I used to tell him that he did not stand for truth. There was no anger in me. I told him this home truth because I loved him. In the same manner I tell the British people that I love them and that I want their association but I want that association on conditions well defined.

I want my self-respect and I want my absolute equality with them. If I cannot gain that equality from the British people, I do not want the British connection. If I have to let the British people go and import temporary disorder and dislocation of national business, I will rather favour that disorder and dislocation than that I should have injustice from the hands of a great nation such as the British nation. . . .

I deny being a visionary. I do not accept the claim of saintliness. I am of the earth, earthly, a common gardener man as much as any one of you, probably much more than you are. I am prone to as many weaknesses as you are. But I have seen the world. I have lived in the world with my eyes open. I have gone through the most fiery ordeals that have fallen to the lot of man. I have gone through this discipline. I have understood the secret of my own sacred Hinduism. I have learnt the lesson that non-co-operation is the duty not merely of the saint but it is the duty of every ordinary citizen, who not knowing much, not caring to know much, but wants to perform his ordinary household functions. The people of Europe teach even their masses, the poor people, the doctrine of the sword. But the *rishis* [sages] of India, those who have held the traditions of India, have preached to the masses of India the doctrine, not of the sword, not of violence but of suffering, of self-suffering. . . .

I am asking my countrymen in India to follow no other gospel than the gospel of self-sacrifice which precedes every battle. Whether you belong to the school of violence or non-violence, you will still have to go through the fire of sacrifice and of discipline. May God grant you, may God grant our leaders the wisdom, the courage and the true knowledge to lead the nation to its cherished goal! May God grant the people of India the right path, the true vision and the ability and the courage to follow this path, difficult and yet easy, of sacrifice.

✦   ✦   ✦

THE ABOLITION OF UNTOUCHABILITY

Gandhi often said that Indians would not be deserving of freedom from subjection from British rule unless they had rid themselves of the evil of Untouchability. He consistently articulated this position through the 1920s and 1930s, as witness the excerpts that follow. The first is from a speech he delivered at a 'Suppressed Classes Conference' in Ahmedabad in April 1921.[5]

✦   ✦   ✦

. . . Hinduism has sinned in giving sanction to untouchability. It has degraded us, made us the pariahs of the Empire. Even the Mussulmans caught the sinful contagion from us, and in S[outh] Africa, in E[ast] Africa and in Canada, the Mussulmans no less than Hindus came to be regarded as pariahs. All this evil has resulted from the sin of untouchability.

I may here recall my proposition, which is this: So long as the Hindus willfully regard untouchability as part of their religion, so long as the mass of Hindus consider it a sin to touch a section of their brethren, Swaraj [freedom] is impossible of attainment. . . .

We are guilty of having suppressed our brethren; we make them crawl on their bellies; we have made them rub their noses on the ground; with eyes red with rage, we push them out of railway compartments—what more than this has British rule done? . . . We ought to purge ourselves of this pollution. It is idle to talk of Swaraj so long as we do not protect the weak and helpless, or so long as it is possible for a single Swarajist to injure the feelings of any individual. Swaraj means that not a single Hindu or Muslim shall for a moment arrogantly think that he can crush with impunity meek Hindus or Muslims. Unless this condition is fulfilled we will gain Swaraj only to lose it the next moment. We are no better than the brutes until we have purged ourselves of the sins we have committed against our weaker brethren. . . .

✦   ✦   ✦

The next excerpt is from an article written by Gandhi in January 1926 titled 'The Crime of Caste'.[6]

✦   ✦   ✦

5. From *Young India*, issues of 27 April and 4 May 1921, as reproduced in *CWMG*, vol. 19, pp. 573–574.

6. From *Young India*, 14 January 1926, as reproduced in *CWMG*, vol. 29, pp. 399–400.

In South Africa it is the crime of colour and race for which we [Indians] are be-ing punished. In India we Hindus punish our co-religionists for the crime of caste. The fifth caste—the Panchama[7]—is the greatest offender deserving the punishment of untouchability, unapproachability, invisibility and what not. An extraordinary case that was tried in a Madras Presidency court brings viv-idly to light the sad plight of our suppressed countrymen. A simple cleanly dressed Panchama entered a temple in a perfectly devotional spirit without the slightest intention of hurting anybody's feeling or insulting any religion. He had been in the habit of paying his respects at this temple every year though he did not enter it. But last year in his ecstatic mood he forgot himself and entered the temple. The priest in charge could not distinguish him from the others and therefore accepted his offering. But when he regained self-possession, he was terrified to find himself in a prohibited place and ran away from the temple. But some who knew him caught him and handed him to the Police. The temple authorities when they discovered the crime, had the temple duly purified. Then followed a trial. A Hindu Magistrate convicted him and imposed a fine of Rs 75 or one month's rigorous imprisonment for insulting his own religion! An appeal was filed. There was an elaborate argu-ment over it. Judgement had to be reserved! And when conviction was set aside, it was not because the court held that poor Panchama had a right to enter the temple but because the prosecution in the lower court had for-gotten to prove the insult. This is no triumph of justice or truth or religion or morality. . . .

It is a curious situation. We resent, and properly, the treatment meted out to our countrymen in South Africa. We are impatient to establish Swaraj. But we Hindus refuse to see the incongruity in treating a fifth of our own co-religionists as worse than dogs. For dogs are not untouchables. Some of us nowadays even keep them as drawing-room pets.

What place shall the 'untouchables' occupy in our scheme of swaraj? If they are to be free from all special restraints and disabilities under swaraj, why can we can not declare their freedom now? And if we are powerless to-day, shall we be less powerful under swaraj? We may shut our eyes and stuff our ears to these questions. But they are of the highest importance to the

---

7. The name by which Untouchables were referred to in South India—it literally means 'of the fifth class', i.e., outside the four orders of the caste system.

Panchamas. Surely judgement will be pronounced against Hinduism, if we as a body do not rise as one man against this social and religious atrocity.

Much has no doubt been done to remove this evil. But it is all too little so long as criminal prosecutions for temple entry are possible and so long as the suppressed classes continue to be denied the right of entering temples, using public wells, and sending their children freely to national schools. We must yield to them the same rights as we would have the Europeans concede to our countrymen in South Africa. . . .

✦ ✦ ✦

In the early 1930s the lawyer and activist B. R. Ambedkar emerged as a leading spokeman for the Untouchables. Ambedkar was a bitter critic of Gandhi and the Congress. In response, Gandhi redoubled his efforts to abolish Untouchability. Notably, in this effort he was opposed not just by Ambedkarites—who thought he was going too slowly—but also by orthodox Hindus—who thought that Untouchability had a divine sanction, and Gandhi had no business to challenge it. The Untouchables had been known variously as Depressed and Suppressed Classes—Gandhi now gave them a new appellation, 'Harijan', or Children of God. He also formed a Harijan Sevak Sangh, or Society for the Service of Harijans. In 1933–1934 Gandhi went on an All-India tour to press for greater rights for Harijans. The excerpt that follows is from his reply to a deputation of Harijans whom he met in the southeastern town of Rajamundry in December 1933.[8]

✦ ✦ ✦

One important question that you have raised is that the Harijan Sevak Sangh should be principally manned and managed by you. That shows that you have not followed the pages of the *Harijan*. That shows also that you have not understood the origin of the Board. The Board has been formed to enable *savarna* [upper-caste] Hindus to do repentance and reparation to you. It is thus a Board of debtors, and you are the creditors. You owe nothing to the debtors, and therefore, so far as this Board is concerned, the initiative has to come from the debtors. You have to certify whether the debtors discharge their

8. From *Harijan*, 5 January 1934, as reproduced in *CWMG*, vol. 56, pp. 393–395.

obligation or not. What you have to do is to enable and help them to discharge their obligations; that is to say, you can tell them how they can discharge their obligation, you can tell them what in your opinion will satisfy the great body of Harijans. They may or may not accept your advice. If they do not, naturally they run the risk of incurring your displeasure. A debtor may go to a creditor and say to him. 'I have brought so much money, will you take it?' The creditor may say. 'Off you go; I want full payment or none.' Or the creditor may say, 'What you have brought is not part payment, but worse.' All these things you, creditors, can do. And so, when this Board was established and some Harijan friends wrote to me, I told them that Harijans should form themselves into advisory boards or boards of inspection. I want you to understand this distinction thoroughly. You will please see that there is no desire not to accept your advice or co-operation or help. I am only putting before you the true and logical position. This is a period of grace that God has given to caste Hindus, and it is during this period of grace that they have to prove their sincerity. And I am moving heaven and earth and am going about from place to place, simply in order that this obligation on the part of *savarna* Hindus may be fully discharged. . . .

✦   ✦   ✦

This next excerpt is from an article entitled 'Our Shame'. It is striking how Gandhi reproduces, in extenso and in his own journal, these sharp criticisms of his work and mission. He was never one to underestimate the uphill task of the reformer.[9]

✦   ✦   ✦

Reference has already been made in these columns to a memorandum which was received by me at Coonoor on behalf of 'Adi-Hindus[10] of Tamil Districts'. It is signed by thirty-six representatives some of whom are members of municipal councils or taluq boards. From this, I condense below the catalogue of their disabilities. In condensing it I have not materially changed their language. Criticism interspersed with the recital has been removed as being superfluous. The list is otherwise untouched.

9. From *Harijan*, 9 March 1934, as reproduced in *CWMG*, vol. 57, pp. 259–262.
10. In South India, Harijans were variously known as Adi-Hindus, Adi-Dravidas, and—as already noted—Panchamas.

1. We have no access to eating-houses, laundries, shaving saloons, coffee and tea clubs, restaurants, choultries [hotels], schools, *agraharams* [Brahmin neighbourhoods], wells, tanks, water-taps, springs, post offices (located in villages) and other places of public resort, not to speak of temples in several places.

2. In some places, holding umbrellas, wearing sandals, wearing dhotis below the knees are considered as a great crime. Wearing jewels made of gold by our women-folk and using clean cloth over their body would be regarded as an ill omen by some caste Hindus.

3. We are not allowed to carry our dead within particular union board areas alongside the highway, simply because there is a temple of a deity on the road-side. We are compelled to carry the dead body through a paddy field even when there is knee-deep mire during [the] rainy season.

4. The Headman of the so-called untouchables within a particular union board area is not allowed by the caste Hindus to get on horseback and pass along the highway during his investiture ceremony as Headman of the said classes.

5. In some village bazaars, bleached cloth cannot be touched by us when we are desirous of buying it for festivals.

6. If cooked bread or other eatables are touched in bazaars knowingly or unknowingly, the whole cost of the food-stuff will be extracted from our people for the sin of touching them.

7. Since a very high percentage of our people living in rural areas have no habitation of their own in most of the districts of the presidency, but are allowed by sufferance to live on the lands of the land-owning classes, any demand for wages for work contributed by our people in their lands is highly resented by their masters. They do not get living wages and the hours of work are unlimited. These are often paid in unwholesome grain in short measures.

8. For marriage occasions or processions of our deity, we cannot get the services of caste Hindu musicians when we cannot find some among us.

9. Young men of our community riding on bicycles are being regarded with severe displeasure. In remotest villages, *jutkas* (horse cabs) cannot ply for us, as the caste Hindu owners refuse to take us. The same is the case with motor buses.

10. In public latrines, built out of public funds in a particular municipal area, the so-called untouchables are actively prevented from using them. After a good deal of assertion, they were provided with separate latrines.

11. In some of the dispensaries run under the control of particular local bodies, our people do not get proper treatment at the hands of caste Hindus employed there.

12. In the temporary water-sheds erected by caste Hindus during the hot season, the distinction made by them in pouring water to the Adi-Hindus for drinking purpose[s] is highly intolerable and offensive.

13. When our people get into local bodies and panchayats the orthodox caste Hindus resign their seats by way of protest, and in some cases our people are given separate seats.

14. When an Adi-Hindu rests on the *pial* [verandah] in front of his house, he should get up and bow his head before a caste Hindu and worship him with due veneration when the caste Hindu happens to pass that way. If this custom is neglected by the Adi-Hindus, they will be taken to task severely by the caste Hindus.

    We are often asked to set our own house in order. This is simply begging the question. Where the Hindu society is one vast system of gradations and degradations based on caste and birth, there is no use in accusing the so-called untouchables of being divided among themselves. After all, the so-called untouchables are themselves victims of circumstances.

15. In municipal areas, separate water-taps are maintained wherever caste Hindus object.

16. To rural elementary schools maintained out of public funds our children have no free access. When they are admitted, they are given separate seats, or they are asked to sit on the floor. If the pupils approach the caste Hindu orthodox teachers employed there, knowingly or unknowingly, to clear some doubts, they are pushed back by the teachers with the help of slates or sticks for fear of pollution. In some cases, our children are made to stand outside the main school premises in all seasons, in order to receive instruction through the window, and hence our children cannot even see the blackboard. When the lower elementary course is completed in the separate schools established for our children,

we are not admitted in the higher elementary schools run under the public management in the same village. Even trained teachers belonging to [the] Adi-Hindu community are not appointed in such higher elementary schools. Our children cannot use the common latrine. It is a great pity that even our representatives serving on different local bodies do not pay surprise visits to such schools, where caste Hindus predominate, for fear of molestation and endless trouble. . . .

In high schools our students cannot take drinking water from the pots used there during [the] hot season; but they must depend upon some caste Hindu students to pour water for our young men and girls. Even vessels are not given to our students, but the students have to use only their hands as vessels for drinking. To the common tiffin [eating] rooms our students have no free access.

17. In post offices located in inaccessible places, we cannot post letters straightaway or transact any other business. Even for buying post cards, covers or stamps, we will have to stand at a great distance from such post offices and beg some caste Hindu passers-by to comply with our request. There are two things involved in this. Firstly, we cannot pass through the public pathway. Secondly, we are prevented from transacting business straightaway in the post office.

18. *We feel sorry that your august person has not taken birth in the Adi-Hindu community to realize our practical difficulties.* (emphasis in original)

This is a formidable catalogue. There is no exaggeration in it, if one or two mental reservations are understood. Every statement is true of some place. No disability is universal. Some are rare. And all are being abated by voluntary effort. . . . The shame of caste Hindus will continue so long as these disabilities are practiced in the name of religion, no matter to how little or great an extent. It is the clear duty of sanatanists [orthodox Hindus] so called to denounce the disabilities in the severest possible language and join hands with the reformers in protecting Harijans from humiliation heaped upon them under the sanction of religious custom. The eighteenth grievance with the signatories have specially underlined I regard as a compliment paid by them to me. Yes, it is quite possible that I would have felt the force of these terrible grievances much more, had I been born an Adi-Hindu. Not having had that luck, I have become one by adoption. There will be no rest for me nor society, so long as untouchability persists.

+ + +

We now excerpt an article in which Gandhi contrasts two approaches to Harijan emancipation, temple entry, and economic uplift.[11]

+ + +

One sees sometimes in the public Press criticism on the temple-entry question. It is double-barrelled, being directed on the one hand by Harijans and on the other by sanatanists. Some of the Harijans say, 'We do not want temple-entry; do not build temples, but use all you receive for economic uplift.' Some Sanatanists say, 'Give up the temple-entry question altogether. You are hurting our feelings by forcing Harijans into temples.' Both are wrong in substance. Not one single pice out of the purse has been or will be spent for building temples. Attempt is being made only to have public temples opened to Harijans on the same terms on which they are open to the other Hindus. It is a matter of choice for the Harijans to visit or not to visit them; *savarna* Hindus have to lift the bar against Harijans. For those millions who regard temples as treasure-chests of spiritual wealth, they are living realities which they hold dear as life itself. If they are truly repentant towards Harijans, they must share these treasures with the latter. I know what the opening of temples means to Harijans. Only last week, between Dharwar and Belgaum, I opened three temples to Harijans in the presence of crowds of *savarna* [upper caste] Hindus and Harijans. If critics had been present at the opening and noticed the pleasure on the countenances of the Harijans present as they bowed before the image and received the *prasad* [holy offering] their criticism would have been silenced. Harijan critics would have realized that, apart from themselves, Harijans at large did desire temple-entry. Sanatanist critics would have realized that temples, wherever they were opened, were being opened with the fullest concurrence of the temple-goers concerned and in the presence of crowds of them. No hole-and-corner opening can do any good whatsoever to Hinduism. To be of spiritual or any value at all, the opening has to be performed with due publicity, solemnity and the

11. From *Harijan,* 16 March 1934, as reproduced in *CWMG,* vol. 57, pp. 285–286.

willing consent of the existing temple-goers, and not of such self-styled reformers as have no faith or interest in temples and for whom temples may
even be a superstition. Temple-entry agitation requires no financial outlay, it
does not lend itself to agitation except by a few workers who have faith in
temples and whose word would command attention from the mass *savarna*
mind. It is, therefore, a question that can only be and is being gently and
cautiously handled. The only insistence is on the right and the duty of the
believing reformer advocating temple-entry and showing that without it the
reformation will not only be incomplete but fruitless. For, without temples
being freely open to Harijans, untouchability could not be said to have been
removed root and branch.

As for the economic uplift, it is altogether wrong to put it in opposition to
temple-entry. Temple-entry can only help such uplift. For, when Harijans are
freely admitted to temples, all the avenues to economic betterment must be
automatically open to Harijans as to others. So far as the moneys received are
concerned, they will *all* be used *only* for economic uplift, if it is admitted that
educational uplift also means economic, in that it makes the educated Harijan fitter for running life's race. I am aware that education among the *savarnas* has often rendered them less fit for the race. But that has been so, because their education has meant contempt for labour. There is not much
danger of such a mishap with the general body of Harijans for some time to
come at least. And the danger can be averted altogether, if those who are in
charge of the movement will take care to purge Harijan education of the evils
of the current method, which ignores the technical side for the most part, if
not altogether.

✦　✦　✦

HINDU-MUSLIM UNITY AND INTER-FAITH DIALOGUE

Gandhi had gone to South Africa at the invitation of a Muslim merchant. In that country, his main clients, and in time his main supporters, were Muslims. From the first he was deeply committed to fostering
better relations between Hindus and Muslims. This commitment he
carried over into his work in India. In April 1919 he drafted this 'vow of

Hindu-Muslim Unity', hundreds of thousands of copies of which were printed and distributed as a 'satyagraha leaflet'.[12]

◆   ◆   ◆

. . . If the Hindu and Muslim communities could be united in one bond of mutual friendship, and if each could act towards the other even as children of the same mother, it would be a consummation devoutly to be wished. But before this unity becomes a reality, both the communities will have to give up a good deal, and will have to make radical changes in ideas held heretofore. Members of one community when talking about those of the other at times indulge in terms so vulgar that they but [ex]acerbate the relations between the two.

In Hindu society we do not hesitate to indulge in unbecoming language when talking of the Mahomedans and *vice versa*. Many believe that an ingrained and ineradicable animosity exists between the Hindus and Mahomedans. In many places we see that each community harbours distrust against the other. Each fears the other. It is an undoubted fact that this anomalous and wretched state of things is improving day by day. . . . But the object of taking a vow is speedily to bring about, by the power of self-denial, a state of things which can only be expected to come in the fullness of time. How is this possible? Meetings should be called of Hindus—I mean the orthodox Hindus— where this question should be seriously considered. The standing complaint of the Hindus against the Mussulmans is that the latter are beef-eaters and that they purposely sacrifice cows on the *Bakr-i-Id* day.[13] Now it is impossible to unite the Hindus and Mahomedans so long as the Hindus do not hesitate to kill their Mahomedan brethren in order to protect a cow. For I think it is futile to expect that our violence will ever compel the Mahomedans to refrain from cow-slaughter. I do not believe the efforts of our cow-protection societies have availed in the least to lessen the number of cows killed every day. I have had no reason to believe so. I believe myself to be an orthodox Hindu and it is my conviction that no one who scrupulously practices the Hindu religion may

12. From *Young India*, 7 May 1919, as reproduced in *CWMG*, vol. 15, pp. 201–203.

13. A major Muslim festival, which commemorates Ibrahim's willingness to sacrifice his son. God permits him to sacrifice a ram instead, for which cattle were later permitted as a substitute.

kill a cow-killer to protect a cow. There is one and only one means open to a Hindu to protect a cow and that is that he should offer himself as a sacrifice if he cannot stand its slaughter. Even if a very few enlightened Hindus thus sacrificed themselves, I have no doubt that our Mussulman brethren would abandon cow-slaughter. . . . If I want my brother to redress a grievance, I must do so by taking upon my head a certain amount of sacrifice and not by inflicting injury on him. I may not demand it as of right. My only right against my brother is that I can offer myself [as] a sacrifice.

It is only when the Hindus are inspired with a feeling of pure love of this type that Hindu-Muslim unity can be expected. As with the Hindus, so with the Mussulmans. The leaders among the latter should meet together and consider their duty towards the Hindus. When both are inspired by a spirit of sacrifice, when both try to do their duty towards one another instead of pressing their rights, then and then only would the long-standing differences between the two communities cease. Each must respect the other's religion, must refrain from even secretly thinking ill of the other. We must politely dissuade members of both the communities from indulging in bad language against one another. Only a serious endeavour in this direction can remove the estrangement between us. Our vow would have value only when masses of Hindus and Mussulmans join in the endeavour. I think I have now made sufficiently clear the seriousness and magnitude of this vow. I hope that on this auspicious occasion and surely the occasion must be auspicious when a wave of *satyagraha* [non-violent resistance] is sweeping over the whole country—we could all take this vow of unity. For this it is further necessary that leading Hindus and Mahomedans should meet together and seriously consider the question and then pass a unanimous resolution at a public meeting. This consummation will certainly be reached if our present efforts are vigorously continued. I think the vow may be taken individually even now and I expect that numerous people will do so every day. My warnings have reference to the taking of the vow publicly by masses of men. If it is taken by the masses, it should, in my humble opinion, be as follows:

'With God as witness we Hindus and Mahomedans declare that we shall behave towards one another as children of the same parents, that we shall have no differences, that the sorrows of each shall be the sorrows of the other and that each shall help the other in removing them. We shall respect each other's religion and religious feelings and shall not stand in the way of our respective religious practices. We shall always refrain from violence to each other in the name of religion'.

+ + +

Gandhi's concern with inter-religious harmony went beyond Hindus and Muslims. The next excerpt is from a speech delivered to an audience of Christians in Calcutta in August 1925.[14]

+ + +

Mr. Chairman and Friends: You, Sir, have just said that probably this is for the first time I am privileged to address a meeting of Indian Christians only. If you refer to my present visit, you are perfectly correct. But if you refer or have referred to the whole of the time that I have been in India since my return from South Africa, then I have to inform you that I had such a privilege in 1915. But my connection with Indian Christian[s] dates back to 1893. That was the time when I went to South Africa and found myself in the midst of a large Christian Indian community. I was agreeably surprised to find so many young men and young women who, whilst they were devoted Christians, were equally devoted to the motherland, and it gave me greater pleasure when I discovered that most of the young men and young women had never seen India. The majority of them were born in Natal; some of them in Mauritius, because it was from Mauritius that the first batch of free Indian settlers found their way to South Africa. They were most of them children of indentured parents. Indentured Indians were those who had gone to work on the sugar estates of Natal under an indissoluble contract to work on those estates for at least five years and, as they had gone under this contract, otherwise called indenture, they were called Indentured Indians. Their state was described during his lifetime by the late Sir William Hunter[15] as a state very near to slavery. . . .

14. From *Amrita Bazar Patrika*, 15 August 1925, as reproduced in *CWMG*, vol. 28, pp. 17–23.

15. William Hunter, civil servant and scholar, was the author of many books on Indian affairs, among them histories of Bengal and of the Indian Muslims. Hunter was also chairman of the Education Commission of 1882 to which both Syed Ahmad Khan and Jotirao Phule testified.

It goes hard with people who have to suffer the disabilities that our countrymen, whom I have just now described to you, have to labour under, to understand that there can be any such thing as 'Brotherhood of Man'. If you are readers of newspapers and if you take any interest in what goes on outside the four corners of India, you may know that, today, in South Africa an attempt is being made by the Government of the country to drive away the Indians, or, as it has been well put by one of the newspapers here, English-owned, to starve them out of South Africa; and in this scheme of starvation are included some of these very men I have described to you. Whether ultimately this thing will come to pass, whether ultimately the Government of India will sanction or tolerate this thing, remains to be seen. But the connection in which I mention this thing to you is, as I have already told you, that it is difficult for such men to realize the meaning of brotherhood; and yet I have undertaken to speak to you on brotherhood at this time because it is in such times of stress and difficulty that one's spirit of brotherhood is really tested. . . .

Brotherhood does not mean loving or sympathizing with those, extending the hand of fellowship to those who will in return love you. That is a bargain. Brotherhood is not a mercantile affair. And my philosophy, my religion teaches me that brotherhood is not confined merely to the human species; that is, if we really have imbibed the spirit of brotherhood, it extends to the lower animals. In one of the magazines issued in England by those great philanthropic societies 30 or 35 years ago, I remember having read some beautiful verses. I think the title of those verses was *My Brother Ox*. In them the writer beautifully described how on a man who loved his fellow men it was obligatory to love his fellow-animals also, taking the word animals to mean the sub-human species. The thought struck me most forcibly. At that time, I had learnt very little of Hinduism. All I knew about it was what I had imbibed from my surroundings, from my parents and others. But I realized the force of that writing. However, I do not intend to dwell upon this broadest brotherhood. I shall confine myself to 'Brotherhood of Man'. I have brought this thing in order to illustrate that our brotherhood is a mockery if we are not prepared to love even our enemies. In other words, one who has imbibed the spirit of brotherhood cannot possibly allow it to be said of him that he has any enemy at all. People may consider themselves to be our enemies, but we should reject any such claim. . . .

The question then arises: how is it possible to love those who consider themselves to be our enemies? Almost every week, I receive letters either from Hindus or from Mussalmans, sometimes from Christians, combating this fundamental position that I have taken up. If it is a Hindu who writes, then he asks me, 'How is it possible for me to love a Mussalman who kills the cow, which is dear to me as my life?' Of if it is a Christian who writes to me, he asks, 'How is it possible to love Hindus who so ill-treat those whom they call untouchables, Hindus who have suppressed a fifth of their own numbers?' and if it is a Mussalman who writes, he asks, 'How is it possible to extend the hand of brotherhood or fellowship to Hindus who are worshippers of stock and stone?' I say to all these three: 'Your brotherhood is of no value to me if you cannot love the respective parties that you have described'. But what does the attitude signify after all? Does it not signify cowardly fear or intolerance? If all of us are God's creation, why should we fear one another or hate those who do not hold the same belief that we do? A Hindu will ask me, is he to sit or look on, while a Mussalman is doing something which is most repugnant to him? My brotherhood replies, 'Yes'. And I add, 'You must sacrifice yourself, or in the language you have just listened to, you must bear the cross. If you want to defend one who is dear to you, you must die without killing'. I have personal experience of such occurrences.

If you have the courage to suffer lovingly, you melt the stoniest heart. You may raise your hand against one whom you regard as a ruffian, but how if he overpowers you? Will not the ruffian be more ferocious because of his victory over you? Does not history show that evil feeds on resistance? History also furnishes instances of men having tamed the fiercest man with their all-embracing love. But I admit that such non-resistance requires far greater courage than that of a soldier who returns two blows against one. I also admit that if a man has anger instead of love in him for the evil-doer, it is better for him to fight clean rather than, in a cowardly manner, to sit still for fear of dying. Cowardice and brotherhood are contradictory terms. I know that the world does not accept the fundamental position that I have endeavoured to place before you. I know that in Christian Europe, this doctrine of non-retaliation is pooh-poohed.

At the present moment, I am privileged to receive precious letters from friends all over Europe and America, some of them asking me to still further expound the doctrine of non-resistance. Some others are laughing at me and telling me: 'It is all right for you to talk these things in India, but you dare not do so in Europe'. Yet others tell me: 'Our Christanity is a whitewash, we do not understand the message of Jesus, it has got to be still delivered to us, so that we can understand it'. All these three positions are more or less right from the standpoint of the writers. But I venture to tell you that there is no peace for this world, and to take the name of brotherhood is a blasphemy, until we arrive at this fundamental position. Men there are who ask and so also women who ask: 'Is it human to refrain from retaliation?' I say it is human. Up to now we have not realized our humanity, we have not realized our dignity; we are supposed to be, if Darwin is to be believed, the descendants of monkeys, and I am afraid that we have not yet shed our original state.

The late Dr. Anna Kingsford[16] in one of her books wrote once: 'As I walk about the streets of Paris, I seem to see before me diverse lions and snakes personified'. She says these animals have only the human form but no more. Man, to realize his full stature, has to become absolutely fearless. This he will do not by being armed from head to foot, but by generating force from within. A *Kshatriya* is one who does not fly from danger, he is not one who strikes a blow for a blow. The *Mahabharata* says also that forgiveness is the quality of a brave man. There is a statue erected, I am told, in the memory of the late General Gordon.[17] The sculptor does not put a sword in his hands, he puts only a stick. It is considered to be a beautiful work of art. If I was born a sculptor and I had the order, I would not have put even a stick in the hands of General Gordon, but I would have pictured him as one with folded arms, with his chest put forward, in all humility telling the world: 'Come, all of you, who want to throw your darts, here is General Gordon to receive them without flinching, without retaliation'. That is my ideal of a soldier. Such soldiers have lived on the earth.

Christianity undoubtedly has given birth to such soldiers, and so has Hinduism, so has Islam. In my opinion, it is not true to say that Islam is a religion of the sword. History does not bear that out. But I am just now speaking to you of individual instances, and what is true of the individual can be true of nations or of groups of individuals; not all at once, I admit, but in the process

16. A nineteenth-century British theosophist and author.

17. A nineteenth-century British army commander who served and died in the Sudan and is one of the four subjects of Lytton Strachey's *Eminent Victorians*.

of evolution, when men after men live this truth in their lives before our very eyes, they cannot but affect us. Such is the history of Quakers. Such is the history of Dukhobors whom Tolstoy has described. I do not know how far the latter, after having gone to Canada, are carrying out their original resolution, but the fact stands that they have lived this life of non-resistance as a community. I, therefore, feel that we are trifling with that sacred name, Brotherhood of Man, unless and until we are ruled by this fundamental fact in life.

What I am just now combating is the position that is taken up by some of the finest writers in Europe and by some of the finest writers even in India: that man, as a class, will never be able to arrive at a stage when he can do without retaliation. I have a fundamental quarrel with that position. On the contrary, I say that man, as man, will not realize his full destiny, and his full dignity, until he has been so far educated as to be able to refrain from retaliation. Whether we like it or whether we do not like it, we are being drawn to it. It would be to our credit if, instead of being driven to the position, we will take ourselves to it, and I have come here this evening to ask you to exercise this privilege, the privilege of voluntarily taking up this idea in practice. Indeed, I ought not to have to be speaking to a Christian audience on this, because some of my friends tell me that I am really a Christian, when I talk about non-retaliation. Little do they know that I have got to strive with the Christians, as I have to with Hindus and my Muslim friends. I do not know many Christians who have adopted this thing as a rule of their life. Some of the very best Christians that I know do not admit that this is the teaching of Christ. I do believe that it is the teaching of Christ. They say it was meant merely for his twelve disciples, not meant for the world, and they quote some passages from the New Testament in support of their contention. The opponents of non-violence as a rule of life say that it can only breed a race of cowards, and if India takes up this message of non-retaliation, she is a doomed country. On the contrary, the fundamental position that I place before you is, that unless India takes up this position, she is a doomed nation and with her all the nations of the world. India is a continent, and when India takes up the doctrine of force, as Europe today seems to have taken it up, then India becomes one of the exploiters of the weaker races of the world. Just imagine what it must mean to the world. . . .

✦   ✦   ✦

THE POSITION OF WOMEN

A modern feminist would have ambivalent feelings about Gandhi. She might deplore his opposition to contraception and his lack of enthusiasm for women in the workforce but perhaps admire his ability to bring women into social movements and his criticisms of the treatment of widows in Hindu society. The following excerpt succinctly states Gandhi's views on the position of women, past, present, and future.[18]

✦ ✦ ✦

A fair friend, who has hitherto successfully resisted the matrimonial temptation, writes:

There was a women's conference yesterday at the Malabari Hall [in Bombay], at which many sound speeches were made and many resolutions passed. The question of the evening was the Sarda Bill.[19] We are so glad you uphold the age of 18 for girls. Another important resolution dealt with the laws of inheritance. What a help it would be, if you wrote a strong article on this subject in *Navajivan* and *Young India*? Why should women have either to beg or to fight in order to win back their birthright? It is strange— and also tragically comic—to hear man born of woman talk loftily of 'the weaker sex' and nobly promising 'to give' us our due! What is this nonsense about 'giving'? Where is the 'nobility' and 'chivalry' in restoring to people that which has been unlawfully wrested from them by those having brute power in their hands? Wherein are women less important than men? Why should their share of inheritance be less than that of men? Why should it not be equal? We were discussing this very heatedly with some people a couple of days ago. A lady said, 'We don't need any change in the law. We are quite content. After all, it is but fair that the son, who carries on the name and family traditions, should have the

18. From *Young India*, 17 October 1929, as reproduced in *CWMG*, vol. 42, pp. 4–6.
19. The Sarda Bill, in a bid to stem the then widespread practice of child marriage, forbade the marriage of girls below the age of fourteen.

greater share. He is the mainstay of the family.' We said, 'And what about the girl?' 'Oh,' intervened a strapping young man who was there, 'the other fellow will look after *her!*' There you are. The 'other fellow'! Always the other fellow! This other fellow is an absolute nuisance! *Why* should there be another fellow? Why should it be taken for granted that there *will* be another fellow? They talk as though a girl were a bale of goods to be tolerated in the parental house until 'the other fellow' comes round, and then coolly handed over to him with a sigh of relief. Really wouldn't *you* be wild, if you were a girl?

I do not need to be a girl to be wild over man's atrocities towards woman. I count the law of inheritance among the least in the list. The Sarda Bill deals with an evil far greater than the one which the law of inheritance connotes. But I am uncompromising in the matter of woman's rights. In my opinion she should labour under no legal disability not suffered by man. I should treat the daughters and sons on a footing of perfect equality. As women begin to realize their strength, as they must in proportion to the education they receive, they will naturally resent the glaring inequalities to which they are subjected.

But to remove legal inequalities will be a mere palliative. The root of the evil lies much deeper than most people realize. It lies in man's greed of power and fame, and deeper still in mutual lust. Man has always desired power. Ownership of property gives this power. Man hankers also after posthumous fame based on power. This cannot be had, if property is progressively cut up in pieces, as it must be if all the posterity become equal co-sharers. Hence the descent of property for the most part on the eldest male issue. Most women are married. And they are co-sharers, in spite of the law being against them, in their husbands' power and privileges. They delight in being ladies this and what not simply for the fact of being the wives of particular lords. Though, therefore, they may vote for radical reform in academic discussions over inequalities, when it comes to acting up to their vote they will be found to be unwilling to part with the privileges.

Whilst, therefore, I would always advocate the repeal of all legal disqualifications, I should have the enlightened women of India to deal with the root cause. Woman is the embodiment of sacrifice and suffering, and her advent to public life should, therefore, result in purifying it, in restraining unbridled ambition and accumulation of property. Let them know that millions of men have no property to transmit to posterity. Let us learn from them that it is better for the few to have no ancestral property at all. The real property that a parent can transmit to all equally is his or her character and educational facilities. Parents should seek to make their sons and daughters self-reliant, well able to earn an honest livelihood by the sweat of the brow. . . . Much of the present imbecility of the children of the wealthy will go, if the latter can but substitute the worthy ambition of educating their children to become independent for the unworthy ambition of making them slaves of ancestral property, which kills enterprise and feeds the passions which accompany idleness and luxury. The privilege of the awakened women should be to spot and eradicate age-long evils.

That mutual lust too has played an important part in bringing about the disqualifications of the fair sex hardly needs any demonstration. Woman has circumvented man in a variety of ways in her unconsciously subtle ways, as man has vainly and equally unconsciously struggled to thwart woman in gaining ascendancy over him. The result is a stalemate. Thus viewed, it is a serious problem the enlightened daughters of *Bharat Mata*[20] are called upon to solve. They may not ape the manner of the West, which may be suited to its environment. They must apply methods suited to the Indian genius and Indian environment. Theirs must be the strong, controlling, purifying, steadying hand, conserving what is best in our culture and unhesitatingly rejecting what is base and degrading. . . .

✦   ✦   ✦

The subject of this next excerpt is contained in its perhaps uncharacteristically strident title, namely, 'Tear Down the Purdah'. Sita is the wife of Lord Rama, the central character of the Ramayana; Draupadi the wife of the five Pandavas (of whom Bhima was one), the heroes of the other great epic, the Mahabharata.[21]

✦   ✦   ✦

20. 'Bharat Mata': literally, Mother India.
21. From *Young India*, 3 February 1927, as reproduced in *CWMG*, vol. 33, pp. 44–45.

Whenever I have gone to Bengal, Bihar or the United Provinces, I have observed the purdah system more strictly followed than in the other provinces. But when I addressed a meeting at Darbhanga late at night and amid calm surroundings free from noise and bustle and unmanageable crowds, I found in front of me men, but behind me and behind the screen were women of whose presence I knew nothing till my attention was drawn to it. The function was in connection with the laying of the foundation-stone of an orphanage, but I was called upon to address the ladies behind the purdah. The sight of the screen behind which my audience, whose numbers I did not know, was seated made me sad. It pained and humiliated me deeply. I thought of the wrong being done by men to the women of India by clinging to a barbarous custom which, whatever use it might have had when it was first introduced, had now become totally useless and was doing incalculable harm to the country. All the education that we have been receiving for the past 100 years seems to have produced but little impression upon us, for I note that the purdah is being retained even in educated households not because the educated men believe in it themselves but because they will not manfully resist the brutal custom and sweep it away at a stroke. I have the privilege of addressing hundreds of meetings of women attended by thousands. . . . I am quite aware of the very high culture of these thousands of sisters whom I get the privilege of addressing. I know that they are capable of rising to the same height that men are capable of, and I know too that they do have occasions to go out. But this is not to be put down to the credit of the educated classes. The question is, why have they not gone further? Why do not our women enjoy the same freedom that men do? Why should they not be able to walk out and have fresh air?

Chastity is not a hot-house growth. It cannot be superimposed. It cannot be protected by the surrounding wall of the purdah. It must grow from within, and to be worth anything it must be capable of withstanding every unsought temptation. It must be as defiant as Sita's. It must be a very poor thing that cannot stand the gaze of men. Men, to be men, must be able to trust their womenfolk, even as the latter are compelled to trust them. Let us not live with one limb completely or partially paralysed. Rama would be nowhere without Sita, free and independent even as he was himself. But for robust independence Draupadi is perhaps a better example. Sita was gentleness incarnate. She was a delicate flower. Draupadi was a giant oak. She bent mighty Bhima himself to her imperious will. Bhima was terrible to everyone, but he was a lamb before Draupadi. She stood in no need of protection from any one of the Pandavas. By seeking today to interfere with the free growth of the womanhood of India we are interfering with the growth of free and independent-spirited men. What we are doing to our women and what we are doing to the 'untouchables' recoils upon our heads with a force [a] thousand times multiplied. It partly accounts for our own weakness, indecision, narrowness and helplessness. Let us then tear down the purdah with one mighty effort.

✦   ✦   ✦

8

THE ROOTED COSMOPOLITAN

RABINDRANATH TAGORE

THE COLLECTED WORKS OF RABINDRANATH TAGORE run to 18,000 printed pages in Bengali. The bulk consists of poems, plays, songs, short stories, and novels; but there are some significant works of non-fiction as well. Although best remembered as a creative writer who transformed the Bengali language and became the first Asian to win the Nobel Prize in literature, Tagore was also a fine essayist, who had interesting and original things to say about the society and politics of India and the world.

Rabindranath Tagore was born in 1861 into a family of scholars, social reformers, and entrepreneurs. His grandfather was a close associate of Rammohan Roy. The family were among the earliest to join Roy's Brahmo Samaj. Later members of the Tagore family started schools, wrote on the Upanishads, and ran the large and profitable family estates in eastern India.

As the fourteenth and youngest child of a rich, cultivated man, Rabindranath was educated at home and through his travels. He spent holidays with a brother in the civil service, whose official duties took him to parts of India very distant and in a cultural sense very different from Bengal. The boy also made regular trips to Europe. He was admitted to a school in England, but soon dropped out to resume his self-education.

Beginning in the 1880s, Tagore published a steady stream of poems, stories, and novels. These had a profound impact in his native Bengal, but were little known outside. In 1912 he carried some translations of his poems to England; these were shown to the Irish poet W. B. Yeats, who helped refine them and, more importantly, gave them his endorsement. The translations, published under the title *Gitanjali,* were a great success, going into ten printings within six months. When the award of the Nobel Prize followed, the Bengali writer had become a world figure. His appeal was enchanced by his appearance—with a handsome oval face and piercing eyes, framed by a flowing white beard, and dressed in long colourful robes, he looked every inch the Oriental guru.

Tagore was a patriot without quite being a nationalist. He was no apologist for colonial rule; after British soldiers fired on an unarmed crowd in Amritsar in 1919 he returned his knighthood to the King. At the same time he was dismayed by the xenophobic tendencies of the populist edge of the Indian national movement. He thought that India had much to learn from other cultures, including (but not restricted to) the West.

Tagore's understanding of countries other than his own was deepened by his extensive travels abroad. He made four trips to the United States and many more to Europe. He visited Japan several times, went to China, travelled through West and Southeast Asia, and also went to South America. In 1930, touching seventy, he spent several weeks in the Soviet Union. Through these trips he deepened an already substantial interest in aesthetics, music, and literature. He was catholic enough to admire both the medieval Persian poet Hafiz and the Anglo-American modernist T. S. Eliot.

Tagore was the most widely travelled Indian of his generation. From what he saw at home and abroad, he arrived at an understanding of India's place in the world that was more nuanced, more layered, more complex, and more profound than that articulated by any of his compatriots. He sought to give this vision an institutional form, founding a university in 1921 on land his family owned in rural Bengal. The curriculum he developed here bridged science and the humanities. Music and art were also taught, and there was a special focus on the study of Japan and China, the two civilisations with which India might, in Tagore's view, share mutually beneficial interactions in a post-colonial future. The campus where these myriad activities took place was named Santiniketan, the Abode of Peace; with the university calling itself Viswa-Bharati, or India in the World. To forestall criticism that this was an elitist or 'ivory tower' vision of learning, Tagore simultaneously started an institute of rural reconstruction.

Tagore died in 1941. Seven decades later, his songs are still sung in Bengal. His stories and poems are now available in decent English translations. One poem serves as the national anthem of India, another as the national anthem of Bangladesh. In his own lifetime, Tagore had a profound impact on Gandhi and Jawaharlal Nehru, who are commonly (and rightly) regarded as the two most influential individuals in modern Indian history. Rabindranath Tagore the poet and novelist would have pride of place in any history of Indian literature; but, as I think the excerpts below demonstrate, Rabindranath Tagore the thinker and prophet is by no means out of place in an anthology of Indian political writing.

INDIA AND THE WEST

Dismayed by the xenophobia of the Swadeshi movement, Tagore wrote a series of essays in Bengali in 1909–1910 advocating a more nuanced understanding of relations between East and West. Excerpts from a later English translation follow.[1]

✦   ✦   ✦

. . . Whether India is to be yours or mine, whether it is to belong more to the Hindu, or to the Moslem, or whether some other race is to assert a greater supremacy than either,—that is not the problem with which Providence is ex-

---

1. From Rabindranath Tagore, *Greater India,* trans. Surendranath Tagore (Madras: S. Ganesan, 1921), pp. 79–101.

ercised. It is not as if, at the bar of the judgment seat of the Almighty, different advocates are engaged in pleading the rival causes of Hindu, Moslem or Westerner, and that the party which wins the decree shall finally plant the standard of permanent possession. It is our vanity which makes us think that it is a battle between contending rights,—the only battle is the eternal one between Truth and untruth. . . .

Of late the British have come in and occupied an important place in India's history. This was not an uncalled for, accidental intrusion. If India had been deprived of touch with the West, she would have lacked an element essential for her attainment of perfection. Europe now has her lamp ablaze. We must light our torches at its wick and make a fresh start on the highway of time. That our forefathers, three thousand years ago, had finished extracting all that was of value from the universe, is not a worthy thought. We are not so unfortunate, nor the universe, so poor. Had it been true that all that is to be done has been done in the past, once for all, then our continued existence could only be a burden to the earth, and so would not be possible. . . .

The Englishman has come through the breach in our crumbling walls, as the messenger of the Lord of the world-festival, to tell us that the world has need of us; not where we are petty, but where we can help with the force of our Life, to rouse the World in wisdom, love and work, in the expansion of insight, knowledge and mutuality. Unless we can justify the mission on which the Englishman has been sent, until we can set out with him to honour the invitation of which he is the bearer, he cannot but remain with us as our tormentor, the disturber of our quietism. So long as we fail to make good the arrival of the Englishman, it shall not be within our power to get rid of him.

The India to which the Englishman has come with his message, is the India which is shooting up towards the future from within the bursting seed of the past. This new India belongs to humanity. What right have we to say who shall and who shall not find a place therein. Who is this 'We'? Bengali, Marathi or Panjabi, Hindu or Mussalman? Only the larger 'We' in whom all these,—Hindu, Moslem and Englishman, and whosoever else there be,—may eventually unite shall have the right to dictate who is to remain and who is to leave.

On us to-day is thrown the responsibility of building up this greater India, and for that purpose our immediate duty is to justify our meeting with the Englishman. It shall not be permitted to us to say that we would rather remain aloof, inactive, irresponsive, unwilling to give and to take, and thus to make poorer the India that is to be.

So the greatest men of modern India have all made it their life's work to bring about an approachment with the West. The chief example is Rammohan Roy. He stood alone in his day for the union of India with the world on the broad base of humanity. No blind belief, no ancestral habit was allowed to obscure his vision. With a wonderful breadth of heart and intellect he accepted the West without betraying the East. . . . Rammohan Roy did not assist India to repair her barriers, or to keep cowering behind them,—he led her out into the freedom of Space and Time, and built for her a bridge between the East and West. That is why his spirit still lives with us, his power of stimulating India's creative energies is not yet exhausted. No blind habit of mind, no pettiness of racial pride, were able to make him commit the folly of rebellion against the manifest purpose of time. . . .

What then are we to make of the antagonism which has arisen of late between the Englishman and the Indian, educated as well as uneducated? Is there nothing real in this? Is it only the machination of a few conspirators? Is this antagonism essentially different in purpose from the constant action and reaction of making and breaking which are at work in the making of Indian History? It is very necessary for us to come to a true understanding of its meaning. . . .

We began with a blind, foolish, insensate begging at the door of Europe, with our critical sense entirely benumbed. That was not the way to make any real gain. Whether it be wisdom, or political rights, they have to be earned, that is to say to be attained by one's own *shakti* [strength] after a successful struggle against obstructing forces. If they be put into our hands by others, by way of alms, they do not become ours at all. To take in a form which is derogatory can only lead to loss. Hence our reaction against the culture of Europe and its ideals. A feeling of wounded self-respect is prompting us to return upon ourselves. . . .

Rammohan Roy was able to assimilate the ideals of Europe so completely because he was not overwhelmed by them: there was no poverty or weakness on his side. He had ground of his own on which he could take his stand and where he could secure his acquisitions. The true wealth of India was not hidden from him, for this he had already made his own. Consequently he had with him the touchstone by which he could test the wealth of others. He did not sell himself by holding out a beggar's palms, but assessed the true value of whatever he took.

This *shakti* which was natural to our first great leader, is steadily developing itself amongst us through constantly conflicting stresses and strains, actions and reactions. Pendulum-wise do our movements touch now this extreme, now the other. An undue eagerness of acceptance and an undue timidity of rejection assail us by turns. . . .

The West has come as India's guest; we cannot send away the visitor while the object of his visit remains unfulfilled; he must be properly accommodated. But, whatever be the reason,—whether it be some defect in our power of recognition, or the miserliness of the West in revealing itself in its truth,—if the flow of this great purpose of Time should receive a check, there is bound to be a disastrous irruption.

If we do not come into touch with what is true, what is best, in the Englishman; if we find in him merely a merchant, or a military man, or a bureaucrat; if he will not come down to the plane in which man may commune with man and take him into confidence;—if, in fine, the Indian and the Englishman needs must remain apart, then will they be to each other a perennial source of unhappiness. In such case the party which is in power will try to make powerless the dissatisfaction of the weaker by repressive legislation, but will not be able to allay it. Nor will the former find any satisfaction in the situation; and feeling the Indian only to be a source of trouble the Englishman will more and more try to ignore his very existence. . . .

All the trouble that we see now-a-days is caused by this failure of East and West to come together. Bound to be near each other, and yet unable to be friends, is an intolerable situation between man and man, and hurtful withal. Therefore the desire to put an end to it must become overwhelming sooner or later. Such a rebellion, being a rebellion of the heart, will not take account of material gains or losses; it will even risk death.

And yet it is also true that such rebelliousness can only be a temporary phase. In spite of all retarding factors our impact with the West must be made good,—there can be no escape for India until she has made her own whatever there may be worth the taking from the West. Until the fruit is ripe it does not get released from the stem, nor can it ripen at all if it insists on untimely release. . . .

Those of us who go to the Englishman's durbar [court] with bowed heads and folded hands, seeking emoluments of office or badges of honour,—we only attract his pettiness and help to distort his true manifestation in India. Those, again, who in a blind fury of passion would violently assail him, succeed in evoking only the sinful side of the Englishman's nature. If, then, it be true that it is our frailty which excites his insolence, his greed, his cowardice or his cruelty, why blame him? Rather should we take the blame on ourselves.

In his own country the Englishman's lower nature is kept under control and his higher nature roused to its fullest capacity by the social forces around him. The social conscience there, being awake, compels each individual, with all its force, to take his stand on a high level and maintain his place there with unceasing effort. In this country his society is unable to perform the same function. Anglo-Indian society is not concerned with the whole Englishman. It is either a society of civilians, or of merchants, or of soldiers. Each of these are limited by their own business, and become encased in a hard crust of prejudice and superstition. So they develop into thorough-going civilians, or mere merchants, or blatant soldiers. We cannot find the man in them. . . .

On the other hand, the decay and weakness of the Indian *Samaj* [society] itself is also a bar to the rousing of the true British spirit, wherefore both are losers. It is our own fault, I repeat, that we meet only *Burra Sahebs*[2] and not great Englishmen. And to this we owe all the sufferings and insults with which we have to put up. We have no remedy but to acknowledge our sin and get rid of it. . . .

Neither tall talk nor violence, but only sacrifice and service are true tests of strength. Until the Indian can give up his fear, his self-interest, his luxury, in his quest for the best and the highest, in his service of the Motherland, our demanding from the Government will but be empty begging and will aggravate both our incapacity and our humiliation. When we shall have made our country our own by sacrifice and established our claim to it by applying our own powers for its reclamation, then we shall not need to stand abjectly and the Englishman need not lower himself. Then may we become colleagues and enter into mutual arrangement.

Until we can cast off our individual or *Samajic* [collective] folly; as long as we remain unable to grant to our own countrymen the full rights of man; as long as our zamindars [landords] continue to look on their tenantry as part of their property, our men in power glory in keeping their subordinates under

2. *Burra Sahebs* is best translated as 'big shots', those who carry and display an excessive arrogance.

their heels, our higher castes think nothing of looking down on the lowest castes as worse than beasts; so long shall we not have the right or power to demand from the Englishman proper behaviour towards ourselves.

At every turn,—in her religion, in her *samaj* [social arrangements], in her daily practice—does the Indian of to-day fail to do justice to herself. She does not purify her soul by sacrifice, and so on every side she suffers futility. She cannot meet the outsider on equal terms and so receives nothing of value from him. No cleverness or violence can deliver her from the sufferings and insults of which the Englishman is but the instrument. Only when she can meet him as his equal, will all reason for antagonism, and with it all conflict, disappear. Then will East and West unite in India,—country with country, race with race, knowledge with knowledge, endeavour with endeavour. Then will the History of India come to an end, merged in the History of the World which will begin.

✦   ✦   ✦

THE EXCESSES OF NATIONALISM

In the middle of World War I, Tagore travelled to Japan and the United States. Everywhere, he warned his audiences against equating love of one's nation with the celebration of military prowess. His lectures were published in a slim book, *Nationalism,* that is perhaps his most powerful and compelling piece of non fiction. Remarkably, the note on Tagore in the official Nobel Prize Web site does not mention this book, thus confirming the popular belief that he should be known by his stories and poems alone. The excerpts presented below suggest otherwise.[3]

✦   ✦   ✦

. . . The political civilization which has sprung up from the soil of Europe and is overrunning the whole world, like some prolific weed, is based upon exclusiveness. It is always watchful to keep the aliens at bay or to exterminate

---

3. From Rabindranath Tagore, *Nationalism* (1917; reprint, New Delhi: Penguin Books, 2009), pp. 15–30, 40–45.

them. It is carnivorous and cannibalistic in its tendencies, it feeds upon the resources of other peoples and tries to swallow their whole future. It is always afraid of other races achieving eminence, naming it as a peril, and tries to thwart all symptoms of greatness outside its own boundaries, forcing down races of men who are weaker, to be eternally fixed in their weakness. Before this political civilization came to its power and opened its hungry jaws wide enough to gulp down great continents of the earth, we had wars, pillages, changes of monarchy and consequent miseries, but never such a sight of fearful and hopeless voracity, such wholesale feeding of nation upon nation, such huge machines for turning great portions of the earth into mince-meat, never such terrible jealousies with all their ugly teeth and claws ready for tearing open each other's vitals. This political civilization is scientific, not human. It is powerful because it concentrates all its forces upon one purpose, like a millionaire acquiring money at the cost of his soul. It betrays its trust, it weaves its meshes of lies without shame, it enshrines gigantic idols of greed in its temples, taking great pride in the costly ceremonials of its worship, calling this patriotism. . . .

I must not hesitate to acknowledge where Europe is great, for great she is without doubt. We cannot help loving her with all our heart and paying her the best homage of our admiration—the Europe who, in her literature and art, pours out an inexhaustible cascade of beauty and truth fertilizing all countries and all time; the Europe who, with a mind which is titanic in its untiring power, is sweeping the height and the depth of the universe, winning her homage of knowledge from the infinitely great and the infinitely small, applying all the resources of her great intellect and heart in healing the sick and alleviating those miseries of man which up till now we were contented to accept in a spirit of hopeless resignation; the Europe who is making the earth yield more fruit than seemed possible, coaxing and compelling the great forces of nature into man's service. Such true greatness must have its motive power in spiritual strength. For only the spirit of man can defy all limitations, have faith in its ultimate success, throw its searchlight beyond the immediate and the apparent, gladly suffer martyrdom for ends which cannot be achieved in its lifetime and accept failure without acknowledging defeat. In the heart of Europe runs the purest stream of human love, of love of justice, of spirit of self-sacrifice for higher ideals. The Christian culture of centuries has sunk deep in her life's core. In Europe we have seen noble minds who have ever stood up for the rights of man irrespective of colour and creed; who have braved calumny and insult from their own people in fighting for humanity's cause and raising their voices against the mad orgies of militarism, against the rage of brutal retaliation or rapacity that sometimes takes possession of a whole people; who are always ready to make reparation for wrongs done in the past by their own nations. . . . There are these knight-errants of modern Europe who have not lost their faith in the disinterested love of freedom, in the ideals which own no geographical boundaries or national self-seeking. These are there to prove that the fountainhead of the water of everlasting life has not run dry in Europe, and from thence she will have her rebirth time after time. . . . Europe is supremely good in her beneficence where her face is turned to all humanity; and Europe is supremely evil in her maleficent aspect where her face is turned only upon her own interest, using all her power of greatness for ends which are against the infinite and eternal in Man. . . .

But while trying to free our minds from the arrogant claims of Europe and to help ourselves out of the quicksands of our infatuation, we may go to the other extreme and bind ourselves with a wholesale suspicion of the West. The reaction of disillusionment is just as unreal as the first shock of illusion. We must try to come to that normal state of mind by which we can clearly discern our own danger and avoid it without being unjust towards the source of that danger. There is always the natural temptation in us of wishing to pay back Europe in her own coin, and return contempt for contempt and evil for evil. But that again would be to imitate Europe in one of her worst features, which comes out in her behaviour to people whom she describes as yellow or red, brown or black. And this is a point on which we in the East have to acknowledge our guilt and own that our sin has been as great, if not greater, when we insulted humanity by treating with utter disdain and cruelty men who belonged to a particular creed, colour or caste. It is really because we are afraid of our own weakness, which allows itself to be overcome by the sight of power, that we try to substitute for it another weakness which makes itself blind to the glories of the West. When we truly know that Europe which is great and good, we can effectively save ourselves from the Europe which is mean and grasping. . . . We must admit that there is a living soul in the West which is struggling unobserved against the hugeness of the organizations under which men, women and children are being crushed, and whose mechanical necessities are ignoring laws that are spiritual and human—the soul whose sensibilities refuse to be dulled completely by dangerous habits of heedlessness in dealings with races for whom it lacks natural sympathy. The West could never have risen to the eminence she has reached if her strength were merely the strength of the brute or of the machine. The divine in her heart is suffering from the injuries inflicted by her hands upon the world—and from this pain of her higher nature flows the secret balm which will bring healing to these injuries. Time after time she has fought against herself and has undone the chains which with her own hands she fastened round helpless limbs. . . . This shows hidden springs of humanity in spots which look dead and barren. It proves that the deeper truth in her nature, which can survive such a career of cruel cowardliness, is not greed, but reverence for unselfish ideals. It would be altogether unjust, both to us and to Europe, to say that she has fascinated the modern eastern mind by the mere exhibition of her power. Through the smoke of cannons and dust of markets the light of her moral nature has shone bright, and she has brought to us the ideal of ethical freedom, whose foundation lies deeper than social conventions and whose province of activity is worldwide.

The East has instinctively felt, even through her aversion, that she has a great deal to learn from Europe, not merely about the materials of power, but about its inner source, which is of the mind and of the moral nature of man. Europe has been teaching us the higher obligations of public good above those of the family and the clan, and the sacredness of law, which makes society independent of individual caprice, secures for it continuity of progress, and guarantees justice to all men of all positions in life. Above all things Europe has held high before our minds the banner of liberty, through centuries of martyrdom and achievement—liberty of conscience, liberty of thought and action, liberty in the ideals of art and literature. And because Europe has won our deep respect, she has become so dangerous for us where she is turbulently weak and false—dangerous like poison when it is served along with our best food. There is one safety for us upon which we hope we may count, and that is that we can claim Europe herself as our ally in our resistance to her temptations and to her violent encroachments; for she has ever carried her own standard of perfection, by which we can measure her falls and gauge her degrees of failure, by which we can call her before her own tribunal and put her to shame—the shame which is the sign of the true pride of nobleness. . . .

This abstract being, the Nation, is ruling India. We have seen in our country some brand of tinned food advertised as entirely made and packed without being touched by hand. This description applies to the governing of India, which is as little touched by the human hand as possible. The governors need not know our language, need not come into personal touch with us except as officials; they can aid or hinder our aspirations from a disdainful distance, they can lead us on a certain path of policy and then pull us back again with the manipulation of office red tape. The newspapers of England, in whose columns London street accidents are recorded with some decency of pathos, need take but the scantiest notice of calamities which happen in India over areas of land sometimes larger than the British Isles. . . .

I have not come here, however, to discuss the question as it affects my own country, but as it affects the future of all humanity. It is not a question of the British government, but of government by the Nation—the Nation which is the organized self-interest of a whole people, where it is least human and least spiritual. Our only intimate experience of the Nation is with the British Nation, and as far as the government by the Nation goes there are reasons to believe that it is one of the best. Then, again, we have to consider that the West is necessary to the East. We are complementary to each other because of our different outlooks upon life which have given us different aspects of truth. Therefore if it be true that the spirit of the West has come upon our fields in the guise of a storm it is nevertheless scattering living seeds that are immortal. And when in India we become able to assimilate in our life what is permanent in western civilization we shall be in a position to bring about a reconciliation of these two great worlds. . . .

I have a deep love and a great respect for the British race as human beings. It has produced great-hearted men, thinkers of great thoughts, doers of great deeds. It has given rise to a great literature. I know that these people love justice and freedom, and hate lies. They are clean in their minds, frank in their manners, true in their friendships; in their behaviour they are honest and reliable. The personal experience which I have had of their literary men has roused my admiration not merely for their power of thought or expression but for their chivalrous humanity. We have felt the greatness of this people as we feel the sun; but as for the Nation, it is for us a thick mist of a stifling nature covering the sun itself.

This government by the Nation is neither British nor anything else; it is an applied science and therefore more or less similar in its principles wherever it is used. It is like a hydraulic press, whose pressure is impersonal, and on that account completely effective. The amount of its power may vary in different engines. Some may even be driven by hand, thus leaving a margin of comfortable looseness in their tension, but in spirit and in method their differences are small. Our government might have been Dutch, or French, or Portuguese, and its essential features would have remained much the same as they are now. Only perhaps, in some cases, the organization might not have been so densely perfect, and therefore some shreds of the human might still have been clinging to the wreck, allowing us to deal with something which resembles our own throbbing heart.

Before the Nation came to rule over us we had other governments which were foreign, and these, like all governments, had some element of the machine in them. But the difference between them and the government by the Nation is like the difference between the hand-loom and the power-loom. In the products of the hand-loom the magic of man's living fingers finds its expression, and its hum harmonizes with the music of life. But the power-loom is relentlessly lifeless and accurate and monotonous in its production.

We must admit that during the personal government of former days there have been instances of tyranny, injustice, and extortion. They caused sufferings and unrest from which we are glad to be rescued. The protection of law is not only a boon, but it is a valuable lesson to us. It is teaching us the discipline which is necessary for the stability of civilization and for continuity of progress. We are realizing through it that there is a universal standard of justice to which all men, irrespective of their caste and colour, have their equal claim.

This reign of law is [how] our present government in India has established order in this vast land inhabited by peoples different in their races and customs. It has made it possible for these peoples to come in closer touch with one another and cultivate a communion of aspiration.

But this desire for a common bond of comradeship among the different races of India has been the work of the spirit of the West, not that of the Nation of the West. . . . In India we are suffering from this conflict between the spirit of the West and the Nation of the West. The benefit of western civilization is doled out to us in a miserly measure by the Nation, which tries to regulate the degree of nutrition as near the zero-point of vitality as possible. The portion of education allotted to us is so raggedly insufficient that it ought to outrage the sense of decency of western humanity. We have seen in these countries how the people are encouraged and trained and given every facility to fit themselves for the great movements of commerce and industry spreading over the world, while in India the only assistance we get is merely to be jeered at by the Nation for lagging behind. While depriving us of our opportunities and reducing our education to the minimum required for conducting a foreign government, this Nation pacifies its conscience by calling us names, by sedulously giving currency to the arrogant cynicism that the East is east and the West is west and never the twain shall meet. If we must believe our schoolmaster in his taunt that, after nearly two centuries of his tutelage, India not only remains unfit for self-government but unable to display originality in her intellectual attainments, must we ascribe it to something in the nature of western culture and our inherent incapacity to receive it or to the judicious niggardliness of the Nation that has taken upon itself the white man's burden of civilizing the East? . . .

We must recognize that it is providential that the West has come to India. And yet someone must show the East to the West, and convince the West that the East has her contribution to make to the history of civilization. India is no beggar of the West. And yet even though the West may think she is, I am not for thrusting off western civilization and becoming segregated in our independence. Let us have a deep association. If Providence wants England to be the channel of that communication, of that deeper association, I am willing to accept it with all humility. I have great faith in human nature, and I think the West will find its true mission. I speak bitterly of western civilization when I am conscious that it is betraying its trust and thwarting its own purpose. The West must not make herself a curse to the world by using her power for her own selfish needs but, by teaching the ignorant and helping the weak, she should save herself from the worst danger that the strong is liable to incur by making the feeble acquire power enough to resist her intrusion. . . .

✦ ✦ ✦

THE PROBLEM WITH NON-CO-OPERATION

In the spring of 1921, when the non-co-operation movement was in full flow, Tagore was travelling in the West, raising money for his university in Santiniketan. Reading reports of Gandhi's movement renewed his reservations about a militant and unthinkingly oppositional nationalism. He expressed his feelings in letters written to his and Gandhi's close friend, the English priest C. F. Andrews, who released them to the press.[4]

✦   ✦   ✦

Lately I have been receiving more and more news and newspaper cuttings from India, giving rise in my mind to a painful struggle that presages a period of suffering which is waiting for me. I am striving with all my power to tune my mood of mind to be in accord with the great feeling of excitement sweeping across my country. But, deep in my being, why is there this spirit of resistance maintaining its place in spite of my strong desire to remove it? . . .

The idea of non-co-operation is political asceticism. Our students are bringing their offering of sacrifices to what? Not to a fuller education, but to non-education. It has at its back a fierce joy of annihilation, which at its best is asceticism, and at its worst that orgy of frightfulness in which human nature, losing faith in the basic reality of normal life, finds a disinterested delight in an unmeaning devastation, as has been shown in the late war and on other occasions which came nearer to us. 'No,' in its passive moral form, is asceticism, and in its active moral form violence. . . .

I remember the day, during the Swadeshi movement in Bengal, when a crowd of young students came to see me in the first floor of our . . . house. They said to me that if I would order them to leave their schools and colleges they would instantly obey. I was emphatic in my refusal to do so, and they went away angry, doubting the sincerity of my love for my motherland. And yet long before this popular ebullition of excitement, I myself had given a thousand rupees, when I had not five rupees to call my own, to open a Swadeshi store and courted banter and bankruptcy.

The reason of my refusal to advise those students to leave their schools was because the anarchy of mere emptiness never tempts me, even when it is resorted to as a temporary measure. I am frightened at an abstraction which is ready to ignore living reality. These students were no mere phantoms to

4. From Rabindranath Tagore, *Letters to a Friend,* ed. C. F. Andrews (London: George Allen and Unwin, 1928), pp. 128–137.

me. . . . I could not lightly take upon myself the tremendous responsibility of a mere negative programme for them which would uproot their life from its soil, however thin and poor that soil might be. The great injury and injustice which had been done to those boys, who were tempted away from their career before any real provision was made, could never be made good to them. . . .

I love my fellow-beings and prize their love. Yet I have been chosen by destiny to ply my boat at that spot where the current is against me. What irony of fate is this, that I should be preaching co-operation of cultures between East and West on this side of the sea just at the moment when the doctrine of non-co-operation is preached on the other side!

You know that I do not believe in the material civilization of the West, just as I do not believe the physical body to be the highest truth in man. But I believe still less in the destruction of the physical body, and the ignoring of the material necessities of life. What is needed is the establishment of harmony between the physical and spiritual nature of man, the maintaining of balance between the foundation and superstructure. I believe in the true meeting of East and West. Love is the ultimate truth of soul. We should do all we can not to outrage that truth, but to carry its banner against all opposition. The idea of non-co-operation unnecessarily hurts that truth. It is not our hearth-fire, but the fire that burns out our hearth and home. . . .

To-day, at this critical moment of the world's history, cannot India rise above her limitations and offer the great ideal to the world that will work towards harmony and co-operation between the different peoples of the earth? Men of feeble faith will say that India requires to be strong and rich before she can raise her voice for the sake of the whole world. But I refuse to believe it. That the measure of man's greatness is in his material resources is a gigantic illusion casting its shadow over the present-day world—it is an insult to man. It lies in the power of the materially weak to save the world from this illusion; and India, in spite of her penury and humiliation, can afford to come to the rescue of humanity. . . .

India has ever nourished faith in the truth of the Spiritual Man, for whose realization she has made in the past innumerable experiments, sacrifices and penances, some verging on the grotesque and the abnormal. But the fact is she has never ceased in her attempt to find it, even though at the tremendous cost of losing material success. Therefore I feel that the true India is an idea, and not a mere geographical fact. I have come into touch with this idea in far-away places of Europe, and my loyalty was drawn to it in persons who belonged to countries different from mine. India will be victorious when this idea wins the victory—the idea of 'Purusham mahantam adityavarnam tama-sah parastat'—'The Infinite Personality, whose Light reveals itself through the obstruction of Darkness.' Our fight is against this Darkness. Our object is the revealment of the Light of this Infinite Personality of Man. This is not to be achieved in single individuals, but in one grand harmony of all human races. The darkness of egoism which will have to be destroyed is the egoism of the Nation. The idea of India is against the intense consciousness of the separateness of one's own people from others, which inevitably leads to ceaseless conflicts. Therefore my own prayer is, let India stand for the co-operation of all peoples of the world. . . .

Our present struggle to alienate our heart and mind from the West is an attempt at spiritual suicide. If, in the spirit of national vainglory, we shout from our housetops that the West has produced nothing that has an infinite value for man, then we only create a serious cause of doubt about the worth of any product of the Eastern mind. For it is the mind of Man, in the East and West, which is ever approaching Truth in her different aspects from different angles of vision. If it can be true that the standpoint of the West has betrayed it into an utter misdirection, then we can never be sure of the standpoint of the East. Let us be rid of all false pride and rejoice at any lamp being lit in any corner of the world, knowing that it is a part of the common illumination of our house. . . .

The West has misunderstood the East. This is at the root of the disharmony that prevails between them. But will it mend matters if the East in her turn tries to misunderstand the West? The present age has been powerfully possessed by the West; it has only become possible because to her is given some great mission for man. We, from the East, have come to her to learn whatever she has to teach us; for by doing so we hasten the fulfillment of this age. We know that the East also has her lessons to give, and she has her own responsibility of not allowing her light to be extinguished. The time will come when the West will find leisure to realize that she has a home of hers in the East where her food is and her rest.

✦   ✦   ✦

9

THE ANNIHILATOR OF CASTE

B. R. AMBEDKAR

OUR NEXT MAKER OF MODERN INDIA had one thing in common with Rabindranath Tagore—he too was the fourteenth and last child of his parents. There the parallels end. Where Tagore's family was rich and upper-caste, Bhimrao Ramji Ambedkar was the son of a small-time military official who hailed from the untouchable Mahar caste. The boy studied in a school in Satara, where a Brahmin teacher changed his surname from Ambavadekar to Ambedkar. After the family moved to Bombay, Bhimrao matriculated from the Elphinstone High School. He then joined the now well-established Elphinstone College, where his fees were paid by the progressive Maharaja of Baroda. He obtained his B. A. in 1912, whereupon he joined the service of the Baroda State.

In 1913 Ambedkar was sent by the Maharaja for higher studies in the United States. He enrolled at Columbia University in New York, where he wrote a master's thesis on the caste system and a doctoral thesis on provincial finance in British India. He was guided in his research by the economist E. R. A. Seligman and came under the influence of the philosopher John Dewey, who also taught at Columbia. Living in New York was an education in itself, broadening the mind and culture of this shy young Indian from an underprivileged background. He read furiously on all subjects, buying, for his personal collection, more than two thousand books from the second-hand stores of the city.

In 1916 Ambedkar moved to London, enrolled at Gray's Inn, and began another doctorate at the London School of Economics. But his scholarship ran out, and he was summoned back to Baroda, where he was appointed Military Secretary to the Maharaja. However, the discrimination he faced (due to his caste) led him to quit the job in disgust and move to Bombay. He started tutoring students for a living (as Gokhale had done before him). By this time he was also politically active. With funds from the Maharaja of Kolhapur (who, like his counterpart in Baroda, was a critic of the Brahmin stranglehold on society and politics in western India), he began a fortnightly paper for the 'Depressed Castes'.

In 1920 Ambedkar went back to London to resume his studies, funding himself from his savings, supplemented by a loan from a Parsi friend. His doctoral thesis on the 'Problem of the Rupee' was accepted in 1923. He also qualified as a Bar-at-Law. On his return to Bombay Ambedkar enrolled at the Bombay High Court, as Gandhi had once done, except that the younger man was able to maintain a successful legal practice. He remained active on other fronts, starting a society to spread education among the 'Depressed Classes' (as the Untouchables were then legally known). In 1927 he was nominated to the Bombay Legislative Council, where his first speech (*pace* Gokhale) asked for the budget to be framed amidst less secrecy. Meanwhile, he had also begun lecturing at the city's Law College (he later served a term as its principal).

Ambedkar was not unsympathetic to the reformers who had preceded him. However, he felt that they had not gone far enough. The medieval saint-poets asked merely for Brahmins and Sudras to be treated on par as devotees of God. Ambedkar argued that religious equality meant little without social and economic equality. As for upper-caste reformers, there was, he thought, an inescapably patronising tinge to their efforts. It was time for the 'Depressed Classes' to assert their own rights under their own leaders.

In 1928 a commission headed by John Simon came to India to examine the question of constitutional reforms. The Congress boycotted its proceedings, in part because its members were all white. In his testimony to the commission, Ambedkar argued that the 'Depressed Classes' should be treated as 'a distinct, independent minority'—as separate from the Hindus, as the Muslims already were. He also advocated direct action for the fulfilment of their rights, launching *satyagrahas* to allow Untouchables to drink water from tanks and to enter temples from which they were excluded. There was determined opposition by the upper castes, leading Ambedkar to conclude that reform could come only through the purposive action of the state. He thus asked, to begin with, for greater representation for the 'Depressed Classes' at all levels of public service.

Through the 1930s and 1940s, Ambedkar wrote a series of tracts excoriating Gandhi and Gandhism. The two men met several times but could not reconcile their differences. In 1932 the British Government awarded separate electorates for Untouchables. Gandhi went on a fast to protest—to save his life, a compromise was reached with Ambedkar (known as the Poona Pact) whereby a joint electorate would remain for Hindus, but with a greater number of seats for the 'Depressed Classes'.

In 1936 Ambedkar formed the Independent Labour Party to fight the elections mandated under the new Government of India Act. (In later years the party changed its name twice, becoming, first, the Scheduled Caste Federation, and later, the Republican Party of India.) In June 1942 he was nominated to the Viceroy's Executive Council, the first Untouchable to be so distinguished. This set him even more firmly in opposition to the Congress, which, in August of the same year, started its Quit India movement.

When India became independent in 1947, the new Congress Government offered Ambedkar the job of law minister. He served in the post for four years, before resigning in September 1951. By now, he had become deeply attracted to the Buddha, whom he referred to as 'my master'. In January 1954 he was asked to be the chief guest at the premier of a feature film on Jotirao Phule produced by the writer-editor P. K. Atre. In October 1956 Ambedkar converted to Buddhism in the city of Nagpur. Six weeks later he died in New Delhi.

Like his great rival Gandhi, Ambedkar had multiple agendas as well as multiple careers. He was, at various times, a lawyer, teacher, legislator, educational organiser, party builder, and cabinet minister. Through all these roles and assignments he continued to be a prolific writer. He published important books on many topics, including federalism, theology and philosophy, finance, language, constitutionalism, and, not least, the sociology, politics, and history of the caste system.

B. R. Ambedkar's life and work are summed up by his biographer Dhananjay Keer as follows:

> What did Ambedkar achieve for the Untouchables? The story of the past life of the Scheduled Caste Hindus was pitch dark.... It was for the first time in the history of the past twenty-five hundred years that the sun of a better future arose on their horizon. Ambedkar, the son of their soil, their kith and kin, focussed the world attention on their civic, social and political rights and liberties, made untouchability a burning topic of the day, raised it to an international importance, and gave it a global publicity. His ceaseless hard struggle and his merciless hammer forced an opening for them, and inaugurated an era of light and liberty. He awakened in them a sense of human dignity, a feeling of self-respect and a burning hatred of untouchability that was worse than slavery. He pulled them out of slough and exorcized despondency and despair from their minds. He infused courage and new life into their demoralized and dehumanized cells. He gave them their soul and re-imbued them with a spirit which enabled them to voice their grievances, and to stand up for justice, equality and liberty. Before the rise of their leadership they were treated worse than animals. His heroic struggle raised them to political equality with other communities in India.

The quaintness of the prose notwithstanding, this is an essentially accurate description of what one man did for his people.

THE REVOLUTION AGAINST CASTE

In 1927 Ambedkar led a protest against a ban on Untouchable castes drinking water from a lake in the town of Mahad. On that occasion he made a speech comparing the struggle against caste with the struggle against absolutism in late eighteenth-century France. Excerpts from that speech follow.[1]

+   +   +

The Hindus are divided, according to sacred tradition, into four castes; but according to custom, into five: Brahmins, Kshatriyas, Vaishyas, Shudras and Atishudras. The caste system is the first of the governing rules of the Hindu religion. The second is that the castes are of unequal rank. They are ordered in a descending series of each meaner than the one before.

Not only are their ranks permanently fixed by the rule, but each is as-signed boundaries it must not transgress, so that each one may at once be recognized as belonging to its particular rank. There is a general belief that the prohibitions in the Hindu religion against intermarriage, inter-dining, inter-drinking and social intercourse are bounds set to degrees of association with one another. But this is an incomplete idea. These prohibitions are in-deed limits to degrees of association; but they have been set to show people of unequal rank what the rank of each is. That is, these bounds are symbols of inequality.

The caste Hindus of Mahad prevent the untouchables from drinking the water of the Chavadar Lake not because they suppose that the touch of the untouchables will pollute the water or that it will evaporate and vanish. Their reason for preventing the untouchables from drinking it is that they do not wish to acknowledge by such a permission that castes declared inferior by sacred tradition are in fact their equals.

Gentlemen! you will understand from this the significance of the struggle we have begun. Do not let yourselves suppose that the Satyagraha Commit-tee has invited you to Mahad merely to drink the water of the Chavadar Lake of Mahad.

It is not as if drinking the water of the Chavadar Lake will make us immor-tal. We have survived well enough all these days without drinking it. We are

1. From Arjun Dangle, ed., *Poisoned Bread: Translations from Modern Marathi Dalit Literature* (Hyderabad: Orient Longman, 1992), pp. 223–233. Ambedkar's speech was transcribed by Changdeo Khairmode and is translated by Rameshchandra Sirkar.

not going to the Chavadar Lake merely to drink its water. We are going to the Lake to assert that we too are human beings like others. It must be clear that this meeting has been called to set up the norm of equality.

I am certain that no one who thinks of this meeting in this light will doubt that it is unprecedented. I feel that no parallel to it can be found in the history of India. If we seek for another meeting in the past to equal this, we shall have to go to the history of France on the continent of Europe. A hundred and thirty-eight years ago, on 24 January 1789, King Louis XVI had convened, by royal command, an assembly of deputies to represent the people of the king-dom. This French National Assembly has been much vilified by historians. The Assembly sent the King and the Queen of France to the guillotine; perse-cuted and massacred the aristocrats; and drove their survivors into exile. It confiscated the estates of the rich and plunged Europe into war for fifteen years. Such are the accusations leveled against the Assembly by the histori-ans. In my view, the criticism is misplaced; further, the historians of this school have not understood the gist of the achievement of the French Na-tional Assembly. That achievement served the welfare not only of France but of the entire European continent. If European nations enjoy peace and pros-perity today, it is for one reason: the revolutionary French National Assembly convened in 1789 set new principles for the organization of society before the disorganized and decadent French nation of its time, and the same principles have been accepted and followed by Europe.

To appreciate the importance of the French National Assembly and the greatness of its principles, we must keep in mind the state of French society at the time. You are all aware that our Hindu society is based on the system of castes. A rather similar system of classes existed in the France of 1789: the difference was that it was a society of three castes. Like the Hindu society, the French had a class of Brahmins and another of Kshatriyas. But instead of three different castes of Vaishya, Shudra and Atishudra, there was one class that comprehended these. This is a minor difference. The important thing is that the caste or class system was similar. The similarity to be noted is not only in the differentiation between classes: the inequality of our caste system was also to be found in the French social system. The nature of the inequality in the French society was different: it was economic in nature. It was, however, equally intense. The thing to bear in mind is there is a great similarity be-tween the French National Assembly that met on 5 May 1789 at Versailles and our meeting today. The similarity is not only in the circumstances in which the two meetings took place but also in their ideals. . . .

That Assembly of the French people was convened to reorganize French society. Our meeting today too has been convened to reorganize Hindu society. . . . The road it marked out for the development of the French nation, the road that all progress[ive] nations have followed, ought to be the road adopted for the development of Hindu society by this meeting. We need to pull away the nails which hold the framework of caste-bound Hindu society together, such as those of the prohibition of intermarriage down to the prohibition of social intercourse so that Hindu society becomes all of one caste. Otherwise untouchability cannot be removed nor can equality be established. . . .

Remember that if the prohibitions on social intercourse and inter-drinking go, the roots of untouchability are not removed. Release from these two restrictions will, at the most, remove untouchability as it appears outside the home; but it will leave untouchability in the home untouched. If we want to remove untouchability in the home as well as outside, we must break down the prohibition against intermarriage. Nothing else will serve. From another point of view, we see that breaking down the bar against intermarriage is the way to establish real equality. Anyone must confess that when the root division is dissolved, incidental points of separateness will disappear by themselves. The interdictions of inter-dining, inter-drinking and social intercourse have all sprung from the one interdiction against intermarriage. Remove the last and no special efforts are needed to remove the rest. They will disappear of their own accord. In my view the removal of untouchability consists in breaking down the ban on intermarriage and doing so will establish real equality. If we wish to root out untouchability, we must recognize that the root of untouchability is in the ban on intermarriage. Even if our attack today is on the ban against inter-drinking, we must press it home against the ban on intermarriage; otherwise untouchability cannot be removed by the roots. Who can accomplish this task? It is no secret that the Brahmin class cannot do it.

While the caste system lasts, the Brahmin caste has its supremacy. No one, of his own will, surrenders power which is in his hands. The Brahmins have exercised their sovereignty over all other castes for centuries. It is not likely that they will be willing to give it up and treat the rest as equals. The Brahmins do not have the patriotism of the Samurais of Japan. It is useless to hope that they will sacrifice their privileges as the Samurai class did, for the sake of national unity based on a new equality. Nor does it appear likely that the task will be carried out by other caste Hindus. . . .

The task of removing untouchability and establishing equality that we have undertaken, we must carry out ourselves. Others will not do it. Our life will gain its true meaning if we consider that we are born to carry out this task and set to work in earnest. Let us receive this merit which is awaiting us.

This is a struggle in order to raise ourselves; hence we are bound to undertake it, so as to remove the obstacles to our progress. We all know how at every turn, untouchability muddies and soils our whole existence. We know that at one time our people were recruited in large numbers into the troops. It was a kind of occupation socially assigned to us and few of us needed to be anxious about earning our bread. Other classes of our level have found their way into the troops, the police, the courts and the offices, to earn their bread. But in the same areas of employment you will no longer find the untouchables.

It is not that the law debars us from these jobs. Everything is permissible as far the law is concerned. But the Government finds itself powerless because other Hindus consider us untouchables and look down upon us, and it acquiesces in our being kept out of Government jobs. Nor can we take up any decent trade. It is true, partly, that we lack money to start business, but the real difficulty is that people regard us as untouchables and no one will accept goods from our hands.

To sum up, untouchability is not a simple matter; it is the mother of all our poverty and lowliness and it has brought us to the abject state we are in today. If we want to raise ourselves out of it, we must undertake this task. We cannot be saved in any other way. It is a task not for our benefit alone; it is also for the benefit of the nation. . . .

Our work has been begun to bring about a real social revolution. Let no one deceive himself by supposing that it is a diversion to quieten minds entranced with sweet words. The work is sustained by strong feeling, which is the power that drives the movement. No one can now arrest it. I pray to God that the social revolution which begins here today may fulfil itself by peaceful means.

None can doubt that the responsibility of letting the revolution take place peacefully rests more heavily on our opponents than on us. Whether this social revolution will work peacefully or violently will depend wholly on the conduct of the caste Hindus. People who blame the French National Assembly of 1789 for atrocities forget one thing. That is, if the rulers of France had not been treacherous to the Assembly, if the upper classes had not resisted it, had not committed the crime of trying to suppress it with foreign help, it would have had no need to use violence in the work of the revolution and the whole social transformation would have been accomplished peacefully.

We say to our opponents too: please do not oppose us. Put away the orthodox scriptures. Follow justice. And we assure you that we shall carry out our programme peacefully.

+ + +

HOW TO ANNIHILATE CASTE

In December 1935 Ambedkar was invited by the Jat Pat Todak Mandal, a Hindu reform organisation based in the Punjab, to deliver the Presidential Address at their annual conference. However, when Ambedkar sent them the text of his address, the invitation was withdrawn. He then published his speech, a brilliant and withering indictment of the caste system, at his own expense. In the preface to this pamphlet Ambedkar wrote of the invitation sent and rescinded that 'what can any one expect from a relationship so tragic as the relationship between the reforming sect of Caste Hindus and the self-respecting sect of Untouchables, where the former have no desire to alienate their orthodox fellows and the latter have no alternative but to insist upon reform being carried out?' Excerpts from his undelivered address follow.[2]

+ + +

It is a pity that Caste even to-day has its defenders. The defences are many. It is defended on the ground that the Caste System is but another name for division of labour and if division of labour is a necessary feature of every civilized society then it is argued that there is nothing wrong in the Caste System.

2. From B. R. Ambedkar, *Annihilation of Caste* (1936; reprint, New Delhi: Arnold Publishers, 1990), pp. 47–84.

Now the first thing [that] is to be urged against this view is that Caste System is not merely division of labour. It is also a division of labourers.

Civilized society undoubtedly needs division of labour. But in no civilized society is division of labour accompanied by this unnatural division of labourers into water-tight compartments.

[The] Caste System is not merely a division of labourers which is quite different from division of labour—it is an hierarchy in which the divisions of labourers are graded one above the another.

In no other country is the division of labour accompanied by this gradation of labourers.

There is also a third point of criticism against this view of the Caste System. This division of labour is not spontaneous[;] it is not based on natural aptitudes. Social and individual efficiency requires us to develop the capacity of an individual to the point of competency to choose and to make his own career.

This principle is violated in the Caste System in so far as it involves an attempt to appoint tasks to individuals in advance, selected not on the basis of trained original capacities, but on that of the social status of the parents. Looked at from another point of view this stratification of occupations which is the result of the Caste System is positively pernicious. Industry is never static. It undergoes rapid and abrupt changes. With such changes an individual must be free to change his occupation. Without such freedom to adjust himself to changing circumstances it would be impossible for him to gain his livelihood.

Now the Caste System will not allow Hindus to take to occupations where they are wanted if they do not belong to them by heredity. If a Hindu is seen to starve rather than take to new occupations not assigned to his Caste, the reason is to be found in the Caste. By not permitting readjustment of occupations, caste becomes a direct cause of much of the unemployment we see in the country.

As a form of division of labour the Caste System suffers from another serious defect. The division of labour brought about by Caste is not a division based on choice. Individual sentiment, individual preferences has no place in it. It is based on the dogma of predestination.

Considerations of social efficiency would compel us to recognize that the greatest evil in the industrial system is not so much poverty and the suffering that it involves as the fact that so many persons have callings which make no appeal to those who are engaged in them. Such callings constantly provoke one to aversion, ill-will and the desire to evade.

There are many occupations in India which on account of the fact that they are regarded as degraded by the Hindus provoke those who are engaged in them to aversion. There is a constant desire to evade and escape from such occupations which they produce upon those who follow them owing to the slight and stigma cast upon them by the Hindu religion. What efficiency can there be in a system under which neither men's hearts nor their minds are in their work? As an economic organization Caste is therefore a harmful institution, in as much as it involves the subordination of man's natural powers and inclinations to the exigencies of social rules.

Some have dug a biological trench in defence of the Caste System. It is said that the object of Caste was to preserve purity of blood. Now ethnologists are of opinion that men of pure race exist nowhere and that there had been a mixture of all races in all parts of the world.

Especially this is the case with the people of India. Mr. D. R. Bhandarkar in his paper on *Foreign Elements in the Hindu Population* has stated that 'there is hardly a class or Caste in India which has not a foreign strain in it. There is an admixture of alien blood not only among the warrior classes—the Rajputs and the Marathas—but also among the Brahmins who are under the happy delusion that they are free from all foreign elements'.

The Caste System cannot be said to have grown as a means of preventing the admixture of races or means of maintaining purity of blood. As a matter of fact [the] Caste System came into being long after the different races of India had commingled in blood and culture. To hold that distinctions of Castes are really distinctions of race and to treat different Castes as though they were so many different races is a gross perversion of facts. What racial affinity is there between the Brahmin of Punjab and the Brahmin of Madras? What racial affinity is there between the untouchable of Bengal and the untouchable of Madras? What racial difference is there between the Brahmin of Punjab and the Chamar of Punjab? What racial difference is there between the Brahmin of Madras and the Pariah of Madras? The Brahmin of the Punjab is racially of the same stock as the Chamar of the Punjab and the Brahmin of Madras is of the same race as the Pariah of Madras. Caste System does not demarcate racial division. . . .

A tree should be judged by the fruits it yields. If Caste is eugenic what sort of a race of men [should it have] produced? Physically speaking the Hindus are a C people. They are a race of pygmies and dwarfs stunted in stature and wanting in stamina. It is a nation 9/10ths of which is declared to be unfit for military service. This shows that the Caste System does not embody the eugenics of modern scientists. It is a social system which embodies the arrogance and selfishness of a perverse section of the Hindus who were superior enough in social status to set it in fashion and who had authority to force it on their inferiors.

Caste does not result in economic efficiency. Caste cannot and has not improved the race. Caste has however done one thing. It has completely disorganized and demoralized the Hindus.

The first and foremost thing that must be recognized is that Hindu society is a myth. The name Hindu is itself a foreign name. it was given by the Mahomedans to the natives for the purpose of distinguishing themselves. It does not occur in any Sanskrit work prior to the Mahomedan invasion. They did not feel the necessity of a common name because they had no conception of their having constituted a community.

Hindu Society as such does not exist. It is only a collection of castes. Each caste is conscious of its existence. Its survival is the be all and end all of its existence.

Castes do not even form a federation. A caste has no feeling that it is affiliated to other castes except when there is a Hindu-Muslim riot. On all other occasions each caste endeavours to segregate itself and to distinguish itself from other castes. Each caste not only dines among itself and marries among itself but each caste prescribes its own distinctive dress. What other explanation can there be of the innumerable styles of dress worn by the men and women of India which so amuse the tourists? . . .

The Caste System prevents common activity and by preventing common activity it has prevented the Hindus from becoming a society with unified life and a consciousness of its own being.

The Hindus often complain of the isolation and exclusiveness of a gang or a clique and blame them for anti-social spirit. But they conveniently forget that this anti-social spirit is the worst feature of their own Caste System. One caste enjoys singing a hymn of hate against another caste as much as the Germans did in singing their hymn of hate against the English during the last war. The literature of the Hindus is full of caste genealogies in which an attempt is made to give a noble origin to one caste and an ignoble origin to other castes. . . .

This anti-social spirit is not confined to caste alone. It has gone deeper and has poisoned the mutual relations of the sub-caste as well. In my province the Gulak Brahmins, Deorukha Brahmins, Karada Brahmins, Palshe Brahmins and Chitpavan Brahmins, all claim to be sub-divisions of the Brahmin Caste. But the anti-social spirit that prevails between them is quite as marked and quite as virulent as the anti-social spirit that prevails between them and other Non-Brahmin castes. . . .

The Brahmin's primary concern is to protect 'his interest' against those of the Non-Brahmins and the Non-Brahmin's primary concern is to protect their interests against those of the Brahmins.

The Hindus, therefore, are not merely an assortment of castes but they are so many warring groups each living for itself and for its selfish ideal. . . .

There is no doubt, in my opinion, that unless you change your social order you can achieve little by way of progress. You cannot mobilize the community either for defence or for offence. You cannot build anything on the foundations of caste. You cannot build up a nation, you cannot build up morality. Anything that you will build on the foundations of caste will crack and will never be a whole.

The only question that remains to be considered is—How to bring about the reform of the Hindu social order? How to abolish Caste? This is a question of supreme importance.

There is a view that in the reform of caste, the first step to take, is to abolish sub-castes. This view is based upon the supposition that there is a greater similarity in manners and status between sub-castes than there is between castes.

I think this is an erroneous supposition. The Brahmins of Northern and Central India are socially of lower grade, as compared with the Brahmins of the Deccan and Southern India. The former are only cooks and water carriers while the latter occupy a high social position. On the other hand, in Northern India, the Vaishyas and Kayasthas are intellectually and socially on a par with the Brahmins of the Deccan and southern India. Again, in the matter of food there is no similarity between the Brahmins of the Deccan and Southern India, who are vegetarians and the Brahmins of Kashmir and Bengal who are non-vegetarians. On the other hand, the Brahmins of the Deccan and Southern

India have more in common so far as food is concerned with such Non-Brahmins as the Gujaratis, Marwaris, Banias and Jains.

There is no doubt that from the standpoint of making the transit[ion] from one caste to another easy, the fusion of the Kayasthas of Northern India and the other Non-Brahmins of Southern India with the Brahmins of the Deccan and the Dravid country [i.e., South India] is more practicable than the fusion of the Brahmins of the South with the Brahmins of the North.

But assuming that the fusion of sub-castes is possible, what guarantee is there that the abolition of Sub-Castes will necessarily lead to the abolition of Castes? On the contrary, it may happen that the process may stop with the abolition of Sub-Castes. In that case, the abolition of Sub-Castes will only help to strengthen the Castes and make them more powerful and therefore more mischievous. This remedy is therefore neither practicable nor effective and may easily prove to be a wrong remedy.

Another plan of action for the abolition of Caste is to begin with inter-caste dinners. This also, in my opinion, is an inadequate remedy. There are many Castes which allow inter-dining. But it is a common experience that inter-dining has not succeeded in killing the spirit of Caste and the consciousness of Caste.

I am convinced that the real remedy is inter-marriage. Fusion of blood can alone create the feeling of being kith and kin and unless this feeling of kin-ship, of being kindred, becomes paramount the separatist feeling—the feel-ing of being aliens—created by Caste will not vanish.

Among the Hindus inter-marriage must necessarily be a factor of greater force in social life than it need be in the life of the non-Hindu where society is already well-knit by other ties, [and] marriage is an ordinary incident of life. But where society is cut asunder, marriage as a binding force becomes a mat-ter of urgent necessity.

The real remedy for breaking Caste is inter-marriage. Nothing else will serve as the solvent of Caste. . . .

Caste may be bad: Caste may lead to conduct so gross as to be called man's inhumanity to man. All the same, it must be recognized that the Hindus ob-serve Caste not because they are inhuman or wrong headed. They observe Caste because they are deeply religious.

People are not wrong in observing Caste. In my view, what is wrong is their religion, which has inculcated this notion of Caste. If this is correct, then obviously the enemy, you must grapple with, is not the people who observe Caste, but the Shastras [sacred texts] which teach them this religion of Caste.

Criticizing and ridiculing people for not inter-dining or inter-marrying or occasionally holding inter-caste dinners and celebrating inter-caste marriages, is a futile method of achieving the desired end. The real remedy is to destroy the belief in the sanctity of the Shastras. . . .

Reformers working for the removal of untouchability, including Mr. Gandhi, do not seem to realize that the acts of the people are merely the results of their beliefs inculcated upon their conduct until they cease to believe in the sanctity of the Shastras on which their conduct is founded. . . .

It is no use seeking refuge in quibbles. It is no use telling people that the Shastras do not say what they are believed to say, grammatically read or logically interpreted. What matters is how the Shastras have been understood by the people. You[3] must take the stand that Buddha took. You must not only discard the Shastras, you must deny their authority, as did Buddha and Nanak. You must have courage to tell the Hindus, that what is wrong with them is their religion—the religion which has produced in them this notion of the sacredness of Caste. Will you show that courage?

+ + +

WHY THE UNTOUCHABLES DISTRUST GANDHI

In 1945 Ambedkar published a book called *What Congress and Gandhi Have Done to the Untouchables,* its title singling out the party and individual he believed to be his main political and personal adversary. A sharp and at times bitter polemic, the book nonetheless makes some telling points, as the following excerpts reveal.[4]

+ + +

The Untouchables have always said that Mr. Gandhi's anti-Untouchability campaign has failed. After 25 years of labour, hotels have remained closed,

3. This 'you' is the upper-caste reformer.

4. As reproduced in Vasant Moon, ed., *Dr Babasaheb Ambedkar, Writings and Speeches,* vol. 9 (Bombay: Government of Maharashtra, 1991), pp. 262–269.

wells have remained closed, temples have remained closed and in very many parts of India—particularly in Gujarat—even schools have remained closed. The extracts produced from the papers[5] form therefore a very welcome testimony especially because the papers are Congress papers. As they fully corroborate what the Untouchables have been saying on the point, nothing further need be said on the subject except to ask one question.

Why has Mr. Gandhi failed? According to me, there are three reasons which [have] brought about this failure.

The first reason is the Hindus to whom he makes his appeal for the removal of Untouchability do not respond. Why is this so? It is a common experience that the words a man uses and the effect they produce are not always commensurate. What he says has its momentum indefinitely multiplied, or reduced to nullity, by the impression that the hearer for good reason or bad happens to have formed of the spirit of the speaker. This gives a clue to know why Mr. Gandhi's sermons on Untouchability have completely failed to move the Hindus, why people hear his after-prayer sermons for [a] few minutes and then go to the comic opera and why there is nothing more to it. The fault is not entirely of the Hindu public. The fault is of Mr. Gandhi himself. Mr. Gandhi has built up his reputation of being a Mahatma on his being an harbinger of political freedom and not on his being a spiritual teacher. Whatever may be his intentions, Mr. Gandhi is looked upon as an apostle of Swaraj. His anti-Untouchability campaign is looked upon as a fad if not a side-show. That is why the Hindus respond to his political biddings but never to his social or religious preaching. . . .

The second reason is that Mr. Gandhi does not wish to antagonize the Hindus even if such antagonism was necessary to carry out his anti-Untouchability programme. A few instances will illustrate Mr. Gandhi's mentality.

Most of Mr. Gandhi's friends give credit to Mr. Gandhi for sincerity and earnestness for the cause of the Untouchables and expect the Untouchables to believe in it on the mere ground that Mr. Gandhi is the one man who keeps on constantly preaching to the Hindus the necessity of removing Untouchability. They had lost sight of the old proverb that an ounce of practice is worth a ton of preaching and have never cared to ask Mr. Gandhi to explain why does he not cease to preach to the Hindus the necessity of removing Untouchabil-

5. Not reproduced here.

ity and launch a campaign of satyagraha or start a fast. If they would ask for such an explanation they would know why Mr. Gandhi merely contents himself with sermons on Untouchability.

The true reasons why Mr. Gandhi will not go beyond sermons were revealed to the Untouchables for the first time in 1929 when the Untouchables in the Bombay Presidency opened a campaign of satyagraha against the Hindus for establishing their civic rights in the matter of temple-entry and taking water from public wells. They hoped to get the blessings of Mr. Gandhi in as much as satyagraha was Mr. Gandhi's own weapon to get wrongs redressed. When appealed to for support, Mr. Gandhi surprised the Untouchables by issuing a statement condemning their campaign of satyagraha against the Hindus. The argument urged by Mr. Gandhi was very ingenious. He stated that satyagraha was to be used only against foreigners; it must not be used against one's own kindred or countrymen and as the Hindus were the kindred and countrymen of the Untouchables by rules of satyagraha the latter were debarred from using the weapon against the former! What a fall from the sublime to the ridiculous! By this Mr. Gandhi made nonsense of satyagraha. Why did Mr. Gandhi do this? Only because he did not want to annoy and exasperate the Hindus.

As a second piece of evidence, I would refer to what is known as the Kavitha incident. Kavitha is a village in the Ahmedabad District in Gujarat. In 1935, the Untouchables of the village demanded from the Hindus of the village that their children should be admitted in the common school of the village along with other Hindu children. The Hindus were enraged at this outrage and took their revenge by proclaiming a complete social boycott. The events connected with this boycott were reported by Mr. A. V. Thakkar,[6] who went to Kavitha to intercede with the Hindus on behalf of the Untouchables. The story told by him runs as follows:-

> The Associated Press announced on the 10th inst. that the Caste Hindus of Kavitha agreed to admit Harijan boys to the village school in Kavitha and that matters were amicably settled. This was contradicted on the 13th instant by the Secretary of the Ahmedabad Harijan Sevak Sangh, who said in his statement that the

6. A. V. Thakkar was a respected social worker, a senior member of the Servants of India Society, and a friend of Gandhi's.

Harijans had undertaken (privately of course) not to send their children to the school. Such an undertaking was not given voluntarily, but was extorted from them by the Caste Hindus, in this case the Garasias of the village, who had proclaimed a social boycott against poor Harijans—weavers, chamars [leather-workers] and others, who number over 100 families. They were deprived of agricultural labour, their animals of grazing in the pasture land, and their children of buttermilk. Not only this, but a Harijan leader was compelled to take an oath by Mahadev [the Hindu god Shiva] that he and others would not hereafter even make an effort to reinstate their children in the school. The so-called settlement was brought about in this way.

But even after the bogus settlement reported on the 10th and the complete surrender by poor Harijans, the boycott was not lifted up to the 19th and partly up to the 22nd from the weavers. It was lifted somewhat earlier from the head of the chamars, as Garasias themselves could not remove the carcasses of their dead animals, and thus had to come to terms with chamars earlier. As if the enormities perpetrated so far were not enough, kerosene was poured into the Harijan's well, once on the 15th instant and again on the 19th instant. One can imagine what terrorism was thus practiced on poor Harijans because they had dared to send their children to sit alongside of the 'princely' Garasia boys.

I met the leaders of the [caste Hindu] Garasias on the morning of the 22nd. They said they could not tolerate the idea of boys of Dheds and Chamars [both untouchable castes] sitting by the side of their own boys. I met also the District Magistrate of Ahmedabad on the 23rd with a view to finding out if he would do something to ease the situation, but without any result. Harijan boys are thus practically banned from the village school with nobody to help them. This has caused despondency among the Harijans to such an extent that they are thinking of migrating in a body to some other village.

This was a report made to Mr. Gandhi. What did Mr. Gandhi do? The following is the advice Mr. Gandhi gave to the Untouchables of Kavitha:—

There is no help like self-help. God helps those who help themselves. If the Harijans concerned will carry out their reported resolve to wipe the dust of Kavitha off their feet, they will not only
be happy themselves but they will pave the way for others who
may be similarly treated. If people migrate in search of employment how much more should they do so in search of self-respect?
I hope that well-wishers of Harijans will help these poor families
to vacate inhospitable Kavitha.

Mr. Gandhi advised the Untouchables of Kavitha to vacate. But why did he
not advise Mr. Thakkar to prosecute the Hindus of Kavitha and help the Untouchables to vindicate their rights? Obviously, he would like to uplift the
Untouchables if he can but not by offending the Hindus. What good can such
a man do to promote the cause of the Untouchables? All this shows that Mr.
Gandhi is most anxious to be good to the Hindus. That is why he opposes
satyagraha against the Hindus. That is why he opposed the political demands
of the Untouchables as he believed that they were aimed against them. He is
anxious to be so good to the Hindus that he does not care if he is thereby becoming good for nothing for the Untouchables. That is why Mr. Gandhi's whole
programme for the removal of Untouchability is just words, words and words
and why there is no action behind it.

The third reason is that Mr. Gandhi does not want the Untouchables to organize and be strong. For he fears that they might thereby become independent of the Hindus and weaken the ranks of Hindus. This is best illustrated by
the activities of the Harijan Sevak Sangh. The whole object of the Sangh is to
create a slave mentality among the Untouchables towards their Hindu masters. Examine the Sangh from any angle one may like and the creation of slave
mentality will appear to be its dominant purpose.

The work of the Sangh reminds one of the mythological demoness Putana
described in the Bhagvat—a companion to the Mahabharat. Kamsa the king
of Mathura, wanted to kill Krishna, as it was predicted that Kamsa will die at
the hands of Krishna. Having come to know of the birth of Krishna, Kamsa
asked Putana to undertake the mission to kill Krishna while he was yet a boy.
Putana took the form of a beautiful woman and went to Yashoda, the foster
mother of Krishna and having applied liquid poison to her breast pleaded to
be employed as a wet nurse for suckling the baby Krishna and thus have the

opportunity to kill it. The rest of the story it is unnecessary to pursue. The point of the story is that the real purpose is not always the same as the ostensible purpose and a nurse can be a murderess. The Sangh is to the Untouchables what Putana was to Krishna. The Sangh under the pretence of service is out to kill the spirit of independence from among the Untouchables. The Untouchables, in the early stages of their agitation, had taken the support of some well-meaning Hindus and had followed their leadership. By the time of the Round Table Conference, the Untouchables had become completely self-reliant and independent. They were no longer satisfied with charity from the Hindus. They demanded what they said was their right. There is no doubt that it is to kill this spirit of independence among the Untouchables that Mr. Gandhi started the Harijan Sevak Sangh. The Harijan Sevak Sangh by its petty services has collected a swarm of grateful Untouchables who are employed to preach that Mr. Gandhi and the Hindus are the saviours of the Untouchables. . . . The Untouchables are too simple-minded to know that the cost of the service which the Harijan Sevak Sangh offers to render is loss of independence. This is exactly what Mr. Gandhi wants.

The worst part of the activities of the Harijan Sevak Sangh is the help rendered to the Untouchable students kept in the hostels maintained by the Sangh. These Untouchable students remind me of Bhishma and Kacha, two prominent characters [who] figure in the Mahabharata. Bhishma proclaimed with great show that the Pandavas were right [but] between the two he fought on the side of the Kauravas and against the Pandavas. When asked to justify his conduct he was not ashamed to say that he fought for the Kauravas because they fed him. Kacha belonged to the community of the Devas who were engaged in a war against the Rakshasas. The spiritual head of the Rakshasas knew a mantra [incantation] by which he could revive a dead Rakshasa. The Devas were losing the battle since their head did not know the mantra and could not revive their dead. The Devas planned to send Kacha to the head of the Rakshasas with instructions somehow to learn the mantra and come back. Kacha in the beginning could not succeed. Ultimately he entered into an agreement with Devayani the daughter of the spiritual head of the Rakshasas that if she helped him to acquire the mantra he would be prepared to marry her. Devayani succeeded in fulfilling her part of the contract. But Kacha refused to perform his part alleging that the interests of his community were more important than his promise to her.

Bhishma and Kacha, in my opinion, are typical of the morally depraved characters who know no other purpose but to serve their own interests for the time being. The Untouchable students in the Harijan hostels are acting the part of both Bhishma and Kacha. During their stay in the hostels they play the part of Bhishma by singing the praises of Mr. Gandhi and the Congress. When they come out of the hostels they play the part of Kacha and denounce Mr. Gandhi and the Congress. I am extremely pained to see this. Nothing worse could happen to the youth of the Untouchables than this moral degeneration. But this is the greatest disservice which his Harijan Sevak Sangh has done to the Untouchables. It has destroyed their character. It has destroyed their independence. This is what Mr. Gandhi wants to happen.

Take a fourth illustration. The Sangh is run by the Caste Hindus. There are some Untouchables who have demanded that the institution should be handed over to the Untouchables and should be run by them. Others have demanded that the Untouchables should have representation on the governing Board. Mr. Gandhi has flatly refused to do either on two very ingenious grounds which no man with the greatest cunning could improve. Mr. Gandhi's first argument is that the Harijan Sevak Sangh is an act of penance on the part of the Hindus for the sin of observing Untouchability. It is they who must do the penance. Therefore the Untouchable can have no place in running the Sangh. Secondly Mr. Gandhi says the money collected by him is given by the Hindus and not by the Untouchables and as the money is not of the Untouchables, the Untouchables have no right to be on the Governing Body. The refusal of Mr. Gandhi may be tolerated but his arguments are most insulting and a respectable Untouchable will be forgiven if he refuses to have anything to do with the Sangh. One should have thought that the Harijan Sevak Sangh was a Trust and the Untouchables its beneficiaries. Any tyro in law would admit that the beneficiaries have every right to know the aims and objects of the Trust, its funds and whether the objects are properly carried out or not. The beneficiaries have even the right to have the Trustees removed for breach of trust. On that basis it would be impossible to deny the claim of the Untouchables for representation on the Managing Board. Evidently Mr. Gandhi does not wish to accept this position. A self-respecting Untouchable who has no desire to cringe and who does not believe in staking the future of the Untouchables on the philanthropy of strangers cannot have any quarrel with Mr. Gandhi. He is quite prepared to say that if meanness is a virtue then Mr. Gandhi's logic is superb and Mr. Gandhi is welcome to the benefit of it. Only he must not blame the Untouchables if they boycott the Sangh.

These however could not be the real reasons for not allowing the Untouchables to run the Sangh. The real reasons are different. In the first place, if the Sangh was handed over to the Untouchables Mr. Gandhi and the Congress will have no means of control over the Untouchables. The Untouchables will cease to be dependent on the Hindus. In the second place, the Untouchables having become independent will cease to be grateful to the Hindus. These consequences will be quite contrary to the aim and object, which have led Mr. Gandhi to found the Sangh. . . . That is why Mr. Gandhi does not wish to hand over the Sangh to the control and management of the Untouchables. Is this consistent with a genuine desire for the emancipation of the Untouchables? Can Mr. Gandhi be called a liberator of the Untouchables? Does this not show that Mr. Gandhi is more anxious to tighten the tie which binds the Untouchables to the apron strings of the Hindus than to free them from the thralldom of the Hindus?

These are the reasons why Mr. Gandhi's anti-Untouchability campaign has failed. . . .

✦   ✦   ✦

10

THE MUSLIM SEPARATIST

MUHAMMAD ALI JINNAH

THROUGH THE 1930S AND 1940S GANDHI and the Congress faced two major challenges that cast doubt on their claim to represent all of India and all Indians. The first was from B. R. Ambedkar, who argued that the Congress was a party of the upper castes. The second was from Muhammad Ali Jinnah, who insisted that the Congress represented only Hindus, and that the Muslims of the sub-continent need look rather to his party, the Muslim League, to protect and advance their interests.

Jinnah was born in Karachi in 1876, into a Gujarati-speaking family of Shia Muslim merchants. He was the eldest of seven children of a successful businessman, who owned his own horse carriages. After studying in a school in Karachi, Jinnah proceeded to London to qualify as a lawyer, enrolling at Lincoln's Inn. In 1896 he returned with his barrister's qualification in hand and joined the Bombay bar.

Thus far there are some conspicuous parallels with Gandhi. Both had Gujarati as their mother tongue, both came from mercantile communities, both studied law in London, and both came back to practice in Bombay. However, Jinnah was very successful at his chosen profession. In a few years he had developed a very lucrative practice. He was offered a place on the bench, which he refused on the grounds that he normally earned in a day what a Judge earned in a month.

At the same time, like other successful and ambitious young Indians, Jinnah was not averse to a career in public life. In 1904 he attended his first Congress session, in Bombay. In another parallel with Gandhi, he attracted the favourable attention of Gopal Krishna Gokhale. He also came close to the great Parsi nationalist Dadabhai Naoroji. Jinnah was elected to the Imperial Legislative Council in 1910 as part of a new quota for Muslims. At thirty-five, he was one of its youngest members. Interestingly enough, one of his first speeches was on the condition of Indians in South Africa.

By 1915 or thereabouts Jinnah was being referred to as the 'Muslim Gokhale'. Like his mentor, he was known for his careful research, his closely argued speeches, and his focus on harmonious relations between Hindus and Muslims. In the politics of the day he occupied a unique position—for he was at once a member of the Congress and of the Muslim League, while simultaneously serving as a member of the Imperial Council.

When Gandhi came home from South Africa in January 1915, Jinnah spoke at a reception for the returning hero in Bombay. Towards the end of the decade, however, the two Gujarati lawyer-politicians fell out over the best means to advance Indian interests. Jinnah preferred the constitutional route, while Gandhi wanted the Congress to adopt his creed of countrywide *satyagraha*. The break became final, and irretrievable, when at the Nagpur Congress of December 1920 Jinnah was booed off the stage by Gandhi's eager (or perhaps over-eager) followers.

Through the 1920s Jinnah tried, with limited success, to organise a moderate alternative to Gandhi's party. In 1925 he was offered a knighthood, and refused, as Gokhale had done before him.

In 1930, Jinnah moved to London, where he ran a successful practice at the Bar while also taking part in the Round Table Conferences of 1930 and 1931 which discussed, abortively, India's political future. At one time he seriously considered standing for the British Parliament. However, in 1934, he was persuaded to return to India to assume leadership of the Muslim League. Over the next few years, he infused life and purpose into a moribund organisation. Under his leadership the membership of the League increased from a few thousand to well over half a million.

Students and professionals flocked to his call. Now, it could no longer be dismissed as a party merely of the Muslim nobility and gentry. Jinnah also laid special focus on strengthening the provincial branches of the League. In all this he was taking a leaf out of his rival's book, for Gandhi had once adopted similar methods to convert the Congress from an elite debating club into a mass-based political party.

In the elections of 1937 the Congress came to power over much of India. Ironically, electoral defeat actually helped the Muslim League, for they were now able to portray the Congress in office as an essentially Hindu party. Questions were raised about the promotion by Congress Ministries of Hindi (as opposed to Urdu) and the singing of religious hymns in state schools. These campaigns helped the League to alienate the Congress from any Muslim support it still enjoyed. Then World War II broke out, and the Congress Ministries resigned. In 1940 the Muslim League formally committed itself to the formation of a separate homeland for Muslims, to be named Pakistan. Jinnah, once known as 'the ambassador of Hindu-Muslim unity', had now come around to the view that Hindus and Muslims could not live together in a single, united, independent, nation.

When Gandhi and his followers went to jail during the Quit India movement, Jinnah used the opportunity to further consolidate the Muslim League. By now, the British were treating the League on par with the Congress. Jinnah demanded, and obtained, a further parity, of himself with Gandhi.

After the end of the war, elections were held to the central and provincial assemblies. The League obtained a resounding 88 percent of the Muslim vote. In the crucial provinces of Punjab and Bengal it won 75 out of 88 and 113 out of 119 Muslim seats respectively. Now Partition and the establishment of Pakistan were more or less inevitable.

In their campaign to create Pakistan, Jinnah and the League were helped by separate electorates, by the arrogance of the Congress, and by the British policy of 'divide-and-rule'. That said, one cannot and must not discount the quality of Jinnah's leadership or the energy and commitment of his cadres and followers. These made what, in 1937, had seemed a very distant dream, into a concrete reality ten years later.

Muhammad Ali Jinnah died in September 1948.

THE STEPS TOWARDS A MUSLIM NATION

The context for this first excerpt is provided by the elections of 1937, in which the Congress did far better than the Muslim League even among Muslim voters. With the rival party now running administrations in six major provinces, the League had to re-group. In the following excerpt from his Presidential Address to the annual session of the Muslim League held at Lucknow in October 1937, Jinnah urges his colleagues to stand firm against the adversary.[1]

✦   ✦   ✦

. . . The present leadership of the Congress, especially during the last ten years, has been responsible for alienating the Musalmans of India more and more by pursuing a policy which is exclusively Hindu, and since they have formed the Governments in six provinces where they are in a majority they have by their words, deeds and programme shown more and more that the Musalmans cannot expect any justice or fair-play at their hands. Wherever they are in a majority and wherever it suited them, they refused to co-operate with the Muslim League Parties and demanded unconditional surrender and signing of their pledges.

The demand was insistent: abjure your part and forswear your policy and programme and liquidate [the] Muslim League; but where they found that they had not a majority, like the North-West Frontier Province, their sacred principle of collective responsibility disappeared, and promptly the Congress Party was allowed in that province to coalesce with any other group. That any individual Musalman member who was willing to unconditionally surrender and sign their pledge was offered a job as a minister and was passed off as a Musalman minister, although he did not command the confidence or the respect of an overwhelming majority of the Musalman representatives in the legislature. These men are allowed to move about and pass off as Muslim ministers for the 'loyal' services they have rendered to the Congress, by surrendering and signing the pledge unconditionally, and the degree of their reward is the extent of their perfidy. Hindi is to be the national language of all

1. As reproduced in Jamil-ud-din Ahmad, ed., *Some Recent Speeches and Writings of Mr. Jinnah,* 4th ed. (Lahore: Sh. Muhammad Ashraf, 1946), pp. 27, 30–35.

India, and that *Bande Matram*[2] is to be the national song, and is to be forced upon all. The Congress flag is to be obeyed and revered by all and sundry. On the very threshold of what little power and responsibility is given, the majority community have clearly shown their hand that Hindustan is for the Hindus. . . . The result of the present Congress Party policy will be, I venture to say, class bitterness, communal war and strengthening of the imperialistic hold as a consequence. . . .

No settlement with [the] majority community is possible, as no Hindu leader speaking with any authority shows any concern or genuine desire for it. Honourable settlement can only be achieved between equals, and unless the two parties learn to respect and fear each other, there is no solid ground for any settlement. Offers of peace by the weaker party always means confession of weakness, and an invitation to aggression. Appeals to patriotism, justice and fair-play and for good-will fall flat. It does not require political wisdom to realize that all safeguards and settlements would be a scrap of paper, unless they are backed up by power. Politics means power and not relying only on cries of just or fair-play or good-will. . . .

I want the Musalmans to ponder over the situation and decide their own fate by having one single, definite, uniform policy which should be loyally followed throughout India. The Congressite Musalmans are making a great mistake when they preach unconditional surrender. It is the height of defeatist mentality to throw ourselves on the mercy and good-will of others and the highest act of perfidy to the Musalman community; and if that policy is adopted, let me tell you, the community will seal its doom and will cease to play its rightful part in the national life of the country and the Government. Only one thing can save the Musalmans and energise them to regain their lost ground. They must first recapture their own souls and stand by their lofty position and principles which form the basis of their great unity and which bind them in one body-politic. . . .

2. The references to Hindi and *Bande Matram* need to be explained. Although written in different scripts, Hindi and Urdu were associated languages; however, from the late nineteenth century, Hindi began to be more closely linked with Hindus, Urdu with Muslims. *Bande Matram* was a patriotic song written by Bankim Chandra Chatterjee; since it celebrated a mother goddess, Muslims opposed to idolatry refused to sing it.

✦ ✦ ✦

In October 1939 the Congress Ministries resigned in protest against the Viceroy, Lord Linlithgow, taking India into World War II without consulting Indian opinion. As the war intensified in Europe, the question of India's political future was intensely discussed in England. The next excerpt is from an article written by Jinnah for the London journal *Time and Tide* and published in January 1940 under the title 'The Constitutional Maladies of India'.[3]

✦ ✦ ✦

The constitutional maladies from which India at present suffers may best be described as symptoms of a disease inherent in the body-politic. Without diagnosing the disease, no understanding of the symptoms is possible and no remedy can suggest itself. Let us, therefore, first diagnose the disease, then consider the symptoms and finally arrive at the remedy.

What is the political future of India? The declared aim of the British Government is that India should enjoy Dominion Status in accordance with the Statute of Westminister in the shortest practicable time. In order that this end should be brought about, the British Government very naturally would like to see in India the form of democratic constitution it knows best and thinks best, under which the government of the country is entrusted to one or other political party in accordance with the turn of the elections.

Such, however, is the ignorance about Indian conditions among even the members of the British Parliament that, in spite of all the experience of the past, it is even yet not realized that this form of government is totally unsuited to India. Democratic systems based on the concept of a homogeneous nation such as England are very definitely not applicable to heterogeneous countries such as India and this simple fact is the root cause of all India's constitutional ills. . . .

The British people must realize that Hinduism and Islam represent two distinct and separate civilizations and, moreover, are as distinct from one another in origin, tradition and manner of life as are nations of Europe. . . .

If, therefore, it is accepted that there are in India a major and a minor nation, it follows that [a] parliamentary system based on the majority principle

3. From Ahmad, *Some Recent Speeches and Writings of Mr Jinnah,* pp. 128–131.

must inevitably mean the rule of the major nation. Experience has proved that, whatever the economic and political programme of any political party, the Hindu, as a general rule, will vote for his caste-fellow and the Muslim for his co-religionist.

The British people, being Christians, sometimes forget the religious wars of their own history and to-day consider religion as a private and personal matter between man and God. This can never be the case in Hinduism and Islam, for both these religions are definite social codes which govern not so much man's relation with his God as man's relation with his neighbour. They govern not only his law and culture but every aspect of his social life and such religions, essentially exclusive, completely preclude that merging of identity and unity of thought on which Western democracy is based. . . .

✦ ✦ ✦

The next excerpt is from Jinnah's famous address to the March 1940 meeting of the Muslim League, held in Lahore, which committed both party and leader to the creation of a separate Muslim homeland to be named Pakistan.[4]

✦ ✦ ✦

. . . The problem in India is not of an inter-communal character but manifestly of an international one, and it must be treated as such. So long as this basic and fundamental truth is not realized, any constitution that may be built will result in disaster and will prove destructive and harmful not only to the Musalmans but to the British and Hindus also. If the British Government are really in earnest and sincere to secure peace and happiness of the people of this sub-continent, the only course open to us all is to allow the major nations separate homelands by dividing India into 'autonomous national states'. There is no reason why these states should be antagonistic to each other. On the other hand, the rivalry and the natural desire and efforts on the part of one to dominate the social order and establish political supremacy over the other in the government of the country will disappear. It will lead more to-wards natural good-will by international pacts between them, and they can

---

4. From the Presidential Address to the annual session of the All-India Muslim League, Lahore, March 1940, in Ahmad, *Some Recent Speeches and Writings of Mr Jinnah*, pp. 176–180.

live in complete harmony with their neighbours. This will lead further to a friendly settlement all the more easily with regard to minorities by reciprocal arrangements and adjustments between Muslim Indian and Hindu India, which will far more adequately and effectively safeguard the rights and interests of Muslims and various other minorities.

It is extremely difficult to appreciate why our Hindu friends fail to understand the real nature of Islam and Hinduism. They are not religions in the strict sense of the word, but are, in fact, different and distinct social orders, and it is a dream that the Hindus and Muslims can ever evolve a common nationality, and this misconception of one Indian nation has gone far beyond the limits and is the cause of most of your troubles and will lead India to destruction if we fail to revise our notions in time. The Hindus and Muslims belong to two different religious philosophies, social customs, literatures. They neither intermarry nor interdine together and, indeed, they belong to two different civilizations which are based mainly on conflicting ideas and conceptions. Their aspects on life and of life are different. It is quite clear that Hindus and Musalmans derive their inspiration from different sources of history. They have different epics, different heroes, and different episodes. Very often the hero of one is a foe of the other and, likewise, their victories and defeats overlap. To yoke together two such nations under a single state, one as a numerical minority and the other as a majority, must lead to growing discontent and final destruction of any fabric that may be so built up for the government of such a state. . . .

History has [shown] to us many geographical tracts, much smaller than the sub-continent of India, which otherwise might have been called one country, but which have been divided into as many states as there are nations inhabiting them. [The] Balkan Peninsula comprises as many as 7 or 8 sovereign states. Likewise, the Portuguese and the Spanish stand divided in the Iberian Peninsula. Whereas under the plea of unity of India and one nation, which does not exist, it is sought to pursue here the line of one central government when we know that the history of the last twelve hundred years has failed to achieve unity and has witnessed, during the ages, India always divided into Hindu India and Muslim India. The present artificial unit of India dates back only to the British conquest and is maintained by the British bayonet, but termination of the British regime . . . will be the herald of the entire break-up with worse disaster than has ever taken place during the last one thousand years under Muslims. Surely that is not the legacy which Britain would bequeath to India after 150 years of her rule, nor would Hindu and Muslim India risk such a sure catastrophe.

Muslim India cannot accept any constitution which must necessarily result in a Hindu majority government. Hindus and Muslims brought together under a democratic system forced upon the minorities can only mean Hindu raj. Democracy of the kind with which the Congress High Command is enamoured would mean the complete destruction of what is most precious in Islam. We have had ample experience of the working of the provincial constitutions during the last two and a half years and any repetition of such a government must lead to civil war. . . .

Musalmans [in India] are not a minority as it is commonly known and understood. . . . Musalmans are a nation according to any definition of a nation, and they must have their homelands, their territory and their state. We wish to live in peace and harmony with our neighbours as a free and independent people. We wish our people to develop to the fullest our spiritual, cultural, economic, social and political life in a way that we think best and in consonance with our own ideals and according to the genius of our people. Honesty demands and the vital interests of millions of our people impose a sacred duty upon us to find an honourable and peaceful solution, which would be just and fair to all. But at the same time we cannot be moved or diverted from our purpose and objective by threats or intimidations. We must be prepared to face all difficulties and consequences, make all the sacrifices that may be required of us to achieve the goal we have set in front of us.

Ladies and gentlemen, that is the task before us. I fear I have gone beyond my time limit. . . . Anyhow, I have placed before you the task that lies ahead of us. Do you realize how big and stupendous it is? Do you realize that you cannot get freedom or independence by mere arguments? I should appeal to the intelligentsia. The intelligentsia in all countries in the world have been the pioneers of any movements for freedom. What does the Muslim intelligentsia propose to do? I may tell you that unless you get this into your blood, unless you are prepared to take off your coats and are willing to sacrifice all that you can and work selflessly, earnestly and sincerely for your people, you will never realize your aim. Friends, I therefore want you to make up your mind definitely and then think of devices and organize your people, strengthen your organisation and consolidate the Musalmans all over India. I think that the masses are wide-awake. They only want your guidance and your lead. Come forward as servants of Islam, organize the people economically, socially, educationally and politically and I am sure that you will be a power that will be accepted by everybody. (Cheers.)

✦   ✦   ✦

The last excerpt is from a speech to the Sudents' Union of the Aligarh Muslim University (AMU) in March 1941, a year after the Pakistan resolution. The AMU was the college of choice for bright young Muslims from all over India. Jinnah is thus addressing those who could play crucial leadership roles in the (as yet hypothetical) state of Pakistan.[5]

✦   ✦   ✦

. . . Mr. Jinnah began by expressing his warmest thanks for the deep affection and regard shown to him by the Aligarh students. Proceeding, he said that when he addressed them last year, the Lahore resolution, popularly known as Pakistan, had not been passed, but he had noticed that they were anxious for the declaration of the ideal embodied in the Lahore resolution. In other parts of India he had noticed the same feeling. What I have done, said Mr. Jinnah, is to declare boldly what was stirring the heart of Muslim India. The whole Hindu press, Hindu leaders and the Congress got hysterical about it. They raised a storm of opposition: but all the press propaganda, vituperation, misrepresentation and hysterical outbursts have not changed our position. I have asserted on numerous occasions that the democratic parliamentary system of government as they have in England and other Western countries is entirely unsuited to India. I was condemned in the Congress press as an enemy of India's freedom! But the truth of the statement is gradually dawning on the minds of all thinking persons. . . .

In everything that is fundamental and essential to life [said Jinnah] Hindus and Muslims differ. It is no use shutting one's eyes to realities. Among Hindus themselves there are schisms and exclusive castes and sub-castes. Between them they make a most undemocratic society yet they have suddenly fallen in love with democracy. They talk of nothing else but democracy. (Laughter.) In Bombay recently a swimming bath on the seashore was opened for the ex-

5. From Ahmad, *Some Recent Speeches and Writings of Mr Jinnah*, pp. 261–269.

clusive use of the Hindus. They are not prepared to swim with the Muslims even in the sea. I do not want to ridicule the feelings of the Hindus. I respect everyone's religious feelings. I am only referring to these things to show how deep is the difference between the Hindus and the Muslims. It would be no wisdom to proceed to build for India a constitution on the assumption as if these differences did not exist. By ignoring the realities and the difficulties in the way of fitting India into a simple democratic system the Hindus will be doing the greatest harm to their own people. Democracy of the kind they want to impose on India is an impossibility, for even the conditions which make diluted democracy possible in other countries are absent from India. The sooner the idea is given up the better.

It was therefore after mature consideration that we passed the Lahore resolution which advocates the establishment of independent sovereign states in regions of Muslim majority, namely, the North-West and the North-East of India and also provides for mandatory safeguards for minorities in the regional states and their units. Now it does not require a great genius or a great constitutionalist to understand the scheme of partition. Without waiting to consider the scheme on its merits the Congress and other Hindu circles became hysterical about it, as if it were a nightmare or some dangerous animal! (Laughter.) As a matter of fact, Pakistan has been there for centuries; it is there to-day, and it will remain till the end of the world. (Cheers.) It was taken away from us; we have only to take it back. What is the title of the Hindus to it? How can we be prevented from claiming what is our own? It is really more in the interest of the Hindus themselves. What, after all, does the League say? Zones with clear Muslim majority are to be demarcated and allowed to establish independent states of their own with the necessary territorial readjustments. Under the scheme two-thirds of India goes to the Hindus where they can have their own states. They should be content with their due share. They can never have the whole of India. . . .

The old slogans against Pakistan, such as vivisection of India, cutting mother India into two, and cutting the mother cow have been given up. They have now begun to ask whether they will be safe if India is partitioned. The Hindu press has raised the bogey that if India is partitioned the Muslims will overrun the entire country. It is a baseless insinuation. For if that is the Hindu fear, may I know how do they then propose to rule over the whole of India? In Pakistan there will be no more than seventy million Muslims. Hindu India will consist of no less than two hundred and twenty million Hindus. Do they mean to say that these 220 million people cannot hold their freedom against a mere seventy million? Then it is said that the future of India will not be safe, as all the invasions have come from the North-West of India, and that Pakistan itself will not be able to ward off such invasions. It is said that a united India, a democratic India, alone can withstand such attacks and, therefore, there should be a central democratic government of India. By having a central government and a majority in the ballot-box they think they can make the country safe from invasion. (Laughter.) Further, our Hindu friends ask the Muslim minorities as to how Pakistan was gong to benefit them and that they would suffer at the hand of the Hindus. As for the invasions from the North-West, may I know where did the Portuguese come from? Where did the French come from, and where did our British masters come from? Was it through the Khyber Pass? They came from the coasts. But we know that, as a matter of fact, modern warfare knows no frontiers. The decisive weapon of modern war is the air-arm. The land and the sea powers have taken a secondary position. Let us, therefore, live as good neighbours; let the Hindus guard the South and West and let the Muslims guard the frontiers. We will then stand together and say to the world, 'Hands off India; India for the Indians'. (Cheers.)

The second objection which concerns Muslim minorities has no force. As a self-respecting people, we in the Muslim minority provinces say boldly that we are prepared to undergo every suffering and sacrifice for the emancipation and liberation of our brethren in regions of Muslim majority. By standing in their way and dragging them along with us into a united India we do not in any way improve our position. Instead, we reduce them also to the position of a minority. But we are determined that, whatever happens to us, we are not going to allow our brethren to be vassalised by the Hindu majority. But the fact is that the creation of these independent states will be the surest guarantee for the fair treatment of the minorities. When the time for consultation and negotiations comes the case of Muslims in the minority provinces will certainly not go by default.

Pakistan is not only a practicable goal but the only goal if you want to save Islam from complete annihilation in this country. We have yet to go a long way. Pakistan is there but we have to take it. It is easier to achieve freedom than to keep it. England and America are independent states but how hard they have to struggle to preserve their independence! We have to prepare ourselves. Make yourselves strong; prepare your people in education, trade, industries, commerce and defence. The problems before us will be how to maintain internal security and ward off external aggression. Freedom cannot be achieved or kept by the spinning of charkhas.[6] We should be prepared to fight and defend our homes and ideals we cherish. (Cheers.) The realization of Pakistan is in your hands. . . . Aligarh is the arsenal of Muslim India and you are its best soldiers. Go to the countryside. Educate our people and uplift them. Explain to our people what is our goal. There are many who are trying to mislead them. Let them understand things and then they will march on to their destined goal. . . .

The time has now come to devote yourselves more and more to the constructive programme. I ask you to spend your vacations in attending to constructive work, like the spread of literacy, social uplift, economic betterment and greater political consciousness and discipline among our people. We want to establish Muslim States in the North-West and the North-East of India, so that the peaceful and neighbourly relations may be maintained between Hindus and Muslims. This is the only way to restore lasting peace and happiness to the country. I have learnt from reliable sources that in responsible circles in England and even in Congress circles this scheme is being seriously considered. Let us, therefore, march on to our goal. The time comes, and when you are ready, I will tell you what to do. (Prolonged cheers.)

✦   ✦   ✦

6. The charkha is the spinning wheel, which Gandhi urged patriotic Indians to use to spin their own yarn.

11

THE RADICAL REFORMER

E. V. RAMASWAMI

In the Tamil country, as in Maharashtra, it was Brahmins who took early advantage of British rule, learning English in order to serve the new rulers as teachers, lawyers, doctors, clerks, and civil servants. When the Congress sought members in South India, once more it was Brahmins who came to the fore. Some joined the new organisation out of a spirit of patriotism and national service, others in the hope that it would help deliver jobs at higher levels of the administration.

Before colonialism, the Brahmin already enjoyed an exalted social status. Whether by accident or design, the policies of the Raj made them dominant in an economic and political sense as well. It was the danger of Brahmin hegemony in all spheres of life that lay behind the activism of Jotirao Phule and B. R. Ambedkar. Their analogue in South India was an equally remarkable thinker-organiser named E. V. Ramaswami.

Ramaswami was born in the town of Erode in 1879. He was a Kannada-speaking Naiker, from a caste that lay in the upper stratum of Sudras. His father was a moderately successful businessman.

We know little about Ramaswami's early life. It is said that he travelled to Banaras as a young man, where he was less than impressed with the city and its religiosity. In particular, he was appalled by the dirt in the streets and by the sight of half-burnt bodies in the river Ganges. On his return home, he joined the family business and also briefly served as the Chairman of the Erode Municipality. In about 1920 Ramaswami became active in the Congress party. He energetically adopted the Gandhian credo, promoting home-spun cloth, temple-entry for the Untouchables, and the like. In 1925 he left the Congress because he found that its leadership was overwhelmingly Brahmin, and with only the rare exception was insensitive to the claims of the lower castes. A catalytic incident related to a Congress-run hostel whose management insisted, despite Ramaswami's protests, on serving food separately to Brahmin and Non-Brahmin students.

Ramaswami now turned to promoting what he called 'Self Respect'. He believed that ancient history and current politics had consolidated the domination of South India by North India, and of Non-Brahmins by Brahmins. Oppressed castes and regions needed thus to regain, or reassert, their self-respect and create conditions where they could be in control of their own affairs. A brilliant orator in Tamil, he also ran a series of widely read political magazines where he promoted his ideas.

(Apart from what he saw around him in the India of the 1920s, Ramaswami seems also to have been influenced by the then very popular American rationalist thinker and propagandist, Robert G. Ingersoll. A visit to the Soviet Union in 1931 reinforced his belief in materialism.)

From the 1930s, Ramaswami was increasingly known as 'Periyar', or 'the great one'. In his speeches and essays, he took radical stands in favour of atheism, women's rights, and contraception. He ran a militant (and eventually successful) campaign against the imposition of Hindi in South India. He wrote critically of the Ramayana and other Hindu epics and texts, which, in his view, promoted the message of Brahmin superiority and endorsed distinctions of caste and gender. Brahmin priests were a particular target of his polemics—they were, he claimed, corrupt and cunning, as well as sexual predators.

In 1944 Ramaswami formed his own party, the Dravida Kazhagam, which asked for the establishment of a separate, sovereign, nation-state in south India to be called Dravida Nadu. When India became independent on 15 August 1947, and when it enacted a democratic constitution and celebrated its first Republic Day on 26 January 1950, Ramaswami observed both events as days of mourning. In his view, they merely formalised the rule of the northern Aryans over the southern Dravidians.

In 1949 a group of Ramaswami's followers broke away to form the Dravida Munnetra Kazhagam (DMK). In 1967 the DMK became the first professedly regional party to come to power in a major provincial election in India. The Congress, once dominant in Tamil Nadu, has never since regained power in that state. Without the ideological and organisational groundwork laid down by Ramaswami, it is hard to see how this could have happened. To be sure, he may have himself seen this as somewhat less than ideal—for he wanted a separate country for the Tamils, not merely greater autonomy within the existing nation-state of India.

Ramaswami's message is nicely captured in a statue of his in Tiruchirapalli which carries this inscription: 'God does not exist at all. The inventor of God is a fool. The propagator of God is a scoundrel. The worshipper of God is a barbarian'.

E. V. Ramaswami died in December 1973.

THE FRAUD OF RELIGION

We present excerpts from two speeches of Ramaswami brilliantly satirising the pretensions of orthodox Hindus and Hinduism. The first is from a talk at Courtallam, Tirunelveli district, in August 1927.[1]

♦   ♦   ♦

The skulduggery that the priestly class or Brahmins indulge in in the name of religion to weaken our unity and expropriate our hard-earned wealth, and ruin our society and country and make us into people without self-respect and living corpses is nothing less than the damage done to us in the name of politics by politicians and so-called nationalists as I have repeatedly stated.

Without realizing this we ourselves are aiding these treacherous acts to continue forever and creating the foundation for making us and our posterity

1. First published in *Kudiarasu*, 11 September 1927. Translated for this volume by A. R. Venkatachalapathy.

their permanent slaves. As I go about explaining this you might feel greatly agitated. But if you give me a patient hearing and apply reason without prejudice the truth of this, whether I am right or wrong, will surely become clear to you.

Further, like the Vedas, puranas and shastras,[2] I am not saying that 'Believe whatever I say! My word is the word of god! If you do not believe me you'll perish in hell! Or you'll become atheists!' Rather I say that 'Brush aside what I say if it does not conform to your reason, knowledge, learning and experience. If it does fit in with these please put them into practice at least to some extent. Redeem your brethren by explaining these to them'. Please realize that I have nothing selfish to gain from this.

I am no agent of any religion. Nor am I the slave to any religion. I am bound only by the concepts of love and knowledge. I therefore speak to you whatever strikes me as is my duty, my desire, my happiness. Otherwise I leave things to your duty, to your free will, to your reason.

What is the purpose of the existence of religion for a country or a society or an individual? Is it meant for disciplining and uniting a society or country or to divide it? Is it bound by the conscience of an individual or is it meant to bind the individual's conscience? Is religion for the sake of man or is it man for the sake of religion? Please ponder over this.

Please think over the nature of religion in this manner. Firstly, how many of those here know anything about what is our, the Hindu, religion? How many of the so-called Hindus understand its philosophy? How many even accept that there is such a religion as Hinduism?

Firstly, to which language does the word 'Hindu' belong? Can anybody say that 'Hindu' occurs in any of the world's languages? If we look into when this word came into our country—does this term occur in the literature and grammar of our Tamil, or for that matter, in the old Tamil writings of the Sangam, or in the Aryan language or in the Vedas, shastras, agamas, sruti, smriti, purana, history, story or any such repository of Aryan civilization or tradition? Or is this term to be encountered in the songs or stories of the venerated Alwars and Nayanmars?[3] Or can we find that at least the Sitthars or sages or rishis have either uttered or employed this term?

---

2. The Hindu scriptures.

3. Medieval saint-poets of the Tamil country.

When we look at what we mean by *matham,* religion, scholars say that 're-ligion is a doctrine'. Even if we accept that, what then is Hindu *matham?*

If we concede there is a Hindu doctrine, what does 'Hindu' mean? All religions, apart from the Hindu religion, prefix the name of an individual to themselves, such as the 'Christian religion', 'Mohammedan religion', 'Buddhist religion', 'Ramanuja religion', 'Sankaracharya religion', etc. In this manner which fellow does 'Hindu' refer to? Whose doctrine is it? Please ponder whether we have not adopted as the name of our religion a term which has no meaning but only a phonic sound.

Secondly, who is the author of the Hindu religion? How old is it? What is its doctrine? What is the authority for all these? Ponder over all these issues.

Some say that 'the Hindu religion is the religion of the vedas. The vedas were spoken by God.' Look at the vulgarity of this proposition. If the vedas were spoken by god then they'd have to be common for all; how is it that the vedas are accepted by some and rejected by some, revealed to some and not revealed to others, and circumscribed by some boundary? If it has been spoken by god, why has it been revealed only in one language? If it was a veda meant for us would it not have been spoken in our language. What do we have to do with the vedic language?[4] Further if it had been meant for us how is it that it is not for us to hear, see, read or understand? . . . Like 'being a wife to every-body' why is it being amenable to every wishful exegesis and a faction to back every such exegesis? If we think of all such questions we have to ask 'Is there such a thing as a veda? If yes, is it is true? If true, can it bind us?' Please think.

How many gods in this world! . . . How many gods! How many symbols representing these gods! How many temples for these gods! How much food offerings for each god! How many marriages! How many children! How many such horrors! Look at all these! How many differences among the devotees! How many castes! How much of hierarchical ranking! Is it just that one section of these, who can be counted on the fingers, should be considered superior and high and entitled?[5]

---

4. The Vedas were composed in Sanskrit, whereas the language of Ramaswami and his readers was Tamil. Tamil speakers are extremely proud of the antiquity of their language and literary traditions and of the fact that these developed independently of Sanskrit.

5. The allusion here is to the Brahmins, who despite their small numbers claimed ritual and spiritual superiority to other Hindus.

If our religion accepts the theory that god is common to all and is omni-present, how is it that such cruelties as we should not go near the deity, enter the temples, while some others can touch the deity, wash it, clothe it can be instituted.

Now please think what is the use of our having accepted such a religion, accepted its gods, built temples for them, endowed our properties, and wor-shipping it daily. . . .

◆ ◆ ◆

The next excerpt is from a talk at Pachaiyappa's Hall, Madras, in Octo-ber 1927.[6]

◆ ◆ ◆

. . . Our religious policies and practices are the reason for our country not at-taining freedom and wallowing in a state without self-respect. Some of those listening to me may be offended by what I say. This is so because selfish persons have inculcated the superstition of religious belief in people to such an extent. . . . It is so ingrained that it is not easy to convince people. . . . However, if I do not speak out I will be either a selfish person or a coward. If you analyse this in a detached manner employing reason, there'd be no need to find fault with what I say. When one talks of religion it becomes imperative as well to talk about the failure of politics as a result. Many here know that I worked extensively in the field of politics. After this experience realising that this was not the path to freedom I left the Congress and not because I was either expelled or out of minor difference of opinion. I did not come from a modest background. I quit at a time when I was in a position of responsibility and power. I quit as I believed that nothing good will come out for the country from this political movement. It was at the Kanchipuram conference [of Novem-ber 1925] that this feeling got strengthened. I was for many years the President and Secretary of the Tamilnadu Congress Committee. It was then [I realised] my service was wasted and that I was only serving our enemies in the task of ruining our country and society that I quit politics.

6. Originally published in *Kudiarasu,* 23 October 1927. Translated for this volume by A. R. Venkatachalapathy.

If you want to know my standing regarding religion, between 1904 and June 1927, . . . I was the secretary and chairman of the Erode Circle Devasthanam [temple board]. The Board of the Hindu Religious Endowments had always written in praise of me. The newly constituted Board, in creating a new Devasthanam committee for four taluks, has again nominated me a member. . . . Many complaints were sent to them by brahmins urging against my nomination. One of the first complaints stated that I am a criminal and that I have been jailed twice. That complaint was forwarded to me. I replied that the charges were all correct and the only error was that I had been jailed thrice and not twice.

Next, signatures were collected from many non-brahmins and brahmins that 'This fellow abuses religion; he abuses only brahmins. Engage a CID inspector to report on him' and a petition was sent to the government. The government again asked for a reply. I stated, 'I do not abuse any one class of people. I abuse everybody. I cannot but abuse any class of people whose ideas come in the way of my work. I am striving only to see that there are equal rights for all'. I was re-nominated. As I keep travelling to Chennai and other places I have delegated my chairmanship to another responsible person and now remain its vice chairman. Some people who have heard me speak say that 'I am an atheist, an abuser of religion', 'an enemy of swaraj' and 'a stooge of the government'. I am yet to see any sign that I am a favourite of the government. The government treats me in the same manner that it has always treated me. Even today I am being shadowed by policemen as before. . . .

The issue I am to speak to you [about] today is the reform of religion. I am not out to defraud you, like the brahmins, by saying that you have to accept all that I say and if you don't then sin will befall you. I set out to speak on the matter of religious reform only after stating that 'Please give me a patient hearing and then do as you wish'. . . .

When did the need for religion originate? Why does one need religion? We need to ponder this. To my mind it seems that religion might have originated when humans began to live as groups and wanted to have some order for their day-to-day life and prevent one from harming others. And when this order began to be established the principles might have been devised in keeping with the knowledge, capabilities, situations, climate, etc. of the people of the times. With the passage of time this order must have grown in tune with the desires and greed and politics of individuals and finally taken the shape of what is called religion today. In our country when religion originated it had little to do with politics. In those days our people did not have a sense of politics. There was little need for it in any case. Why? Analyse the history of thousands of years ago. In those days, agriculture flourished. There was enough and more for the needs of everybody.

The one who had paddy gave it to the one who had cotton and got cotton or cloth in exchange. This was so for other needs as well. This is what is called barter. During their free time our people indulged in contemplation and created some laws and religious stipulations. However the brahmins who came to our land later, fooled our carefree people, manipulated them to their benefit, enslaved everyone and became their creators and lords. . . . If this state continues how will we ever progress? How can we escape a life of thraldom and live with self-respect? Therefore we should destroy all those who are hurdles to a life of self-respect of a nation or country. We should forsake obstinacy and act according to the state of the people and our reason, remove the obstacles in the path and become free by attaining self-respect.

Some call themselves 'Hindus'. But if you ask them 'What does it mean to be a Hindu?', ninety out of a hundred would have no answer. Yet, their love for religion based on superstition is beyond description. Of Muslims, ninety out of a hundred are well aware of their religion. Unlike other religionists we do not have an understanding of our religion. If you ask our people such questions as 'What is your religion? Who founded it? When did it originate?' there is no one to answer them. But if you ask Muslims or Christians or Buddhists or others they are ready with an answer. The antiquity attributed to the Hindu religion by these people is not simple. If you buy all the paper available, put the number one and fill it with egg-shaped zeroes all over, yet the age attributed to it would be higher and not lower. Nobody is able to answer who is its head. Some say it was created by god. If we ask for evidence they cite the veda. If we ask them what it says, they reply, 'You cannot see it; hear it; read it!' Is it possible that god could have composed it? No. Because if it was god who created it everyone in this world should accept it. Anyone should be able to see it. So how can we believe in the veda? How can we follow it? People of other religions have translated their scriptures into various languages, printed them and have ensured that it is available even to people of other religions.

It was because Muslims and Christians took such efforts that they could spread their religion and their scriptures and there are seven and a half crores of Muslims and a crore of Christians in our country. Can anybody say that these seven and a half crores came from countries such as Arabia or Turkey? . . . Every week four thousand of the so-called Hindus convert to other religions. The reason is that [Muslims and Christians] propagate their religion. To the people who have so converted they teach their religion and also give them education. Then they provide a vocation for leading a good life and this creates a feeling that their religion should rule the world. For this they spend very little money for the sake of religion. They do not spend even one per cent of what we spend for our religion. No other religion spends as much as we do. Within a short time of their coming Christians have rallied our people, given them education, and have made themselves our masters. . . .

But our religion, said to be made by god and millions and millions of years old, says that a majority of the people should not read its scriptures; and if one violates it, there are punishments such as the cutting of the tongue that studies, the pouring of molten lead into ears that hear, and the gouging out of the heart that learns. As a result, only with the advent of the white government 5% are now literate. Of them, 90% are Brahmins. But some say that 'We never forbade anyone from studying; we only forbade the studying of the vedas'. The education of vedic times is not like the histories of England, Europe or Arabia. Nor is it the books written by Shakespeare or Macaulay. The education of those days was that of morals. These moral maxims became the vedas. And we are not supposed to read the vedas. . . . If the white government had not come would religion have permitted the education of even one out of a thousand among us? Well if we cannot read the vedas can we not at least learn Sanskrit? No, they say. If we ask why, they say it will not come to our tongue. If I say, let me try they say that the morals of the vedas occur intermittently in them and therefore that too is not permitted. Thus are untold travails and insults heaped upon us in the name of religion. But the expenses incurred in this regard are beyond calculation. No other religion expends so much money. In other religions one or two persons may endow a thousand or four thousand pounds. That will be used to propagate their religion. That means the spreading of education among people, ameliorating disease and discovering the new. But in our religion everyone is forced to pay a tax for religion. In our province alone, according to government statistics, temples and

monasteries have an annual revenue of 2 crores of rupees. If you add inde-
pendent monasteries and temples the figure would be many times over. The
Tirupathi temple alone has an annual income of 20 lakhs. In the district of
Tirunelveli alone three or four temples have an annual revenue of 2–3 lakhs.

If you include renowned temples such as those in Chidambaram,
Rameswaram and Srirangam this figure will be much higher. Apart from these
there are other unaccounted sums. Suppose if one goes from here to Tirupathi to offer two thousand rupees, what are the other expenses involved. He
has to take his relatives with him. He has to wear the ritual yellow cloth. He
has to go in a procession with drums. He has to collect alms on the streets
crying out 'Govinda, Govinda'. Why does he do all this to make his offering of
two thousand rupees? It's a votive offering. What was the vow? Earlier when
he was sick or distressed and god saved him from disease in answer to his
prayers. Therefore he has to now empty the promised sum without a shortfall
of a single anna. And there are other expenses as well. Just think how much
money is spent on such things. Imagine how many people from the Himalayas
to Kanyakumari make such pilgrimage. Many go not only for votive offerings
but for festivals as well. How much is spent on that? I am not saying anything
about the faith. I am giving these figures only to ask what is the outcome.
What is the use of the money thus spent? Just think who gains from all this. All
this money goes into raw rice, green gram, ghee, badam and sugar. Who eats
them? . . .

Let's now turn to rituals. How much do we spend on rituals? Our people
think that men are made for rituals. . . . Even before we are conceived the rituals begin. A priest is required to conduct the rituals. He has to come and
burn the firewood and create smoke and soot. Only if he says that a healthy
child will be born do we believe that such a child will be born. We believe that
only if we instruct the child in the womb will it become intelligent. If the child
trips and falls we have to perform a ritual. To cast the horoscope, to put it in a
cradle, to feed it, to tie a nappy, to tonsure, to pierce the ears, to send it to
school—rituals have to be performed for each one of these. Even if the child
develops a fever a ritual is needed. For every ritual the brahmin has to be
called in. Money has to be coughed up. Even if one falls ill, he says 'Saturn is
turning towards Venus and has to be propitiated'. Shelling out money is the
propitiation. For the ritual of marriage matching [of horoscopes] has to be
done. . . . If another man desires the woman he winks at the priest offering to

pay five hundred or a thousand rupees, the priest says that the match is not right even if it is. He fixes the time and day according to his own whims. He murmurs death mantras or such thing at the marriage ritual and takes money. In some cases the bride is widowed after ten days of marriage. The horrors inflicted by the mother-in-law are unutterable. There's no limit to the troubles and misfortune caused by the husband. And if you ask the priest why did this happen even after matching all aspects [of their horoscopes] he says, 'That's her karma, what can anybody do about that?' And if you ask 'Why then did you compare so many horoscopic attributes, perform rituals and take away money?' he replies, 'You are stupid'. If the couple are childless, he says, 'You must have a child. Go to Kashi, go to Rameswaram, perform charities, make propitiations, . . . or else you will go to hell'. Partaking food at a child-less home is a big sin, he asserts.

You should have a child even if you have to make your wife cohabit with your brother. What is the secret behind this? Only if a family has at least one heir can the brahmin perform rituals and fill his stomach. Otherwise his line will perish without anyone to give to him. Finally, does he leave us alone even at the time of death? Like the carts are permitted to pass at tollgates only after the toll is paid, even the dead man has to pay a toll to the brahmin.

Let's now consider religious preceptors and gurus. People gain nothing from these. In the name of the Hindu religion, there are many Sankaracharyas, and Saiva and Vaishnava pontiffs. They go about with their retinue in processions on elephants and camels, camp at a place, advertise through their men about ritual washing of their feet and giving alms, charge a rupee or a pound for their feet to be washed and to let people drink that dirty water, and move out to a different camp after people there are milked dry, doing expiatory ritual and taking a ritual dip with our money for having set eyes on a shudra, another rit-ual and dip for the shudra's shadow falling on them, one more ritual and dip for having spoken in [demotic or colloquial] Tamil. Some of them are called 'loka guru' [people's preceptor]. And then there's the kula guru [family preceptor]. He sends his man to let people know of his coming. The disciples rush to him with family and children and are ordered to fall at this feet.

KULA GURU: How many children do you have?

DISCIPLE: Three. Two of whom are married.

KULA GURU: Two sons are two units. You are one unit. That makes it three units. Three units make three. Three quarters makes three-quarters. So of three and three-quarters you have remitted only one and a quarter!

DISCIPLE: Lord, forgive me. But I've submitted one and a quarter as a fine in my ignorance because my two sons are not employed.

KULA GURU: But was it not your father who willed that it's one and a quarter for each unit? Look at this writ.

And after the money is taken, his man says 'Swamigal's [the preceptor's] home needs a bit of repair. Come and get it done soon for Swamigal is inconvenienced'. . . .

+ + +

ON THE RIGHTS OF WIDOWS

Ramaswami was an early and consistent advocate of widow-marriage. The excerpt that follows is from an article published in August 1926.[7]

+ + +

. . . Intelligent people will agree that the creator has not endowed men and women with different faculties. Is it possible to find any difference between men and women, setting aside the physical features, in sharpness of intellect or in qualities of courage and heroism? It is not possible at all. There are, in both men and women, intellectuals, courageous people as well as stupid and cowardly people. While this is the case, it is unfair and wicked on the part of the haughty male population to continue to denigrate and enslave the female population.

Among the atrocities perpetrated by the Hindu male population against women, here we have to consider the treatment meted out to widows alone.

7. Originally published in *Kudi Arasu*, 22 August 1926, reproduced from K. Veeramani, ed., *Periyar on Women's Rights* (Madras: Emerald Publishers, 1994), pp. 26–31. Translated by R. Sundara Raju.

Even a very old man who is already satiated with worldly pleasures tries to marry again, as soon as his wife is dead. He also selects a very beautiful and graceful maid to be his bride. But, if a girl loses her husband, even before knowing anything of worldly pleasures, she is compelled to close her eyes to everything in the world and die broken-hearted. What a great injustice!

It is extremely cruel on the part of the Hindu brethren to witness the gradual destruction suffered by one half of their society, without taking any action.

In the past, it was customary for a woman who lost her husband, to jump into his funeral pyre. . . . When efforts were being taken to stop this practice of self-immolation, called *Sati,* the orthodox people indulged in a great agitation saying that Hindu religion was in danger and the orthodoxy was getting destroyed. But in course of time, the agitation died out and the practice of *Sati* also stopped altogether.

Now, the practice of preventing widows from marrying again is a partial and cruel one. Allowing an old man who has lost his wife to marry again and preventing even a young childless widow from getting married again—this attitude is far from impartial and just.

It is reasonable to say that the remarriage of a widow interferes with her chastity. Widows lose their chastity and get destroyed only because we don't get them remarried. Some young widows who seek to satisfy their physical passion become pregnant and seek to destroy the child in the womb. To whom will this sin of infanticide go? It will go only to the parents who compel young widows to continue to be widows and not get remarried. Leaving alone the young women who do not wish to marry again, it is always good to get the other young widows remarried.

When some friends read such ardent advocacy of widow remarriage, they may wonder if my support of this proposition is only verbal or if I have taken active participation in any widow-remarriage. Just to clear this doubt at least, I wish to record what I have done in practice.

I belong to the Karnataka Balijavar Community. The women of my community are [not] permitted to marry again, in case they become widows. The family in which I was born was extremely orthodox and rigorously devoted to Vaishnava religious principles. In spite of this family background, from my seventh year onwards I was ridiculing the artificial distinctions between the high and the low in society and also the practice of not eating any item of food touched by others. Not satisfied with this, I broke these bans deliberately and touched anybody and ate food from any house.

For these reasons, I was prevented from entering our kitchen and excepting my father, nobody used any vessel touched by me, without washing it. Those who were envious of the rigid orthodox practices in our family, derived some comfort from my rebellious attitude. They used to remark, 'Naicker has been blessed with a son for his orthodoxy and he is a gem of boy!' From my sixteenth year I attributed to male arrogance the special training given to girl children and the restrictions imposed on them.

In these circumstances, my sister died, leaving a male child and a girl child. When the girl, whom we called Ammayi, was ten years old, we celebrated her marriage on a grand scale. Sixty days after the marriage, the husband of the young girl died of cholera. He was only 13 years old then. When Ammayi heard about his death, she ran up to me crying bitterly, 'Uncle, did I ask you to get me married? You have thrown a boulder on my head!' and fell violently at my feet injuring her head. Six hundred to seven hundred men and women who had come there for condolence looked at me and the girl alternately and shed tears profusely. I too cried uncontrollably. And when I lifted the prostrate girl from the ground, I resolved to get her married again.

A year after the girl came of age, my brother-in-law and I took steps to arrange for her marriage. As soon as this news reached my parents and others, they were upset, thinking that their community was in great danger, and made the parties whom we had contacted, withdraw from the talk of marriage alliance. Finally, we selected the brother of my brother-in-law's second wife. The young man and the girl were secretly taken to Chidambaram, and their marriage was conducted in the temple. I did not go to Chidambaram, simply to keep our relatives off the scent, regarding our plans. I was afraid that if those people got the least suspicion, they would force the bridegroom to withdraw from the alliance. As a result of this remarriage for the girl, there was division among our relatives, communal discipline was enforced for some time and later our relationships became normal.

The boy and the girl live together and begot a male child. But, unfortunately, after some time, my niece lost her second husband also. Now, the mother and the son are living together fairly comfortably. Still, in my community there are some widowed girls below 13 years. It is a touching sight to see the parents of those widowed children treating them like untouchables.

Whenever I think of the lot of widows and when I witness their sufferings, I come to the conclusion that it is the law of nature for the strong to dominate over the weak and ill-treat them. We are tempted to think that when Hindu Society came under the domination of some people, there was neither religion nor any kind of discipline in that society, that some kind of discipline arose among them and that the strong shaped that discipline to suit their self-interest. But, whatever may be the reason for the present state of the Hindu Society, my firm belief is that the low position given permanently to widows may prove to be the reason for the utter ruin of the Hindu religion and the Hindu society.

I crave your forgiveness for my frank statement that most of the people who claim to be involved in politics, social welfare, social reformation and the improvement of women's lot are working only for the improvement of their lives and for building their own reputation and not for the causes to which they claim to be devoted.

Further, even if in these spheres there is some improvement, most of those who appear to be working there are actuated not by convictions but only by a love of popularity. Those who speak about the improvement of the status of women keep the women in their own families under 'purdah'; those who speak about the remarriage of widows, keep the widows in their own families well guarded and protect their widowhood carefully. There is no connection between what they preach and what they practice. If we try to find the reason for such conduct, we will have to conclude that they instinctively feel that women are slaves, subservient to men and that they must be kept under control. That is why these people treat women like animals. They seem to feel that giving freedom to women is equivalent to committing a very serious crime. The result of this attitude is that there is no independence or freedom to one half of the human race. This wicked enslavement of half of the human race is due to the fact that men are physically a little stronger than women. This principle applies to all spheres of life and the weaker are enslaved by the stronger.

If slavery has to be abolished in society, the male arrogance and wickedness which lead to the enslavement of women must be abolished first. Only when this is achieved, the tender sprouts of freedom and equality will register growth. . . .

✦　✦　✦

THE CASE FOR CONTRACEPTION

Ramaswami supported contraception as a means of enhancing the rights and freedoms of women. This set him apart from other Indian reformers, such as Gandhi, who advocated celibacy as a means of birth control. The excerpts that follow are from an article published in 1930.[8]

◆   ◆   ◆

What I wrote two years ago on contraception shocked many people. But, now it has become an ordinary matter to be talked about everywhere. . . . But, there are basic differences between the reasons given by us for contraception and the reasons given by others for this. We say that contraception is necessary for women to gain freedom. Others advocate contraception taking into consideration many problems like the health of women, the health and energy of the children, the poverty of the country and the maintenance of the family property. Many Westerners also support contraception for the same reasons. Our view is not based on these considerations. We recommend that women should stop delivering children altogether because conception stands in the way of women enjoying personal freedom. Further, begetting a number of children prevents men also from being free and independent. This truth will be clear if we listen to talk of men and women when their freedom is hampered.

When a man is in difficulties, he generally says, 'If I were a single man without encumbrances, I would face any difficulty boldly. But, because I am now the father of 4 or 5 children, out of anxiety of looking after them, I have to bow to the words of others'. So too, when a woman is subjected to suffering by the husband or by some adverse circumstances, she generally says, 'If I were free, I would get away from this place or drown myself in a river or a tank. My temperament will not allow me to face this kind of suffering even for a minute. But how can I go away, leaving these children to fend for themselves?' Therefore, it is these children that stand in the way of the freedom of both men and women.

When people in the world have to work hard and also subordinate themselves, sacrificing personal freedom, just in order to earn a living, if they are

8. Originally published in *Kudi Arasu*, 6 April 1930, reproduced from Veeramani, *Periyar on Women's Rights*, pp. 45–47. Translated by R. Sundara Raju.

burdened with the responsibility of looking after children also, how can they be free and independent? Therefore, conception and delivery of children obstruct the freedom of both men and women. Conception proves to be the wicked enemy of women's freedom. That is why we say that women must definitely put a stop to delivering children. Conception is the root cause of women becoming sickly, developing signs of old age too soon and meeting with death early. Further, it is this conception that stands in the way of women becoming ascetics, religious leaders and heads of religious institutions and *mutts,* while men are free to become any of these. That is why we advocate contraception. . . .

✦   ✦   ✦

THE CONSTRAINTS OF MARRIAGE

Our final excerpt from the feminist, or proto-feminist, writings of E. V. Ramaswami speaks of the burdens placed on women by that most durable of human institutions, marriage.[9]

✦   ✦   ✦

The married life of a man and a woman in our country is very bad; in no other country it is so bad. The marriage principle, briefly, involves the enslavement of a woman by her husband, and it is nothing else. We conceal this enslavement under cover of marriage rites and we deceive the women concerned by giving the wedding the meaninglessly false name of a divine function.

Generally speaking, not merely in our country, but in almost all countries of the world, as far as marriage is concerned, women are subjected to unnaturally harsh treatment. This will be accepted as true by all impartial people. But, in this, our country is far worse than other countries.

If this wickedness against women continues, in the near future, that is, within another fifty years, marriage rites and connected relationships will cease to be; we can be sure of that. Realising this, intelligent people in other

9. Originally published in *Kudi Arasu,* 17 August 1930, reproduced from Veeramani, *Periyar on Women's Rights,* pp. 68–71. Translated by R. Sundara Raju.

countries are gradually relaxing the harsh treatment of women. Our country alone is obstinately clinging to the old practices. Therefore an unconventionally drastic agitation of women has to take place.

Last year (1929) at the Chengalpattu conference a resolution was passed stating that men and women should have the right to be divorced from their partners. And then in the Women's Conference held in Madras recently there was a demand for a law to enable women to have divorce when necessary. The so called social reformers raised a hue and cry against the resolutions in the two conferences. But after the Chengalpattu resolution, in some part[s] of India and in other countries divorce laws have been enacted. In Russia marriage itself is treated as a daily contract. All of us know that in Germany, if there is no agreement between a man and his wife, they can be divorced without assigning any reason. The Baroda government[10] also has enacted such a law. In many countries of the West, such a law is in force. We have to say that it is foolish on the part of the government in our country not to have enacted such a law. Newspapers report that in South India many husbands have killed their wives suspecting immoral behaviour. Sometimes the husband's suspicion of his wife's character has led to many murders. Those who believe in divine dispensation do not have the brains to ask themselves why marriages conducted according to religious rites and the approval of god, end in this fashion. If the world of the women should progress, if the human element should develop in women and if men should have contentment and happiness and if they should experience real love, it is essential that we should give our people the right to seek divorce when it is necessary. Otherwise men and women will have no scope for independent living.

Many of our 'social reformers' raise a violent cry of protest if a man marries two wives. It is not clear what makes them raise this cry. Is it their devotion to religion or rationalism or their interest in the welfare of women or the freedom of human beings or the righteous conduct of human beings? We will discuss this question on another occasion.

Now, I wish to ask the people who object to a man marrying more than one wife these questions: Is marriage intended to give pleasure and satisfaction to man or is it just a formal rite? If by chance a man gets as his wife a woman

10. The princely state of Baroda was known for its progressive Maharaja and its progressive administration.

whom he does not like, who does not cooperate with him and who cannot give him physical pleasure, then what should the man concerned do? In the same way, if a woman happens to get a man unsuitable to her in every way, then, what is her lot? What is she to do? If marriage has anything to do with divinity, and if it is really dissoluble, will such complications arise in it? When these things are considered it will be clear to any kind of man, that the talk of divinity is utter falsehood. Therefore, if divorce is not facilitated in our country by law as it is done in other countries, we will have to do propaganda against marriage and also for more than one partner for each married man and woman. That apart, at present, we wish to urge the men who find their wives non-cooperative, and useless for giving pleasure and satisfaction, to come forward to marry the women they like. Only then the suffering that results from bringing together, in the name of divine sanction, men and women who do not know each other and who have not given their consent for the alliance will end. Why man is born and why he dies are questions with which we are not concerned. What we are convinced about is that as long as human beings live, they must enjoy pleasure and satisfaction. For this, a woman must have a man and a man must have a woman.

When this is accepted, if difficulties which cause sorrow between the couple crop up, it is the first duty of any sensible man to get rid of those difficulties. Those who work for the pleasure and satisfaction of other human beings must do this service. Without getting rid of the difficulties if men and women suffer dissatisfaction and pain, telling themselves that simply because they are married, they must patiently put up with everything, I would say that they betray absence of the essential human qualities and also want of self-respect.

+   +   +

12

THE SOCIALIST FEMINIST

KAMALADEVI CHATTOPADHYAY

WHEREAS AMBEDKAR, JINNAH, AND RAMASWAMI WERE critics of Gandhi, our next maker of modern India was a critical sympathiser. In this she was somewhat akin to Tagore. While the poet urged Gandhi not to reject other cultures when demanding national independence, Kamaladevi Chattopadhyay[1] asked him to be more sensitive to the rights of women, as well as to be more attentive to the economic bases of social strife.

Kamaladevi was born in 1903, the youngest child of a middle-class Brahmin family from the southwestern port city of Mangalore. Her commmunity of Chitrapur Saraswats had taken early to modern education and reaped its rewards accordingly. Her own father was in the colonial civil service. Growing up, Kamaladevi was deeply influenced by her mother, who read Tamil, English, Hindi, and Marathi and also played the classical violin.

Kamaladevi was married and widowed in her teens. Her mother encouraged her to study in Madras, where she fell in love with and later

---

1. Kamaladevi's last name is sometimes rendered as Chattopadhyaya.

married Harindranath Chattopadhyay, who was a brother of the poet-patriot Sarojini Naidu and a versifier and actor of some talent himself. The theatre seemed to be a common bond—for Kamaladevi liked to act in and promote plays, particularly those with social themes. In 1926, still in her early twenties, she stood for election to the Madras Legislative Council but lost narrowly. By now she was a convinced nationalist in the Congress mould. In 1928 she was elected to the prestigious All India Congress Committee.

Kamaladevi became better known when, in 1930, she prevailed upon Gandhi not to restrict the Salt Satyagraha to men alone. She herself made packets of salt and sold them outside the Bombay stock exchange, shouting 'Mahatma Gandhi ki jai' (Glory to Mahatma Gandhi). Then she repeated the procedure in the High Court. For this breach of the law, she was arrested and sent to jail, the first of several prison terms she was to—the word is inescapable—enjoy.

In 1934 a group of idealistic and brilliantly gifted young men and women formed the Congress Socialist Party (CSP). This urged the Congress to be more sensitive to the rights of workers and peasants. At the same time, these Congress Socialists detested the so-called Socialist Fatherland, the Soviet Union. Condemning its one-party state and its brutal treatment of political dissidents, the CSP stood rather for a marriage of democracy and socialism. Kamaladevi was active in the CSP from the beginning, becoming its president in 1936. She had also become increasingly involved in the women's movement, lobbying for better working conditions for women in factories and farms as well as for their right to paid maternity leave.

Kamaladevi was arrested during the Quit India movement of 1942 and spent more than a year in jail. However, after India became independent in 1947, she refused to enter formal politics. With her abilities, and her record as a fighter for freedom, a place in Parliament and in the Union Cabinet was hers for the asking. If she wished, she could have been a governor of a large state or ambassador to an important country. Offers were made in these directions—she rejected them all—in favour of social work. In the first, difficult years of freedom she worked to resettle refugees in northern India. Through her Indian Co-operative Union she helped the displaced refugees acquire land, build homes, and set up small workshops and factories. Under her direction, the Co-operative Union ran schools and hospitals as well.

From the 1950s Kamaladevi turned increasingly to the revival and promotion of India's rich, varied, and endangered craft traditions. She established the All India Handicrafts Board and headed it for twenty years. She travelled through the country, studying existing traditions of weaving, pottery, sculpture, metalwork, toy-making, and so forth. She formed cooperatives to market the products of craftsmen and to provide them credit. She instituted awards to motivate them. She urged state governments to cut out middlemen and to deal directly with craftsmen, source their products, and sell them through their own emporia. A healthy competitive rivalry between the states was thereby created. That Indian crafts are still alive and, moreover, have a visible national and international presence, is owed more to Kamaladevi Chattopadhyay than to any other individual.

Among the other institutions that Kamaladevi helped create and nurture were the National School of Drama, the Sangeet Natak Akademi, and the India International Centre. She is now chiefly known for her work for handicrafts and through the institutions that she founded. But, as the excerpts below demonstrate, Kamaladevi was also an original thinker, whose writings on politics and social reform continue to speak to us today.

Kamaladevi Chattopadhyay died in 1988, having lived through the most part of a century she helped define and whose finest tendencies she embodied.

THE WOMEN'S MOVEMENT IN PERSPECTIVE

In 1942 Kamaladevi Chattopadhyay was elected president of the All-India Women's Conference. Because she was then in jail she could not assume office. However, after her release from prison in 1944, she presided over the annual conference of the Women's Conference held that year in Bombay. Excerpts from her address are presented below. Her educated, urbane, and modern style makes for an interesting contrast with the more direct and earthy prose of Tarabai Shinde, her fellow worker in the cause of gender equality.[2]

+ + +

Although the women's movement has fairly advanced and matured, I feel the need today more than ever to restate its case, because of the continued misunderstanding of its nature and growth by a large number of men and quite a few women alike. The women's movement . . . operates as an integral part of the progressive movement in the broadest sense, and is not a sex war as so many mechanically believe or are led to believe. For the issues round which it revolves, such as right of votes, inheritance, entry into professions and the like, are an intrinsic part of the bigger issues striving to overcome the prevailing undemocratic practices that deny common rights to certain sections of society. It is therefore a comrade to the struggle of the backward castes and the long-oppressed classes alike, seeking to regain the lost inheritance of man's inalienable rights. To give it any other interpretation or shear it off to isolate it from the main current, is socially injurious. It is equally erroneous to hold the 'nature of man' responsible for women's disabilities and give the women's movement an anti-man twist. It is the nature of our society which is at fault and our drive has to be directed against faulty social institutions.

The women's movement, therefore, does not seek to make women either fight men or imitate them. It rather seeks to instill into them a consciousness of their own faculties and functions and create a respect for those of the other sex. Thus alone can society be conditioned to accept the two as equals. To fit women theoretically and practically into this scheme, women have to be encouraged to develop their gifts and talents. This has therefore to be one of the main planks of the movement.

Closely allied to a false conception of the women's movement is also the false value allotted to the women's economic worth. The correct premise to start from is the recognition of the social division of labour between the sexes, which gives the lie direct to the middle and upper-class conception of women

2. From the Presidential Address to the All-India Women's Conference, Bombay, 7 April 1944, reproduced in Kamaladevi [Chattopadhyay], *At the Crossroads,* ed. Yusuf Meherally (Bombay: The National Information and Publications Ltd., 1947), pp. 90–99.

as domestic and social parasites, living on their husbands and contributing nothing. Woman power is basic and the woman must be recognized as a social and economic factor on her own, not as an assistant to man. Little recognized are the tremendous labours of the housewife, and even in the most highly industrialized countries house-keeping still remains the major industry, and the housewives still form the majority. To state blandly that woman produces children and rears them, cooks food, cleans, washes, is not enough. . . . The housewife is as much of a working woman as a factory worker. She expends more energy and time and skill in the production of commodities than the unionized, legally protected worker, for her hours are unlimited and her tools countless. Tradition has always tended to place a lower value on home pro-duction and services. One reason may be because such goods and services do not come on the market but only cater to the family group as consumers. Yet, really speaking, this very fact should make them, as one writer says, 'priceless'. For, since society depends upon the family not only for biological perpetuation but cultural as well, woman as the guardian of the home and one of its stabilizing factors, will also continue to remain 'priceless'. The trag-edy is that its very non-pecuniary and non-competitive character has lowered the prestige of the woman's role. Husbands who claim they 'support' their wives simply because the latter do not bring home a pay cheque, are being anti-social, upsetting the harmonious social equilibrium and breaking social solidarity. For it is time society recognized that every housewife supports herself though she may not scratch at a desk or run a machine, by the social labour she performs and the contribution she makes towards the mainte-nance of the home and its happiness.

The entrance of women into extra-domestic activities has to be welcomed, for it provides a wider field for their talents, breaks the relative segregation of the women as a sex, relaxes the restrictions that otherwise narrow women's functions. What is strange is that as long as woman confines herself to her domestic duties, she is censured as a burden on man, whereas if she tries to earn a livelihood outside the home, she is equally condemned as a competi-tor of man, trying to take his livelihood away from him. . . .

The field of operations that lie before the Conference is ever-widening. Many varied activities beckon and the temptation to rush in all directions is great. But like an autumnal matron who has developed a high sense of dis-crimination but not lost her youthful vigour and enthusiasm, the Conference

would do well to concentrate on a few items and do them well. First in importance I would place the training of social services, so eminently needed yet
so grievously neglected. . . . Closely allied to this is the necessity for training women in handicrafts and fostering hand[made] industries. Those of our
branches which are already working in this direction, one of them even turning out paper, will testify to the utility of such ventures. They will provide a
means of livelihood to many helpless women. Incidentally, they will add to
the industrial production of our country at a time when it is not able to meet
our needs. Every branch should initiate and run whatever industries it is best
in a position to introduce. In such undertakings, I am sure, we can always
count on the help and co-operation of other experienced bodies who are already in the field but who do not attempt the special training and employment of women, a task this Conference is best fitted for.

As essential and as scarce are the health-services, particularly nursing. . . .
The maternity and child welfare movement is mostly a week-end show and
the entire country can boast of only 800 centres to cater to such a vast area
and population. All this makes an appalling picture. While admitting that the
Women's Conference is not the body which can build up a complete health-
service to meet the country's requirements, I feel sure it can make a small but
appreciable contribution. It can recruit women to the nursing profession, encourage many more girls to take courses in public health-nursing, first aid,
industrial hygiene, etc., and also get more of such courses introduced in our
educational and social institutions. It can help to organize shorter courses in
the general principles of nursing to meet the present emergency in the country. At the same time it should agitate to raise the standard of housing, allowances, training and pay of the nursing staff, with a view to popularizing
and securing social recognition to this long-despised but most noble of
professions. . . .

Although the food problem is the most frightening at the moment and
tends to overshadow most others, its causes are beyond the Conference's
power to remedy. As long as India's economy continues to be throttled and
perverted by foreign interests, hunger and starvation must stalk this land of
plenty. Only a careful development of its vast untapped wealth, based on an
economy designed to meet the needs of the people by a free India[n] people's
government, can aspire to overcome this dreadful scourge of perpetual famines. But that can't by any means be our final word on it. As women happen to

be the regulators of food in the home they should be more sensitive now than ever to the care and preservation of food, avoid waste in daily consumption as also in lavish hospitality which in the present setting strikes one as painfully incongruous. Working out balanced diets with the limited things available, would also help. The worst sufferers in this tragic drama are the children. In every responsible society they have the first claim on the available resources, particularly milk. But today in our country the man who pays the price gets the milk. So, while adults who are not wholly dependant on this article are able to get large supplies and sometimes even thoughtlessly waste it, children who solely subsist on it are forced to go without it if they do not have sufficient means. Ways and methods must be sought by us to alter this and see that our children, which in reality means several future generations to come, are not hopelessly undermined. We shall be guilty of a grave crime if we do not get this righted immediately.

In catering to the daily needs of [humans] we too often grossly neglect the cultural side, the delicate creations in word, song and colour in which the dreams of mankind find expression. The Conference must realize its responsibility in fostering creative work. It can encourage women artists and introduce them to the public. It can place their writings with publishers, articles with editors, it can organize concerts and exhibitions and help playwrights produce their plays. This would help release floods of creative streams and direct them into useful channels, thereby enriching the cultural wealth of our country, a wealth which can only be measured by the happiness it brings to them that give and them that receive.

Two happenings affecting women have considerably agitated the public mind—the re-employment of women in mines and the Bills emerging from the deliberations of the Rau Committee and now before the Central Assembly.[3] The former, an act perpetrated in violation of an international agreement and intense national feeling, has raised such a storm of protest both in India and abroad as to bear ample testimony to its unpopularity. The Government arguments that no compulsion is applied and that wages have been increased, have no reality. Poverty drives people to any risks. The very fact that three

3. This is a reference to the reforms of Hindu personal laws recommended by a committee headed by the civil servant B. N. Rau. The reforms, aimed at greatly enhancing the rights of Hindu women, came into operation a decade later, in the mid-1950s.

annas a day is paid for surface work as against eight annas[4] underground is explanation enough. The wage even after this grand increase is about Rs. 15 [per month], while the average in other industries in the neighbourhood is around Rs. 25 to 30. In addition, the general conditions are very bad, housing deplorable and inadequate. Although the agitation against this measure has been considerable, it has not been effective, and none of us can rest while it continues. The Women's Conference, if it is to prove an effective instrument for safeguarding women's interests, must get women out of the mines as speedily as possible.

All progressive elements in India have long dreamed of the establishment of a common national legal code, operating irrespective of caste or creed. It is as a step towards this that we welcome the codification of the Hindu Law under-taken by the Rau Committee, and not as an end in itself. I hope this attempt will fructify in the near future and give us the entire codification as a com-plete picture, instead of in bits and pieces which so easily lend themselves to distortion when isolated from the whole. The Conference has supported the Intestate Succession Bill in spite of its inadequate nature, because it seeks to give recognition to the principle of women's right. It is regrettable that in the Marriage Bill the barriers of caste and gotra which have lost most of their sig-nificance in modern society, have not been overcome. The clause on monog-amy is welcome though it would not serve the purpose without certain other changes which are envisaged. The Women's Conference, along with other liberal sections of society has always stood for the institution of marriage. The strong allegiance of women to this institution hardly needs reiteration, for it is proverbial. . . . But all societies including the Hindu, have recognized the need for modification, in its legal attitudes. Laws have had to change from time to time under changing conditions. Those who seek relaxation of a rigid marriage law or of a law that makes difference between the sexes in dispensing justice, do not do so on flimsy grounds but on a deep respect for and understanding of the function of law which is to enable harmonious liv-ing. Where it becomes a social injustice, the need for an adjustment has to be recognized by society as imperative. . . .

Our insular peninsular outline has widened into the global, with an in-creasing awareness that we and the rest of the world are but part of a single

4. A rupee then contained sixteen annas.

sphere, that our destinies are inevitably linked, our paths interlocked. Therefore, world policies and events are as much our concern as our affairs, their responsibilities. War as much as peace reveals that the world cannot be divided into islands of freedom and slavery, that the present system of one people holding another down by armed might, no matter with what smooth explanations, leads ultimately to world enslavement by fear and violence, and to colossal human, material and moral destruction. Just as national freedom is but an extension of social freedom the Conference is fighting for, the establishment of the same principle all the world over is of equal interest to us. Until this present system is not only outlawed in principle but abolished in practice, all talk of peace and freedom becomes transitory and meaningless. For peace is not to be achieved by armed victories or by refusing to bear arms, but by the removal of the root causes: imperialism and colonial exploitation that menace peace. Today we witness the fantastic spectacle of big world-powers claiming to fight for the larger freedom and greater happiness of mankind feeling no sense of shame or humiliation in denying those very principles to millions of the people they still continue to exploit and dominate over.

It is not idle curiosity or cheap sentiment which shapes the question that haunts and harasses every diplomat like a family ghost: 'What about India?' We may well say 'Everything', for while England continues to hold India in political and economic bondage, the [Allied] Nations do nothing short of perpetrating a colossal lie on humanity. India is more than a test, it is a symbol. It is the mirror in which the world sees the shape of things to be. Today we are witnessing the fantastic spectacle of two warring groups [i.e., the Allied and the Axis powers], each assiduously claiming to fight for the larger freedom and greater happiness of mankind. It is towards a world which recognizes the right of every nation to determine and rule its own destiny but in a co-operative world order, that the women of India and of the world have to strive for, if humanity is ever to enjoy decency, peace and happiness, and world wars banished from amongst our seasonal pests.

Before closing, I should like to send my thoughts to those millions all over the world whose homes have been gripped by the plight of death and destruction, and whose spirits are lacerated by untold suffering, and offer them sincerest sympathies. In particular, my thoughts turn to the distressed areas within our own homeland and I take this opportunity to pay my humble tribute to the various organizations, volunteer corps and individuals who are so selflessly serving to alleviate suffering. I should like in particular to congratulate our Bengal branch for its splendid work in this terrible distress.[5]

The air is heavy with gloom, the sky rent with cries of pain. Civil liberties, one of the main planks of the Conference, are under perpetual assault. Shadows of suspicion and insincerity deepen and lengthen, blacking out those neon lights mankind had succeeded in lighting through the ages, a growing disregard for the common courtesies and human decencies and a ruthless flouting of popular feeling make a mockery of life. The continued detention of our valued and irreplaceable leaders and comrades[6] who alone at the helm could transform the scene from despair to hope and weave order out of chaos, often dulls our spirit and stays our hand. But this very tragedy should in truth galvanise us into greater and mightier action, for our responsibility becomes doubly greater. There are some who turn to post-war reconstruction as an escape from the terrors of the present. Others believe that in large-scale industrialization lies the cure. Those who have faith in these patent pills have only to glance at some of the highly industrialized countries to note the havoc wrought out of priceless natural resources and marvelous technical opportunities. Hunger, unemployment, slums, human degradation, all bear eloquent testimony to this tragedy. It is not enough to produce more. It is more important to determine its basis and the principles that will guide the distribution; in short, who controls and directs the economy. We cannot surely subscribe to a system in which many produce but few enjoy the benefit, in which artificial scarcity is created by arbitrarily denying men the right to produce, and destroying natural wealth.

Women can have real freedom only in a society which will uphold the sanctity of life and the dignity of labour, a society which will give every child the fullest opportunities for development, enforce and practise those fundamental economic and social rights that entitle every individual to a decent life, the fruits of his or her labour, and the benefits of science and culture. To achieve this the Women's Conference should ally itself with all the progressive forces in the country and develop a vital identity with other oppressed sections of

5. In 1943 there had been a serious famine in Bengal, in which several million died as a result of starvation.

6. This refers to the fact that many congressmen who had participated in the Quit India movement of 1942 were still in prison.

the society to pull its full weight on the side of progress in order to overcome reaction. Thus alone can it meet the present challenge and play an accredited role in the national regeneration of the country.

✦   ✦   ✦

A SOCIALIST VIEW OF THE COMMUNAL QUESTION

The next excerpt presents a socialist's view of the growing divide be-tween Hindus and Muslims in the 1940s. It argues that the solution to the conflict lay not in a separate Muslim homeland but in a model of economic growth that focused on the elimination of poverty.[7]

✦   ✦   ✦

The larger communal tangle or triangle as it has also been called, is not a natural, political, or social phenomenon in this country. It is a device con-ceived and carried out by British imperialism to maintain itself in security in this vast land. As a matter of fact any of India's major problems can only be posed and appraised against her colonial background—that is her retarded economy. Had India been able to industrialise in the course of her normal economic evolution, the fuel for the current raging conflagration could never have been provided. The real communal problem has under its thin veneer of religiosity a stark economic core.

Let us glance back at history. With the destruction of Indian indigenous industries, the [colonial] Government's vast secretariat became the only job-offering agency. . . . In the period immediately following the 1857 Indian War of Independence, the British definitely encouraged the Hindu element to sup-ply the large army of clerical staff that it needed. This meant a rapid re-orientation of the Hindu community by the swift creation of the nucleus of the present Indian middle-class. The impact of the new English education and its influence on those who resorted to it, too, was swift and far-reaching. The newly growing middle-class, faced with even a more rapidly growing scarcity

7. From a speech to the Provincial Socialist Convention, Mangalore, April 1947, reprinted in Kamaledevi [Chattopadhyay], *At the Crossroads,* ed. Yusuf Meherally (Bombay: The National Information and Publications Ltd., 1947), pp. 90–99.

of jobs, now cut off from the old rural and feudalized occupations, had . . . to turn to modern business and, where possible, industry.

The Muslims, who at the very start got left behind in this race, . . . remained tied to their ancient feudal moorings a longer time. As the new middle-class which, thanks to the nature of the early British policy was predominantly Hindu, began from the early twentieth century to form the spearhead of the nationalist revolt, the British decided to reverse their old policy and now court the Muslims instead. . . . So communal electorates, communal ratios in services, etc., were introduced for this purpose.

As greater and greater frustrations overtook the Hindu middle-class with rising unemployment facing its educated youth, and as the budding industrialists kept forever coming up against the British commercial interests, the discontentment commenced flowing into the national tide from all sides swelling it into a mighty flood. In this context the communal problem began to show up its political character more and more. Under a retarded national economy, opportunities were few and the rush on those few terrific. The British who had created the situation, now used it to pit one community against the other, ever widening the gulf between the two. But the logical national march towards freedom could not be arrested. The anti-British sentiment spread like wild-fire and the Muslim masses were soon caught in it too.

As the progressive and radical forces gather strength, proportionately the elements of reaction too muster strength to beat back the new challenge. In different countries it assumes different guises. But the commonest and most feasible is that of religion or of race. It would perhaps be more correct to say perversions of both. We have seen in recent years how in spite of the vast strides made by science and its dispassionate pursuit by objective minds, the very findings of anthropology and ethnology are perverted to reinforce brutal reactionary forces as in the case of the Nazi rule; the oppression of the coloured peoples in Asia and Africa; the discrimination against negroes in America and the Harijans in India; the widespread anti-Sem[i]tism in Europe. . . .

Often these are availed of by a third interested party in order to bolster itself up. The British in India have all along played that role, putting community against community, religious groups against religious groups through bribery, favouritism, distribution of patronage and the like, successfully cutting across that gigantic national unity wrought by the 1857 revolution. In course of time these were followed by constitutional procedures to perpetuate fur-

ther the growing cleavages, such as the introduction of communal electorates, communal composition of legislatures, communal ratios in appointment
to offices, admission to educational and other institutions, sanctioning of
grants; and a host of such equally unhealthy practices. . . .

It is against this background that the role of the Muslim League gets clear,
for ironically it was on [the] very anti-British and intense patriotic feeling of
the Muslims and not on any religious sop, that the concept of Pakistan was
founded. The Muslims wanted freedom as passionately as the Hindus. Mohamed Ali Jinnah was going to get it for them; only he told them that he
wanted them to be free from not merely the British oppressors but the even
worse Hindu exploiters. Here like Hitler who used the weapon of Aryan purity
and anti-Sem[i]tism to drive his people to frenzy, Jinnah used his clever idiom
of a 'Muslim nation' as the driving force. The Muslim masses were economically and socially too backward and too ignorant to understand the true nature of the many problems that weighed them down. . . . For Mr. Jinnah had
realized only too well that the rising mass discontent could only be met by
some concrete political factor, however distorted or perverted it be, and not
mere empty religious shibboleths.

It is very important for us to remember that Pakistan has been raised on the
hunger of the Muslim masses for freedom. At the same time Jinnah has been
able to rally and keep tied to the League the younger intellectuals and the other
growing middle-classes by getting Government favours, offices, posts distributed to them and preventing thereby their joining the nationalist movement.

The League has no record of any constructive work for the amelioration of
the Muslim masses. The League ministries[8] can take no credit for any such
special services. The rule of the League has been to aid the British directly or
indirectly to enable them to continue their stranglehold and stall the freedom
movement through deliberate obstruction of the nationalist tide. It is in the
very nature of the League, constituted as its leadership is, of big vested interests, that it cannot serve the Indian masses, be they Hindus or Muslims. Had
the Congress from the earliest days countered this by courageously pursuing
an economic programme for the masses and identified itself completely with
the peasantry as against the landlords, it would have effectively undermined
the League's efforts at disruption and the two-nation theory would have failed

8. The Muslim League had been in power in provinces such as Sind and Bengal.

to find the soil in which to implant its poisonous stem. Unfortunately, the Congress failed to follow any such scientific line and the Muslim masses fell a prey to medievalism—fanatical, irrational religious fervour that can have never any reality in their day-to-day struggle.

The Hindu section on the other hand, partly through ignorance but more so because of the frustration caused partly by the absence of any positive programme of mass contact and social reconstruction work and partly by the acute tension produced by the long delay in the attainment of power due to Britain's reluctance to part with power, plunged deeper and more recklessly into a similar abyss of fanatical passions, unable and too ill-equipped to face the logic of a rapidly changing situation. It has however sought refuge in a demagogic past. It tries to cover the complex present with the veil of a vague past, tinting the harsh realities with illusive shades and the gross angles with sentimental contours, conjuring up in short by-gone ghosts to lend heroics to commonplace sentiments. Unfortunately as the aggressiveness of the Muslim League has advanced, proportionately has the lure of this Hindu mirage deepened, ensnaring in its meshes raw immature minds who, thwarted by an overpowering present, fill the imagination with past achievements, which at least for the fleeting moment give them a sense of security. This is how Nazism raised itself on the ruins of a prostrate Germany, feeding young and old alike on the rosy illusion of an all-conquering Aryan race. The Indian youth[,] which is rapidly falling victim to similar antics, must beware of its dangers. India can neither save itself nor solve its problems by donning the faded armour of memories, however glorious they be. The menace of the present cannot be met by a reorientation to the past. Rather is it a bold and courageous reckoning up of the existing conditions and their appraisal which alone can steer us along the proper path.

The crux of the modern world problem is its illogical economic system. . . . A society so blatantly based on violence and exploitation where the majority is unable to secure in spite of its hard industry, even bare minimum subsistence, and denied normal opportunities for cultivating its talents or giving expression to its creative urge, is the common enemy of [all] irrespective of caste, creed or religion. Similarly poverty is not the monopoly of any one particular community. It is common to all exploited people. For the exploiting elements, the landlords and capitalists are also distributed amongst every community. The exploitation of the masses by the vested interests is common to all sections. A Hindu landlord is no kinder to a Hindu kisan [peasant] than a Muslim landlord to a

Muslim kisan; nor does a Hindu or a Muslim employer pay any higher wages to his workers simply because they belong to his community. . . . Employers demand the same hard hours of labour from their employees quite irrespective of the latters' caste, creed or community. The Hindu landlords of Bihar have exploited their Hindu tenants even as the Muslim landlords of Sind have exploited their Muslim tenants. The class character is not altered or modified by religious or cultural factors—and that is really the inherent weakness of a communal movement. It can only thrive on the ignorance of the masses and must collapse before socially aware, understanding minds. Neither the Muslim nor the Hindu businessmen had any compunction in making fortunes out of the Bengal famine that destroyed millions of Muslims and Hindus alike. For when famine comes it laps up all communities like a hungry flame. The Muslims of Bengal died like flies in spite of a Muslim Ministry in power. . . .

Unreal issues are therefore raised to divert the growing consciousness of the masses into futile channels and by this deflection dissipate their mounting strength. The 'Two-Nation' theory so ardently pressed by the League is meant therefore to confuse the Muslim masses and camouflage the real social issues. These people are led into believing that all their miseries spring from only one source, a Hindu-dominated country, and if only they could get 'their territory' separated from the Hindu tyranny, all their troubles would instantly disappear. In the absence of any real political or economic education, they are inclined to swallow this sop and lend themselves to working up frenzied agitations in support of what is known as Pakistan. . . .

The incitement to organized violence through mass frenzy by a reactionary leadership, marks a significant phase in our political history—as always and everywhere it has sought to camouflage its real character under the guise of religion. The Christian crusader fought no more for the Christian holy land than do the Muslim masses for their sacred Pakistan. As the challenge of a growing, conscious people becomes more pronounced, its assertive qualities more determined, the traditional citadels of economic and social power must strive to deal the rising new order a death blow. The core of all religious wars has been economic and political domination. If religion be faith, then it is outside its very nature to lend itself to fratricidal orgies. For faith is a stream that springs from within and is neither protected nor destroyed from without. The very act of coercion is a complete negation of all that religion has stood for or meant emotionally for people. . . .

It is obvious that the waves of violence which are rocking the country cannot be abated by either hitting back with greater violence or by a mere appeal to cold reason. The old order has been set adrift from its old moorings. We have now to fall back with greater earnestness and effort on all the available social and cultural material out of which more positive structures can be raised, and new avenues cut which time and patience can convert into abiding channels like new veins in a system through which continued streams of creative and invigorating activities can be made to flow until the organism heaves up anew and functions as a normal, healthy mechanism. Every nerve must be bent to foster scientific thinking and rational analysis through every resource available, administrative or public or private. Activities of a national character must be encouraged on a nation-wide basis with all the emphasis on its universal character, especially so with organisations of the masses which must be converted from their present local units coloured aggressively by the emotions of local environments into large national bodies with national objectives. Very intensive education of the masses must be undertaken where the conflagration has not spread, and the real nature of their political and social problems explained. . . .

History, reason and commonsense are with us. For the very violence is but the sign of desperation; it shows the gathering pressure of social forces which can neither be abated nor overcome. The fact also remains that the basic economic problem of India, even as its political problem, is one and indivisible. The measures that can solve poverty and ignorance in one province, can solve them in another. The class that oppresses one section of the community can also oppress another. Religion, community nor even caste identity is a safeguard against class exploitation, much less artificial frontiers. Neither the Muslim landlords of Sind nor the Muslim capitalists of Bengal will cease to exploit the Muslim masses the moment Pakistan walls them off from 'Hindu' India. But it is when these Muslim masses peep over that wall apprehensively and shyly and see what is happening on the other side that they will determine whether the wall is to continue to stand or go. The onus of that responsibility rests on us. . . . There are not two nations—there are only two forces, those that create and those that destroy—the former have a future, the latter none. . . .

+   +   +

13

THE RENEWED AGENDAS OF

M. K. GANDHI

THE NINETY VOLUMES OF the *Collected Works of Mahatma Gandhi* run chronologically from the 1880s to the 1940s. On many subjects, a later statement of Gandhi appears to diverge from or even contradict an earlier statement. Gandhi himself urged that in these cases the reader should take his most recent pronouncement as reflecting his correct view of the question.

As noted in the prologue to this book, Gandhi was rare among modern politicians in his readiness to engage in argument and in his willingness to change or modify his opinions in the light of criticism. His critics were sometimes fanatics and cranks, whose angry and abusive letters were often reprinted in his journals *Young India* and *Harijan*, alongside Gandhi's good-tempered replies. At other times these critics were thinkers and actors of more substance. These too he responded to, at greater length, and perhaps more substantively.

This chapter presents Gandhi's considered views on three important subjects—nationalism, caste, and Hindu-Muslim relations. Here, he is responding to criticisms we have encountered in previous chapters. We end with two short statements which outline Gandhi's hopes for a free India.

RE-VISITING NATIONALISM

In this first excerpt, Gandhi responds to Rabindranath Tagore's worry, printed in Chapter 8, that non-co-operation would foster an unreasoning hostility against the foreigner and foreign culture.[1]

✦   ✦   ✦

The Poet of Asia, as Lord Hardinge[2] called Dr. Tagore, is fast becoming, if he has not already become, the Poet of the world. Increasing prestige has brought to him increasing responsibility. His greatest service to India must be his poetic interpretation of India's message to the world. The Poet is, therefore, sincerely anxious that India should deliver no false or feeble message in her name. He is naturally jealous of his country's reputation. He says he has striven hard to find himself in tune with the present movement. He confesses that he is baffled. He can find nothing for his lyre in the din and the bustle of Non-cooperation. In three forceful letters, he has endeavoured to give expression to his misgivings, and he has come to the conclusion that Non-cooperation is not dignified enough for the India of his vision, that it is a doctrine of negation and despair. He fears that it is a doctrine of separation, exclusiveness, narrowness and negation.

No Indian can feel anything but pride in the Poet's exquisite jealousy of India's honour. It is good that he should have sent to us his misgivings in language at once beautiful and clear.

In all humility, I shall endeavour to answer the Poet's doubts. I may fail to convince him or the reader who may have been touched by his eloquence, but I would like to assure him and India that Non-cooperation in conception is not any of the things he fears, and he need have no cause to be ashamed of his country for having adopted Non-cooperation. If, in actual application, it appears in the end to have failed, it will be no more the fault of the doctrine, than it would be of Truth, if those who claim to apply it in practice do not appear to succeed. Non-cooperation may have come in advance of its time. In-

---

1. 'The Poet's Anxiety', *Young India*, 1 June 1921, as reproduced in K. Swaminathan, ed., *The Collected Works of Mahatma Gandhi* (New Delhi: Publications Division, 1958 [hereafter *CWMG*]), vol. 20, pp. 161–164.

2. A former Viceroy of India.

dia and the world must then wait, but there is no choice for India save between violence and Non-cooperation.

Nor need the Poet fear that Non-cooperation is intended to erect a Chinese wall between India and the West. On the contrary, Non-cooperation is intended to pave the way to real, honourable and voluntary co-operation based on mutual respect and trust. The present struggle is being waged against compulsory co-operation, against one-sided combination, against the armed imposition of modern methods of exploitation, masquerading under the name of civilization.

Non-cooperation is a protest against an unwitting and unwilling participation in evil.

The Poet's concern is largely about the students. He is of the opinion that they should not have been called upon to give up Government schools before they had other schools to go to. Here I must differ from him. I have never been able to make a fetish of literary training. My experience has proved to my satisfaction that literary training by itself adds not an inch to one's moral height and that character-building is independent of literary training. I am firmly of [the] opinion that the Government schools have unmanned us; rendered us helpless and Godless. They have filled us with discontent, and providing no remedy for the discontent, have made us despondent. They have made us what we were intended to become—clerks and interpreters. A Government builds its prestige upon the apparently voluntary association of the governed. And if it was wrong to cooperate with the Government in keeping us slaves, we were bound to begin with those institutions in which our association appeared to be most voluntary. The youth of a nation are its hope. I hold that, as soon as we discovered that the system of Government was wholly, or mainly evil, it became sinful for us to associate our children with it. . . .

I, therefore, think that the Poet has been unnecessarily alarmed at the negative aspect of Non-cooperation. We had lost the power of saying 'no'. It had become disloyal, almost sacrilegious to say 'no' to the Government. This deliberate refusal to co-operate is like the necessary weeding process that a cultivator has to resort before he sows. Weeding is as necessary to agriculture as sowing. Indeed, even whilst the crops are growing, the weeding fork, as every husbandman knows, is an instrument almost of daily use. The nation's Non-cooperation is an invitation to the Government to co-operate with it on its own terms as is every nation's right and every good government's duty. Non-cooperation is the nation's notice that it is no longer satisfied to be in tutelage. The nation had taken to the harmless (for it) natural and religious doctrine of Non-cooperation in the place of the unnatural and irreligious doctrine of violence. And if India is ever to attain the *swaraj* of the Poet's dream, she will do so only by Non-violent Non-cooperation. Let him deliver his message of peace of the world, and feel confident that India, through her Non-cooperation, if she remains true to her pledge, will have exemplified his message. Non-cooperation is intended to give the very meaning to patriotism that the Poet is yearning after. An India prostrate at the feet of Europe can give no hope to humanity. An India awakened and free has a message of peace and goodwill to a groaning world. Non-cooperation is designed to supply her with a platform from which she will preach the message.

✦ ✦ ✦

RE-VISTING CASTE

In Chapter 9 we printed excerpts from a pamphlet by B. R. Ambedkar called 'The Annihilation of Caste'. Ambedkar's frontal attack on the organizing principles of Hindu society prompted a rejoiner by Gandhi, which he printed in his journal, *Harijan*. Ambedkar's indictment, thought Gandhi, was a challenge to Hindus to put their house in order.[3]

✦ ✦ ✦

. . . Dr Ambedkar was to have presided last May at the annual conference of the Jat-Pat-Torak Mandal of Lahore. But the conference itself was cancelled because Dr. Ambedkar's address was found by the Reception Committee to be unacceptable. How far a Reception Committee is justified in rejecting a President of its choice because of his address that may be objectionable to it is open to question. The Committee know Dr. Ambedkar's views on caste and the Hindu scriptures. They knew also that he had in unequivocal terms decided to give up Hinduism. Nothing less than the address that Dr. Ambedkar

---

3. 'Dr Ambedkar's Indictment', in two parts, *Harijan*, 11 and 18 July 1936, as reproduced in *CWMG*, vol. 63, pp. 134–136, 153–154.

had prepared was to be expected from him. The Committee appears to have deprived the public of an opportunity of listening to the original views of a man who has carved out for himself a unique position in society. Whatever label he wears in future, Dr. Ambedkar is not the man to allow himself to be forgotten.

Dr. Ambedkar was not going to be beaten by the Reception Committee. He has answered their rejection of him by publishing the address at his own expense. . . .

No reformer can ignore the address. The orthodox will gain by reading it. This is not to say that the address is not open to objection. It has to be read if only because it is open to serious objection. Dr. Ambedkar is a challenge to Hinduism. Brought up as a Hindu, educated by a Hindu potentate, he has become so disgusted with the so-called *savarna* Hindus for the treatment that he and his have received at their hands that he proposes to leave not only them but the very religion that is his and their common heritage. He has transferred to that religion his disgust against a part of its professors.

But this is not to be wondered at. After all one can only judge a system or an institution by the conduct of its representatives. What is more, Dr. Ambedkar found that the vast majority of *savarna* [upper caste] Hindus had not only conducted themselves inhumanly against those of their fellow religionists whom they classed as untouchables, but they had based their conduct on the authority of their scriptures, and when he began to search them he had found ample warrant for their belief in untouchability and all its implications. The author of the address has quoted chapter and verse in proof of his threefold indictment—inhuman conduct itself, the unabashed justification for it on the part of the perpetrators, and the subsequent discovery that the justification was warranted by their scriptures.

No Hindu who prizes his faith above life itself can afford to underrate the importance of this indictment. Dr. Ambedkar is not alone in his disgust. He is its most uncompromising exponent and one of the ablest among them. He is certainly the most irreconcilable among them. Thank God, in the front rank of the leaders he is singularly alone and as yet but a representative of a very small minority. But what he says is voiced with more or less vehemence by many leaders belonging to the depressed classes. Only the latter, for instance Rao Bahadur M. C. Rajah and Dewan Bahadur Srinivasan, not only do not threaten to give up Hinduism but find enough warmth in it to compensate for the shameful persecution to which the vast mass of Harijans are exposed.

But the fact of many leaders remaining in the Hindu fold is no warrant for disregarding what Dr. Ambedkar has to say. The *savarnas* have to correct their belief and their conduct. Above all, those who are by their learning and influence among the *savarnas* have to give an authoritative interpretation of the scriptures. The questions that Dr. Ambedkar's indictment suggests are:

1. What are the scriptures?
2. Are all the printed texts to be regarded as an integral part of them or is any part of them to be rejected as unauthorized interpolations?
3. What is the answer of such accepted and expurgated scriptures on the question of untouchability, caste, equality of status, inter-dining and intermarriages?

. . . The Vedas, Upanishads, *Smritis* and Puranas including *Ramayana* and *Mahabharata* are the Hindu scriptures. Nor is this a finite list. Every age or even generation has added to the list. It follows, therefore, that everything printed or even found handwritten is not scripture. The *Smritis,* for instance, contain much that can never be accepted as the word of God. Thus many of the texts that Dr. Ambedkar quotes from the *Smritis* cannot be accepted as authentic. The scriptures properly so called can only be concerned with eternal verities and must appeal to any conscience, i.e., any heart whose eyes of understanding are opened. Nothing can be accepted as the word of God which cannot be tested by reason or is not capable of being spiritually experienced. And even when you have an expurgated edition of the scriptures, you will need their interpretation. Who is the best interpreter? Not learned men surely. Learning there must be. But religion does not live by it. It lives in the experiences of its saints and seers, in their lives and sayings. When all the most learned commentators of the scriptures are utterly forgotten, the accumulated experience of the sages and saints will abide and be an inspiration for ages to come.

Caste has nothing to do with religion. It is a custom whose origin I do not know and do not need to know for the satisfaction of my spiritual hunger. But I do know that it is harmful both to spiritual and national growth. . . . The law of varna[4] teaches us that we have each one of us to earn our bread by following the ancestral calling. It defines not our rights but our duties. It necessarily has reference to callings that are conducive to the welfare of humanity and to no other. It also follows that there is no calling too low and none too high. All are good, lawful, and absolutely equal in status. The callings of a Brahmin—spiritual teacher—and a scavenger are equal, and their due performance carries equal merit before God and at one time seems to have carried identical reward before man. Both were entitled to their livelihood and no more. Indeed one traces even now in the villages the faint lines of this healthy operation of the law. Living in Segaon with its population of 600, I do not find a great disparity between the earnings of different tradesmen including Brahmins. I find too that real Brahmins are to be found even in these degenerate days who are living on alms freely given to them and are giving freely of what they have of spiritual treasures. It would be wrong and improper to judge the law of varna by its caricature in the lives of men who profess to belong to a varna whilst they openly commit a breach of its only operative rule. Arrogation of a superior status by any of the varnas over another is a denial of the law. And there is nothing in the law of varna to warrant a belief in untouchability. (The essence of Hinduism is contained in its enunciation of one and only God as Truth and its bold acceptance of ahimsa [non-violence] as the law of the human family.)

I am aware that my interpretation of Hinduism will be disputed by many besides Dr. Ambedkar. That does not affect my position. It is an interpretation by which I have lived for nearly half a century and according to which I have endeavoured to the best of my ability to regulate my life.

In my opinion the profound mistake that Dr. Ambedkar has made in his address is to pick out the texts of doubtful authenticity and value and the state of degraded Hindus who are no fit specimens of the faith they so woefully misrepresent. Judged by the standard applied by Dr. Ambedkar, every known living faith will probably fail.

In his able address, the learned Doctor has over-proved his case. Can a religion that was professed by Chaitanya, Jnanadeya, Tukaram, Tiruvalluvar, Ramakrishna Paramahamsa, Raja Ram Mohan Roy, Maharshi Devendranath

---

4. Varna is the classical four-fold division of Hindu society into Brahmins (priests), Kshatriyas (warriors), Vaishyas (merchants), and Shudras (peasants and labourers).

Tagore, Vivekanand and a host of others who might be easily mentioned, be so utterly devoid of merit as is made out in Dr. Ambedkar's address? A religion has to be judged not by its worst specimens but by the best it might have produced. For that and that alone can be used as the standard to aspire to, if not to improve upon.

*   *   *

Chapter 9 also excerpted a sharp personal attack on Gandhi by Ambedkar, written in 1945. Gandhi did not reply to the book, but the excerpt below demonstrates that he had taken aboard Ambedkar's criticisms. In the 1920s Gandhi said that while untouchability must go, the injunctions against inter-dining and inter-marriage could stay. By the 1940s, as suggested below, he had abandoned these positions.[5]

*   *   *

A friend from Patidar Ashram, Surat, writes to Shri Narhari Parikh[6]:

'If Harijan girls are to marry Caste Hindus it should be on condition that the couple will devote their lives to the service of the Harijans. . . . If Caste Hindu girls live amongst Harijans as Harijans, Harijan sisters will be able to learn a lot from them'.

If an educated Harijan girl marries a Caste Hindu the couple ought to devote themselves to the service of Harijans. Self-indulgence can never be the object of such a marriage. That will be improper. I can never encourage it. It is possible that a marriage entered into with the best of intentions turns out to be a failure. No one can prevent such mishaps. Even if one Harijan girl marries a Caste Hindu with a high character it will do good to both the Harijans and Caste Hindus. They will set up a good precedent and if the Harijan girl is really worthy, she will spread her fragrance far and wide and encourage others to copy her example. Society will cease to be scared by such marriages. They will see for themselves that there is nothing wrong in them. If children born of such a union turn out to be good, they will further help to remove untouchability. Every reform moves at the proverbial snail's pace. To be dissatisfied with this slowness of progress betrays ignorance of the way in which reform works.

5. From *Harijan*, 7 July 1946, as reproduced in *CWMG*, vol. 84, pp. 388–389.
6. A close and long-time associate of Gandhi, based in Gujarat.

It is certainly desirable that Caste Hindu girls should select Harijan husbands. I hesitate to say that it is better. That would imply that women are inferior to men. I know that such inferiority complex is there today. For this reason I would agree that at present the marriage of a Caste Hindu girl to a Harijan is better than that of a Harijan girl to a Caste Hindu. If I had my way I would persuade all Caste Hindu girls coming under my influence to select Harijan husbands. That it is most difficult I know from experience. Old prejudices are difficult to shed. One cannot afford to laugh at such prejudices either. They have to be overcome with patience. And if a girl imagines that her duty ends by marrying a Harijan and falls a prey to the temptation of self-indulgence after marriage, the last state would be worse than the first. The final test of every marriage is how far it develops the spirit of service in the parties. Every mixed marriage will tend in varying degrees to remove the stigma attached to such marriages. Finally there will be one caste, known by the beautiful name Bhangi, that is to say, the reformer or remover of all dirt. Let us all pray that such a happy day will dawn soon.

The correspondent must realize that even the best of my wishes cannot come true on the mere expression. I have not succeeded in marrying off a single Harijan girl to a Caste Hindu so far after my declaration. I have a Caste Hindu girl who at her father's wish has offered to marry a Harijan lad of her father's selection. The lad is at present under training at Sevagram. God willing, the marriage will take place after a short time.

✦ ✦ ✦

RE-VISITING HINDU-MUSLIM CO-OPERATION

In Chapter 10 we printed several speeches made by M. A. Jinnah, who argued that the Congress was biased against Muslims and that Hindus and Muslims could not peaceably live together in a single nation. Gandhi sought to rebut these criticisms in a speech on the eve of the Quit India Movement, delivered to a meeting of the All India Congress Committee. The speech is excerpted below.[7]

7. Reproduced in *CWMG*, vol. 76, pp. 385–391.

✦   ✦   ✦

Hindu-Muslim unity is not a new thing. Millions of Hindus and Mussalmans have sought after it. I consciously strove for its achievement from my boyhood. While at school, I made it a point to cultivate the friendship of Muslim and Parsi fellow students. I believed even at that tender age that the Hindus in India, if they wished to live in peace and amity with the other communities, should assiduously cultivate the virtue of neighbourliness. It did not matter, I felt, if I made no special effort to cultivate the friendship with Hindus, but I must make friends with at least a few Mussalmans. It was as counsel for a Mussalman merchant that I went to South Africa. I made friends with other Mussalmans there, even with the opponents of my clients, and gained a reputation for integrity and good faith. I had among my friends and co-workers Muslims as well as Parsis. I captured their hearts and when I left finally for India, I left them sad and shedding tears of grief at the separation.

In India, too, I continued my efforts and left no stone unturned to achieve that unity. It was my life-long aspiration for it that made me offer my fullest co-operation to the Mussalmans in the Khilafat movement. Muslims throughout the country accepted me as their true friend. . . .

In those days I shocked the Hindus by dining with the Mussalmans, though with the passage of time they have now got used to it. Maulana Bari[8] told me, however, that though he would insist on having me as his guest, he would not allow me to dine with him, lest some day he should be accused of a sinister motive. And so, whenever I had occasion to stay with him, he called a Brahmin cook and made special arrangements for separate cooking. Firangi Mahal, his residence, was an old-styled structure with limited accommodation; yet he cheerfully bore all hardships and carried out his resolve from which I could not dislodge him. It was the spirit of courtesy, dignity and nobility that inspired us in those days. The members of each community vied with one another in accommodating members of sister communities. They respected one another's religious feelings, and considered it a privilege to do so. Not a trace of suspicion lurked in anybody's heart. Where has all that dignity, that nobility of spirit, disappeared now? I should ask all Mussalmans, including Qaid-

8. A famous Muslim scholar from Lucknow, who had worked with Gandhi in the 1920s.

e-Azam Jinnah,[9] to recall those glorious days and to find out what has brought us to the present impasse. Qaid-e-Azam Jinnah himself was at one time a Congressman. If today the Congress has incurred his wrath, it is because the canker of suspicion has entered his heart. May God bless him with long life, but when I am gone, he will realize and admit that I had no designs on Mussalmans and that I had never betrayed their interests. Where is the escape for me if I injure their cause or betray their interests? My life is entirely at their disposal. They are free to put an end to it, whenever they wish to do so. Assaults have been made on my life in the past, but God has spared me till now, and the assailants have repented for their action. But if someone were to shoot me in the belief that he was getting rid of a rascal, he would kill not the real Gandhi, but the one that appeared to him a rascal.

To those who have been indulging in a campaign of abuse and vilification I would say, 'Islam enjoins you not to revile even an enemy. The Prophet treated even enemies with kindness and tried to win them over by his fairness and generosity. Are you followers of that Islam or of any other? If you are followers of the true Islam, does it behove you to distrust the words of one who makes a public declaration of his faith? You may take it from me that one day you will regret the fact that you distrusted and killed one who was a true and devoted friend of yours'. It cuts me to the quick to see that the more I appeal . . . the more intense does the campaign of vilification grow. To me, these abuses are like bullets. They can kill me, even as a bullet can put an end to my life. You may kill me. That will not hurt me. But what of those who indulge in abusing? They bring discredit to Islam. For the fair name of Islam, I appeal to you to resist this unceasing campaign of abuse and vilification.

Maulana Saheb[10] is being made a target for the filthiest abuse. Why? Because he refuses to exert on me the pressure of his friendship. He realizes that it is a misuse of friendship to seek to compel a friend to accept as truth what he knows is an untruth.

To the Qaid-e-Azam I would say: 'Whatever is true and valid in the claim for Pakistan is already in your hands. What is wrong and untenable is in nobody's gift, so that it can be made over to you. Even if someone were to succeed in

9. Jinnah was known to his followers as Qaid-e-Azam (The Great Leader).

10. This is Maulana Abul Kalam Azad, then the most prominent Muslim in the Congress.

imposing an untruth on others, he would not be able to enjoy for long the fruits of such coercion. God dislikes pride and keeps away from it. God would not tolerate a forcible imposition of an untruth'.

The Qaid-e-Azam says that he is compelled to say bitter things but that he cannot help giving expression to his thoughts and his feelings. Similarly I would say: I consider myself a friend of the Mussalmans. Why should I then not give expression to the things nearest to my heart, even at the cost of displeasing them? How can I conceal my innermost thoughts from them? I should congratulate the Qaid-e-Azam on his frankness in giving expression to his thoughts and feelings, even if they sound bitter to his hearers. But even so why should the Mussalmans sitting here be reviled, if they do not see eye to eye with him? If millions of Mussalmans are with you, can you not afford to ignore the handful of Mussalmans who may appear to you to be misguided? Why should one with the following of several millions be afraid of a majority community, or of the minority being swamped by the majority? How did the Prophet work among the Arabs and the Mussalmans? How did he propagate Islam? Did he say he would propagate Islam only when he commanded a majority? I, therefore, appeal to you for the sake of Islam to ponder over what I say. There is neither fair play nor justice in saying that the Congress must accept a thing even if it does not believe in it and even if it goes counter to principles it holds dear. . . .

The Congress has no sanction but the moral one for enforcing its decisions. It believes that true democracy can only be the outcome of non-violence. The structure of a world federation can be raised only on a foundation of non-violence, and violence will have to be totally abjured from world affairs. If this is true, the solution of the Hindu-Muslim question, too, cannot be achieved by resort to violence. If the Hindus tyrannize over the Mussalmans, with what face will they talk of a world federation? It is for the same reason that I do not believe in the possibility of establishing world peace through violence as the English and American statesmen propose to do. The Congress has agreed to submitting all the differences to an impartial international tribunal and to abide by its decisions. If even this fairest of proposals is unacceptable, the only course that remains open is that of the sword, of violence. How can I persuade myself to agree to an impossibility? To demand the vivisection of a living organism is to ask for its very life. It is a call to war. The Congress cannot be party to such a fratricidal war. Those Hindus who, like

Dr. Moonje and Shri Savarkar,[11] believe in the doctrine of the sword may seek to keep the Mussalmans under Hindu domination. I do not represent that section. I represent the Congress. You want to kill the Congress which is the goose that lays golden eggs. If you distrust the Congress, you may rest assured that there is to be a perpetual war between the Hindus and the Mussalmans, and the country will be doomed to continue warfare and bloodshed. If such warfare is to be our lot, I shall not live to witness it. . . .

India is without doubt the homeland of all the Mussalmans inhabiting this country. Every Mussalman should therefore cooperate in the fight for India's freedom. The Congress does not belong to any one class or community; it belongs to the whole nation. It is open to Mussalmans to take possession of the Congress. They can, if they like, swamp the Congress by their numbers, and can steer it along the course which appeals to them. The Congress is fighting not on behalf of the Hindus but on behalf of the whole nation, including the minorities. It would hurt me to hear of a single instance of a Mussalman being killed by a Congressman. In the coming revolution, Congressmen will sacrifice their lives in order to protect the Mussalman against a Hindu's attack and *vice versa*. It is a part of our creed, and is one of the essentials of non-violence. You will be expected on occasions like these not to lose your heads. Every Congressman, whether a Hindu or a Mussalman, owes this duty to the organization to which he belongs. The Mussalman who will act in this manner will render a service to Islam. Mutual trust is essential for success in the final nation-wide struggle that is to come.

+ + +

In the end, Gandhi's attempts to forge a common political front of Hindus and Muslims failed. The Muslim League was successful in creating a separate state of Pakistan. This, however, was achieved at the cost of bloody riots between Hindus and Muslims across large parts of north and east India. After Partition, millions of Muslims chose to stay behind in India. In these excerpts from a speech to the All India Congress Committee (A. I. C. C.) on 15 November 1947, Gandhi urges his party

11. B. S. Moonjee and V. D. Savarkar were leaders of the Hindu Mahasabha, a right-wing party that believed that India was (or should be) a state for Hindus only.

colleagues to ensure that Muslims in India were granted the rights of equal citizenship.[12]

* * *

I have come in your midst today. I came to Delhi not to stay for long, but since my arrival many things have happened which should not have happened. And so I have had to prolong my stay here instead of proceeding to the Punjab. This explains my presence in your midst today.

I had made a vow to do or die. When the occasion comes I shall indeed either do or die. I have seen enough to realize that though not all of us have gone mad, a sufficiently large number have lost their heads. What is responsible for this wave of insanity? Whatever the cause, it is obvious to me that if we do not cure ourselves of this insanity, we shall lose the freedom we have won. You must understand and recognize the gravity of the plight we are in. Under the shadow of this impending misfortune the A. I. C. C. has met today. You have to face very serious problems and apply your minds to them.

There is the General Body of the Congress which meets once every year, but it is more or less demonstrative in character. The real Congress is the All-India Congress Committee, in whose keeping is the honour of the Congress. It is for you to give a lead to the Congress and to see that it functions effectively and without any disruption within its ranks. That is why I want you to be true to the basic character of the Congress and make Hindus and Muslims one, for which ideal the Congress has worked for more than sixty years. This ideal still persists. The Congress had never maintained that it worked for the interest of the Hindus only. Must we now give up what we have claimed ever since the Congress was born and sing a different tune? Congress is of Indians, of all those who inhabit this land, whether they are Hindus, Muslims, Christians, Sikhs or Parsis. There have been Muslims, Christians and Parsis as Presidents of the Congress. But today we hear a different cry. Let me tell you that what we hear today is not the voice of the Congress.

You represent the vast ocean of Indian humanity. You will not allow it to be said that the Congress consists of a handful of people who rule the country. At least I will not allow it. I am an Indian to the last. Ever since I returned from South Africa I have tried to serve the Congress in every way and have done

12. Reproduced in *CWMG*, vol. 90, pp. 37–42.

nothing else. I have tried to understand Indians from different walks of life, have lived with them, eaten with them and loved them. I have seen no difference between Harijans and other Hindus. That is how I am made.

The Congress is held responsible for whatever happens today. The situation has changed since August 15.[13] I am leaving out of consideration what happened before that date. I do not wish to hear what part you played in the events that have happened since August 15. I have not the right to sit here. I have much work to do outside this hall. That is why I had requested that I might be allowed to have my say and then take your leave. You might ask me any questions you like at the end of my speech, though there ought to be no necessity for such questions. I wish only to show you a little of the way so that you might find it easier to carry on your deliberations.

When we were fighting for our freedom, we bore a heavy responsibility, but today when we have achieved freedom, our responsibility has grown a hundred-fold. What is happening today? Though it is not true of the whole of India, yet there are many places today where a Muslim cannot live in security. There are miscreants who will kill him or throw him out of a running train for no reason other than that he is a Muslim. There are several such instances. I will not be satisfied with your saying that there was no help for it or that you had no part in it. We cannot absolve ourselves of our responsibility for what has happened. I have to fight against this insanity and find out a cure for it. I know and I confess that I have not yet found it.

I am ashamed of what is happening today; such things should never happen in India. We have to recognize that India does not belong to Hindus alone, nor does Pakistan to Muslims. I have always held that if Pakistan belongs to Muslims alone, then it is a sin which will destroy Islam. Islam has never taught this. It will never work if Hindus as Hindus claim to be a separate nation in India and Muslims in Pakistan. The Sikhs too have now and again talked of a Sikhistan. If we indulge in these claims, both India and Pakistan will be destroyed, the Congress will be destroyed and we shall all be destroyed.

I maintain that India belongs both to Hindus and Muslims. You may blame the Muslim League for what has happened and say that the two-nation theory is at the root of all this evil and that it was the Muslim League that sowed the

13. This refers to 15 August 1947, the day of the Partition and Independence of India.

seed of this poison; nevertheless I say that we would be betraying the Hindu religion if we did evil because others had done it. Ever since my childhood I have known that Hinduism teaches us to return good for evil. The wicked sink under the weight of their own evil. Must we also sink with them? My own experience of sixty years has confirmed what Hinduism has taught me and my study of other religions has revealed the same thing. Islam too says the same thing. It is the basic creed of the Congress that India is the home of Muslims no less than of Hindus. . . .

It is held by some that if we perpetrate worse atrocities on Muslims here than what have been perpetrated on Hindus and Sikhs in Pakistan, it will teach the Muslims in Pakistan a salutary lesson. They will indeed be taught a lesson, but what will happen to you in the mean while? You say that you will not allow Muslims to stay in India, but I hold it to be an impossibility to drive away three-and-a-half crores[14] of them to Pakistan. What crime have they committed? The Muslim League indeed is culpable, but not every Muslim. If you think that they are all traitors and fifth-columnists, then shoot them down by all means, but to assume that they are all criminals because they are Muslims is wrong. If you bully them, beat them, threaten them, what can they do but run away to Pakistan? After all, life is dear to them. But it is unworthy of you to treat them so. Thereby you will degrade the Congress, degrade your religion and degrade the nation.

If you realize this, then it is your duty to recall all those Muslims who have been obliged to flee to Pakistan. Of course those of them who believe in Pakistan and wish to seek their happiness there are welcome to migrate. For them there is no bar. They will not need military protection to escort them. They go of their own will and at their own expense. But those who are leaving today have to be provided with special transport and special protection. Such unnatural exodus under artificial conditions must cause us shame. You should declare that those Muslims who have been obliged to leave their homes and wish to return are welcome in your midst. You should assure them that they and their religion will be safe in India. This is your duty, this is your religion. You must be humane and civilized, irrespective of what Pakistan does. If you do what is right Pakistan will sooner or later be obliged to follow suit.

14. One crore is 10 million.

As things are we cannot hold our heads high in the world today and have to confess that we have been obliged to copy Pakistan in its misdeeds and have thereby justified its ways. How can we go on like this? What is happening is a provocation to war on both sides and must inevitably lead to it. You will then have to part company with [Prime Minister] Jawaharlal [Nehru]. And yet it is because of him that we are held in high esteem in the world today. He is respected outside India as one of the world's greatest statesmen. Many Europeans have told me that the world has not known such a high-minded statesman. I have known Americans who hold Jawaharlal in higher esteem than they hold President Truman. Even those who have fabulous wealth, vast armies and the atom bomb respect the moral worth of Jawaharlal's leadership. We in India ought to have due appreciation for it.

I repeat to you that it is your prime duty to treat Muslims as your brothers, whatever may happen in Pakistan. We will not return blow for blow but will meet it with silence and restraint. Restraint will add to your strength. But if you copy what happens in Pakistan, then on what moral basis will you take your stand? What becomes of your non-violence? If you approve of what has happened, then you must change the very creed and character of the All-India Congress Committee. This is the basic issue before you. Until you have faced it, you cannot solve any of the problems that are before you. When your house is on fire you must first put out the flames before you can do anything else. That is why I have taken so much of your time. Let all Muslims who have left their homes and fled to Pakistan come back here. India is big enough to keep them as well as the Hindu and Sikh refugees who have fled from Pakistan. What I wish to emphasize to you is that if you maintain the civilized way, whatever Pakistan may do now, sooner or later, she will be obliged by the pressure of world opinion to conform. Then war will not be necessary and you will not have to empty your exchequer. . . .

✦   ✦   ✦

Continuing on the theme of Hindu-Muslim harmony in independent India, here are excerpts from a talk by Gandhi at a prayer meeting in New Delhi on 7 December 1947. He spoke in Hindi—the translation is by the editorial team of the *Collected Works of Mahatma Gandhi*.[15]

15. Reproduced in *CWMG*, vol. 90, pp. 191–194.

✦ ✦ ✦

BROTHERS AND SISTERS,

Today I wish to talk to you about a very complicated matter, which is also rather sensitive. It has appeared in the newspapers. You will have seen that yesterday some Hindu women workers went to Lahore and met some Muslim women there. They discussed the question of what ought to be done about the Hindu women abducted by Muslims in Pakistan and the Muslim women abducted by Hindus and Sikhs in East Punjab. A very large number of Muslims have already left India and it is possible some more may yet leave. We should now resolve that not a single Muslim will be compelled to leave. If they voluntarily opt for Pakistan that is a different matter. But the fact is that no one wants voluntarily to leave India. Why should anyone want to give up one's house and property? It is not as if they had houses and properties waiting for them in Pakistan. Those voluntarily opting for Pakistan or going for the sake of jobs are very few, which is natural because there are not enough jobs for them in Pakistan. And if their established businesses in India are not affected, there is no reason for them to go.

But what of the women? This is a complicated question. Some say that about 12,000 women had been abducted by Hindus and Sikhs and twice that number had been abducted by Muslims in Pakistan. Some others say that this estimate is too low. I would say 12,000 is not a small number. Why, a thousand, or even one, is not a small number. Why should even a single woman be abducted? It is barbaric for a Hindu woman to be abducted by a Muslim or a Muslim woman to be abducted by a Hindu or a Sikh. Some people believe that 12,000 represents a very conservative figure. Let us say that 12,000 women had been abducted by Muslims of Pakistan and another 12,000 women had been abducted by Hindus and Sikhs of East Punjab. The problem is how to recover them. The women workers had been to Pakistan to consider how to solve this problem. The Hindu and Sikh women carried away by force should be restored to their families. Similarly the Muslim women taken away should be restored to theirs. This task should not be left to the families of the women. It should be our charge. . . .

We have become barbarous in our behavior. It is true of East Punjab as well as of West Punjab. It is meaningless to ask which of them is more barbaric. Barbarity has no degrees. . . . It is not necessary to ask who has been more guilty. Atrocities have taken place on a mass scale and it is irrelevant who took the first step. The need is for women who have been abducted and harassed to be taken back to their homes. It is my belief that the police cannot do this. The army cannot do this. Yes, a team of women workers could be sent to East Punjab and another team to West Punjab but I do not think that would be effective. I can say as a man of experience that this is not the way to do this work. This is a task for the Governments to tackle. I am not saying that the Governments were behind the abductions. It was not the Government of East Punjab which organized abductions. In East Punjab Hindus and Sikhs were responsible for them and in West Punjab Muslims were responsible. What further investigation is required? Whatever the number—I put it at 12,000 at least—East Punjab and West Punjab should return them.

It is being said that the families of the abducted women no longer want to receive them back. It would be a barbarian husband or a barbarian parent who would say that he would not take back his wife or daughter. I do not think the women concerned had done anything wrong. They had been subjected to violence. To put a blot on them and to say that they are no longer fit to be accepted in society is unjust. At least this does not happen among Muslims. At least Islam is liberal in this respect, so this is a matter that the Governments should take up. The Governments should trace all these women. They should be traced and restored to their families. The police and women social workers cannot effectively deal with this. The problem is difficult, which means to say that public opinion is not favourable. You cannot say that all the 12,000 women were abducted by ruffians. I do not think that is the case. It is good men that have become ruffians. People are not born as goondas; they become so under certain circumstances. Both the Governments had been weak in this respect. Neither Government has shown enough strength to recover the abducted women. Had both the Governments exercised authority, what happened in East Punjab and West Punjab would not have happened. But our independence was born only three months ago. It is still in its infancy.

In my view Pakistan is responsible for spreading this poison. But what good can come from apportioning responsibility? There is only one way of saving these women and that is that the Governments should even now wake up to their responsibility, give this task the first priority and all their time and accomplish it even at the cost of their lives. Only thus can these women be rescued. Of course we should help the Government if it requires help. . . .

✦ ✦ ✦

VILLAGE RENEWAL AND POLITICAL DECENTRALISATION

Gandhi and Karl Marx resemble one another in only two respects— that each has had a deep and enduring influence, and that neither left behind any real blueprint for the just society they envisaged and worked for. Marx's idea of a future communist society is contained only in a few pages of his 'Critique of the Gotha Programme', whereas Gandhi's vision of a free India is manifest only in passing thoughts here and there. For example, when the Congress came to power in several provinces of British India in 1937, Gandhi offered these reflections on his ideal village.[16]

✦ ✦ ✦

'A Humble Villager of Birbhum' living in Santiniketan sends me through Deenabandhu Andrews[17] the following questions:

1. What is an ideal Indian village in your esteemed opinion and how far is it practicable to reconstruct a village on the basis of an 'Ideal Village' in the present social and political situation of India?
2. Which of the village problems should a worker try to solve first of all and how should he proceed?
3. What should be the special theme of village exhibitions and museums in a miniature form? How should such exhibitions be best utilized for the reconstruction of villages?

1. An ideal Indian village will be so constructed as to lend itself to perfect sanitation. It will have cottages with sufficient light and ventilation built

16. From *Harijan*, 9 January 1937, reproduced in *CWMG*, vol. 64, pp. 217–218.

17. C. F. Andrews, an English priest and writer, an intimate friend of Gandhi's (and Tagore's), and a long-time supporter of freedom for India, was known affectionately as 'Deenbandhu' (friend of the poor).

of a material obtainable within a radius of five miles of it. The cottages will have courtyards enabling householders to plant vegetables for domestic use and to house their cattle. The village lanes and streets will be free of all avoidable dust. It will have wells according to its needs and accessible to all. It will have houses of worship for all; also a common meeting place, a village common for grazing its cattle, a co-operative dairy, primary and secondary schools in which industrial education will be the central fact, and it will have panchayats [village councils] for settling disputes. It will produce its own grains, vegetables and fruits, and its own khadi [home-spun cloth]. This is roughly my idea of a model village. In the present circumstances its cottages will remain what they are with slight improvements. Given a good zamindar [landlord], where there is one, or co-operation among the people, almost the whole of the programme other than model cottages can be worked out at an expenditure within the means of the villagers including the zamindar or zamindars, without Government assistance. With that assistance there is no limit to the possibility of village reconstruction. But my task just now is to discover what the villagers can do to help themselves if they have mutual co-operation and contribute voluntary labour for the common good. I am convinced that they can, under intelligent guidance, double the village income as distinguished from individual income. There are in our villages inexhaustible resources not for commercial purposes in every case but certainly for local purposes in almost every case. The greatest tragedy is the hopeless unwillingness of the villagers to better their lot.

2. The very first problem the village worker will solve is its sanitation. It is the most neglected of all the problems that baffle workers and that undermine physical well-being and breed disease. If the worker became a voluntary Bhangi [sweeper], he would begin by collecting night-soil and turning it into manure and sweeping village streets. He will tell people how and where they should perform daily functions and speak to them on the value of sanitation and the great injury caused by the neglect. The worker will continue to do the work whether the villagers listen to him or no.

3. The spinning-wheel should be the central theme of all such village exhibitions and the industries suited to the particular locality should revolve round it. An exhibition thus arranged would naturally become an

object-lesson for the villagers and an educational treat when it is accomplished by demonstrations, lectures and leaflets.

✦   ✦   ✦

In the elections of 1946, Congress Ministries once more came to power in several provinces. The departure of the British was now imminent. In this context, Gandhi outlined in an interview his hopes for the political system of free India.[18]

✦   ✦   ✦

Q. You have said in your article in the *Harijan* of July 15, under the caption 'The Real Danger', that Congressmen in general certainly do not know the kind of independence they want. Would you kindly give them a broad but comprehensive picture of the Independent India of your own conception?

A. I do not know that I have not, from time to time, given my idea of Indian independence. Since, however, this question is part of a series, it is better to answer it even at the risk of repetition.

Independence of India should mean independence of the whole of India, including what is called India of the States and the other foreign powers, French and Portuguese, who are there, I presume, by British sufferance. Independence must mean that of the people of India, not of those who are today ruling over them. The rulers should depend on the will of those who are under their heels. Thus, they have to be servants of the people, ready to do their will.

Independence must begin at the bottom. Thus, every village will be a republic or *panchayat* having full powers. It follows, therefore, that every village has to be self-sustained and capable of managing its affairs even to the extent of defending itself against the whole world. It will be trained and prepared to perish in the attempt to defend itself against any onslaught from without. Thus, ultimately, it is the individual who is the unit. This does not exclude dependence on and willing help from neighbours or from the world. It will be free and voluntary play of mutual forces. Such a society is necessarily highly cultured in which every man and woman knows what he or she wants

18. From *Harijan*, 28 July 1946, as reproduced in *CWMG*, vol. 85, pp. 32–34.

and, what is more, knows that no one should want anything that others cannot have with equal labour. . . .

In this structure composed of innumerable villages, there will be ever-widening, never-ascending circles. Life will not be a pyramid with the apex sustained by the bottom. But it will be an oceanic circle whose centre will be the individual always ready to perish for the village, the latter ready to perish for the circle of villages, till at last the whole becomes one life composed of individuals, never aggressive in their arrogance but ever humble, sharing the majesty of the oceanic circle of which they are integral units.

Therefore the outermost circumference will not wield power to crush the inner circle but will give strength to all within and derive its own strength from it. I may be taunted with the retort that this is all Utopian and, therefore, not worth a single thought. If Euclid's point, though incapable of being drawn by human agency, has an imperishable value, my picture has its own for mankind to live. Let India live for this true picture, though never realizable in its completeness. We must have a proper picture of what we want, before we can have something approaching it. If there ever is to be a republic of every village in India, then I claim verity for my picture in which the last is equal to the first or, in other words, no one is to be the first and none the last.

In this picture every religion has its full and equal place. We are all leaves of a majestic tree whose trunk cannot be shaken off its roots which are deep down in the bowels of the earth. The mightiest wind cannot move it.

In this there is no room for machines that would displace human labour and that would concentrate power in a few hands. Labour has its unique place in a cultured human family. Every machine that helps every individual has a place. But I must confess that I have never sat down to think out what that machine can be. . . .

Q. Do you believe that the proposed Constituent Assembly[19] could be used for the realization of your picture?

A. The Constituent Assembly has all the possibilities for the realization of my picture. Yet I cannot hope for much, not because the State Paper holds no

19. It had been announced that an Assembly, representing the widest possible spectrum of Indian opinion, would be convened to frame a Constitution for free India.

such possibilities but because the document, being wholly of a voluntary nature, requires the common consent of the many parties to it. These have no common goal. Congressmen themselves are not of one mind even on the contents of Independence. I do not know how many swear by non-violence or the charkha [spinning-wheel] or, believing in decentralization, regard the village as the nucleus. I know on the contrary that many would have India become a first-class military power and wish for India to have a strong centre and build the whole structure round it. In the medley of these conflicts I know that if India is to be [a] leader in clean action based on clean thought, God will confound the wisdom of these big men and will provide the villages with the power to express themselves as they should.

Q. If the Constituent Assembly fizzles out because of the 'danger from within', as you have remarked in the above-mentioned article, would you advise the Congress to accept the alternative of general country-wide strike and capture of power, either non-violently or with the use of necessary force? What is your alternative in that eventuality if the above is not approved by you?

A. I must not contemplate darkness before it stares me in the face. And in no case can I be a party, irrespective of non-violence, to a universal strike and capture of power. Though, therefore, I do not know what I should do in the case of a breakdown, I know that the actuality will find me ready with an alternative. My sole reliance being on the living Power which we call God. He will put the alternative in my hands when the time has come, not a minute sooner.

✦　✦　✦

PART FOUR

DEBATING DEMOCRACY

INTRODUCTION TO PART IV

PERHAPS NO NEW NATION WAS BORN in more difficult circumstances than India. When the British finally relinquished control over the sub-continent, they left behind not one new nation but two—India and Pakistan, the latter created as a homeland for the Muslim minority. Independence and Partition had been accompanied by massive religious rioting, which claimed more than a million lives. The Government of India had to contend with the anger and desperation of some 8 million refugees who had fled across the border from East and West Pakistan. Their discontent threatened to unleash a fresh wave of violence between Hindus and Sikhs on the one hand and the Muslims who had chosen to stay behind in India on the other.

An equally portentous problem was that of the princely states. The British had controlled some two-thirds of the sub-continent directly, the rest being divided into more than five hundred chiefdoms and principalities whose rulers owed allegiance to the King-Emperor in London but were largely free to govern as they pleased. In the 1930s, an All India States Peoples Conference (AISPC) promoted by the Congress sought to involve the subjects of these chiefdoms in the nationalist struggle. The princes themselves they disparaged as reactionary feudals. Now, however, they had to be persuaded—or coerced—to join the new nation, a process that was to take more than two years.

The refugees had to be placated and the princely states integrated. Beyond these immediate concerns, a larger future for the new nation had to be designed. Between December 1946 and November 1949 some 200 individuals served as elected members of the Constituent Assembly of India, and collectively they designed a democratic Constitution which guaranteed freedom of speech, association, and worship; enshrined special privileges for disadvantaged social groups such as those of low castes and tribals; identified the respective powers of the Centre and the States; and adopted a parliamentary system of governance based on universal adult franchise.

In 1946, the year the Constituent Assembly was convened in New Delhi, a group of Americans designed the Japanese Constitution. In 1949, when the Assembly concluded its deliberations, a Communist Party led by Mao Zedong established control over China. The new political system of India was thus in marked contrast to that adopted by these other Asian nations. Unlike the case of Japan, it was chosen and designed by Indians; unlike the case of China, it allowed its citizens to speak their minds freely and to vote for whichever party they pleased. But there was a contrast with the advanced Western democracies as well, namely, that in India the right to elect one's leaders had been granted to all adults in one fell swoop, rather than in stages. That some two-thirds of the electorate was illiterate made the choice even more striking.

Between 15 August 1947, when India acquired Dominion Status within the British Empire, and 26 January 1950, when the Constitution making it a democratic Republic came into operation, the unity of the new nation was sorely tested. There were several serious problems other than that of the refugees and the princely states. In September 1947 an armed conflict broke out with Pakistan over the disputed territory of Kashmir. In March 1948 the Communist Party of India launched an insurrection, hoping to capture power on the Chinese model and instal a one-party state. There was discontent in the north-eastern borderlands, with a large section of Nagas and Manipuris unwilling to join the Indian Union.

It was against this background of dissent and discord that India held its first general elections in January-February 1952. Polls were held simultaneously to the national Parliament and to the various State Assemblies. A variety of parties contested, some regionally based, others with national ambitions. (Among them were the Communists who had laid down arms and accepted the Constitution.) The party of the freedom struggle, the Indian National Congress, was elected to power with a comfortable majority. But it still faced major challenges—including the forging of an economic policy that could lift the masses out of poverty; and the forging of a foreign policy that could assert India's place in a world increasingly defined by the rivalry between the United States and the Soviet Union.

Many observers—not all of them cynical Westerners—had thought that India's first general elections would be its last. They did not think that democracy could take root in an illiterate and hierarchical society. Surely it would give way soon to rule by a strongman or, at the least, by a strong, centralized institution such as the Indian Army. Other commentators were sceptical of the ability of India to stay together as a single nation. They thought it would balkanize again, perhaps after a bloody civil war based this time on language rather than religion; or that it would return to the pattern of pre-colonial India, with the Government in Delhi controlling territory within a radius of a few hundred miles (at best), with the more far-flung areas slowly seceding to form a series of independent nations or kingdoms.

The fears were to be falsified. The General Elections of 1952 were followed by nation-wide polls in 1957 and 1962. Elections to the State Assemblies were also held regularly. The processes of democracy were consolidated and upheld by an independent judiciary and a free press. At the same time, despite discontent in the borderlands, national unity was also maintained. The writ of the central government ran over the whole of India.

Through the 1950s and 1960s the specific contours of democracy and national unity were intensely debated in all parts of the country. The Congress won successive general elections but had still to answer its critics on left and right who were represented in Parliament. It also met strong opposition in the states themselves; not least in the southernmost state of Kerala, where Congress dominance was successfully challenged first by the socialists and then by the communists. Apart from this political opposition, individuals and groups within civil society were also vocal in their criticisms of the policies of the Congress government.

This part of the book features the major debates on politics and social policy that took place in the first decades of Indian independence. These arguments covered a wide range of topics, including the ideals and institutions of democracy; the relations between different religious communities; the respective roles of the state and private enterprise in promoting economic development; India's place in the world; the place of the English language in India; the honourable integration within the nation-state of small ethnic minorities; and more.

The range of topics discussed in the pages that follow is commensurate with the scale of the enterprise, namely, the building of a single, united, nation out of so many disparate fragments; the nurturing of a democratic ethos in a poor and divided society; the promotion of industrial development in an agrarian economy; and the safeguarding of national honour and dignity in an increasingly polarized international climate. I think that the quality of the interlocutors is worthy of note too. As in other parts of the book, these makers of modern India combine subtlety of argument with intensity of expression—the first marking them out as original political thinkers, the second as focused political actors. There may be one exception to this characterisation, which I shall leave to the reader to identify, only remarking here that what this particular 'maker' lost by way of intellectual sophistication, he perhaps made up by way of social and political influence.

14

THE WISE DEMOCRAT

B. R. AMBEDKAR

As we have seen in Chapter 9, B. R. Ambedkar had been a bitter critic of Gandhi and the Congress. Remarkably, despite twenty years of intense personal and political rivalry, when India became independent Ambedkar was offered the job of law minister in the Union Cabinet. This was an extraordinary act of reconciliation, for which Gandhi seems to have been personally responsible. It is said that he told the pre-eminent Congress leaders, Jawaharlal Nehru and Vallabhbhai Patel, that freedom had come not to a single party but to all of India. In this spirit the first Cabinet also included representatives of the Akali Dal and the Justice Party, who had likewise previously opposed the Congress.

To facilitate Ambedkar's entry into the Cabinet, the Congress elected him to the Constituent Assembly of India from a safe seat in Bombay. As law minister, he was made chairman of the committee formed to draft the Indian Constitution. As the thirteen volumes of the proceedings of the Assembly demonstrate, Ambedkar handled criticism with tact and authority. He also made some quite brilliant speeches on the significance of the Constitution for the future of democracy.

Apart from piloting the Constitution of India through a sometimes fractious Assembly, Ambedkar made one other important contribution as law minister. This was to oversee the drafting of a new law that would, for the first time, allow Hindu women to choose their marriage partners, to divorce them if necessary, and to inherit a fair share of ancestral property. These reforms only came into effect after Ambedkar resigned from the Cabinet in 1951. But he was their principal architect, as he was of the Constitution itself.

THE INDIAN CONSTITUTION DEFENDED AND INTERPRETED

We print excerpts of two important speeches made by Ambedkar to the Constituent Assembly of India. The first introduced the draft of the Constitution and outlined the meanings of 'constitutional morality'.[1]

✦ ✦ ✦

. . . One likes to ask whether there can be anything new in a Constitution framed at this hour in the history of the world. More than [one] hundred years have rolled over when the first written Constitution was drafted. It has been followed by many countries reducing their Constitutions to writing. What the scope of a Constitution should be has long been settled. Similarly what are the fundamentals of a Constitution are recognized all over the world. Given these facts, all Constitutions in their main provinces must look similar. The only new things, if there can be any, in a Constitution framed so late in the day are the variations made to remove the faults and to accommodate it to the needs of the country. The charge of producing a blind copy of the Constitutions of other countries is based, I am sure, on an inadequate study of the Constitution. I have shown what is new in the Draft Constitution and I am sure that those who have studied other Constitutions and who are prepared to consider the matter dispassionately will agree that the Drafting Committee in

1. Speech in Constituent Assembly on 4 November 1948, as reproduced in *Constituent Assembly Debates: Official Report,* vol. 7 (reprint, New Delhi: Lok Sabha Secretariat, 1988), pp. 31–44.

performing its duty has not been guilty of such blind and slavish imitation as it is represented to be.

As to the accusation that the Draft Constitution has produced a good part of the provisions of the Government of India Act, 1935, I make no apologies. There is nothing to be ashamed of in borrowing. It involves no plagiarism. Nobody holds my patent rights in the fundamental ideas of a Constitution. What I am sorry about is that the provisions taken from the Government of India Act, 1935, relate mostly to the details of administration. I agree that administrative details should have no place in the Constitution. I wish very much that the Drafting Committee could see its way to avoid their inclusion in the Constitution. But this is to be said on the necessity which justifies their inclusion. Grote, the historian of Greece, has said that:

'The diffusion of constitutional morality, not merely among the majority of any community but throughout the whole, is the indispensable condition of government at once free and peaceable; since even any powerful and obstinate minority may render the working of a free institution impracticable, without being strong enough to conquer ascendency for themselves.'

By constitutional morality Grote meant 'a paramount reverence for the forms of the Constitution, enforcing obedience to authority acting under and within these forms yet combined with the habit of open speech, of action subject only to definite legal control, and unrestrained censure of those very authorities as to all their public acts combined too with a perfect confidence in the bosom of every citizen amidst the bitterness of party contest that the forms of the Constitution will not be less sacred in the eyes of his opponents than in his own.' *(Hear, hear.)*

While everybody recognizes the necessity of the diffusion of Constitutional morality for the peaceful working of a democratic Constitution, there are two things interconnected with it which are not, unfortunately, generally recognized. One is that the form of administration has a close connection with the form of the Constitution. The form of the administration must be appropriate to and in the same sense as the form of the Constitution. The other is that it is perfectly possible to pervert the Constitution, without changing its form by merely changing the form of the administration and to make it inconsistent and opposed to the spirit of the Constitution. It follows that it is only where people are saturated with Constitutional morality such as the one described by Grote the historian that one can take the risk of omitting from the Constitution details of administration and leaving it for the Legislature to prescribe them. The question is, can we presume such a diffusion of Constitutional morality? Constitutional morality is not a natural sentiment. It has to be cultivated. We must realize that our people have yet to learn it. Democracy in India is only a top-dressing on an Indian soil, which is essentially undemocratic.

In these circumstances it is wiser not to trust the Legislature to prescribe forms of administration. This is the justification for incorporating them in the Constitution.

Another criticism against the Draft Constitution is that no part of it represents the ancient polity of India. It is said that the new Constitution should have been drafted on the ancient Hindu model of a State and that instead of incorporating Western theories the new Constitution should have been raised and built upon village Panchayats and District Panchayats.[2] There are others who have taken a more extreme view. They do not want any Central or Provincial Governments. They just want India to contain so many village Governments. The love of the intellectual Indians for the village community is of course infinite if not pathetic *(laughter)*. It is largely due to the fulsome praise bestowed upon it by Metcalfe[3] who described them as little republics having nearly everything that they want within themselves, and almost independent of any foreign relations. The existence of these village communities each one forming a separate little State in itself has according to Metcalfe contributed more than any other cause to the preservation of the people of India, through all the revolutions and changes which they have suffered, and is in a high degree conducive to their happiness and to the enjoyment of a great portion of the freedom and independence. No doubt the village communities do not care to consider what little part they have played in the affairs and the des-

2. A panchayat was a council of elders (usually upper-caste, always male), which had traditionally exercised authority in Indian villages.

3. C. T. Metcalfe was an influential colonial administrator of the early nineteenth century, who had served as governor of Agra, lieutenant-governor of the north-western provinces, and acting Governor-General of India.

tiny of the country; and why? Their part in the destiny of the country has been well described by Metcalfe himself who says:

'Dynasty after dynasty tumbles down. Revolution succeeds to revolution. Hindoo, Pathan, Mogul, Maratha, Sikh, English are all masters in turn but the village communities remain the same. In times of trouble they arm and fortify themselves. A hostile army passes through the country. The village communities collect their little cattle within their walls, and let the enemy pass unprovoked.'

Such is the part the village communities have played in the history of their country. Knowing this, what pride can one feel in them? That they have survived through all vicissitudes may be a fact. But mere survival has no value. The question is on what plane they have survived. Surely on a low, on a selfish level. I hold that these village republics have been the ruination of India. I am therefore surprised that those who condemn Provincialism and Communalism should come forward as champions of the village. What is the village but a sink of localism, a den of ignorance, narrow-mindedness and communalism? I am glad that the Draft Constitution has discarded the village and adopted the individual as its unit. . . .

Some critics have taken objection to the description of India in Article 1 of the Draft Constitution as a Union of [States]. . . . Some critics have said that the Centre is too strong. Others have said that it must be made stronger. The Draft Constitution has struck a balance. However much you may deny powers to the Centre, it is difficult to prevent the Centre from becoming strong. Conditions in [the] modern world are such that centralization of powers is inevitable. One has only to consider the growth of the Federal Government in the U.S.A. which, notwithstanding the very limited powers given to it by the Constitution, has out-grown its former self and has overshadowed and eclipsed the State Governments. This is due to modern conditions. The same conditions are sure to operate on the Government of India and nothing that one can do will help to prevent it from being strong. On the other hand, we must resist the tendency to make it stronger. It cannot chew more than it can digest. Its strength must be commensurate with its weight. It would be a folly to make it so strong that it may fall by its own weight. . . .

The Constitution has been discussed in some of the Provincial Assemblies of India. It was discussed in Bombay, C. P., West Bengal, Bihar, Madras and East Punjab. It is true that in some Provincial Assemblies serious objections were taken to the financial provisions of the constitution. . . . But excepting this, in no Provincial Assembly was any serious objection taken to the Articles of the Constitution. No Constitution is perfect and the Drafting Committee itself is suggesting certain amendments to improve the Draft Constitution. But the debates in the Provincial Assemblies give me courage to say that the Constitution as settled by the Drafting Committee is good enough to make in this country a start with. I feel that it is workable, it is flexible and it is strong enough to hold the country together both in peace time and in war time. Indeed, if I may say so, if things go wrong under the new Constitution, the reason will not be that we had a bad Constitution. What we will have to say is, that Man was vile. Sir, I move.

✦   ✦   ✦

A year after a draft had been introduced and discussed, a final Constitution was agreed upon. In his last speech to the Assembly, Ambedkar offered some prophetic warnings about the course of Indian democracy.[4]

✦   ✦   ✦

. . . The credit that is given to me does not really belong to me. It belongs partly to Sir B. N. Rau, the Constitutional Adviser to the Constituent Assembly who prepared a rough draft of the Constitution for the consideration of the Drafting Committee. A part of the credit must go to the members of the Drafting Committee who, as I have said, have sat for 141 days and without whose ingenuity to devise new formulae and capacity to tolerate and to accommodate different points of view, the task of framing the Constitution could not have come to so successful [a] conclusion. Much greater share of the credit must go to Mr. S. N. Mukherjee, the Chief Draftsman of the Constitution. His ability to put the most intricate proposals in the simplest and clearest legal form can rarely be equaled, nor his capacity for hard work. He has been an acquisition to the Assembly. Without his help, this Assembly would have

4. Speech in Constituent Assembly, 25 November 1949, as reproduced in *Constituent Assembly Debates: Official Report*, vol. 11, pp. 972–981.

taken many more years to finalise the Constitution. I must not omit to mention the members of the staff working under Mr. Mukherjee. For, I know how hard they worked and how long they have toiled sometimes even beyond midnight. I want to thank them all for their effort and their co-operation. *(Cheers.)*

The task of the Drafting Committee would have been a very difficult one if this Constituent Assembly had been merely a motley crowd, a tessellated pavement without cement, a black stone here and a white stone there in which each member or each group was a law unto itself. There would have been nothing but chaos. This possibility of chaos was reduced to nil by the existence of the Congress Party inside the Assembly which brought into its proceedings a sense of order and discipline. It is because of the discipline of the Congress Party that the Drafting Committee was able to pilot the Constitution in the Assembly with the sure knowledge as to the fate of each article and each amendment. The Congress Party is, therefore, entitled to all the credit for the smooth sailing of the Draft Constitution in the Assembly.

The proceedings of this Constituent Assembly would have been very dull if all members had yielded to the rule of party discipline. Party discipline, in all its rigidity, would have converted this Assembly into a gathering of 'yes' men. Fortunately, there were rebels. They were Mr. Kamath, Dr. P. S. Deshmukh, Mr. Sidhva, Prof. Saxena and Pandit Thakur Das Bhargava. Along with them I must mention Prof. K. T. Shah and Pandit Hirday Nath Kunzru. The points they raised were mostly ideological. That I was not prepared to accept their suggestions, does not diminish the value of their suggestions, nor lessen the service they have rendered to the Assembly in enlivening its proceedings. I am grateful to them. But for them, I would not have had the opportunity which I got for expounding the principles underlying the Constitution which was more important than the mere mechanical work of passing the Constitution.

Finally, I must thank you Mr. President[5] for the way in which you have conducted the proceedings of this Assembly. The courtesy and the consideration which you have shown to the Members of the Assembly can never be forgotten by those who have taken part in the proceedings of this Assembly. There were occasions when the amendments of the Drafting Committee were sought

---

5. The president of the Constituent Assembly was the senior Congress leader, Rajendra Prasad.

to be barred on grounds purely technical in their nature. Those were very anxious moments for me. I am, therefore, specially grateful to you for not permitting legalism to defeat the work of Constitution making.

As much defence as could be offered to the Constitution has been offered by my friends Sir Alladi Krishnaswami Ayyar and Mr. T. T. Krishnamachari. I shall not therefore enter into the merits of the Constitution. Because I feel, however good a Constitution may be, it is sure to turn out bad because those who are called to work it, happen to be a bad lot. However, bad a Constitution may be, it may turn out to be good if those who are called to work it, happen to be a good lot. The working of a Constitution does not depend wholly upon the nature of the Constitution. The Constitution can provide only the organs of State such as the Legislature, the executive and the Judiciary. The factors on which the working of those organs of the State depend are the people and the political parties they will set up as their instruments to carry out their wishes and their politics. Who can say how the people of India and their parties will behave? Will they uphold constitutional methods of achieving their purposes or will they prefer revolutionary methods of achieving them? . . .

The condemnation of the Constitution largely comes from two quarters, the Communist Party and the Socialist Party. Why do they condemn the Constitution? Is it because it is really a bad Constitution? I venture to say 'no'. The Communist Party wants a Constitution based upon the principle of the Dictatorship of the Proletariat. They condemn the Constitution because it is based upon parliamentary democracy. The Socialist[s] want two things. The first thing they want is that if they come in[to] power, the Constitution must give them the freedom to nationalize or socialize all private property without payment of compensation. The second thing that the Socialists want is that the Fundamental Rights mentioned in the Constitution must be absolute and without any limitations so that if their Party fails to come into power, they would have the unfettered freedom not merely to criticize, but also to overthrow the State.

These are the main ground[s] on which the Constitution is being condemned. I do not say that the principle of parliamentary democracy is the only ideal form of political democracy. I do not say that the principle of no acquisition of private property without compensation is so sacrosanct that there can be no departure from it. I do not say that Fundamental Rights can never be absolute and the limitations set upon them can never be lifted. What I do say is that the principles embodied in the Constitution are the views of the present generation or if you think this to be an over-statement, I say they are the views of the members of the Constituent Assembly. . . .

If we wish to maintain democracy not merely in form, but also in fact, what must we do? The first thing in my judgment we must do is to hold fast to constitutional methods of achieving our social and economic objectives. It means we must abandon the bloody methods of revolution. It means that we must abandon the method of civil disobedience, non-cooperation and satyagraha. When there was no way left for constitutional methods for achieving economic and social objectives, there was a great deal of justification for unconstitutional methods. But where constitutional methods are open, there can be no justification for these unconstitutional methods. These methods are nothing but the Grammar of Anarchy and the sooner they are abandoned, the better for us.

The second thing we must do is to observe the caution which John Stuart Mill has given to all who are interested in the maintenance of democracy, namely, not 'to lay their liberties at the feet of even a great man, or to trust him with powers which enable him to subvert their institutions'. There is nothing wrong in being grateful to great men who have rendered life-long services to the country. But there are limits to gratefulness. As has been well said by the Irish patriot Daniel O'Connell, no man can be grateful at the cost of his honour, no women can be grateful at the cost of her chastity and no nation can be grateful at the cost of its liberty. This caution is far more necessary in the case of India than in the case of any other country. For in India, Bhakti or what may be called the path of devotion or hero-worship, plays a part in its politics unequalled in magnitude by the part it plays in the politics of any other country in the world. Bhakti in religion may be a road to the salvation of the soul. But in politics, Bhakti or hero-worship is a sure road to degradation and to eventual dictatorship.

The third thing we must do is not to be content with mere political democracy. We must make our political democracy a social democracy as well. Political democracy cannot last unless there lies at the base of it social democracy. What does social democracy mean? It means a way of life which recognizes liberty, equality and fraternity as the principles of life. These principles of liberty, equality and fraternity are not to be treated as separate items in a trinity. They form a union or trinity in the sense that to divorce one from the other is to defeat the very purpose of democracy. Liberty cannot be divorced from equality, equality cannot be divorced from liberty. Nor can liberty and equality be divorced from fraternity. Without equality, liberty would produce the supremacy of the few over the many. Equality without liberty would kill individual initiative. Without fraternity, liberty and equality could not become a natural course of things. It would require a constable to enforce them. We must begin by acknowledging the fact that there is complete absence of two things in Indian society. One of these is equality. On the social plane, we have in India a society based on the principle of graded inequality which means elevation for some and degradation for others. On the economic plane, we have a society in which there are some who have immense wealth as against many who live in abject poverty. On the 26th of January 1950, we are going to enter into a life of contradictions. In politics we will have equality and in social and economic life we will have inequality. In politics we will be recognizing the principle of one man one vote and one vote one value. In our social and economic life, we shall, by reason of our social and economic structure, continue to deny the principle of one man one value. How long shall we continue to live this life of contradictions? How long shall we continue to deny equality in our social and economic life? If we continue to deny it for long, we will do so only by putting our political democracy in peril. We must remove this contradiction at the earliest possible moment or else those who suffer from inequality will blow up the structure of political democracy which this Assembly has so laboriously built up.

The second thing we are wanting in is recognition of the principle of fraternity. What does fraternity mean? Fraternity means a sense of common brotherhood of all Indians—if Indians being one people. It is the principle which gives unity and solidarity to social life. It is a difficult thing to achieve. How difficult it is, can be realized from the story related by James Bryce . . . about the United States of America.

The story is—I propose to recount it in the words of Bryce himself—that—

> 'Some years ago the American Protestant Episcopal Church was occupied at its triennial Convention in revising its liturgy. It was thought desirable to introduce among the short sentence prayers a prayer for the whole people, and an eminent New England divine proposed the words "O Lord, bless our nation". Accepted

one afternoon, on the spur of the moment, the sentence was brought up next day for reconsideration, when so many objections were raised by the laity to the word "nation" as importing too definite a recognition of national unity, that it was dropped, and instead there were adopted the words "O Lord, bless these United States".'

There was so little solidarity in the U.S.A. at the time when this incident occurred that the people of America did not think that they were a nation. If the people of the United States could not feel that they were a nation, how difficult it is for Indians to think that they are a nation. I remember the days when politically-minded Indians resented the expression 'the people of India'. They preferred the expression 'the Indian nation'. I am of opinion that in believing that we are a nation, we are cherishing a great delusion. How can people divided into several thousands of castes be a nation? The sooner we realize that we are not as yet a nation in the social and psychological sense of the word, the better for us. For then only we shall realize the necessity of becoming a nation and seriously think of ways and means of realizing the goal. The realization of this goal is going to be very difficult—far more difficult than it has been in the United States. The United States has no caste problem. In India there are castes. The castes are anti-national. In the first place because they bring about separation in social life. They are anti-national also because they generate jealousy and antipathy between caste and caste. But we must overcome all these difficulties if we wish to become a nation in reality. For fraternity can be a fact only when there is a nation. Without fraternity equality and liberty will be no deeper than coats of paint.

These are my reflections about the tasks that lie ahead of us. They may not be very pleasant to some. But there can be no gainsaying that political power in this country has too long been the monopoly of a few and the many are not only beasts of burden, but also beasts of prey. This monopoly has not merely deprived them of their chance of betterment, it has sapped them of what may be called the significance of life. These down-trodden classes are tired of being governed. They are impatient to govern themselves. This urge for self-realization in the down-trodden classes must not be allowed to devolve into a class struggle or class war. It would lead to a division of the House. That would indeed be a day of disaster. For, as has been well said by Abraham

Lincoln, a House divided against itself cannot stand very long. Therefore the sooner room is made for the realization of their aspiration, the better for the few, the better for the country, the better for the maintenance for its independence and the better for the continuance of its democratic structure. This can only be done by the establishment of equality and fraternity in all spheres of life. That is why I have laid so much stress on them.

I do not wish to weary the House any further. Independence is no doubt a matter of joy. But let us not forget that this independence has thrown on us great responsibilities. By independence, we have lost the excuse of blaming the British for anything going wrong. If hereafter things go wrong, we will have nobody to blame except ourselves. There is great danger of things going wrong. Times are fast changing. People including our own are being moved by new ideologies. They are getting tired of Government by the people. They are prepared to have Government for the people and are indifferent whether it is Government of the people and by the people. If we wish to preserve the Constitution in which we have sought to enshrine the principle of Government of the people, for the people and by the people, let us resolve not to be tardy in the recognition of the evils that lie across our path and which induce people to prefer Government for the people to Government by the people, nor to be weak in our initiative to remove them. That is the only way to serve the country. I know of no better.

✦ ✦ ✦

15

THE MULTIPLE AGENDAS OF

JAWAHARLAL NEHRU

As PRIME MINISTER FOR the first formative years after Independence, Jawaharlal Nehru had a defining impact on the politics and society of his country. In India the 1940s and 1950s were the Age of Nehru, just as the 1920s and 1930s had been the Age of Gandhi. To be sure, Nehru was not as original a thinker as Gandhi. On the other hand, Gandhi never held political office. As head of Government from 1947 to 1964, Nehru had a colossal influence on the directions taken—and not taken—by this new, large, diverse, and very conflicted nation.

Jawaharlal Nehru was born in Allahabad in 1889. His father, Motilal, was a successful and wealthy lawyer who doted on his only son. He was sent to Harrow, which he did not enjoy very much; and to Cambridge, where he developed what was to become a lifelong fascination with modern science. He also qualified as a barrister. Returning home shortly before World War I, he ran a desultory law practice before throwing himself full-time into nationalist politics.

Nehru venerated Gandhi. The older man, in turn, showered more affection on his disciple than on his four biological sons. The two men differed in temperament and attitudes to modernity. Nehru was indifferent to religion, whereas Gandhi believed deeply in his own version of

God. Nehru thought that industrialisation was the only solution to the endemic poverty of India; Gandhi called instead for the renewal of the village economy. Nehru had great faith in the powers of the modern state to uplift and reform society; Gandhi was sceptical of state power, trusting instead to the conscience and will of individuals and communities.

Beyond these differences were some fundamental similarities. Both men were patriots in the most inclusive sense, who identified with all of India, rather than with a particular caste, language, region, or religion. Both abhorred violence and strongly preferred democratic forms of government to dictatorships. It may have been these parallels, as well as Nehru's own independent appeal to the young, that led Gandhi to anoint him his political successor.

In December 1929, having just turned forty, Nehru was elected to the first of four terms as president of the Congress. Through the decade of the 1930s he was the party's voice abroad, taking the message of Indian freedom to not always receptive audiences in the West. In the elections of 1937 and 1946, both held under colonial auspices and under a restricted franchise, he was the chief vote-gatherer for the Congress. When India became independent in August 1947 he was the natural choice for prime minister.

Nehru shared one other attribute with Gandhi—the ability, and desire, to set down his ideas on the printed page. He founded and for a time edited a daily newspaper, the *National Herald,* and wrote often for other Indian and foreign periodicals. He also published three major books: *Glimpses of World History* (1934), *An Autobiography* (1936), and *The Discovery of India* (1946). These books are all extremely well written. They have all been continuously in print since their first publication.

Nehru the writer is known chiefly through his three books. Notably, all were published *before* Indian Independence. They are thus far less pertinent to his statecraft than his writings and speeches after 1947. These, however, are little known. They lie in volumes and anthologies assembled by diverse hands and published under the imprimatur of government departments and trusts who do not know how to deliver their books to a wider audience. (By contrast, *Glimpses, Autobiography,* and *Discovery* were published by astute and aggressive commercial presses in India and abroad—they are currently available under the Penguin Classics imprint.)

Of these obscure writings of Nehru, the most important are his *Letters to Chief Ministers*. Soon after Independence, he inaugurated the practice of writing every fortnight to those in charge of running State Governments. The series ran continuously from October 1947 to December 1963. In the 1980s these letters were published in five fat volumes (each exceeding five hundred pages)—these are long out of print and not easily available in libraries outside Delhi (this editor's own set was assembled, one by one, from various second-hand book dealers).

That these *Letters to Chief Ministers* are so little known is a shame. They cover an astonishing range of subjects. Economic development, linguistic and religious politics, the ethics of governance, the Cold War, the passing of literary giants—Nehru writes about all these subjects, and more, in a tone that is alternatively reflective and exhortative. The letters represent Nehru's attempt to make sense of sixteen tumultuous years in the history of India and the world. They are contemporary history at its best. And, as the excerpts below show, they continue to speak to us today.

Aside from these letters, I have also drawn upon Nehru's speeches, which were more carefully structured and perhaps less evocative. But these too dealt with matters of fundamental importance to the nation that, under Nehru's direction, was being made.

Jawaharlal Nehru died in New Delhi on 27 May 1964.

THE TREATMENT OF MINORITIES

In the aftermath of Partition, Nehru was deeply concerned with the state and place of Muslims in independent India. The creation of Pakistan as a homeland for Muslims, and the subsequent flight of Hindus and Sikhs from that country, had led to a rise of intolerance among certain sections of the Hindus. Nehru, however, insisted that Muslims be treated as equal citizens in a secular state and that they be made to feel safe and secure by the administration of the provinces they lived in. The excerpts on this subject that follow on are all from the prime minister's fortnightly letters to chief ministers.

From a letter dated 15 October 1947:[1]

◆ ◆ ◆

I know there is a certain amount of feeling in the country . . . that the Central Government has somehow or other been weak and following a policy of appeasement towards Muslims. This, of course, is complete nonsense. There is no question of weakness or appeasement. We have a Muslim minority who are so large in numbers that they cannot, even if they want to, go anywhere else. They have got to live in India. That is a basic fact about which there can be no argument. Whatever the provocation from Pakistan and whatever the indignities and horrors inflicted on non-Muslims there, we have got to deal with this minority in a civilized manner. We must give them security and the rights of citizens in a democratic State. If we fail to do so, we shall have a festering sore which will eventually poison the whole body politic and probably destroy it. Moreover, we are now on a severe trial in the international forum. I have it on the authority of our delegates to the U[nited] N[ations] O[rganisation] that the friendliness towards India which existed before the recent tragedy [i.e., Partition] has changed and we are looked upon with distrust and almost with a certain degree of contempt. We cannot afford to ignore this feeling. We are dependent for many things on international goodwill—increasingly so since partition. And pure self-interest, apart from moral considerations, demands that world opinion should be on our side in this matter of treatment of minorities.

I would ask you, therefore, as a matter of great importance, to take steps to put across to the public the true basis of our policy. How exactly you should do so is a matter which I must leave to your judgment; it must depend on local factors.

The other important question to which I would draw your attention is the paramount importance of preserving the public services from the virus of communal politics. There is a great deal of evidence that the services in Paki-

1. See Jawaharlal Nehru, *Letters to Chief Ministers, 1947–1964*, 5 vols., ed. G. Parthasarathi (New Delhi: Jawaharlal Nehru Memorial Fund, 1985–1989) (hereafter *LCM*), vol. 1, pp. 2–4.

stan have got out of hand and are not amenable to the control of their government. You will have noticed that Mr. Jinnah[2] himself referred, in a recent address in Karachi, to the indiscipline that has set in in the services. This is
already a serious headache for Pakistan, and will probably be more serious in
future. Fortunately for us, taking an overall picture, . . . we have been able,
generally speaking, to preserve the integrity of the services against the communal virus. But there have been lapses in East Punjab specially in the police; and unless we are vigilant the disease may spread. We would then be
faced with a situation of the utmost gravity, viz., of having a government in
office which could not get its decrees executed by its own servants; the sort
of thing that is happening so frequently in the South American Republics. I
would ask you, therefore, to allow no laxity in the loyal execution of government's policy by its servants, particularly in the matter of just and fair treatment to minorities. If we condone lapses in this respect, we shall be storing
up serious trouble for the country in the future.

✦   ✦   ✦

From a letter dated 7 December 1947:[3]

✦   ✦   ✦

Reports have reached me of big demonstrations organized by the R[ashtriya
S[wayamsevak] S[angh][4] in some provinces. Often these demonstrations
have been held in spite of prohibitory orders. . . . Some provincial authorities
have taken no action in this matter and apparently accepted this defiance of
orders. I do not wish to interfere with your discretion in this matter. But
I would like to draw your attention to the fact that this acquiescence in defiance is likely to have grave consequences.

We have a great deal of evidence to show that the R.S.S. is an organization which is in the nature of a private army and which is definitely proceeding on the strictest Nazi lines, even following the technique of organization.
It is not our desire to interfere with civil liberties. But training in arms of

2. M. A. Jinnah, then governor-general of Pakistan.

3. *LCM*, vol. 1, pp. 33–34.

4. Established in 1925, the Rashtriya Swayamsewak Sangh is an organisation committed to the establishment of a Hindu state in India.

large numbers of persons with the obvious intention of using them is not something that can be encouraged. The fact that the R.S.S. is definitely and deliberately against the present central and provincial governments need not be considered enough for any action to be taken against them and any legitimate propaganda might certainly be allowed. But their activity more and more goes beyond these limits and it is desirable for provincial governments to keep a watchful eye and to take such action as they may deem necessary. . . .

I have some knowledge of the way the Nazi movement developed in Germany. It attracted by its superficial trappings and strict discipline considerable numbers of lower middle class young men and women who are normally not too intelligent and for whom life appeared to offer little to attract them. And so they drifted towards the Nazi party because its policy and programme, such as they were, were simple, negative and did not require an active effort of the mind. The Nazi party brought Germany to ruin and I have little doubt that if these tendencies are allowed to spread and increase in India, they would do enormous injury to India. No doubt India would survive. But she would be grievously wounded and would take a long time to recover.

✦ ✦ ✦

From a letter dated 17 January 1948:[5]

✦ ✦ ✦

Since I last wrote to you, everything that has happened has been completely overshadowed by Gandhiji's fast.[6] . . . The last prolonged fast which Gandhiji undertook was in 1943 when he was a prisoner. That fast was for a purpose which the man in the street understood and wholly sympathised with. His recent fast in Calcutta was also for an easily understood purpose which had the support of the overwhelming bulk of the people. The fast which he has now undertaken is less easy for the general public to understand; and in fact there are sections of them more particularly among the refugees, who do not sym-

5. *LCM*, vol. 1, pp. 48–49.
6. Gandhi had just gone on a fast in protest against the continuing attacks on Muslims in Delhi and East Punjab.

pathise with it and are in a sense antagonistic to it. Therein lies its significance and supreme courage.

We are faced, particularly in East Punjab and Delhi, with the psychological problem created by the events of the last few months. These have created in the minds of people, not merely among the refugees but also among others, a bitterness, a sense of desperation and a desire for retaliation—in short, a serious spiritual malaise. This is wholly understandable but nonetheless extremely dangerous. We have all of us done our best to cure it but have not succeeded except only to a limited extent. The difficulties have been partly due to our inability effectively to tackle the problem of rehabilitation [of refugees] and partly to the continuing evidence of hostility and barbaric conduct towards the minorities in Pakistan. The result has been that sections of the Hindu community are not in tune with and do not understand Gandhiji's approach to the Muslim problem in India. They resent his approach and think that it is somehow or other inimical to their own interests. And yet any person with vision can see that Gandhiji's approach is not only morally correct, but is also essentially practical. Indeed it is the only possible approach if we think in terms of the nation's good, both from the short and long distance points of view. Any other approach means perpetuating conflict and postponing all notions of national consolidation and progress.

This is not the occasion to analyse—no one can analyse them—the complex of urges which must have driven Gandhiji to take this supreme step but quite clearly its main purpose is to make the majority community in India search its heart and purge itself of hatred and the desire to retaliate. In the atmosphere in which it has been undertaken, it displays a degree of heroism of which only Gandhiji is capable. The ordeal has been made worse for him by the tragic events that have occurred in Pakistan in the last few days—the murder and wholesale looting in Karachi and the revolting attack on a non-Muslim refugee train in Gujrat in West Punjab. But these incidents, in Gandhiji's conception, are not merely wholly irrelevant but only increase the urgency of the step that he has taken.

I am sure you will mobilize all your resources to emphasise to the people of your province, by every possible means, the meaning and purpose of the fast and thus help to create a situation in which Gandhiji may break it. I regard the emergency created by the fast as at least as grave as the disease that has given rise to it; and if we do not go all out to meet it, history will not forgive us.

✦ ✦ ✦

From a letter dated 20 September 1953:[7]

✦ ✦ ✦

. . . I want to share with you a certain apprehension that is growing within me. I feel that in many ways the position relating to minority groups in India is deteriorating. Our Constitution is good and we do not make any distinction in our rules and regulations or laws. But, in effect, changes creep in because of administrative practices or officers. Often these changes are not deliberate, sometimes they are so.

In the Services, generally speaking, the representation of the minority communities is lessening. In some cases, it is very poor indeed. It is true that some of the highest offices in the land are occupied by members of these minority communities. They occupy high places also in our foreign missions. But in looking through Central Government figures, as well as some others, I am distressed to find that the position is very disadvantageous to them, chiefly to the Muslims and sometimes others also.

In our Defense Services, there are hardly any Muslims left. In the vast Central Secretariat of Delhi, there are very few Muslims. Probably the position is somewhat better in the provinces, but not much more so. What concerns me most is that there is no effort being made to improve this situation, which is likely to grow worse unless checked.

It is all very well for us to say that we shall not pay any attention to communal and like considerations in appointments. I am no lover of communalism and its works. Indeed, I think it is the most dangerous tendency in India and has to be combated on all fronts. But, at the same time, we have to realize that in a vast and mixed country like India we must produce a sense of balance and of assurance of a square deal and future prospects in all parts of the country and in all communities of India. If the tendency is to upset any balance or to emphasize one aspect at the cost of another, the result is a lack of equilibrium and dissatisfaction and frustration among large groups. . . .

I have referred to Muslims above, but this applies to Christians and others also. Unfortunately there is a feeling of apprehension among a large number

7. *LCM*, vol. 3, pp. 375–380.

of our Christian countrymen and countrywomen, and many of them feel uncertain of their place in India in the future. We have always to remember India as a composite country, composite in many ways, in religion, in customs, in languages, in ways of life, etc. An attempt by the majority groups to impose itself on others can only lead to inner conflicts, which are as bad as outer conflicts. The basic problem for us today in India is to build up a united India in the real and inner sense of the word, that is, a psychological integration of our people. . . .

The feeling of nationalism is an enlarging and widening experience for the individual or the nation. More especially, when a country is under foreign domination, nationalism is a strengthening and unifying force. But, a stage arrives when it might well have a narrowing influence. Sometimes, as in Europe, it becomes aggressive and chauvinistic and wants to impose itself on other countries and other people. Every people suffer from the strange delusion that they are the elect and better than all others. When they become strong and powerful, they try to impose themselves and their ways on others. In their attempt to do so, sometime or other, they overreach themselves, stumble and fall. That has been the fate of the intense nationalism of Germany and Japan.

But a more insidious form of nationalism is the narrowness of mind that it develops within a country, when a majority thinks itself as the entire nation and in its attempt to absorb the minority actually separates them even more. We, in India, have to be particularly careful of this because of our tradition of caste and separatism. We have a tendency to fall into separate groups and to forget the larger unity.

Communal organizations are the clearest examples of extreme narrowness of outlook, strutting about in the guise of nationalism. In the name of unity, they separate and destroy. In social terms they represent reaction of the worst type. We may condemn these communal organizations, but there are many others who are not free from this narrow influence. Oddly enough, the very largeness of India, which is a world in itself, tends to make the people living in it complacent, rather ignorant of the rest of the world, and narrowminded. We have to contend against these forces. . . .

✦　✦　✦

ON PLANNING AND ECONOMIC POLICY

In recent years, Jawaharlal Nehru has come under attack for having promoted the belief that the state should occupy the 'commanding heights' of the economy. These policies are said to have stifled private enterprise. It is true that Nehru had an aesthetic aversion to big business and a perhaps too rosy picture of the alleged successes of centralised planning in the socialist countries. That said, the criticisms are somewhat anachronistic. At the time of Independence, even the private sector in India had called for massive state investment in the economy. In any case, Nehru's economic philosophy was more complex than is sometimes supposed—for instance, he saw planning as necessary not merely to augment productivity but also to overcome the sectarian affiliations of caste, language, and religion. The two excerpts on this subject that follow are from his letters to chief ministers.

From a letter dated 22 December 1952:[8]

✦ ✦ ✦

. . . This relatively short session of Parliament did substantial work and many important problems were discussed. The most important discussion was that on the Five Year Plan. By approving of it in Parliament, we have given the final seal to this Plan and now the time comes to implement it. It is true that implementation has been going on all the time and nearly two years out of the five are over. Nevertheless, we have to make a new approach now, a more positive, concentrated and integrated one. More particularly, we have to rely on public co-operation.

On the State Governments lies a special responsibility in this respect and we have no interval to rest before we start on the next stage of the journey. There is no resting place for any of us who are in positions of responsibility, for the world and India move on and if we delay, we are likely to be left behind.

The first thing to be done is to give the widest publicity to this Plan or to its essential features and its basic outlook. . . . There is material enough in the printed summary that they have produced and we must remember that the best approach still in India is the personal one, through public meeting or

8. *LCM*, vol. 3, pp. 203–206.

group discussion. Now that Parliament and most of our State Assemblies are not in season, members should go to their constituencies and make an intensive drive on the subject of the Five Year Plan. Unfortunately and rather unreasonably, most of the Opposition groups have criticized or even condemned the Plan. They have often done so for entirely contradictory reasons, the same person criticizing it for not going far enough and for going too far, having regard to our resources. The responsibility of those who believe in the Plan is thus all the greater.

People in the States and in districts will naturally be interested chiefly in their own part of this Plan and what they can do. This part should be explained, but the approach should always be an all-India approach and an attempt should be made to explain this great conception of planning for the whole country. Behind the Plan lies the conception of India's unity and of a mighty co-operative effort of all the people of India. That should always be stressed and the inter-relation of one part of India with another pointed out. If we adopt this approach, we shall be dealing with the major disease or weakness of India, i.e., the fissiparous tendencies and parochial outlook that often confront us in this country. The more we think of this balanced picture of the whole of India and of its many-sided activities, which are so interrelated with one another, the less we are likely to go astray in the crooked paths of provincialism, communalism, casteism and all other disruptive and disintegrating tendencies. That is a hard task, for it means changing the mentality of large numbers of people. It is a task which will not be completed within these three remaining years of the Plan, but will have to be continued till we root out and put an end to these tendencies. . . .

The Plan is comprehensive and there lies a tremendous deal of thought and discussion behind it. It is, on the whole, a cautious Plan, even a moderate one, and yet it is far-reaching and, if we so will it, we can take it as far as we like. It is a challenge to all of us and in the measure that we meet that challenge, we build the new India and justify our work. We have, therefore, to take this up in all earnestness and try to infuse in our work something of the spirit of a missionary for a cause. We have to remember always that it is not merely the governmental machinery that counts in this, but even more so the enthusiasm and co-operation of the people. Our people must have the sensation of partnership in a mighty enterprise, of being fellow-travellers towards the next goal that they and we have set before us. The Plan may be, and has to be, based on the calculations of economists, statisticians and the like, but figures and statistics, very important as they are, do not give life to the scheme. That breath of life comes in other ways, and it is for us now to make this Plan, which is enshrined in cold print, something living, vital and dynamic, which captures the imagination of our people.

◆ ◆ ◆

From a letter dated 3 March 1953:[9]

◆ ◆ ◆

. . . More and more it is being realized in other parts of the world that we in India are engaged in a mighty adventure. To build up this country and to solve the problems of poverty and unemployment in a democratic way on this scale is something that has not been done anywhere. The magnitude of the task and the difficulties we have to overcome may sometimes oppress us, but, at the same time, they should fill us with the enthusiasm that great undertakings bring with them. Probably the next five to ten years are the critical years for us. If we carry on during this period as a stable, progressive country, making good and advancing, then we have succeeded and we have little to fear in the future. Even if the pace is not quite so fast as we would like it to be, the mere fact of continuous progress on a stable basis would be a triumph for large-scale democratic working. There is danger in our becoming static and slow-moving; there is equally danger in trying to go faster than circumstances or our resources permit us to do. The middle course, the golden mean is always difficult.

We have set before us the ideal of the welfare State. . . . The welfare State means welfare for all and not for a section of the community only. It means productive and gainful employment for all and the removal of the grave disparities in incomes and methods of living that exist in India today. We get used to these, but every foreigner who comes here is struck even now by these great disparities. How are we to get rid of them? Some of our friends suggest, as if that was some magic remedy, nationalization all round or a reduction of higher salaries, etc. Except for a few, salaries are not high in India now. Where possible, we should try to reduce them. But merely to distribute

9. *LCM*, vol. 3, pp. 252–255.

poverty does not mean progress. In order to go ahead, we have to try to maintain some standards somewhere. That does not mean affluence for some and poverty for the rest, still less does it mean vulgar display which unfortunately is still rather common with a few of our people. As for nationalization, the real test is how far this adds to our productive capacity as well as to the smoother working of our Plan. Mere nationalization does not add to that productive capacity much, if at all. It might indeed mean a lessening of it. At the most it means a transfer of ownership with the same production and the available resources being utilized for compensation. It is far better to use our resources for new State enterprises, leaving the old ones to carry on as they are, subject to some kind of control by the State. Thus production grows and the public sector grows till it becomes the dominant sector.

The problems of today in India or elsewhere cannot be solved by some purely academic approach or by a dogmatic creed of yesterday. Most of us, I suppose, believe in a socialistic approach and in socialistic ideals. But when these are thought of in terms of some rigid formulae, developed in Europe in the nineteenth century, they need not necessarily apply to India in the middle of the twentieth century. Even economic science is not so static and conditions have changed greatly.

Thus far we see a full-blooded socialism, if that is the right term, working in Communist countries, together with an accompaniment of authoritarian control and an absence of the democratic approach. That is, practically everything is State-controlled and that develops bureaucracy in an extreme measure, apart from suppressing individual freedom. Certain economic results are undoubtedly obtained that way, but the price paid is heavy. In other countries which aim at socialism, though of a different variety, inevitably, there is some kind of a mixed economy, though the quality of the mixture may vary. Indeed, I am inclined to think that in a democratic society, a so-called mixed economy is inevitable, though the public sector may grow and be the dominant partner. The private sector however will continue to have an important place, but the major industries would tend to be in the public sector. We have laid down that in a planned economy the private sector has to conform to the national plan and therefore has to be controlled to some extent. That appears to be obvious if we are to have any planning. But this leads to a difficulty. The private sector has a different outlook and approach and cannot easily function if there is too much control. It thus ceases to have the advantages attaching to the public sector as well as to the private sector. The other day some industrialists came to see me and said that they would be very happy to co-operate fully with the Five Year Plan. But it was becoming increasingly difficult for them to function effectively with so many restrictions and controls. It was better they said, that an industry was taken over by the public sector completely than left in a hamstrung condition in the private sector. These people exaggerated somewhat, but I think there was some truth in what they said. It is better to take over an industry in the public sector and organize it as such as to allow the industries left to the private sector some freedom of movement, subject of course to some basic considerations. I am mentioning these matters to you so that we might give thought to them.

As for our resources, it is clear that we have to depend essentially on our country and our own people. We can welcome help from abroad, but it cannot take us far. I have a feeling that we have enough in this country provided we can reach it. The difficulty is that it is spread out and not easily accessible. We have, of course, the small savings scheme and this is important and should be encouraged. But perhaps some additional approach would bring in larger resources at our disposal. If we had a large number of rural banks, they would not only serve as agencies for giving credit to the farmer, and thus replacing the old *bania* [village moneylender], but they would also attract small pools of money which, in the aggregate, may amount to a very big sum. . . .

+   +   +

ASIA REDUX

In the seventeen years that he was prime minister, Jaswaharlal Nehru served simultaneously as India's foreign minister. In March 1947, with India's independence imminent, Nehru took the lead in organising a conference of Asian countries that were free or still under the colonial yoke. Twenty-eight countries sent delegates to participate in the meeting, which was held in the shadow of the Purana Qila (Old Fort) in Delhi. In his inaugural address, excerpted below, Nehru explored the idea of a pan-Asianism which would not turn its back on the West. This formulation owed a great deal to the work of Rabindranath Tagore, a thinker Nehru greatly admired.[10]

✦ ✦ ✦

FRIENDS AND FELLOW ASIANS! What has brought you, the men and women of Asia, here? Why have you come from various countries of this mother continent of ours and gathered together in this ancient city of Delhi? Some of us, greatly daring, sent you invitations for this Conference and you gave a warm welcome to that invitation. And yet it was not merely the call from us, but some deeper urge that brought you here.

We stand at the end of an era and on the threshold of a new period of history. Standing on this watershed which divides two epochs of human history and endeavour, we can look back on our long past and look forward to the future that is taking shape before our eyes. Asia, after a long period of quiescence, has suddenly become important again in world affairs. If we view the millennia of history, this continent of Asia, with which Egypt has been so intimately connected in cultural fellowship, has played a mighty role in the evolution of humanity. It was here that civilization began and man started on his unending adventure of life. Here the mind of man searched unceasingly for truth and the spirit of man shone out like a beacon which lighted up the whole world.

This dynamic Asia from which great streams of culture flowed in all directions gradually became static and unchanging. Other peoples and other continents came to the fore and with their new dynamism spread out and took possession of great parts of the world. This mighty continent became just a field for the rival imperialisms of Europe, and Europe became the centre of history and progress in human affairs.

A change is coming over the scene now and Asia is again finding herself. We live in an age of tremendous transition and already the next stage takes shape when Asia assumes her rightful place with the other continents.

It is at this great moment that we meet here and it is the pride and privilege of the people of India to welcome their fellow Asians from other countries, to

10. From Jawaharlal Nehru, *India's Foreign Policy: Selected Speeches, September 1946—April 1961* (1961; reprint, New Delhi: Ministry of Information and Broadcasting, 1971), pp. 249–253.

confer with them about the present and the future, and lay the foundation of our mutual progress, well-being and friendship. . . .

We welcome you, delegates and representatives from China, that great country to which Asia owes so much and from which so much is expected; from Egypt and the Arab countries of West Asia, inheritors of a proud culture which spread far and wide and influenced India greatly; from Iran whose contacts with India go back to the dawn of history; from Indonesia and Indo-China whose history is intertwined with India's culture, and where recently the battle of freedom has continued, a reminder to us that freedom must be won and cannot come as a gift; from Turkey that has been rejuvenated by the genius of a great leader; from Korea and Mongolia, Siam, Malaya and the Philippines; from the Soviet Republics of Asia which have advanced so rapidly in our generation and which have so many lessons to teach us; and from our neighbours Afghanistan, Tibet, Nepal, Bhutan, Burma and Ceylon to whom we look especially for co-operation and close and friendly intercourse. . . . We also welcome observers from Australia and New Zealand, because we have many problems in common, especially in the Pacific and in the south-east region of Asia, and we have to co-operate together to find solutions.

As we meet here today, the long past of Asia rises up before us, the troubles of recent years fade away, and a thousand memories revive. But I shall not speak to you of these past ages with their glories and triumphs and failures, nor of more recent times which have oppressed us so much and which still pursue us in some measure. During the past two hundred years we have seen the growth of Western imperialisms and of the reduction of large parts of Asia to colonial or semi-colonial status. Much has happened during these years, but perhaps one of the notable consequences of the European domination of Asia has been the isolation of the countries of Asia from one another. India always had contacts and intercourse with her neighbour countries in the north-west, the north-east, the east and the south-east. With the coming of British rule in India these contacts were broken off and India was almost completely isolated from the rest of Asia. The old land routes almost ceased to function and our chief window to the outer world looked out on the sea route which led to England. A similar process affected other countries of Asia also. Their economy was bound up with some European imperialism or other; even culturally they looked towards Europe and not to their own friends and neighbours from whom they had derived so much in the past.

Today this isolation is breaking down because of many reasons, political and other. The old imperialisms are fading away. The land routes have revived and air travel suddenly brings us very near to one another. This Conference itself is significant as an expression of that deeper urge of the mind and spirit of Asia which has persisted in spite of the isolationism which grew up during the years of European domination. As that domination goes, the walls that surrounded us fall down and we look at one another again and meet as old friends long parted.

In this Conference and in this work there are no leaders and no followers. All countries of Asia have to meet together on an equal basis in a common task and endeavour. It is fitting that India should play her part in this new phase of Asian development. Apart from the fact that India herself is emerging into freedom and independence, she is the natural centre and focal point of the many forces at work in Asia. Geography is a compelling factor, and geographically she is so situated as to be the meeting point of Western and Northern and Eastern and South-East Asia. Because of this, the history of India is a long history of her relations with the other countries of Asia. Streams of culture have come to India from the West and the East and been absorbed in India, producing the rich and variegated culture which is India today. At the same time, streams of culture have flowed from India to distant parts of Asia. If you would know India, you have to go to Afghanistan and West Asia, to Central Asia, to China and Japan and to the countries of South-East Asia. There you will find magnificent evidence of the vitality of India's culture which spread out and influenced vast numbers of people.

There came the great cultural stream from Iran to India in remote antiquity. And then began that constant intercourse between India and the Far East, notably China. In later years South-East Asia witnessed an amazing efflorescence of Indian art and culture. The mighty stream which started from Arabia and developed as a mixed Irano-Arabic culture poured into India. All these came to us and influenced us, and yet so great was the powerful impress of India's own mind and culture that it could accept them without being itself swept away or overwhelmed. Nevertheless, we all changed in the process and in India today all of us are mixed products of these various influences. An Indian, wherever he may go in Asia, feels a sense of kinship with the land he visits and the people he meets.

I wish to speak to you not of the past, but rather of the present. We meet here not to discuss our past history and contacts, but to forge links for the future. And may I say here that this Conference, and the idea underlying it, is in no way aggressive or against any other continent or country? Ever since news of this Conference went abroad some people in Europe and America have viewed it with doubt, imagining that this was some kind of a pan-Asian movement directed against Europe or America. We have no designs against anybody; ours is the great design of promoting peace and progress all over the world. Far too long have we of Asia been petitioners in Western courts and chancelleries. That story must now belong to the past. We propose to stand on our own legs and to co-operate with all others who are prepared to co-operate with us. We do not intend to be the playthings of others.

In this crisis in world history Asia will necessarily play a vital role. The countries of Asia can no longer be used as pawns by others; they are bound to have their own policies in world affairs. Europe and America have contributed very greatly to human progress and for that we must yield them praise and honour, and learn from them the many lessons they have to teach. But the West has also driven us into wars and conflicts without number and even now, the day after a terrible war, there is talk of further wars in the atomic age that is upon us. In this atomic age Asia will have to function effectively in the maintenance of peace. Indeed, there can be no peace unless Asia plays her part. There is today conflict in many countries, and all of us in Asia are full of our own troubles. Nevertheless, the whole spirit and outlook of Asia are peaceful, and the emergence of Asia in world affairs will be a powerful influence for world peace.

Peace can come only when nations are free and also when human beings everywhere have freedom and security and opportunity. Peace and freedom, therefore, have to be considered in both their political and economic aspects. The countries of Asia, we must remember, are very backward and the standards of living are appallingly low. These economic problems demand urgent solution or else crisis and disaster may overwhelm us. We have, therefore, to think in terms of the common man and fashion our political, social and economic structure so that the burdens that have crushed him may be removed, and he may have full opportunity for growth.

We have arrived at a stage in human affairs when the ideal of One World and some kind of a World Federation seem to be essential, though there are many dangers and obstacles in the way. We should work for that ideal and not for any grouping which comes in the way of this larger world group. We, therefore, support the United Nations structure which is painfully emerging from its infancy. But in order to have One World, we must also, in Asia, think of the countries of Asia co-operating together for that larger ideal.

This Conference, in a small measure, represents this bringing together of the countries of Asia. Whatever it may achieve, the mere fact of its taking place is itself of historic significance. Indeed, this occasion is unique in history, for never before has such a gathering met together at any place. So even in meeting we have achieved much and I have no doubt that out of this meeting greater things will come. When the history of our present times is written, this event may well stand out as a landmark which divides the past of Asia from the future. And because we are participating in this making of history, something of the greatness of historic events comes to us all. . . .

We seek no narrow nationalism. Nationalism has a place in each country and should be fostered, but it must not be allowed to become aggressive and come in the way of international development. Asia stretches her hand out in friendship to Europe and America as well as to our suffering brethren in Africa.

We of Asia have a special responsibility to the people of Africa. We must help them to their rightful place in the human family. The freedom that we envisage is not to be confined to this nation or that or to a particular people, but must spread out over the whole human race. That universal human freedom also cannot be based on the supremacy of any particular class. It must be the freedom of the common man everywhere and full opportunities for him to develop.

We think today of the great architects of Asian freedom—Sun Yat-sen, Zaghlul Pasha, the Ataturk Kemal Pasha and others, whose labours have borne fruit.

We think also of that great figure whose labours and whose inspiration have brought India to the threshold of her independence—Mahatma Gandhi. We miss him at this Conference and I yet hope that he may visit us before our labours end. He is engrossed in the service of the common man in India, and even this Conference could not drag him away from it.[11]

All over Asia we are passing through trials and tribulations. In India also you will see conflict and trouble. Let us not be disheartened by this; this is

---

11. Towards the end of the Conference, Gandhi did come and address the delegates. See *CWMG*, vol. 87, pp. 190–193.

inevitable in an age of mighty transition. There are powerful creative impulses and a new vitality in all the peoples of Asia. The masses are awake and they demand their heritage. Strong winds are blowing all over Asia. Let us not be afraid of them, but rather welcome them; for, only with their help can we build the new Asia of our dreams. Let us have faith in these great new forces and the dream which is taking shape. Let us, above all, have faith in the human spirit which Asia has symbolized for those long ages past.

+   +   +

INDIA IN THE WORLD

In August 1947 India achieved Dominion status within the British Empire; in January 1950 it became a republic, with Jawaharlal Nehru serving as both prime minister and foreign minister. The excerpt that follow is from a speech Nehru made in Parliament on 7 December 1950. At this time, he was perhaps more open to the United States than to the Soviet Union, in part because, in March 1948, the Communist Party of India had mounted an insurrection against the state. This was to change in later years, as the Communists came overground and made their peace with 'bourgeois' democracy, and the Americans themselves chose to ally strongly with Pakistan.[12]

+   +   +

. . . I should like the Members of this House to consider the last five or six years of diplomatic history. In spite of every effort, the world has repeatedly failed to achieve harmony. The astonishing thing is that failure does not teach us a lesson and we make the same mistakes over again. This is really extraordinary. I should have thought that the lessons of the two great world wars [were] obvious enough to anybody willing to give thought to it.

It may be that the crisis today is due to the fault of a nation or a group of nations. It may be Russia's fault or the fault of the communist group of nations. What do we do when a group of nations functions in an objectionable way?

12. From Nehru, *India's Foreign Policy,* pp. 50–55.

People talk a great deal about communism and as an hon. Member pointed out, some Members thought that we had turned this discussion into an anti-communist conference. Communism is certainly an interesting subject and one that is worthy of discussion but it does not have much bearing on the issue. I am sure that those who think only in terms of communism and anti-communism are going hopelessly astray and will never reach any goal. The difficulty is that much of the thinking—not so much here as elsewhere—revolves round these words.

The House knows very well what the policy of the Government of India has been in regard to communist activities in this country. It has not been a tender policy and it is not going to be a tender policy. We must look at the world as it is and recognize that mighty forces are at work and millions of people have come under their influence. We must try to understand them and try as far as we can to divert them into right channels and prevent them from going into wrong ones. That is our problem. Some hon. Members seem to think that I should issue an ultimatum to China, that I should warn them not to do this or that or that I should send them a letter saying that it is foolish to follow the doctrine of communism. I do not see how it is going to help anybody if I act in this way. Remember, the world has many countries. Some of them are called great powers by virtue of their influence. They are nations with great resources behind them and inevitably play a significant part in the world's history today.

The United States of America is a great democratic power. The United Kingdom and the U.S.S.R., even though their policies differ, greatly influence the world's history and no one can deny China the status of a great power today. China is in a position to shape her own destiny and that is a great thing. It is true that she is controlled by communists as Russia is. It would be interesting to know whether or not her type of communism is the same as Russia's, how she will develop and how close the association between China and Russia will be.

The point at issue is that China is a great nation which cannot be ignored, no matter what resolution you may pass. Nor can you ignore the United States of America. Some people talk of American imperialism and American dollars in a hostile fashion. You cannot condemn or ignore the whole nation just because you do not approve of some aspect of the myriad shapes of American life. We have to take facts as they are. The most relevant fact at the moment is that there are some great nations in the world with concentrated power in their hands that influence all the other nations. That being so, there is a conflict between these powerful nations—an ideological conflict as well as a political conflict. Either these nations will have a war and try to suppress or defeat one another or one group will triumph over the other. . . .

The only way seems to be the avoidance of war. All nations must be free to develop as they like without any external interference. This does not mean that they will not influence one another in a variety of ways. It is possible that the existing contradictions may gradually be solved in that manner. On the other hand, they may not. I am not a prophet; I do not know. In any case, the way of war does not solve them. The concentration of power in the hands of these great nations and the fact that the power is not too unevenly matched, means a very disastrous war. It also means no ultimate victory. There may be a military victory; but there will be no real victory, if by victory you mean the achievement of certain objectives.

I doubt if, after the terrible disaster of a world war, democracy can survive. The democratic nations may win the war—mind you, I have little doubt that they will—but I doubt if after the disaster of a world war democracy can survive at all. I even doubt whether any high standards of living can survive. I have no doubt that the great nations wish to avoid war because they are aware of its consequences. No one can assert that America wants war. I cannot imagine anything more unlikely. If America wanted war, who could have stopped her? She obviously does not. She wants to avoid war because she is aware of the great disasters a world war will cause. England also wants to avoid war. In spite of this, forces are impelling these nations in a direction which may lead to war. The biggest task today is to prevent that and that is the task for England, for America, for us and for all other countries. . . .

+   +   +

This next excerpt is from a letter from Nehru to chief ministers, dated 16 June 1952.[13]

+   +   +

. . . It is important that we should be clear about our foreign policy. Some people imagined that there was some shift of it or some variation. As a matter

13. *LCM,* vol. 3, pp. 13–20.

of fact, we have adhered to our policy and we intend to continue to do so. People, judging from some odd incident, come to wrong conclusions. If we take aid from the United States of America or are otherwise friendly to them, we are said to incline towards that particular group of nations in the cold war that is going on. If we send a cultural mission to China and express our appreciation of some of the activities of the new regime in China, we are said to have inclined towards the other group of nations. As a matter of fact, we try our best, within the limits of our policy, to be friendly and co-operative with the countries of both these groups. We have intimate relations—political, cultural and economic—with the United Kingdom. That is not a legacy from the past but is to our interest today. Our whole political structure is largely fashioned after that of the United Kingdom. We use their language extensively. It is natural, therefore, that those connections should continue. That does not mean in the slightest that we subordinate ourselves to the U.K. in any way. Even the Commonwealth relationship does not lessen in the slightest our complete independence of policy or action, as can be seen by anybody who is acquainted with current affairs. . . .

With the United States of America, our associations are also fairly close, though not as close as those with the U.K. We trade with them. We have received help from them and we have many students there. As I have pointed out previously, there is always a certain risk involved in receiving substantial help from any one country. Therefore we have to be careful. It would be folly not to receive the help we so badly need, because we cannot rely upon ourselves.

With the U.S.S.R., our contacts are friendly but not close, that is, we have not got much business or other dealings. That is not because we avoid such dealings, but because, in the nature of things, it is more difficult for us to deal with them. Where an opportunity offers, we take it. With China, partly the same considerations apply, But I think it is true that a variety of circumstances pull India and China towards each other, in spite of differences of forms of government. This is the long pull of geography and history and, if I may add, of the future. I do not see why we should be alarmed at this. Here also we should be careful. All this means that we should look at current history in some perspective of both the past and the future. There is far too much entanglement with the present with all its passions and conflicts for most countries to develop this perspective. We claim no special virtue for ourselves. But, situated as we are, we are perhaps in a better position to look at things at long range and fashion our policy accordingly. . . .

On the return of our cultural mission to China, Delhi heard a great deal about the new China from the members of this mission. On the whole, what we heard was highly appreciative of China, though there were criticisms also. In regard to one matter there was complete agreement and that was the new spirit and enthusiasm of the Chinese people. For any people that is a great asset. For the Chinese with their amazing capacity for hard work and co-operative endeavour, that means something even more. Although we have heard a great deal about recent developments in China, our knowledge still remains vague and the picture is not clear. It would be helpful if we knew more about the background of events there, of their economy, their engineering success, their education, etc., because we might be able to learn something from all this. China started a period of civil wars and internal conflicts forty years ago. During these years, she had no real peace and she had major wars. Because of this obviously no development could take place and large parts of the country were devastated. When the new Government came into power, they had to deal with this accumulated ruin of forty years of conflict and had to start almost from scratch. Only in Manchuria there was a highly industrialized area, built up by the Japanese. But even there part of the equipment had been removed after the last war, mostly by the Russians. Thus the new regime in China started with every disadvantage except that of faith and enthusiasm. Immediately after there was friction with other countries and they were unable to get any kind of help from any outside country excepting the U.S.S.R. What they have done in these difficult conditions is, therefore, of great interest to us. It is true that authoritarian methods yield results rather quickly, whatever their immediate or long-distance disadvantages might be. Nevertheless, it is a feat to face these manifold difficulties and overcome them, chiefly with their own efforts.

We cannot compare India to the European countries or the American. These latter countries have had a long period of growth and industrialization and they have much smaller populations. Even a comparison with the Soviet Union is not fair because the Soviet Union has had over thirty years of building up. Also the Soviet Union has vast areas and, compared to India, a smaller population. But there are far more points of similarity between India and China, among them being enormous populations and economic backwardness.

How the Chinese overcome these economic conditions, industrialize their country and produce more wealth and distribute it more evenly, is therefore of great interest to us. We are committed, and I think rightly so, to democratic and parliamentary institutions. That does not necessarily mean that democracy must be rigid and unable to adapt itself to changing conditions. Democracy, apart from its institutions, is a way of Government and life itself. I firmly believe that it is a better way than a dictatorship or authoritarianism. In the long run, dictatorships must, I think, rather stunt the growth of the country. There are initial advantages which are obvious and the outward speed of progress appears to be fast. But it is very doubtful if the essential quality which underlies human progress, that is the creative spirit of man, can develop adequately under an authoritarian system. To some extent, of course, such authoritarian systems as have economic equality as their goal, are initially liberating forces and release tremendous popular energy. That is a great advantage. But if dictatorship continues, the creative spirit may gradually fade away.

Democracy is supposed to nurture this creative spirit but if it cannot bring about a release from poverty of large masses of human beings, then that creative spirit can only function in a few. Poverty is after all more restrictive and limiting than anything else. If poverty and low standards continue then democracy, for all its fine institutions and ideals, ceases to be a liberating force. It must therefore aim continuously at the eradication of poverty and its companion unemployment. In other words, political democracy is not enough. It must develop into economic democracy also. The problem before India is to bring about this development as rapidly as possible. In the ultimate analysis, the world will not be governed by theories but by actual results achieved. If India succeeds in achieving these results under a system of political democracy, that indeed would be a great victory not only for India but for democracy. If China succeeds by her own methods, undoubtedly those methods will then attract large numbers of people.

Some countries of the West, notably the United Kingdom, tried their utmost since the war to develop this economic democracy under the parliamentary system. They tried to find a middle path between unrestrained private enterprise and . . . the socialistic order. I think that the progress made by England, in spite of enormous difficulties, was remarkable and does every credit to her Government and people. It is said that in developing her social schemes, she lived beyond her means and is now suffering because of this.

This may partly be true, but I am sure that if she had not done so, her fate would have been worse. She had to bring about a tremendous transformation from the days of the old empire when tribute in various forms flowed to her from all over the world, to her new condition which was very different, in spite of some relics of the empire still continuing. Her government decided to spend their money and energy on improving the lot of the people generally, and putting an end to unemployment, in greater production, etc. They succeeded in a large measure. Perhaps the effort was a bit too great, but it must be remembered that, in addition to all this, England had to spend large sums of money on armaments. Whether this was justified or not, it is not for me to say. It is this additional burden of armaments that hastened the grave crisis that she has to face today. Even so, England is today a far more stable and disciplined and in a way contented country than almost any in Europe. Parliamentary democracy has justified itself there more than elsewhere. It may be that the burden is too great for her to bear. But I feel that she has still great resources of strength in her and a great capacity to adapt herself.

When we consider the problems of India, we have to keep these changing, dynamic, fascinating and sometimes rather terrifying aspects of the modern world before us and try to learn from them and avoid the pitfalls. We may discuss various policies but whatever policy we may adopt, our choice is ultimately limited by our capacity in the present. That capacity will no doubt grow. That takes time and there can be no magic solution of our problems. The main thing is that we have the right objective, that we go in that direction, and that we go as fast as circumstances permit us. We can, to some extent, measure and weigh these circumstances but there are ever so many uncertain factors in them, both national and international. The biggest uncertain factor is the response of our own people to any particular policy. It is not ultimately money that counts but the labour, enthusiasm and the will of the people. . . .

✦   ✦   ✦

THE CONFLICT WITH CHINA

In the late 1940s, as his speech to the Asian Relations Conference showed, Nehru hoped for very close political and cultural ties with China. By the late 1950s relations between India and China had begun to sour. The border between the two countries was under dispute, both in the West, in the Indian district of Ladakh, and in the East, in the Indian-administered North-east Frontier Agency (NEFA). The two sides met several times to try to resolve the disputes, but no agreement could be reached. In March 1959 the Dalai Lama fled across the border to India after the failure of an uprising against Chinese rule in Tibet. China expressed its displeasure at India's offering refuge to the Tibetan leader. Meanwhile, there were sporadic clashes between troops along the border. The excerpt that follows is from a letter written by the prime minister to his chief ministers on 1 October 1959.[14]

✦   ✦   ✦

. . . This tension that has arisen between India and China is, of course, of great concern to us. That does not mean that we should get alarmed in the present or fear any serious consequences. I do not think any such development is likely in the foreseeable future. But the basic fact remains that India and China have fallen out and, even though relative peace may continue at the frontier, it is some kind of an armed peace, and the future appears to be one of continuing tension. It is this future that troubles me because it will involve both a mental and a physical strain on our country, and it will somewhat come in the way of our basic policies. . . .

We have . . . to continue those basic policies and, at the same time, show firmness in our dealing with frontier developments. No principle and no policy can be pursued through weakness or fear. I have no fear of China, great and powerful as that country is. China will undoubtedly grow in physical might. Even so, there is no need for us to be afraid and, indeed fear is never a good companion. But we shall have to be vigilant all the time and balance firmness with a continuation of our policy.

Behind all this frontier trouble, there appears to me to be a basic problem of a strong and united Chinese State, expansive and pushing out in various directions and full of pride in its growing strength. In Chinese history, this kind of thing has happened on several occasions. Communism as such is only an added element; the real reason should be found to lie deeper in history

14. *LCM,* vol. 5, pp. 285–288.

and in national characteristic[s]. But it is true that never before have these two great countries, India and China, come face to face in some kind of a conflict. By virtue of their very size and their actual or potential strength, there is danger in this situation, not danger in the present, but rather in the future. That danger may be minimized by other developments and by the world moving gradually towards peace. But the danger will still remain, partly because of the tremendous rate of increase of the population of the Chinese State. Apart from population, there has been and is a certain homogeneity among the Chinese people which probably we lack. I have no doubt, however, that in the face of danger there will be much greater cohesion in India than we have at present. Perhaps, that may be one of the good effects of this new and unfortunate development. . . .

Minor controversies about the frontier might or might not be of importance. What we have to face, however, is something much deeper and more serious. This is a demand for considerable areas, more especially in the NEFA. All this means the Chinese want to come down on this side of the Himalayan barrier. This has two vitally important aspects: one that if a foreign Power comes down on this side of the Himalayas, our basic security is greatly endangered; the other that a sentiment which has been the life-blood of India through past ages is shattered. That sentiment appertains to the Himalayas. . . . The Himalayas are perhaps a more vital part of India's thought and existence throughout the ages than almost anything else. They are vital for our security even in the present age of extra-modern weapons; they are vital for our cultural inheritance.

✦   ✦   ✦

In the second week of October 1962, fighting broke out between the armies of the two countries. The Indians were no match militarily for the Chinese, who easily overcame their resistance and made deep inroads into Indian territory. Having made their point, the Chinese declared a cease-fire and returned to their side of the border. In this letter to chief ministers, dated 22 December 1962, Nehru sought to explain this humiliating defeat at the hands of a country he had once sought to befriend.[15]

15. *LCM*, vol. 5, pp. 544–552.

＋　＋　＋

It seems to me that the major reasons for our reverses were the choice of the terrain on which we had to fight the Chinese. This was all to the advantage of the enemy and very disadvantageous for us, the main disadvantage for us being that there was no easy access to it by road or other means of communications. We had thus to send everything by dropping from the air. This included ammunition, other supplies, clothing, etc. Our Air Force did a very fine job of work, but this lack of proper communications was a great disadvantage. The Chinese, on the other hand, had easy communications behind them as the road system in Tibet came right up to our frontier. Looked at from a purely military point of view, we should have selected a much more effective line of defence which was connected by road at least to our main supply centres. This, however, would have entailed retiring to our own territory and allowing the Chinese to march along it without major fighting. Although this was the wiser thing to do, it was not a pleasant course to follow.

A second major disadvantage to our Army was the fact that our forces had been sent rather hurriedly from low altitudes near sea level to an altitude of about 14,000 feet. Anyone who has done any mountaineering knows the effect of this sudden change to high altitudes. It produces severe headaches and sleepless nights and generally devitalizes one. It is always desirable to acclimatize people at various stages before they reach the high altitude. We could not do so because the Chinese had already crossed our border and were massing their forces there.

It may be said that we ought to have thought of this and placed our forces at that high altitude long before. Even that was not very feasible because that would have meant supplying them with everything a large Army wanted by air dropping. The only course was to build up good roads right up to the frontier. This was undertaken two years or more ago and many roads have been built. But the process was not completed. The terrain is difficult and road building requires high engineering skill. It takes time.

It is interesting to note the difference in the fighting quality of our troops in Ladakh and those in N.E.F.A. In Ladakh they had been acclimatized to the high altitudes for some time past. They fought, therefore, extraordinarily well and inflicted very heavy casualties on the Chinese. Even when they had to withdraw because of superior numbers of the Chinese, they did so gradually and did not allow the Chinese forces to advance much. In N.E.F.A., they had not been acclimatised and could not fight as they normally do.

It is easy to be wise after the event. It is easier to criticize what has happened. But I do think that the two major causes for our reverses were those two that I have mentioned. Some of our Generals have been heavily criticized and have been retired from Service. Many unkind things are said about them without much justification. It was right perhaps that they offered their resignation as honourable men. But the fault was hardly theirs. The faults, such as occurred, were of the local Commanders of Brigades and the like who had to decide on the spur of the moment what they should do when they were being overwhelmed by large numbers of the enemy. The Chief of the Army Staff and the Army Commander who have resigned could hardly be said to be directly responsible. They were competent and brave men and it is very unfair to them to accuse them for something that was due to a large number of circumstances, many of them outside their control.

There was also the fact that the Chinese, after many long years of warfare, are experts at mountain fighting and have been trained specially for this purpose. Their methods of fighting are a mixture of regular orthodox warfare and guerilla war. In Korea, with much worse weapons, they showed what they could do against armies which had the latest modern weapons. Since then the Chinese had got much better weapons and had perfected their methods of mountain warfare. It is evident that they had been preparing for some such invasion for a long time past in Tibet. They had accumulated large supplies and their troops were living all the time at a high altitude.

We have learnt by our experiences and misfortunes and we shall take good care that they do not repeat themselves. The present position is, as I have said above, that our armies, both in N.E.F.A. and Ladakh, hold their positions strongly and even if the Chinese attack them where they are, the positions would still be held. There is no chance, as far as one can see, of any further retreat by our forces. Assam, therefore, is safe from any invasion and as the days go by, our strength increases. Meanwhile, we are not only raising additional forces of various kinds, but also adding as speedily as we can to our equipment and fighting apparatus. For the present, we have to get much of this fighting material from abroad and we are doing so. But, real strength can only come from our manufacturing and producing all this equipment in our own country.

It is of the highest importance, therefore, that our manufacture of munitions and other war material should be speeded up as rapidly as possible. At the same time, we shall continue trying to get such material as we require and as is available from abroad. There is a slight danger of the tempo of our work gradually becoming slower because the excitement of day to day fighting may not be there to keep up the sense of urgency. We have to guard against it because the danger that threatens us is not of today or tomorrow, but will last a considerable time, whether there is actual fighting or not. We can afford to take no more risks for the future.

What were the motives that drove the Chinese to attack us in a big way? To say that this was just a desire to expand their territories or to take possession of the areas they claimed is not wholly an adequate answer, though there is something in it. Countries do not take such action involving dangerous consequences without a much deeper reason. The world today is in a state of cold war between the two major blocs of nations led respectively by the Soviet Union and the United States of America, both of which are nuclear powers, with a tremendous capacity for destruction. A certain balance of terror has been struck up between them which exercises a restraining influence, but which also brings the ever-present danger of a deliberate move or an accident which might bring nuclear war and the ultimate catastrophe. Between these two blocs, there is fear on both sides resulting in an attempt at continuous arming with the latest weapons of mass destruction. There are also attempts being made at some approach to a peaceful settlement of the problems that face them. Recently, we came very near to a nuclear war over Cuba. It almost seemed for a few days that at any moment the atomic and hydrogen bombs might start bursting in various parts of the world bringing death and destruction to millions or even perhaps hundreds of millions. Fortunately, that crisis passed because both of the major parties concerned wanted to avoid such a war. Ever since then there has been a certain relaxation of tension, though that is not very great yet. Still it is noticeable, and for the first time in many years the hopes of people are reviving.

Besides these two major blocs of heavily armed powers there are a number, and a growing number of countries, weak in armed power but still exercising some influence in favour of peace. Perhaps they cannot by themselves make the ultimate decision in favour of peace. But they can and they have in the past made just that little difference which prevents a war from breaking out. They have become symbols, to some extent, of peaceful co-existence and their policy of non-alignment to military blocs has gradually been appreciated more and more even by the big blocs. Both the United State of America and the Soviet Union have appreciated this policy of non-alignment and peaceful co-existence, even though they cannot adopt it for themselves because of their fear of each other. And yet, inevitably almost the world moves towards peaceful co-existence and should ultimately realize that objective unless war overwhelms it before that realization comes. . . .

But to this desire for peace and co-existence there is one major exception, and that is China. China has repudiated the doctrine of peaceful co-existence, even though sometimes it repeats it. It believes in the inevitability of war and, therefore, does not want the tensions in the world to lessen. It dislikes non-alignment and it would much rather have a clear polarization of the different countries in the world. It is not afraid even of a nuclear war because as it is often said, they can afford to lose a few hundred million people and yet have enough numbers left.

Because of this difference of opinion, there is a wide and growing rift between the Soviet Union and China, even though they are military allies. They condemn bitterly each other's policies. It is obviously of high importance to the world as to how far this rift has gone and whether ultimately it will result in a complete break. Every chancellery in the world is deeply interested in this and tries to find out what the exact relationship of the two great countries is. Latterly this inner conflict has come out into the open, and there has been much public cursing of each other.

China, for all its belligerency and the progress it has made in the past dozen years, is still by and large an underdeveloped country and during the last three years or so, has had bad harvests. This has weakened it greatly although its war apparatus may for the present be fairly strong. It realizes, however, that strength comes from industrial development and this is a difficult and slow process. However hard it may work, it requires a great deal of aid from outside. The only country from which it can get substantial aid is the Soviet Union; to some extent also from the East European Communist countries. Russia's softening down, in its opinion, in revolutionary ardour and its thinking of peace and peaceful co-existence, more and more annoys China greatly. This is partly because of their ideological differences, partly also because this leads Russia to help India and like countries in their industrial development. To that extent Russia cannot help China, and indeed because of ideological differences, it has stopped helping it at all and has withdrawn all its technicians and experts from China. Many of the factories built with Russian help now lie deserted in China.

It was possible for China to fall into line with Russian thinking and present policy, and thus perhaps get more aid. But they are too proud to do this and trained too much in the old revolutionary tradition to accept defeat in this matter. What else then could they do? The other course was to heighten tensions in the world and to make non-alignment and peaceful co-existence more and more difficult to maintain. This was a direct assault on Russian policy. It can only be indulged in if they demonstrate that there was no such thing as real non-alignment by breaking those countries which practise it, and thus by increasing the polarization of the world. India was said to be the chief non-aligned country in the world, and a country which constantly preached the virtues of peaceful co-existence. If India could be humiliated and defeated and perhaps even driven into the other camp of the Western Powers, that would be the end of non-alignment for other countries also, and Russia's policy would have been broken down. The cold war would be at its fiercest and Russia would be compelled then to help China to a much greater degree and to withdraw help from the nations that did not side with it completely in the cold war. . . .

This analysis of course is a limited one. There are other factors which work too. The internal difficulties in China have made it more rash and adventurist and the extreme elements in the Government there have taken control. They see that unless some such action is taken and China's industrial progress speeded up very greatly, it will weaken and the pace of progress will slow down. The only way, therefore, to prevent this is to create a situation in which the Soviet Union would be forced to come to China's help. In order to do this, India appeared to be the safest target for the present. . . .

✦   ✦   ✦

THE RIGHTS OF WOMEN

In the late 1940s, B. R. Ambedkar, then law minister of the Government of India, sought to introduce reforms in Hindu personal law, which would give women the right to choose their marriage partner, the right to divorce, and a right to a share of their father's property. Nehru, as prime minister, strongly supported these measures. However, the progress of the 'Hindu Code Bill' was stalled by more conservative-minded politicians. However, after his position had been strengthened by his party's emphatic victory in the general elections of 1952, Nehru revived the reforms and had them passed into law in a modified form, but only after an extended and often very bitter debate in both Houses of Parliament. The excerpt that follows is from a speech made by Nehru in Parliament on 5 May 1955. These echo, probably unconsciously, Ambedkar's warnings that political democracy would have no meaning unless complemented by social and economic democracy.[16]

✦ ✦ ✦

JAWAHARLAL NEHRU: Mr. Deputy Speaker, during the last few days I have not spoken at the various stages of this Bill. But I have taken a deep interest in these discussions and followed them. As, perhaps, the House knows, I have been deeply interested not only in this Bill, but in certain matters connected therewith, and it is a matter of great gratification to me that we have arrived at this stage now, the third reading stage of this Bill and I have every hope that this House will finalise it in the course of the next few hours.

I approve of this Bill, of course. It is not merely what is incorporated in this Bill but rather something more than that which this Bill represents. It appeals to me greatly, I think it is highly important in the context of our national development. We talk about five year plans, of economic progress, industrialization, political freedom and all that. They are all highly important. But I have no doubt in my mind that the real progress of the country means progress not only on the political plane, not only on the economic plane, but also on the social plane. They have to be integrated, all these, when the great nation goes forward. . . .

Now I venture to ask: can any law, whether it is social or economic, be equally applicable when society has changed completely? Let us take India, broadly speaking, a thousand or two thousand years ago. The population of India in those days was one hundredth of what the population today is and India was a community of a large number of villages and some small towns. Now surely modern conditions are entirely different. In the cities of Delhi, Calcutta, Bombay and Madras industries are growing and new social rela-

16. Lok Sabha Debates (New Delhi), vol. 4, part 2, 22 April–7 May, cols. 7954–7968.

tions are growing up. Can anyone say that while all these changes are taking place—tremendous changes—in our social set-up, certain things must remain unchanged? The result is that they will not fit in; the result is a very bad one—that while you appear to hold on to something, that something which has gone, or is in the process of going, cracks up, because it does not fit in with the changed conditions.

This Bill has taken a few days in discussion here, but behind it lies years and years of investigation. . . . No subject, I take it, has been so much before the public, has been discussed so much and opportunities given for its consideration by the public as this particular subject in its various aspects—the question of the reform of the Hindu law in regard to personal relationships. Now that was right because it was important. After all, politics are important, economics are important, very important, but in the final analysis human relations are the most important.

This morning a fact came to my notice, that in the small state of Saurashtra, one of our smallest states, one, if I may say so, of our advanced states in many ways, socially speaking, there is on an average one suicide a day among the women because of maladjustments in human relationships. The figure was 375 in a year; 375 in a population of 40 lakhs, men, women and children. You can calculate the proportion it works out in that state. These are regular authentic figures which the chief minister of that state gave me. This shows the maladjustment and the difficulties that more especially the women have to face. I have no doubt that such similar statistics may be collected from other parts of India. One has to face that situation.

I had the privilege of listening to the speech of the honourable Member opposite, Shri N. C. Chatterjee. The more I listened to it, the more confused I got and surprised. He dealt at great length with what is a sacrament and what is a samskara[17] and other things. . . . A sacrament, I take it, is something which has religious significance, a religious ceremony. A Hindu marriage is a religious ceremony, undoubtedly. Nobody doubts that. It has a religious significance. But, does it mean that it is a sacrament to tie up people who bite, who hate each other, who make life hell for each other? Is that a sacrament or a samskara—I do not understand. Obviously, that is not the question, I admit. I would go a step further. I think all human relationships should have an element

17. 'Samskara' may be translated loosely as (cultural or ritual) tradition.

of sacrament in them. If so, the intimate relationship of husband and wife, apart from other relationships, should have an element of sacrament in it. There is something rather fine in human relationships provided they are good relationships. Otherwise, that relationship is the reverse of fine. It is awful. If they cannot fit into each other, if they are compelled to carry on together, they begin to hate each other and their life is bitter. The whole foundations of their existence are bitter. Surely that is not a sacrament.

He quoted, he referred to [the ancient law-makers] Manu and Yagnyavalkya, very great men in our history, who have shaped India's destiny. We admire them. They are among the heroes of our history. But, is it right for Shri N. C. Chatterjee or anyone to throw Manu and Yagnyavalkya at me and say what they would have done in the present conditions of India?

N. C. CHATTERJEE: I am sorry, the Prime Minister was not here; [Law Minister] Shri Pataskar threw them on me and I only reciprocated rightly.

JAWAHARLAL NEHRU: The point is, it is very unfair for Manu or Yagnyavalkya or anybody else to be brought in as a witness as to what should be done in the present conditions of India. The conditions are completely and absolutely different. I admit that there should be, and there are, undoubtedly, certain principles of human life which, normally speaking, do not change and should not change. There are certain bases of human life. But, in adapting them in legislation and other things, you have to consider the conditions as they are and not as they were 1,000 or 2,000 years ago. . . .

Now, we are often told, reminded, of the high ideals of Indian womanhood, Sita and Savitri. Well, everyone here, I take it, admires those ideals and thinks of Sita and Savitri and other heroines of India with reverence and respect and affection. Sita and Savitri are mentioned as ideals of womanhood for the women. I do not seem to remember men being reminded of Ramchandra and Satyavan, to behave like them. It is only the women who have to behave like Sita and Savitri,[18] the men may behave as they like. No example is put forward before them. I do not know if Indian men are supposed to be perfect, incapable of any further effort or further improvement, but it is bad

18. Sita and Ramchandra, and Savitri and Satyavan, were two couples from the epics legendary for their mutual love and devotion.

that this can be so. It cannot remain so, you cannot have it so under modern conditions, either modern democratic conditions or any conditions of modern life. You simply cannot have it. You cannot have a democracy, of course, if you cut off a large chunk of humanity, fifty per cent or thereabouts of the people, and put them in a separate class apart in regard to social privileges and the like. They are bound to rebel, and rightly rebel against that. . . .

Then again, it is said: 'it is all very well. We are in favour of it, but it is not good enough unless you create economic conditions for the women'. That is an argument which may be considered valid logically, but, when applied to these things, it simply means: 'Do not do this and you start the other. You have not done the first, you are doing the second'. So, the real, basic approach is that nothing need be done. It is quite absurd. You have to make some beginnings somewhere. Of course, I entirely agree that the basic thing is economic condition, equality of economic opportunity. To some extent, I hope, another Bill which is following will do it. Let us go forward still in that line, but to stop a good Act because it does not completely meet the demands of the situation is never to do anything at all.

The House will remember how it tried at first—that was not in this Parliament, but in the previous Parliament—how the then Government brought forward what they called the Hindu Code Bill, a huge document of hundreds of hundreds of pages. We considered it in various ways, introduced it in the House, referred it to committees. It was so big that we could never get through it. In fact, we never started properly with it, and it was patent that if we went through it, it might take a few years—all committee sittings and all that clause by clause consideration could not be done. Therefore, it was decided to split it up into several compartments and deal with each separately. This is the first part of it. The second I hope will be dealt with and sent to the Select Committee later. This is the only way to deal with human life. You cannot take every aspect, the condition of Indian women, all together, and improve it some way. Apart from the complication, the difficulty involved is that, simply the time element comes in and you rub up so many other groups and things and they object and say it is not practicable at all. Therefore, you have to take [them] one by one. We take this here now, and I hope we shall take something else next.

I referred to Indian women and I said that I am no admirer of certain tendencies which are visible. They are not visible in Indian women only, they are visible elsewhere too, but I would beg of you again not to fall into the trap of appearing to criticize other countries or other women or other people in other countries about whom we know very little. . . . Some of us may have gone abroad, spent two or three weeks or months abroad, and formed some opinions. Is that the way you would like a foreigner to come to India and form an opinion of Indian society? You would not. When he comes here for two months and writes a book, you object highly because he has picked out some things which he dislikes and runs you down. He does not know the background of it. As I have often said, the man goes to Banaras, from Western Europe or America and all that. Now, if I go to Banaras, there are many things that I do not like in Banaras. The streets are not clean and this and that—there are many things. But Banaras evokes in me a thousand pictures of India's history, of Buddha preaching in Sarnath, and a hundred other things happening, the whole seat of India's culture and development and this and that. I am filled with India's past history when I go to Banaras. When some tourist comes from abroad he sees the filth and dirt of the lanes of Banaras. They are both true, but it is something deeper than that. When we go abroad then we too fall into the same trap. We see some filth—social and otherwise—and think that that is the basis of society there. Do you think that the civilization of the West or your civilization or the civilization of any country has been built on these weak foundations, immoral foundations, low foundations? Do you think that any civilization, any culture, can be built up on that loose basis? Obviously not. They may have been colonial powers—they have been colonial powers; they may have dominated over us—they have done so; they have done injury to us, but the fact is that they have built a great civilization in the last 200 or 300 or 400 years and you must find out the good and take the good from them. After all we have got to build ourselves on our own soil, basically on our own ideas, but keeping the windows of our minds open to the ideas, to the winds, that come from other countries, accepting them, because the moment we close ourselves up, that moment we become static. Whether we close ourselves up by law, by dogma, by religious dogma or any other kind of closure, it is preventing the growth of the spirit of man, and it is bad, for the individual, for the group and for the country. And it has been the greatness, I think, of the basic Hindu approach of life that it was not rigid. Whether in philosophy or anything else, as everybody knows, we have a way of civilization or a way of orthodoxy completely opposed to each other. We accept them: it is a good thing. There is a spirit of tolerance; a man may be an atheist and still not cease to be a Hindu. Maybe it is not religion in the ordinary sense of the word. But in regard to certain social practices, rigidity comes in. Rigidity comes in when you say you must not eat with so and so, you must not touch so and so. That rigidity is a thing which has weakened and brought many disasters on Hindu society. Now, we have to break that rigidity. I am glad we have broken and we are continuing to break the rigidity in regard to untouchability. I hope we shall break the rigidity due to these caste divisions. Now, in that context, it becomes important that you should break this rigid statute law or interpretation of law by judges which has brought about rigidity in regard to human relations in Hindu society. It is because of that that I welcome this, because it breaks that rigidity, as anybody who has read this Bill can see the conditions provided for divorce, etc., are not easy. They are pretty difficult. For any one to say that this is something which will let loose licentiousness all over India is fantastic. There is no basis in fact for that.

So far as I am concerned, I do not propose to say anything about women in other countries. They are good or bad, as the case may be. About the social fabric of other countries, I am not competent to judge. Though I may be a little more competent perhaps, because of the opportunities I have had of travel abroad, than many Members here, yet I am not competent to judge. But I can say with considerable confidence, expressing my own faith, that the womanhood of India is something of which I am proud. I am proud of their beauty, grace, charm, shyness, modesty, intelligence and their spirit of sacrifice and I think if anybody can truly represent the spirit of India, it can be truly represented by the women of India and not by the men. So it is, and I may tell you that even now in the modern age, some women of India—not many—go out of India, maybe on some official or unofficial work, in commissions and the like. Every time that a woman has been sent, she has done well, not only done well, but produced a fine impression of the womanhood of India.

✦   ✦   ✦

16

THE HINDU SUPREMACIST

M. S. GOLWALKAR

IN THE EARLY YEARS OF INDEPENDENCE, while the country was being united, the refugees of Partition being re-settled, the princely states being integrated, and the Constitution being forged, Nehru worked shoulder-to-shoulder with Vallabhbhai Patel, who was home minister as well as deputy prime minister in the Government of India. After Patel's death in December 1950, Nehru had no equals in both party and government. He towered over the other members of his Cabinet, who were in no position really to challenge him or his ideas. However, he had plenty of critics outside Government, among them Mahadev Sadashiv Golwalkar.

Golwalkar was born in February 1906, son of a headmaster. He studied in schools in small towns in Central India before joining the Banaras Hindu University, where be received bachelor's and master's degrees in zoology. Later he also qualified as a lawyer from Nagpur. Golwalkar was well read in science and in the Hindu scriptures. He was also a formidable linguist, fluent in—among other tongues—Sanskrit, Bengali, Marathi, Hindi, and English.

In 1931, Golwalkar met the founder of the Rashtriya Swayamsewak Sangh (RSS), who was a doctor from Nagpur named K. B. Hedgewar.

The RSS stood for a militant and muscular brand of Hinduism. It recruited young men who would prepare themselves for a lifetime of service to the 'Hindu Rashtra', namely, to the creation of a nation-state run for and by Hindus. Golwalkar's intelligence and energy attracted Hedgewar, who adopted him as his protégé. He left Banaras and moved to Nagpur, where he took charge of running the RSS's organisation. On his mentor's death in 1940, he was appointed the *sarsanghchalak* or chief organiser of the RSS.

Golwalkar was influenced by Swami Vivekananda's call to worship the Motherland. He also admired Bal Gangadhar Tilak, for making culture so central to national identity and self-assertion. However, his love for India and Hindu culture went hand-in-hand with a demonisation of the West and for what he saw as the enemy within. In his suspicion of individualism and his celebration of the organic community, Golwalkar, writes the political theorist Jyotirmaya Sharma, 'displays a deep distrust of diversity'.

Golwalkar saw three principal threats to the formation of a Hindu nation—Muslims, Christians, and Communists. All three were foreign in origin, and the last was Godless to boot. Golwalkar saw Muslims, Christians, and Communists as akin to the demons or *rakshashas* of Indian mythology, with the Hindus as the avenging angels who would slay them and thus restore the goodness and purity of the motherland. The RSS itself was projected by Golwalkar as the chosen vehicle for this national and civilisational renewal of the Hindus.

After Gandhi's murder, in January 1948, Golwalkar was arrested and the RSS banned. This was because Gandhi's assassin, Nathuram Godse, had once been a member of the RSS, and because Golwalkar had himself made very provocative speeches against Muslims and the Congress. He was released from prison and the organisation unbanned in July 1949 after they agreed to abjure violence and accept the democratic principles of the Indian Constitution then being framed.

In 1952 the Bengali politician Syama Prasad Mookerjee formed the Jana Sangh as a 'Hindu-first' political alternative to the Congress. Although it claimed to be a purely cultural organisation, the RSS worked closely with the Jana Sangh, deputed workers to it, and directed its ideology. (This link continues with the Jana Sangh's successor, the Bharatiya Janata Party.) In its early years, the RSS was strong in Maharashtra, the home territory of both Hedgewar and Golwalkar. However, in the run-up to and aftermath of Partition, it greatly expanded its reach and influence in northern India. The communal riots had deeply polarised community and public opinion, as had Pakistan's invasion of Kashmir. A campaign to target the enemy within and the enemy without attracted considerable support in an atmosphere of tension and suffering. In the 1950s and 1960s, as tempers cooled in northern India, Golwalkar and the RSS worked to make their presence felt in the southern parts of the country as well.

In the 1930s the RSS had professed admiration for the policies of the National Socialists in Germany. There are certainly some parallels between Golwalkar's ideas and those of the Nazis—the mystical love of the Motherland, for example, and the hatred of the alien or the culturally impure (the Jews there, the Muslims here). Although references to the Nazis naturally disappeared in later years, Golwalkar's speeches of the 1950s and 1960s still affirmed a *blut-und-boden* (Blood and Soil) kind of nationalism, in which the Hindus were the only true lovers of the nation. The philosophy of the RSS also promised the Hindus that, were they devoted and determined enough, they would enjoy a glory in the future that had apparently been theirs in the past.

There were important Hindu right-wing thinkers before Golwalkar, such as V. D. Savarkar and Madan Mohan Malaviya. These may been more subtle or sophisticated, but scarcely as effective or influential. Through his three decades as the head of the RSS, Golwalkar exercised a deep influence on the society and politics of modern India. A lifelong *brahmachari,* or celibate, he acquired, in the fashion of a typical Hindu guru, a cult of younger male acolytes. These went on to become chief ministers of large Indian states. Others acquired even more power, directing the affairs of the Central Government in New Delhi. Thus Atal Behari Vajpayee, prime minister of India between 1998 and 2004, and Lal Krishna Advani, home minister and deputy prime minister during the same period, were both, in a personal as well as ideological sense, disciples of the long-time head of the RSS.

M. S. Golwalkar died in 1973.

THE HINDU NATION AND ITS ENEMIES

Golwalkar worked chiefly in the oral mode, giving talks to groups of RSS workers in different parts of the country. His speeches were compiled in a book published in 1966 and entitled *Bunch of Thoughts*. The excerpts below define the elements of a putative Hindu nation and identify the threats to its coming into being.[1]

✦ ✦ ✦

The first requisite for a nation is a contiguous piece of land delimited as far as possible by natural boundaries, to serve as the substratum on which the nation has to live, grow and prosper. Then the second requisite is, the people living in that particular territory should have developed love and adoration for it as their motherland, as the place of their sustenance, their security and prosperity. In short, they should feel that they are the children of that soil.

Then, that people should not be just a mass of men, just a juxtaposition of heterogeneous individuals. They should have evolved a definite way of life moulded by community of life-ideals, of culture, of feelings, sentiments, faith and traditions. If people thus become united into a coherent and well-ordered society having common traditions and aspirations, a common memory of the happy and unhappy experiences of their past life, common feelings of friendship and hostility, and all their interests inter-twined into one identical whole— then such people living as children of that particular territory may be termed a 'nation'.

If we apply this definition acknowledged by all the learned men in the world to our own country, we find that this great country of ours extending in the north from the Himalayas—with all its branches spreading north, south, east and west, and with the territories included in those great branches— right up to the Southern ocean inclusive of all the islands, is one great natural unit. As the child of this soil, our well-evolved society has been living here for thousands of years. This society has been known, especially in modern times, as the Hindu Society. This also is a historical fact. For, it is the forefathers of the

1. From M. S. Golwalkar, *Bunch of Thoughts* (Bangalore: Vikrama Prakashan, 1966), pp. 122–135.

Hindu People who have set up standards and traditions of love and devotion for the motherland. They also prescribed various duties and rites with a view to keep aglow in the people's mind for all time to come, a living and complete picture of our motherland and devotion to it as a Divine Entity. And again it is they who shed their blood in defence of the sanctity and integrity of the motherland. That all this has been done only by the Hindu People is a fact to which our history of thousands of years bears eloquent testimony. It means that only the Hindu has been living here as the child of this soil. . . .

When we say, 'this is the Hindu Nation', there are some who immediately come up with the question, 'What about the Muslims and the Christians dwelling in this land? Are they not also born and bred here? How could they become aliens just because they have changed their faith?' But the crucial point is whether THEY remember that they are the children of this soil. What is the use of merely OUR remembering? That feeling, that memory, should be cherished by THEM. . . . But the question before us now is, what is the attitude of those people who have been converted to Islam or Christianity? They are born in this land, no doubt. But are they true to its salt? Are they grateful towards this land which has brought them up? Do they feel that they are the children of this land and its tradition and that to serve it is their great good fortune? Do they feel it a duty to serve her? No! Together with the change in their faith, gone are the spirit of love and devotion for the nation.

Nor does it end there. They have also developed a feeling of identification with the enemies of this land. They look to some foreign lands as their holy places. They call themselves 'Sheikhs' and 'Syeds'. Sheikhs and Syeds are certain clans in Arabia. How then did these people come to feel that they are their descendants? That is because they have cut off all their ancestral national moorings of this land and mentally merged themselves with the aggressors. They still think that they have come here only to conquer and to establish their kingdoms. So we see that it is not merely a case of change of faith, but a change even in national identity. What else is it, if not treason, to join the camp of the enemy leaving their mother-nation in the lurch? . . .

Everybody know[s] that only a handful of Muslims came here as enemies and invaders. So also only a few foreign Christian missionaries came here. Now the Muslims and Christians have grown in number. They did not grow just by multiplication as in the case of fishes. They converted the local population. We can trace our ancestry to a common source, from where one portion was taken away from the Hindu fold and became Muslim and another became Christian. The rest could not be converted and they have remained as Hindus. Now, how did they leave their ancestral home? Was it out of their own sweet will, and out of conviction of the superiority of those faiths? Well, history does not record a single notable instance of that sort.

On the contrary, history tells us that the reason was the fear of life or coercion or the various temptations of power, position etc., and the desire to please the powers that be by adopting their ways and customs and finally even taking to their faiths. There was a lot of deception also. A piece of beef or a loaf used to be thrown into the water reservoir and the villagers, ignorant of what had happened, used to take the water as usual. On the next morning the missionary or the moulvi[2] would come and declare that since they had used the polluted water they had all lost their religion and the only way left for them was to join his fold! In this way whole villages have been converted to Islam in the North and to Christianity on our West Coast. This is deception, pure and simple. Thus it was the mad zeal for increasing their numbers for political domination. It was not propagation of religion, but a political strategy under the garb of religion. The foreign invader not only subjugated them politically and culturally but ultimately converted them to his faith. That too is foreign domination. There are political, economic and cultural dominations and this is religious domination.

It is our duty to call these our forlorn brothers, suffering under religious slavery for centuries, back to their ancestral home. As honest freedom-loving men, let them overthrow all signs of slavery and domination and follow the ancestral ways of devotion and national life. All types of slavery are repugnant to our nature and should be given up. This is a call for all those brothers to take their original place in our national life. And let us all celebrate a great Diwali[3] on the return of these prodigal sons of our society. There is no compulsion here. This is only a call and request to them to understand things properly and come back and identify themselves with the Hindu way of life in dress, customs, building homes, performing marriage ceremonies and funeral rites and such other things.

2. A Muslim cleric.

3. The Hindu festival of lights, said to commemorate the return home of the victorious God-King Ram.

There are some people who declare that they have achieved unity of Hindus, Muslims, Christians and all others on the political and economic plane. But why limit the oneness only there? Why not make it more wide and more comprehensive so as to fuse them all in the Hindu way of life, in our *dharma* and take them back as lost brothers? For those who speak of unity on the political and economic plane, we say that we stand not only for political and economic unity but also for cultural and religious unity. . . .

Today we often hear our political leaders speaking of 'national integration', 'emotional integration' and so on. But what is that 'common emotion', that common basis on which all can come together? What are those eternal life-springs of our national life that go to make it unified, resurgent and glorious?

- In the first place, the feeling of burning devotion to the land, which from times immemorial we have regarded as our sacred *Matrubhoomi* [motherland],
- in the second place, the feeling of fellowship, of fraternity, born out of the realization that we are the children of that one great common Mother,
- in the third place, the intense awareness of common current of national life, born out of common culture and heritage, of common history and traditions, of common ideals and aspirations,
- this trinity of values or, in a word, Hindu Nationalism, forms the bedrock of our national edifice.

✦   ✦   ✦

THE MUSLIM THREAT

For Golwalkar, Indian Muslims were an unreliable fifth column who threatened the unity and strength of the Hindu nation. He counted as them as the chief among three enemies—the others, as noted, being Christians and Communists. The excerpt below targets the Muslims in particular.[4]

4. From Golwalkar, *Bunch of Thoughts*, pp. 166–175.

✦   ✦   ✦

It has been the tragic lesson of the history of many a country in the world that the hostile elements within the country pose a far greater menace to national security than aggressors from outside. Unfortunately, this first lesson of national security has been the one thing which has been consistently ignored in our country ever since the British left this land. Wishful thinking born out of lack of courage to face realities, mouthing of high-sounding slogans by the persons at the helm of affairs to cover up the tragedies overtaking us one after another, and opportunistic alliances of parties and groups with the hostile elements to further their narrow self-interests, have all combined to make the threat of internal subversion to our national freedom and security very acute and real.

First, let us take the case of Muslims.

Even to this day, there are so many who say, 'now there is no Muslim problem at all. All those riotous elements who supported Pakistan have gone away once and for all. The remaining Muslims are devoted to our country. After all, they have no other place to go and they are bound to remain loyal'. . . .

Have those who remained here changed at least after [the Partition of India]? Has their old hostility and murderous mood, which resulted in widespread riots, looting, arson, raping and all sorts of orgies on an unprecedented scale in 1946–47, come to a halt at least now? It would be suicidal to delude ourselves into believing that they have turned patriots overnight after the creation of Pakistan. On the contrary, the Muslim menace has increased a hundredfold by the creation of Pakistan which has become a springboard for all their future aggressive designs on our country.

Their aggressive strategy has always been twofold. One is direct aggression. In the pre-independence days, Jinnah called it 'Direct Action'. The first blow got them Pakistan. Our leaders who were a party to the creation of Pakistan may try to whitewash the tragedy by saying that it was a brotherly division of the country and so on. But the naked fact remains that an aggressive Muslim State has been carved out of our own motherland. From the day the so-called Pakistan came into being, we have been declaring that it is a clear case of continued Muslim aggression. The Muslim desire ever since they stepped on this land some 1200 years ago to convert and enslave the entire country could not bear fruit, in spite of their political domination for several centuries, because the conquering spirit of the nation rose in the form of great and valiant men from time to time, who sounded the death-knell of their kingdoms here. But even though their kingdoms lay shattered, their desire for domination did not break up. In the coming of the British they found an opportunity to fulfil their desire. They played their cards shrewdly, sometimes creating terror and havoc, and ultimately succeeded in browbeating our leadership into panicky surrender to their sinful demand of Partition. . . .

The second front of their aggression is increasing their numbers in strategic areas of our country. After Kashmir, Assam is their next target. They have been systematically flooding Assam, Tripura and the rest of Bengal since long. It is not because, as some would like us to believe, East Pakistan is in the grip of a famine that people are coming away into Assam and West Bengal. The Pakistani Muslims have been infiltrating into Assam for the past 15 years. Does it mean then that famine has been stalking East Pakistan all these 15 years? The Muslims are entering Assam surreptitiously and the local Muslims are sheltering them. What else is this but a conspiracy to make Assam a Muslim majority province so that it would automatically fall into the lap of Pakistan in course of time? As a result, the percentage of Muslims there which was only 11% in 1950, has now more than doubled. . . .

In fact, all over the country wherever there is a masjid or a Muslim mohalla,[5] the Muslims feel that it is their own independent territory. If there is a procession of Hindus with music and singing, they get enraged saying that their religious susceptibilities are wounded. If their religious feelings have become so sensitive as to be irritated by sweet music then why don't they shift their masjids to forests and pray there in silence? Why should they insist on planting a stone on the roadside, whitewash it, call it a prayer spot and then raise a hue and cry that their prayers are disturbed if music is played?

◆ ◆ ◆

NOT SOCIALISM BUT HINDURASHTRA

In 1962, after India's humiliating defeat at the hands of China, Golwalkar argued that the nation's weakness was a consequence of its in-

---

5. A masjid is a Muslim shrine; a mohalla is a city neighbourhood.

sufficient commitment to a Hindu ethos. In the following excerpt, he juxtaposes the 'foreign' ideology of socialism, upheld by his political adversary, Jawaharlal Nehru, to the 'indigenous' model of nationalism. It is based on speeches delivered in South India in November 1963.[6]

+ + +

. . . Our great leaders are quite intelligent and educated. They also realize that without a high ideal, there can be no inspiration for the people to work. Hence they too have placed an ideal before the people. In their view, all that is old is mere ignorant credulousness and superstition and only that which is modern deserves to be an ideal. To them, all that come from Europe and America are modern. If it is Russian, then it must be ultra-modern! But since everything of our land is old and ancient, it is retrogressive and hence unworthy of their consideration. And so, they looked to the West for some ideal. The most modern 'ism' of all the western 'isms' being 'Socialism', our leaders opted for it as the ideal to be placed before our people. The logic of these votaries of modernism is simply wonderful! Anything new, i.e., modern must be superior to things of old. The mere fact of its later birth gives a thing an inherent superiority! So from that point of view, death is superior to life! For, does not death follow life? Likewise, any son is greater than his father! . . .

Now, let us see if Socialism can be an ideal for our country. Firstly it is not a product of this soil. It is not in our blood and tradition. It has absolutely nothing to do with the traditions and ideals of thousands of years of our history. That is why it is thought alien to the millions of our people here. As such it does not have the power to thrill their hearts, and is incapable of inspiring them to a life of dedication and character. Thus we see that it does not possess even the primary qualification to serve as an ideal for our national life.

Further, the very idea of Socialism was born in rank selfishness, in a spirit of envy and hatred. In the European countries, the ushering-in of democracy practically synchronized with the coming of the industrial age. In democracy, all people had equal opportunities. Those who were gifted with more intelligence and more ability pounced upon all these industrial developments of science and became extremely rich. With their riches, they also controlled the

6. Excerpts from M. S. Golwalkar, *Not Socialism but Hindurashtra* (Bangalore: Kesari Press, 1964), pp. 15–45.

Governments to an extent and thus became virtually masters of the people. The rest of the people had only to grudge, having been reduced to the position of slaves. They could not bear to see other people enjoying their wealth when they themselves could not get two square meals. So, a spirit of envy burnt in them and therefore, they rose against that system to ensure a better distribution of wealth. This is how Socialism was born.

This is not to say that the previous system was in any way good, or that the common mass of people should have continued to submit meekly to the oppression of the rich. Far from it. Democracy, which was born as a reaction against the despotic kingship of those times, had fastened new chains in place of old. The high sounding concept of 'individual freedom' meant only freedom for the talented few to exploit the rest of the common people. That was, indeed, an unbearable situation. But Socialism, which was born in that context, was again a mere reaction solely inspired by hatred towards the exploiting class. Then later on political philosophers came forward and said, 'No, no, this is not merely hatred and selfishness. This is the dialectics of materialism, this is social justice'. All these external get-up to give a decent look were added later on. However, its entire theory is based on hate—class hatred and class conflict. Thus, born and based on the sole motive force of hate and envy, it cannot be expected to build up good character in any human being following that theory. . . .

So we have to find out a proper ideal which beats in our hearts, throbs in our blood, and which has been with us for generations. It is no use placing before the people a formless spirit as an ideal. It may be all right for the enlightened. But ordinary men like us require an ideal which we can easily see, understand and experience. Then only will everyone develop in himself a devotion for that ideal, and the ambition to lead a life of pure character will be roused in his heart. Such an ideal is our Nationhood—the great 'Hindu Rashtra'. Now, many of our leaders are emphasizing a number of 'isms'. But the one 'ism' that transcends them all is the real, thorough-going 'nationalism' and that nationalism, in its pristine purity, is our ideal. The *Hindu Rashtra* is therefore our ideal.

'I am a part and parcel of this *Rashtra*. For generations, my forefathers have been striving to do their mite for the propagation of this great national life. I will also do my utmost for the same purpose.' This is the natural attitude we have inherited. But, this attitude we have allowed to be forgotten. We

have to forget this forgetfulness, reawaken in ourselves a dominant understanding and love for our national life and build upon that sure foundation our
strength to meet the challenge of the times. . . .

We, the Hindus, have been living here as the children of this land. We love
this land as our mother. It has protected us like a father. It is in this holy atmosphere of our land that our forefathers were able to unravel the mysteries of
existence and realize the Ultimate Reality which is called by various names.
Nothing can be holier to us than this land. Every particle of dust, everything
living or non-living, animate or inanimate, every stream and reservoir is holy
for us. This training is being given here from times immemorial, from generation to generation. When a child tramples on the ground in play, the mother
says, 'Do not kick the Mother-Earth, dear child'. Or if a nail is driven into the
earth, she says, 'Oh, no! dear child, Mother will be pained'. Such is our tradition. This is not a mere lip expression. It has been developed in us as an experience in our daily life. . . .

But today, there are people in our country who contemptuously consider
this concept of motherland as a meaningless concept belonging to a bygone
age. They consider themselves to be intellectuals and progressives. So far as
we are concerned, we, out of gratitude, call everything that supports and bring
up, as mother. The woman who gave birth to us is our mother. The life-giving
river is our mother. The cow that nourishes us by her life-juice right through
our lives is our mother. In fact, this feeling is a sign of true blossoming of culture, a sign of expansion of mind. What a divine and sublime outlook of mind
it is to view the whole creation as a manifestation of the Great Mother! But for
some, intellect is everything. They forget that even intellectual reasoning has
got a limit. For instance, the human body is after all material. The body of one's
mother also is as much material as any other body. Then why should any one
consider his mother as different from other women? Why have devotion for
her? An intellectual has no answer for this. Take another instance. The human
body requires for its nourishment starch, protein, fat, salt and water. And
these food contents are readily available in human flesh. After all, biologically
man is nothing but blood, flesh and bones. So, why not eat up our neighbour?
But if a person [talks] like this, he may be called a scholarly logician, but certainly not a civilized man. Such intellectualism leads only to cannibalism. . . .

It is therefore that we have to revitalize that love which will make us say,
'Every inch, every particle of our motherland, we will defend with our life-blood.

Our fore-fathers did it, we will do it'. This determination must throb in the heart of every one of us. Day-in and day-out, in our wakeful condition or in our deep sleep, whatever the work we are engaged in, this must be the supreme idea to spur us on to every activity. We are her children. We have been her children for thousands of years. It is we who say that She is our Mother. It is we who say that She is our *Dharma Bhumi, Karma Bhumi, Punya Bhumi, Moksha Bhumi, Pitru Bhumi and Matru Bhumi.*[7] The *Bhumi* is the holies of the holy for us. Before this even heaven has no charms for us. This, we Hindus have said. Who else? . . .

And again, we have to realize one more truth, that we Hindus have been a nation in the fullest sense of the term all along. We have had an ideal, to realize the Ultimate Truth. . . . A whole galaxy of great people have been born from the very ancient times right up to this day, who have been equally worshipful to all of us because they have set before us the ideal life by which man can attain the highest goal of human existence. We have our interests joined to one another. We have the same friends and foes. All the impressions that we have from our past history are common in our hearts. . . .

It has been in our hearts from the very beginning that this is our Hindu Nation. We are nowadays trying to forget it, saying that it is a communal and narrow-minded idea. Had we from the very beginning emphasized that this is Hindu Rashtra, we would have known how to behave with the rest of the people and how to win them over for the rebuilding of this Hindu Rashtra. But we gave up this truth. We thought that we could do without this truth. That is why we are today face to face with all the evils at present infesting our life.

This ideal of the Hindu Rashtra, we have to place before our people. They feel it in our blood. And therefore, if we place this idea of devotion for the Hindu Rashtra, then for the purpose of serving this great national existence in which all of them have been living from generations, they will curb their selfishness, become men of character and be able to stand foursquare before the present day dangers which threaten our very existence. . . .

✦　✦　✦

7. These terms may be translated as, respectively, 'the Land of our Traditions and Ethos', 'the Land of our Work', 'the Land of our Worship', 'the Land of our Salvation', 'the Land of our Fathers', and 'the Land of our Mothers'.

17

THE INDIGENOUS SOCIALIST

RAMMANOHAR LOHIA

FROM ITS BEGINNINGS IN 1925, the Rashtriya Swayamsewak Sangh had set itself in opposition to the Congress. It saw that party as too sympathetic to the Muslims, and its leaders as too appreciative of the West. It stayed apart from the campaigns against colonial rule conducted by the Congress. Our next maker of modern India, on the other hand, was for very many years a member of the Indian National Congress. After Independence, however, he left the party and became an uncompromising critic of the policies of the party's leader and the country's prime minister, Jawaharlal Nehru.

This rebel and heretic was named Rammanohar Lohia. Lohia was born in 1910 in the town of Faizabad, in present-day Uttar Pradesh, into a family of hardware merchants. He was educated in Bombay, where he picked up Marathi, in Calcutta, where he learnt fluent Bengali, and in Benares, where he may have been most comfortable, since Hindi was his mother tongue. By the time he reached his teens, he was a convinced nationalist—thus in 1928, he took part in demonstrations against the all-white Simon Commission for constitutional reforms.

Lohia then went to Berlin for higher studies. Watching Gandhi's Salt March from afar, he wrote a doctoral dissertation, in German, on the economics of salt. His supervisor was the great sociologist Werner Sombart (the author of, among other works, a classic study of why the United States has no indigenous socialist tradition). Lohia left Germany just as the Nazis were coming to power. Had he stayed, he would surely have fallen foul of the new rulers on political, if not racial, grounds.

Lohia returned to India in 1934, an anti-imperialist and socialist. He was an early recruit into the Congress Socialist Party. In 1936 Lohia became Secretary of the Congress's new department of foreign affairs, where he became very interested in the fate of Indians overseas and in freeing the enclave of Goa from Portuguese rule.

Lohia was jailed in 1940 for his speeches against British rule. Two years later he became a hero of the Quit India movement, operating underground for a year and nine months, issuing pamphlets and letters from his secret locations. He was finally arrested in Bombay in May 1944, and taken to Lahore Fort, where he was tortured and kept in solitary confinement. Released in 1946 as part of a general amnesty, he went to Goa to campaign for its freedom. He was arrested, tortured, and deported back to British India.

After India became independent, the socialists in the party left the Congress to form their own organisation. In 1952 the Socialist Party merged with the Kisan Mazdoor Praja Party (founded by the veteran Gandhian J. B. Kripalani) to form the Praja Socialist Party (PSP). Lohia served briefly as General Secretary. In 1955 a radical group led by him left the PSP. The two factions were reunited in 1964 to form a Samyukta (or United) Socialist Party (SSP). In 1965 the party split again—Lohia's group kept the SSP label, whereas his critics started a fresh PSP.

In and out of British jails, Rammanohar Lohia was also arrested several times in independent India—for opposing tax laws, for entering the restricted areas of the North East Frontier Agency without a valid permit, for protesting a rise in prices. Once, in 1964, he was even arrested in the United States of America, for defying the laws of racial segregation in Mississippi and entering the all-white section of a hotel.

After several unsuccessful attempts, Lohia entered the Indian Parliament through a by-election in 1963. Here, he made many provocative speeches against the Congress and against Nehru and his legacy. He believed that the ruling party and its leaders had deliberately distanced themselves from the people of India, economically, linguistically, and sartorially. They were a new elite, brown in colour, but white in language, customs, and manners.

On the economic front, Lohia was a critic of both capitalism and communism. He argued, precociously, for a third way, for a new political and economic system based on the decentralisation of political power, on the use of small-scale technology, and on fulfilling the basic needs of the poor rather than on the creation of wealth per se.

Lohia was both brilliant and sectarian. His critics within the socialist movement accused him of fostering a personality cult around himself. One can see him, with qualifications, as an Indian Trotsky—scholarly, well-read, articulate in many languages, and with a deep interest in literature and the arts. Like Trotsky, he attracted the attention and devotions of many gifted writers and artists. Like Trotsky, for much of his life he was marginalised by politicians he believed to be greatly inferior to himself. There was one notable difference, however—while Trotsky was unashamedly elitist, Lohia affected a love of the popular and the demotic.

Rammanohar Lohia died in 1967, aged fifty-seven.

CASTE AND CLASS

In 1956 Lohia and B. R. Ambedkar met to discuss the possibility of their parties collaborating for the next year's general elections. Unforunately, Ambedkar died soon afterwards. But, as the following excerpt shows, Lohia's thought had much in common with Ambedkar's, notably in its identification of caste, rather than class, as the chief organising principle of Indian society. In this essay of 1958, Lohia brilliantly analysed the continuing hold of the higher castes in independent India.[1]

✦　✦　✦

1. From Rammanohar Lohia, *The Caste System* (1964; reprint, Hyderabad: Rammanohar Lohia Samata Vidyalaya Nyas, 1979), pp. 81–105.

. . . Castes have endured over thousands of years. They have bred certain traits and aptitudes. Some kind of a selection has taken place that is socially as significant as a natural selection. Certain skills of trade, craft, husbandry or administration or handling of principles have become hereditary. A real break-through is almost always the work of a genius. With such caste-wise determination of skills, one might expect great advantages to flow out of such age long selections. That would have been so if all skills fetched an equal social status or monetary reward. They obviously do not. Some skills are believed to be unbelievably superior to others and there is an interminable series of steps in the ladder. Castes of inferior skills are downgraded. They congeal into an almost life-less mass. They cease to be the reservoir from which the nation may refresh and renew itself. Numerically small castes of the most superior skills are the habitual providers of the nation's leadership. In order to maintain their most unnatural dominance, they become a seething mass of chicanery but surfacially most smooth and cultured. The masses are lifeless, the elite are chicane. Caste has done that. . . .

The system of castes is a terrifying force of stability and against change, a force that stabilises all current meanness, dishonor and lie. An unholy fear prevails, lest, if some meanness or lie were to tumble the whole structure might topple. Post-freedom India is but a strict continuance of British India in most essential ways. The Indian people continue to be disinherited. They are foreigners in their own land. Their languages are suppressed and their bread is snatched away from them. All this is done for the alleged sake of certain high principles. And these principles tie up with the system of caste, the great chasm between the few high castes and the four hundred million of the lower castes. These high castes must maintain their rule, both political and economic and, of course, religious. They cannot do it alone through the gun. They must instill a sense of inferiority into those whom they seek to govern and exploit. This they can best do by turning themselves into a select caste with speech, dress, manners and living of which the lower castes are incapable. The attitude of India's political parties is governed by this supreme consideration of having to instill a complex of inferiority among the mass of the people. Peoples' languages are undeveloped, their housing and general styles of living incapacitate them from good or great action and their mind is not worth considering. So must the high castes weave the net of illusion. Current political opinions in India, because they reflect the false and unnatural interests of the high castes, are not worthy of consideration.

The political behaviour of the lower caste is amazing. Why they should become a willing part of this conspiracy is beyond understanding. One reason is clear enough. Caste gives them insurance, indeed, on less than an animal level, more than it does to the high-castes. They would feel helpless without it. Oft times, one gets the impression about these lower castes as though their strenuous labour of the day were but a preparation for the caste feasts and rituals that are to follow. They are the real thing and all else is but a shadow. Anything that interferes with them must appear to them as highly undesirable. They have in fact legends and myths that justify their lowly situation and transform it into a symbol of sacrifice and luster. The Kahars, variously known as Mallahs, Kaivarts, Naviks, who probably number more than a crore, tell stories about their mythical ancestors, who were simple, ungreedy, brave and generous and who lost to other ancestors of Kshatriyas and other high castes because of their greater greed, wiliness and deceit. Taken so, their current life of misery must appear to the lower castes as an unending succession of sacrificial acts for the sake of high principles. . . .

The political behaviour of the lower castes would appear to be a little less inexplicable on the assumption that a long tradition of ideological subjection has made them stagnate. This assumption is wholly founded. Centuries have instilled into them a meek acceptance of the existing [order], aversion to change, sticking with the caste in times of adversity as of good luck, and the search for high life through worship, rituals and general politeness. This can change. In fact, this must change. The revolt against caste is the resurrection of India or, shall we say, the bringing into being of a unique and a hitherto unrealised occasion, when India shall be truly and fully alive. Is such a revolt possible? Scholars may . . . deny it. Men of action will continue to affirm it. Some hope of success arises at the present time. The attack on caste is not single-barrelled. It does not climax into a shrill cry devoid of action. It is in fact as political as it is social. From the political attack on caste, in the sense of drawing the nation's leadership from all the castes in the country, may come that revolution which gives to all Indian society the solidarity and reinsurance now given to smaller groups by caste.

Elsewhere may be found extracts from the constitution and the annual report of the Calcutta Club.[2] This club is the top meeting ground of the Calcutta bourgeoisie, which is the largest segment of the Indian bourgeoisie. Its main activity centres around wine bibbing, while its patron is the President of the Republic. India's Republic is pledged to the policy of prohibition with very considerable police repression as a consequence in certain areas. That the President of an alcohol repressing republic should be the patron of an alcohol drinking club, is a measure of fraud and perfidy which India's higher castes are practicing upon the country and themselves. The President, but more so, the government which advises him are guilty of treason against the republic in a yet more major way. Europeans in India are one in three thousand and more of the population. Of Calcutta's population, they are surely no more than one in four hundred. They enjoy far greater comfort and security than any section of India's population. And yet they are accorded equal representation on the committee of this club. This equality of representation is guaranteed by the club's statutes. The club continues to think that England's monarch still rules India through her viceroy, although the President of the Republic is its patron. Some may be inclined to pass this over as a relic of the past which has escaped notice. These acts are in reality the result of deliberate design. India's bourgeoisie is ever imperiled. A vast sea of miserable humanity surges around it. It clutches at all kinds of symbols old and new and all kinds of authority both substantial and empty in order to keep itself afloat. India's higher castes and their government have therefore to practice continually treason against their Republic. . . .

Foreign rule set the Hindu against the Muslim, but that does not rub out the discord which native religions had created in the country. The policy of divide and rule, which governments pursue, must fasten on already existing elements of division. British rule in India had made use of the element of caste in the same manner that it made use of the element of religion. As the divisive force of caste was not nearly as strong as that of religion, the effort met limited success. The Maratha Party in Western India and also that of the Scheduled Castes, the Justice Party in the South and the mission-led block of Adivasis in Eastern India were fruits of this effort. To them must also be added the block of native princes and big landlords in Eastern India, which

2. Not reproduced here.

followed the lead of foreign rule and, during its last days, appeared discredited beyond recovery.

At the time the British made this effort, they were justifiably condemned. Foreign rule habitually accentuates and widens differences; it does not compose them. It must be condemned. But such condemnation does not remove the ground on which differences originate and thrive. British rule has ended but the caste parties that it gave birth to have continued into free India and are enjoying fresh access of strength. The Workers and Peasants Party and the Republican Party of Western India, the Dravida Munetra Kazhagam of South India and the Jharkhand Party of Eastern India alongside of the Ganatantra and Janata parties are not only regional parties but also caste parties. In fact, they represent and embody regional castes. These regional castes are decisively numerous in their area. The Adivasis of Chota Nagpur are the life-blood of the Jharkhand, the Mahars of the Republicans, the Marathas of the Workers and Peasants, the Mudaliars but also other non-Brahmins of the Dravida Munetra, and the Kshatriyas, not nearly as much of the Ganatantra and the Janata.[3] . . .

The castes that want to form the Maratha, Justice or Scheduled Caste parties suffered ill-treatment from society. The British rulers made use of this sense of grievance and injury, a very bad use indeed, but they did not and could not have created it. That is why the problem has persisted. In some cases, the caste that has suffered the injury and that which has caused it have changed places. But that does not solve the problem of injury. Furthermore, numberless castes have yet to make themselves vocal and effective and are today content to play a passive or a subsidiary role to the contending giants. This is the chief source of injury and injustice.

The political inter-play of castes has unfolded itself fascinatingly in Maharashtra and the drama is not yet over. Until 1930 and a little after, the Maharashtra scene was baffling simple, and its backdrop was Brahmin versus the rest. . . . The Maratha was the spearhead of the revolt against the Brahmin in Maharashtra although other down-graded castes assisted him in varying degrees. The revolt was pro-British in the beginning, because the Brahmins were on the whole anti-British, but the nationalist movement proved strong

---

3. The regional parties mentioned in these paragraphs were very active in the 1950s; some continue to be active still.

enough to absorb it. The Maratha entered the party of nationalism, the Congress Party, and almost took it over. The phenomenon of caste exclusion was witnessed again, with the roles changed. On the one hand, the Brahmin began gradually to lose his monopoly of political power and, on the other, the Maratha did not share his new found authority with the other down-graded castes. . . . They [the Marathas] proved to be as greedy for power and monopolistic as any. They used the revolt of the down-graded castes for the assertion of their own supremacy and not for the destruction of castes as such and the injustice that goes with them. Ever and ever again, the revolt of the down-graded castes has been misused to upgrade one or another caste rather than to destroy the entire edifice of caste. . . .

The exclusion of the high caste from political power does not necessarily imply their exclusion from economic and other types of power. In the first place, such political exclusion has nowhere been total, not even in the South. The Brahmins have in recent years, as the sole representative of the high caste, been increasingly eliminated from legislative and administrative power in Tamilnad. Even so, they still occupy a fantastically privileged position. Although only 4 per cent of the population, their share in the gazette services of the administration must be around forty per cent. At one time, it was nearly seventy per cent. A second more remarkable development is the acquisition of economic power by the Tamil Brahmin. He has increasingly been buying up Mount Road[4] from the retiring British. It would therefore be not correct to describe the high castes in terms of any general decline or to bemoan their fate in any part of the country. . . .

Three distinct types of opposition to caste may be noted, one wordy, the second low level and mixed, and the third real. The wordy opposition is the loudest in respect of such generalised condemnation of caste as leaves the existing structure almost intact. It condemns the caste system as wholly evil, but would equally condemn those who resort to active steps to destroy the system. It sanctifies the principles of rising standards of living and of merit and equality of opportunity as solvents of caste. Raise everybody economically; give everybody an equal opportunity! So say these false advocates of destruction of caste, as though rising standards and opportunities

---

4. Mount Road, now Anna Salai, is the chief thoroughfare of Madras (now Chennai), with land adjacent to it commanding the highest prices.

would be restricted to the low caste. When everybody has an equal opportunity, castes with the five thousand year old traditions of liberal education would be on top. Only the exceptionally gifted from the lower castes would be able to break through this tradition. This is what India's political parties, Congress, Communist and Praja Socialists, under Mr. Nehru's leadership have in mind. They would want men and women of exceptional ability from the lower castes to join their ranks. But they would want the structure as a whole to be kept intact. They are themselves drawn overwhelmingly from the higher castes. They have no hesitation in denouncing their caste or the distinction of high and low castes, so long as their social group based on traditions, ability and manners is left unaffected. If anybody qualifies in ability and manners from among the lower castes, he is welcome. But how many would qualify! Very few. It would be the battle of five thousand years of oppressive training and tradition against an individual talent. Only the genius or the exceptionally able would win in this battle. . . .

A vested interest socialism talks of political and economic revolution alone, meaning the award of increased wages or bonus on the lowest level and the destruction of private property in factories and the like on the highest level. Even in the Europe of changing classes, such a revolution would keep intact the distinction between manual workers and those with the brain. In [an] India of fixed castes, this distinction would spell ruin to the health of society. Workers with the brain are a fixed caste in Indian society; together with the soldier caste, they are the high-caste. Even after the completed economic and political revolution they would continue to supply the managers of the state and of industry. The mass of the people would be kept in a state of perpetual physical and mental lowliness, at least comparatively. But the position of the high-caste would then be justified on grounds of ability and in economic terms as it is now on ground of birth or talent. That is why the intelligentsia of India which is overwhelmingly high-caste, abhors all talk of a mental and social revolution of a radical change in respect of language or caste or the bases of thought. It talks generally and in principle against caste. In fact, it can be most vociferous in its theoretical condemnation of caste, so long as it can be allowed to be equally vociferous in raising the banner of merit and equal opportunity. What it loses in respect of caste by birth, it gains in respect of caste by merit. Its merit concerning speech, grammar, manners, capacity to adjust, routine efficiency is undisputed. Five thousand years have gone into the building of this undisputed merit. A true doctrine of equal opportunity would have to undo the work of five thousand years by giving preferential treatment to the lower castes over a period of at least a few decades. . . .

On no account do the high castes comprise more than one-fifth of India's population. But they keep to themselves almost four-fifths of the nation's leadership. In respect of the top leadership of the four main departments of national activity, business, army, high civil services and political parties, the high-castes easily comprise four-fifths. . . . When more than four-fifths of a nation's vital leadership is traditionally selected from among one-fifths of its population, a state of atrophy is bound to ensure. Four-fifths of its population sinks into a state of listlessness and inefficiency. The nation is sick and continually on the point of death. To revitalize such a nation, a designed selection of leadership has to be made. At least half or sixty per cent of the nation's top leadership must be selected by design from among the lower castes. This need not be done by law. It had better be done through a purposeful understanding. . . . The attempt to revitalize the nation's leadership in terms of caste must be made again and again until it succeeds. . . .

The first wordy war on caste, led by the Dwija,[5] is evenly matched by the second empty struggle against caste led by select Sudra groups. Among the Sudras, certain castes are numerically powerful, even overwhelming in some areas. The age of adult franchise has placed power in their hands. Some castes like the Reddys and Mudaliars of south India and the Marathas of west have made use of it. They, and not the Dwija, are the political overlords of their areas, though, even here the high-caste has strengthened his economic grip and is making most clever and deceptive efforts to stage a political comeback. This is possible chiefly because these are empty struggles against caste. They do not change the social order in the sense of making it more just, mobile or active. They do not give power to all the lower castes, but only to the largest single section within them. They do not therefore destroy caste, but merely cause a shift in status and privileges. Some of the trappings of the high-caste belonging to the Brahmin or Vaishya are stripped off

---

5. The three highest castes, Brahmins, Kshatriyas, and Vaishyas, were collectively known as the Dwija. Traditionally, the males of these castes were allowed to wear the sacred thread, a privilege denied the Sudras and the Untouchables.

them and patched on to the Maratha or the Reddy. This solves no problem. Rather, it disgusts all the other lower castes and enrage[s] the high caste. Caste, with all its debility and some more of its irritations, remains. . . .

Sectional elevation is dangerous in yet another way. Those among the lower castes who rise to high positions tend to assimilate themselves to the existing high-castes. In this process, they inevitably appropriate the baser qualities of the high-caste. Everybody knows how the lower castes, on their rise, tend to segregate their women, which again is a quality not of the top high-caste but of the medium high-caste. Also the lower castes that rise begin to wear the sacred thread of the Dwija, which has so long been denied to them but which the true high caste has begun discarding. All this has an additional result of perpetuating the distinction. Furthermore, such a rise does not cause a general ferment among the lower castes. The risen are alienated from their own groups; instead of fermenting their own original lower groups they seek to become part of the higher castes to whose positions they rise. This process of an extremely sectional and superficial rise gives birth to another misfortune. The lever to the rise is supplied not by the cultivation of good qualities or talent but by the arousing of bitter caste jealousies and the play of intrigues. . . .

This brings us to the third and true struggle against caste now on the agenda of India's history. This struggle aims to pitch-fork the five downgraded groups of society, women, Sudras, Harijans, Muslims and Adivasis,[6] into positions of leadership, irrespective of their merit as it stands today. This merit is at present necessarily low. The tests of merit are also such as to favour the high-caste. What long ages of history have done must be undone by a crusade. The inclusion of all women, including Dwija women, which is but right, into the downgraded groups of society raises their proportion to the entire population to 90%. This vast sea of submerged humanity, nine out of every ten of India's men and women, has drowsed into silence or, at best, some routine noises of seeming life. Economic and political uplift, by itself, may put some fat on their lean limbs. A restoration of self-respect through the abolition of caste, of course, when it goes side by side with economic uplift, can rouse them into the activity of full men and awakened peoples. Let it not be

---

6. Harijan was Gandhi's name for the erstwhile Untouchables; Adivasis are the tribal communities of central India.

forgotten that the high-castes, Dwija, have also suffered grievously from this atrophy of the people, [for] their education and culture hides, under the veneer of good speech and manners, the deadly poison of the lie and self-advancement through deceit. A crusade to uplift the downgraded groups would revive also the high-caste, would set right frames and values which are all askew today. This crusade must never be confused with the niggardly award of preferential positions to a few scores among the lower castes. This only irritates the high-caste. A howl goes up. It does not at all ferment the lower castes. What matters if a dozen or two of the lower castes are added to the high-caste oligarchy of several thousands in any sphere of life? There is need to add them by the hundred and the thousand. That will turn into a crusade what is today only a vote-catching, quarrel-making and jealousy-inspiring device. . . .

This policy of uplift of downgraded castes and groups is capable of yielding much poison. In fact, care may only mitigate some of the worst aspects of the poison; it cannot be totally eliminated. A first poison may come out of its immediate effects on men's minds; it may speedily antagonize the Dwija without as speedily influencing the Sudras. With his undoubted alertness to developments and his capacity to mislead, the Dwija may succeed in heaping direct or indirect discredit on the practitioners of this policy long before the Sudra wakes up to it. Secondly, the colossi among the lower castes like the Chamars and Ahirs may want to appropriate the fruits of this policy without sharing them with the myriad other low castes, with the result that the Brahmin and Chamar change places but caste remains intact. Thirdly, the policy may be misused by selfish men among the lower castes for individual advancement, who may additionally use weapons of intrigue and caste jealousies. This would rend society further apart and subject it to grosser selfishness without bringing it any benefits of weakening and expansion. Fourthly, every single case of election or selection between a Sudra and Dwija may become the occasion for acrimonious exchanges. The baser elements among the downgraded castes would use it as a constant weapon. In their overweening desire to eliminate the particular Dwija against whom they are ranged, they would in total seek to oust all Dwijas or to fill the air with darker suspicions when they fail. . . .

Such is the poison that this policy may bring forth. Continual awareness of this poison may check it in great measure. But the fear of the poison should not blind us to the miraculous power of this policy to create and cure. India will know the most invigorating revolution of her history. The people will have become alive as never before. She may also have indicated in the process a lesson or two to mankind. Karl Marx tried to destroy class, without being aware of its amazing capacity to change itself into caste. . . . For the first time, an experiment shall have been made in the simultaneous destruction of class and caste.

The young high-caste must now rise to his full measure. Instead of seeing in this policy an attack on his interest, he should view it for its capacity to renew the people. . . . The young high-caste must decide to turn himself into manure for the lower castes, so that the people may for once flower into their full glory. If human nature were capable of infinite sacrifice, we would have the high-caste become advisers, while the executives are all low-caste. If this is not possible everywhere, let it be so in as many places as possible. With faith in the great crucible of the human race and equal faith in the vigour of all the Indian people, let the high-caste choose to mingle tradition with mass. Simultaneously, a great burden rests on the youth of the lower castes. Not the aping of the high-caste in all its traditions and manners, not dislike of manual labour, not individual self-advancement, not bitter jealousy, but the staffing of the nation's leadership as though it were some sacred work should now be the supreme concern of women, Sudras, Harijans, Muslims, and Adivasis.

✦   ✦   ✦

BANISH ENGLISH

In the 1950s, Lohia called for the formation of, among other things, a 'Caste Abolition Committee', a 'Price Fixation Committee', and an 'English Removal Committee'. He saw English as a foreign language, promoted by the Indian elite merely to further their interests. He once timed an 'English Removal' convention to coincide with the visit of the British monarch, Queen Elizabeth II, to India. The following excerpts explain why he was opposed to English being used in administration and as a medium of instruction in schools and colleges.[7]

7. From Rammanohar Lohia, *Language* (Hyderabad: Rammanohar Lohia Samata Vidyalaya Nyas, 1986), pp. 10–20.

✦   ✦   ✦

In our own country, I often feel—and perhaps you too feel that way—as if we have been evicted from our fields and homes and that some intruder has usurped the lands and we, the real occupants, are thrown out wringing our hands helplessly in despair. One can reconcile to such an ugly situation after having failed to settle one's land arrears or answer one's debts. But when such a condition is intrigued and forced upon one through forged documents and book-manoeuvring, it is a grave assault on justice. India today faces such an impossible situation. Sitting tight on the high pedestal of offices the top-men advocate a 'go-slow' policy regarding the removal of English. Having been deprived of all our belongings, we have become strangers in our own homes. The ten years of our freedom have committed us to a very paradoxical situation. The real owners of the soil have been estranged and a foreign Fuhrer with all his might and authority lords over us. . . .

You are an employee in the tramways, you organize your own unions. But what is the language in which you carry on your everyday work and correspondence? Obviously English. But how many among you, 9,000 workmen, know this foreign language? Problems concerning labour are talked from the platform and discussed in the press on behalf of the labour, in a medium which a worker is unable to understand. All Indian languages are outlawed. This has its attendant evil. A leadership is hardly evolved from among the rank and file of the workers themselves. Thus the very roots are cut, not the earth alone on which a common wage-earner stands and aspires to use it as a spring-board to leadership. Company management, trade union and civil service have conspired into a triple alliance. In times of emergency, they unite their forces to thwart the just claims of labour. This triple league is bound to continue its oppression over them as long as English continues.

If the entire administrative work of the government and its intellectual activities continue to be carried on in the language of the minority then whose interests will such a government defend? On which side, will it lean? Out of 40 crores, English has touched a fringe of 40 lakh Indians only. The government has its eyes set on this privileged class of 40 lakhs.[8] Towards the rest it has turned its back. The problems that concern the 40 crore underdogs go ne-

8. A lakh is 100,000; a crore is 10 million.

glected, their needs remain unanswered. What matters to the government are the interests of 40 lakhs which alone seem to assume an all India character and, hence, national importance.

Problems relating to prices of foodgrains and hunger will remain unsolved while English continues to thrive on the Indian soil. The bureaucracy till that date will stand at the beck and call of 40 lakhs alone. The dumb masses will never attract its attention and their cries shall ever fall on its deaf ears. At least a crore or a crore and a half inhabitants of this subcontinent take their daily dip in the waters of the Ganga and the Kaveri. Another fifty lakhs depend for their drinking water on their perennial streams. But is not their water polluted by the gutters that drain the cities? And yet there is no one to take up this issue. To the administrative bosses these are but minor problems and of no consequence. Representatives of the forty lakh English versed aristocracy are enthroned in power. The banishment of English will be their dethronement. For these drowning big-wigs English serves as a last straw. They know well that with the removal of English, the government, the law of the land, the trade unions, public institutions and the leading men will have to take cognizance of the forty crores. This would mean a great revolution. It will shake the very foundation of their feudal empire. Take for instance, the defence services. What are the necessary merits for an Indian soldier to rise above the rank of a colonel? Undoubtedly, it is not being conversant in the art of warfare, but a thorough proficiency in [the] English language. The ability to dictate notes in English, the adeptness with which one can converse in English at the dining table and the ease with which one can hold the knife and the fork are some of the few decisive factors. Not gallantry, nay, not the knowledge of warfare, but the mere acquaintance of the English language, is the sole criterion. . . .

Let us now come to the problem of the belly. Who dominate[s] the economic life of the country today? An overwhelming majority of Indians use 'neem-sticks' and charcoal powder to clean their teeth. Who are generally the consumers of toothpaste, automobiles, facepowder, cream and other cosmetics? Newspapers overflow with their advertisements. In modern India, the sale of these fashionable articles of use is confined to the forty to fifty lakhs of English-educated people. A section of the rural population in the cities may swell this figure say at the most to a crore or so. It is to meet the needs of these fashionable people that our daily press advertisers display their wares.

It is now left to you and your judgment to decide which way the economic life of the nation really moves. Whether in the sphere of production or that of consumption, the economic life of the nation stands tuned to this limited section of forty lakhs. The problems of these few become the problems of all.

These forty lakhs provide a fertile soil for the growth of leadership of all political opinions. These leaders are at the helm of affairs of all political parties. This explains the reactionary and conservative nature of their leadership. Modernization is the cry of India today, it is a high and laudable ideal. This privileged class of forty lakhs supported by the leadership in various political groups is unanimous in its view and voice—this is an indication of its corrupt and reactionary mind—that the sale of these articles of luxury should not only be maintained but further encouraged simultaneously with the retention and propagation of English. These two trends are heading the nation towards ruination. The forty crores will have to be alert. They must stand firm to their ground and forge ahead towards a revolution. . . .

Many a ridiculous argument is heard in this respect. One of them is that Bengali, Hindi, Marathi, Tamil and several other native languages are still undeveloped. They, therefore, cannot give us up to date ideas and information. A well-developed Western language thus becomes indispensable. Such a plea is untenable. Compared with French, Indian languages possess a treasure four or five times richer. The vocabulary of Hindi or Bengali is twice as rich as that of English. With the help of Sanskrit these languages wield an inexhaustible mine to coin new words. Admittedly, there is one marked difference. In the last century and a half, western languages have acquired a precise vocabulary, depicting all specific shades and hues. Indian languages are still wanting in this quality. Their coinage suffers from a lack of stability and precision. It is wrong to say that knowledge cannot be imparted through Indian languages. If the Russian Scientists were to learn English obligatorily, perhaps the world would not have heard of the Sputnik.[9] . . .

An Indian child is driven mad right from the age of five and he suffers this disability throughout his life. Overburdened with the learning of a foreign language, he hardly reaches the core of a subject and attains depth. Our university scholars suffer a similar fate. They have been reduced into beasts of

9. Sputnik was the first satellite in space, launched by the Soviet Union in October 1957.

burden. This is clearly shown by a contrast with other peoples. Scientists of Russia and Japan are not burdened with the task of acquiring a foreign language and so their knowledge of subjects becomes deep so that they are enabled to make great discoveries and inventions on the strength of such knowledge. We should understand the difference between the learning of a language and the knowledge of a subject. If the child in India is relieved from this burden of learning a foreign language, his knowledge will be widened and deepened, undoubtedly.

Rescue the Indian schoolboy, his mind and body, from the inhuman burden of English. . . . English is a compulsory subject in our educational curriculum. A majority of candidates fail in it and their careers are shipwrecked. What a colossal waste of national wealth and time! Launching a nation wide campaign in July and August you[10] must frankly proclaim. 'Rid our minds of the impediment of English. We want to acquire knowledge in subjects. That is how we can build a strong nation.' . . .

2500 million souls inhabit our planet. 300 million out of these know English. Some people are infatuated by a mirage that English will become the international vehicle of thought and commerce. Such will-of-the-wisp has haunted people in all times. In the 19th century, it was believed that French was an international language. In the atomic age there are some who claim that place for English. In the 8th and 9th centuries world opinion might have attributed similar credit to Arabic. Two thousand years ago Sanskrit would have been the choice. The river has changed its course[,] rendering the bridge of English useless. [The] Russian language is also making huge strides. The down stream of public opinion is flowing towards it. After some time, [the] Russian language will flaunt the same claim. The clash between English and Russian may lead to a dual race. That English will rise to the level of an international medium is a myth. . . .

✦   ✦   ✦

10. 'You' are his party workers.

18

THE GRASSROOTS SOCIALIST

JAYAPRAKASH NARAYAN

Founded in 1934, the Congress Socialist Party had a formal existence until the Quit India movement of 1942. In this brief period it nurtured a group of men and women who went on to play pivotal roles in the politics and culture of independent India. However, the contributions of the socialists tend to be underplayed in Indian historiography, which has been dominated by schools owing allegiance to the official Congress movement and the Communists, respectively. The Congress has been in power for much of the period since Independence, whereas Marxism has been hegemonic within the academy. The one has offered patronage to scholars; the other, the seductions of an oppositional worldview with global ramifications. The long defunct Congress Socialists can offer neither; with the consequence that the brilliance and originality of their work and thought has had no trumpeters—within the community of professional historians, at any rate.

This book has already paid tribute to two remarkable Congress Socialists—Kamaladevi Chattopadhyay and Rammanohar Lohia. We now turn to a third, Jayaprakash Narayan. Narayan was born in rural Bihar in 1902, into a family of Kayasths, scribes who had traditionally worked as officials, teachers, and lawyers. Narayan's own father worked in the state irrigation department. The boy studied in a village school and was then sent to Patna, where he matriculated with distinction in 1918.

In 1920 Narayan married Prabhavati, a daughter of a Gandhian, who had became a disciple of the Mahatma herself. When the non-co-operation movement started, he left college following its call, attracting the anger of his career-minded parents. However, the movement was called off after protesters set fire to a police station in the United Provinces in February 1922. Soon afterwards, Gandhi was jailed. The young Narayan was greatly disillusioned, since freedom had not come, as promised, within a year. At this stage a friend in America suggested that he overcome his disappointment by going to study there.

So in the summer of 1922, Narayan set out for the United States. He spent seven years in that country, studying successively at universities in California, Iowa, Wisconsin, and Ohio. To make ends meet, he did a variety of odd jobs, including cleaning grapes in a vineyard and washing dishes in a restaurant. This was his first experience of manual labour, which surely would never have come his way had he stayed behind in India. At the University of Wisconsin, then (as now) a centre of progressive thinking, he became a socialist. His studies confirmed his political orientation, since the subjects he specialised in were sociology and political science.

In 1929 Narayan was awarded a master's degree. He wanted to carry on for a PhD, but learning that his mother was seriously ill, he chose to return home. As his biographers Allan and Wendy Scarfe write, 'Jayaprakash returned from America to India convinced that the central problem of human society was inequality of wealth, property, rank, culture and opportunity'.

On returning to India, Narayan was reunited with his wife. She was now part of Gandhi's inner circle, which posed a particular problem—namely, that she had, at her master's instance, taken a vow of celibacy. There were other reasons why Gandhi was not so appealing to Narayan. He saw Gandhi as an economic conservative and was attracted instead to the modernism and socialism of Jawaharlal Nehru. Under Nehru's guidance Narayan joined the Congress and urged the party to take a more active interest in the problems of industrial labour.

Narayan was arrested in 1932 during the civil disobedience movement. In jail he came into contact with Communists, whose worship of a foreign country (Russia) disgusted him. He sought with his friends to marry socialism with patriotism, an endeavour that resulted in the formation, when they were released from jail in 1934, of the Congress Socialist Party.

Now known by the diminutive 'JP', Narayan was arrested again in 1941. In November 1942 he escaped from Hazaribagh jail and went underground. From his various hiding places he issued a series of letters calling for a socialist rebellion. He travelled incognito all over north India, spent time in Nepal, and was finally detected and arrested in September 1944. Like his friend Rammanohar Lohia, he was dispatched to Lahore Fort, tortured, but released at the end of World War II, as part of a deal between the Congress and the Government.

In 1948 JP helped form the new Socialist Party. He served as the president of All-India unions of railway, postal, and defence workers, thus being, in effect, the leader of more than a million men. After the Congress defeated all comers in the 1952 elections, Nehru called Narayan for talks to explore the possibility of the socialists rejoining the Congress. The talks failed, but by this time Narayan was losing interest in party politics altogether. He had become increasingly attracted to the programmes of the Gandhian Vinoba Bhave, who was campaigning for rich landlords to donate, to the poor, excess land *(bhoodan)* and, where possible, entire villages *(gramdan)*. Narayan was inspired to do a *jivandan,* namely, to offer his own life to the service of this social movement. He was also reconsidering his approach to Gandhi, who now appealed to him for his advocacy of village self-rule and his critique of greed and materialism in economic life.

Through the 1950s, JP toured the villages of Bihar trying to get land for the landless. In the 1960s this activity was coupled with attempts to reconcile the people of India's borderlands to the Indian Constitution. All through this period he kept in touch with politicians and politics, writing frequently to Jawaharlal Nehru, and, when she became prime minister in 1966, to his daughter Indira Gandhi. He also remained in contact with his old socialist friends who were in opposition.

After two decades in social service, Narayan dramatically re-entered politics in 1974, to lead an all-India movement against the government of Indira Gandhi, which he (and his associates) held to be corrupt, authoritarian, and indifferent to the needs of the poor. When a State of Emergency was declared in June 1975, Narayan was arrested along with other opposition politicians. He was released after a few months, owing to his ill-health (he had a serious diabetic condition), but remained unreconciled to the rule of Indira Gandhi. When elections were called in March 1977 he campaigned, despite his age and ill health, for a now united opposition. This new 'Janata Party' came to power with JP's blessings, but its disintegration into rival factions deeply disheartened him. He died in October 1979.

In the historiography of modern India, Jayaprakash Narayan is remembered chiefly for his heroic role in the 1942 Quit India movement and his leadership, thirty years later, of the 'Indira, Quit' movement. This is because protest and opposition have a certain glamour attached to them. It may be, however, that Narayan's quiet, patient work at the grassroots shall be of more enduring significance. That is certainly the view of this writer, who has, for this anthology, disregarded his fiery and angry speeches of 1942 and 1974 in favour of his more reflective writings of the 1950s and 1960s.

A PLEA FOR POLITICAL DECENTRALISATION

In 1959 Jayaprakash Narayan published a tract advocating an alternate political system for India, based on the revival and renewal of the village council or panchayat. This system would invert the top-down model of parliamentary democracy by working from the base upwards. Narayan's scheme was an elaboration of Gandhi's idea of oceanic circles, outlined in Chapter 13. Narayan's proposals were ignored at the time, but in the 1990s a Constitutional Amendment mandated the countrywide creation of a modified scheme of Panchayati Raj, or village self-government. The italics in the excerpt that follows are the author's.[1]

1. Jayaprakash Narayan, *A Plea for the Reconstruction of the Indian Polity* (Kashi: Akhil Bharat Sarva Seva Sangh Prakashan, 1959), pp. 91–107. The emphases in this excerpt are in the original.

+ + +

. . . The *foundation* [of our polity] must be self-governing, self-sufficient, agro-industrial, urbo-rural, local communities. The highest political institution *of the local community* should be the General Assembly—*the Gram Sabha*—of which all the adults should be considered members. The selection of the Executive—the Panchayat—should be by general consensus of opinion in the Sabha. There should be no 'candidates', *i.e.*, no one should 'stand' for any post. There should be clear-cut qualifications, as in ancient times, laid down for all selective posts. *No individual should hold the same post for more than a defined period of time.* The panchayat should function through sub-committees, charged with different responsibilities. There should be no official or member appointed or nominated by the State government in the panchayat or its sub-committees.

It may be questioned if there can ever be a general consensus of opinion amongst villagers who are divided into castes and factions and have conflicting interests. We have seen already how for thousands of years the villages of India elected their executive councils by general agreement. Those villages were by no means homogeneous and ideal communities. Therefore, there is no reason to believe that the experience of centuries can not be repeated again. We may also recall that the *only alternative method of election* of village councils or panchayats was that of *drawing lots. There is nothing undemocratic in selection by lots.* . . . . Therefore, *I am emphatically of the view* that the villages should be given an option to choose between the *methods of selection by general agreement or by drawing lots* or, alternatively, it might be provided that the villages first try the former method, and failing therein take recourse to the latter. . . .

The question may also be asked if the village panchayats, as they are to-day, would be able to function in the manner visualized above. There is no better way to teach the young except by giving them responsibility. In the same manner the only way to make the villages self-governing, self-reliant and self-sufficient is to throw upon them real responsibilities. There *was a time* when the *Indian village* republics were *self-created,* like the Swiss communes and their powers and functions were not given to them from above. But *in the present conditions they have to be re-created by a deliberate and bold process of devolution and decentralization,* if Indian democracy has to have a firm base and living reality. I believe that the responsibility given to the gram sabha and the panchayat should be in things that really do matter. For instance, it should be the responsibility of the gram sabha and its panchayat to ensure that no one in the village went without food, clothing and shelter; no child went without primary education; every one received primary medical care. The sabha and panchayat should see that the village became self-sufficient in the matter of food and clothing as soon as possible. Further, they should so plan that within five years, let us say, there was no unemployment in the village and every family reached a minimum standard of living. Self-government, to be real, should be about essential problems of life. . . .

The development of the rest of the polity need not wait till the villages and townships become real communities as visualized here. *Our work must begin at all levels simultaneously,* otherwise it will not succeed at any level.

The next level of the political structure would obviously be that of the regional community. Here, . . . the gram panchayats [village councils] will have to be integrated into the Panchayat Samiti [regional council]. . . . The nature and functions of the Samiti should be those of an autonomous self-governing community . . . : the Samiti should have powers and obligations to do all that may be within its competence.

There is one important point which I wish to emphasise in connection with the *formation of the panchayat samiti. The samiti should be elected by the gram panchayats and not by their members.* This at first might appear to be a distinction between six and half-a-dozen. But that is not so. We have here a major principle of communal life involved. It is the gram panchayat *as a body* that represents the village community and not its members. The panchayat samiti, in its turn, is a representative of the gram panchayats, and it is the latter that should be represented as such and not their members. . . .

The political structure would rise storey by storey from the foundation. The next storey above the panchayat samiti would be that of the District Council (or whatever name be given to it), which will be formed by the integration of the panchayat samitis of the district—again the samitis, as such electing their representatives and not their members. The district councils, in their turn, should have all the powers and obligations necessary to do everything that may be within their competence.

In a similar manner all the district councils of a State would come together to create the State Assembly. The State Assemblies, in like manner, would bring into being the Lok Sabha [National Parliament]. Thus the political institution at each level is an integration of all the institutions at the lower level. . . .

My aim here is not to write a new Constitution for India. I have tried merely to discuss some underlying principles and to indicate the general pattern of the social and political organization. However, it may be useful to deal with a few points of detail by way of further clarification.

First, let me take the question of the *Executive at the different levels.*

At the *Primary Community* level the *Panchayat is the executive:* it might allot different executive functions to its individual members or to small committees.

At the Regional Community level, the Panchayat Samiti is the executive body and it would function through committees.

At the level of the District Community, the District Council would be the executive body, and it would also function through committees.

At the level of the Provincial Community, the Pranta Sabha [Regional Council] would appoint committees which would be the executive bodies, responsible to the Sabha.

Likewise, at the level of the National Community, the Rashtra Sabha [National Council] would appoint committees which would be the executive bodies, responsible to the Sabha.

Who would exercise the legislative powers, it may be asked. According to my conception, each community has powers to make rules and laws in order to manage its internal affairs, provided they do not conflict with the interest of other communities *at the same level* and with the rules and laws laid down *by the communities at higher levels. The higher communal bodies will legislate in their allotted spheres.* Rules and laws may be passed by other communal bodies too, such as educational and economic associations.

The committees should be small, workable bodies with powers to co-opt experts who would participate fully but without the right of vote.

Each committee would have a chairman and a secretary, but, apart from performing the functions of their office, they would enjoy no special powers or privileges.

Each committee would be directly responsible to the general body which would appoint it.

In order to coordinate the work of the different committees, there would be a Co-ordinating Committee, constituted of one representative from each committee: the representative may be the chairman, secretary or any member of the committee concerned. The decisions of the Coordinating Committee would be binding on every other committee.

Up to the district level, the co-ordinating committee would be the panchayat, the panchayat samiti and the district council, which would meet at fixed times.

Every committee would have collective responsibility.

The representative communal bodies would meet periodically, but the committees would be in perpetual session.

Matter[s] of policy would be decided upon, on the motion of a committee or an individual member, by the representative bodies concerned. The committees would execute the policies.

It should be clear from this that at the Provincial and National levels there would be no Ministers, Chief Ministers or Prime Minister as at present. As stated above, *government would be conducted by committees* of the representative bodies. The institution of Prime Minister and Chief Minister, which concentrates too much power into the hands of single individuals is *undemocratic* and smacks of the gun-powder of totalitarianism. It further leads to such dangerous psychological developments as the 'hero-cult' or the 'cult of the individual'.

The President of the different representative communal bodies will have no administrative functions. But it would be his responsibility to see that the representative body of which he is president functions properly and according to the rules laid down. He would also have extraordinary emergency powers in case of the break-down of the democratic apparatus of the community concerned.

The President of the Rashtra Sabha, in addition to the powers mentioned in the last para[graph], would also be the Commander-in-Chief of the armed forces and responsible to the Sabha for the defence of the Nation. He would be assisted by a committee for defence, of which he would be the chairman.

In their task of administration the Committees would be assisted by paid Civil Servants. *At each level the civil servants would be appointed by the corresponding Authority* created for that purpose by the representative body concerned and on terms laid down by the latter. This will be a *sovereign right of the communities: to appoint and dismiss its servants.* At the level of the primary community the civil servant might be an honorary, part-time or full-time volunteer. Even at higher levels there might be honorary civil servants.

It should be pointed out here that because of the decentralized pattern of the social, political and economic organization, the administration would not be top-heavy and far-removed from the people as at present.

In the light of the above, it might be useful to turn for a moment to what is perhaps one of the most serious problems of the present day: the *problem of bureaucracy and corruption.* Some think that one solution of corruption is dictatorship. But even dictatorship is no solution of bureaucracy. To the contrary, we know that dictatorship breeds bureaucracy faster than other systems of government, and, in the bargain, makes it all-powerful.

Even as regards corruption, it is not generally realized that there is corruption on a gigantic scale in the dictatorships—only its form is changed. Instead of corruption in the sense of bribery and the like, there is grosser corruption in the form of lying, deceit, intrigue, terror, enslavement of the human mind, crucification of the dignity of man. All this corrupts human life far more than bribery and similar things.

The only true solution of the problem both of bureaucracy and corruption is direct self-government of the people and direct and immediate supervision and control over the civil servants by the people and their elected organs. In the primary communities, as I have said above, there need be no paid civil servants. In the larger communities the civil servant would be directly under the control and supervision of the communal body concerned. Further, it would obviously be in the interest of the communities to keep the cost of the administration as low as possible. So, there will be a natural check on proliferation of the bureaucracy. Thus as self-government develops, the civil servant becomes either unnecessary or subject to the immediate elected authority.

There may, however, be one danger in all this. If the communal representative bodies and their members themselves become corrupt, there would be little check on corruption in this scheme of things. I admit that it is quite likely that in the beginning it might well be so, but I refuse to believe that such a situation could last long. If the responsibility were really thrown upon the people so that they could see clearly that their suffering was due to the fact that they had chosen the wrong type of people to manage their affairs, the relationship between the people, their representatives and civil servants would be so intimate and direct that it should not take long for the people to remedy the situation. . . .

It is not possible in this paper to consider *what departments* of administration are *to be entrusted to which community.* I have emphasized the general principle that every community would have powers to do all that may be within its natural competence. Since there is general inertia among the people at present, this may not be much. Powers would have to be *'given'* from above. I should therefore say that I would take courage in both hands and give to the communities the utmost powers possible. Some of the powers might not be used, some might be abused. But the people would learn and it would be the job of the voluntary social workers to help them to learn.

I should therefore say that police, justice, taxation, collection, social services, planning, should all be decentralized to the maximum possible extent. As the people learn and acquire self-confidence, the process of decentralization, instead of starting from above, would be normalized and begin to operate from below.

A new political structure like the one envisaged here will not be built in a day, if for nothing else, for the reason that the foundation will have to be laid first and the structure built from below, storey by storey. The economic structure too would have to be built along with. All this would take time, so there will have to be a period of transition.

Village panchayats have been established in the greater part of the country. These have to be remodeled according to the principles put forward in this paper.

The next stage would be the establishment of Panchayat Samitis. This has also been started already, such as in Rajasthan. But again the conception behind it has to be radically changed.

When panchayat samitis are established, the District Councils would have to be constituted.

The economic institutions would also have to be organized side by side.

Planning and the whole system of education would have to be reoriented. . . .

The picture drawn here of the polity for India, and of social organization in general, might perhaps appear to be idealistic. If so, I would not consider that to be a disqualification. An ideal cannot but be idealistic. The question is if the ideal is impractical, unscientific or otherwise ill-conceived. I have tried in the preceding pages to show that all relevant considerations lead irresistibly towards it.

The achievement of this ideal would, however, be a colossal task. Thousands, perhaps hundreds of thousands of voluntary workers would be needed over [a] number of years to accomplish it.

The governments should lend their full support; but it is necessary to remember that the main burden of the task would have to be borne by voluntary political and social workers and institutions. The heart of the problem is to create the 'spirit of community', without which the whole body politic would be without life and soul. This is a task of moral regeneration to be brought about by example, service, sacrifice and love. Those who occupy high places in society—in politics, business, the professions—bear the heavy responsibility of leading the people by personal example.

The task also is one of social engineering, needing the help of the State; of scientists, experts, educationists, businessmen, experimenters; of men and women; of young and old.

It is a task of dedication; of creation; of self-discovery.

It is a task that defines India's destiny. It spells a challenge to India's sons and daughters. Will they accept the challenge?

✦　✦　✦

THE TRAGEDY OF TIBET

In 1959 the Chinese government came down heavily on a rebellion in Tibet, forcing tens of thousands of Tibetans to flee into India. Simultaneously, they strengthened their military presence in and political control over that territory. In these excerpts from speeches he made at the time, Jayaprakash Narayan outlines the implications of the crisis in Tibet for India, China, and the world. This remains a compelling critique of totalitarianism in theory and practice. The italics in the excerpt that follows are the author's.[2]

✦　✦　✦

2. From *The Tragedy of Tibet: Speeches and Statements of Jayaprakash Narayan* (New Delhi: Afro-Asian Committee on Tibet, 1959), pp. 8–21.

... One of the great tragedies of history is being enacted in full view of the world. Tibet is being gobbled up by the Chinese dragon. A country of less than ten million souls is being crushed to death by a country of six hundred and fifty million people. Patriotism, courage, faith can perform miracles. The Tibetans love their country; they are brave; they are devoted to their religion and their Dalai Lama. Yet, 1 to 65 is an odd that even a nation of Herculeses will find it difficult to overcome.

The attention of the world is currently turned elsewhere. Moreover, Tibet for most countries of the world, except its immediate neighbours, is an obscure, distant, benighted land—not worth bothering about. This makes the tragedy of Tibet deeper.

India, as an immediate neighbor of Tibet, and as a country regarded for its moral position, its detachment and freedom from power politics has a great responsibility in this matter. The world looks to India for a lead and India must not fail.

It is not only a question of the fate of ten million people. That of course is important and would be so whatever the number. But there is also the question—and this is of much greater importance—of the basis of international justice and peace. Is world peace possible if the strong are free to oppress the weak with impudence? Such a world would be dominated by a few powerful nations and peace would consist in any uneasy balance of power between them and the small nations would be at their mercy.

This surely is not the picture of the future world order that India has in view. We believe that just as inside nations the rule of law must be established to secure human rights, so in the international community too must the rule of law be enforced so as to ensure the freedom and rights of nations. That rule of law can only be based on an international morality which is universally accepted. Even the strongest power then might find it difficult to go against the moral verdict of the world. From my point of view, the greatest virtue of our foreign policy of non-attachment and independence of judgment is that it enables us to contribute, because of that very non-attachment, to the development of international morality.

India therefore must not shirk her responsibility at this testing moment. Her responsibility is far greater at this time than it was at the time of Hungary. This is so not only because Tibet is on our frontier and what happens there affects our security, nor only because of our spiritual and cultural bonds with

Tibet. The Panchen Lama, by the way, twitted us the other day for showing such solicitude for Bud[d]hism abroad when we had not cared to preserve it at home. The learned Lama forgets that the Bud[d]ha's teachings have very largely become a part of Hindu life and thought and the Bud[d]ha himself is worshipped as our last *Avatar* [of Vishnu]. . . . Our bonds with Tibet are there and they no doubt determine our attitude towards their present plight. But our concern for and responsibility towards Tibet spring mainly from the fact that Tibet is a neighbour who has been wronged. The responsibility is increased when it is recalled that the neighbour had put trust in our assurances.

In this connection, there has been some glib talk of war. If you do this or that, it would mean war with China, it is said. It is amazing that people should talk of war in this loose manner. The whole world knows, and China more than them all, that India has no desire whatever to start a war with anyone. On the other hand, India has repeatedly reiterated her firm desire to continue her bonds of friendship with China. But if China seeks to exploit that desire for unjust purposes, India cannot be party to it. Nor can India be brow-beaten into doing something that she considers wrong nor prevented by threats from doing right.

The main elements of the Tibet situation have been clear enough from the beginning.

Tibet is not a region of China. It is a country by itself which has sometimes passed under Chinese suzerainty by virtue of conquest and never by free choice. Chinese suzerainty has always been of the most nominal kind and meant hardly more than some tribute paid to Peking by Lhasa. At other times Tibet was an independent sovereign country. For some time in the 8th century Peking paid a yearly tribute of 50,000 yards of Chinese brocade to Tibet.

After the fall of the Manchu empire in 1911, Tibet functioned as an independent country till 1950, when the Chinese Communist Government invaded it. In between there were attempts to re-impose Chinese suzerainty by treaty in which the British Government took a leading hand. Pressed from both sides by two powerful forces, Tibet had little choice. Nevertheless nothing came out of these attempts and till the communist invasion, Tibet was a free country.

The British had their own selfish motive for agreeing to China's suzerain powers in Tibet. Being imperialists themselves they had, of course, no qualms in the matter. Their motive was to bribe the Chinese into recognizing the monopoly economic rights of Britain in Tibet.

It was this policy born in imperialist sin that free India inherited. Very rightly India renounced all the rights she enjoyed in Tibet by virtue of that inheritance. But curiously she re-affirmed that part of the sinful policy that related to China. India gave her assent to China's suzerain position in Tibet.

That was a major mistake of our foreign policy. The mistake was twofold. The first was that we accepted an imperialist formula. The very idea that one country may have suzerain powers over another is imperialist in conception. The second mistake was to believe that a powerful totalitarian state could be trusted to honour the autonomy of a weak country.

It is true that we could not have prevented the Chinese from annexing Tibet. But we could have saved ourselves from being party to a wrong. That would have been not only a matter of moral satisfaction, but it would have also set the record right, so that world opinion, particularly in the Afro-Asian part of the world, could have asserted itself. That might have even halted the Chinese. The communists are anxious to present themselves as liberators, so when Afro-Asian opinion would have condemned their Tibet action as aggression they would have found it immensely difficult to go on with it. India's acceptance of the suzerainty formula gave to the Chinese action a moral and legal sanction and prevented the formulation of an Afro-Asian opinion on the question. It thus prevented the true aggressive character of Chinese communism from being realized by the backward peoples of Asia, aggravating the danger of their being enslaved in the name of liberation.

It has been said, more in whisper than aloud, that non-recognition of China's claims of suzerainty would have earned for us the hostility of the Chinese Government. In the first place, issues of right and wrong cannot be decided on considerations of pleasure or displeasure of the parties concerned. In the second place, it should have been foreseen that sooner or later the Chinese would try to destroy the Tibetan autonomy and then a conflict of policies would become inevitable.

Furthermore, we could have made it clear that even though we were opposed to China's suzerainty over Tibet, we were, on our side, keen and determined to pursue our policy of friendship. India had strongly opposed recent Anglo-French aggression in Egypt, but on that account she did not change her policy of friendship towards England and France. Nor was India's action construed by those powerful countries as hostile, nor did they themselves on that account become hostile to India.

There are some who say that facts of history must be taken into account and if Tibet has sometimes been under China, it is irrelevant to raise the question of Tibetan independence now. This is an amazing argument. Anyone who believes in human freedom and the right of all nations to independence, should be ashamed to talk in this fashion. According to the logic of this viewpoint, Hungary, for example, having long been a part of the Austro-Hungarian Empire should never be entitled to independence. Would any sensible person agree with this view? Let us not therefore slip into the habits of lazy thought and give approval to wrongs of history.

For years an illusion was in the making. It was said that China was different. It had an ancient civilization. Therefore Chinese communism was different from Russian and so on and on. That illusion has been shattered to the great good fortune of the peoples of Asia, who have been warned in time.

China rants incessantly about imperialists and expansionists. But China herself has been revealed as a cruel imperial power. If communism had been a truly liberating and anti-imperialist force, the Chinese communists, on assumption of power, should themselves have proclaimed the independence of Tibet and foresworn the old imperialist notion of suzerainty and made a treaty with Tibet of equality and friendship. But communism under Russian and Chinese guidance has become expansionist and aggressive, just as nineteenth century capitalism under the leadership of Britain, France, Germany had become aggressive and expansionist. Somewhere or the other Marxism has gone wrong. Lenin wrote a famous thesis on imperialism as the last phase of capitalism. Some one should write another thesis on communism as the first phase of a new imperialism! . . .

Having annexed Tibet by invoking an outworn, imperialist formula, the Chinese communists were in no hurry to go on with their plans of subjugating the country. They also needed time to build roads and military establishments and to haul up arms to the roof of the world. When they had sufficiently entrenched themselves, they began to tighten the screws. It was not a question of reforms. The question plainly was that of subjugation of Tibet. The Chinese interfered in everything, in the matter of religion as well as administration. Revered Lamas were purposely ill-treated, humiliated, imprisoned, tortured. The sanctity of shrines and images were violated. Monasteries were demolished and their properties confiscated. A new system of administration was imposed, in which Chinese were posted at all key points. The Post & Telegraph, the Mint, the Hydro-electric plant were taken over. Printing of Tibetan currency was prohibited. Chinese Postal stamps were introduced. The powers and functions of the Dalai Lama were clipped. A vast scheme of colonization by China was set on foot, so that large parts of Tibet should cease to be Tibetan and become Chinese. That was a process of stealing Tibet from the Tibetans that caused deep anxiety and aroused bitter resentment. Centuries old granaries, some of them with grain reserves to last for years, were emptied and the grain seized by the Chinese. Reserves of gold and silver bullion were appropriated on the pretext of taking it on loan. The so-called land reforms were introduced, softly at first, but later with the usual communist disregard for popular feeling. Forced labour, so foreign to Tibetan tradition, was introduced on a big scale. The Press and all other means of information were taken over by the Chinese.

All this was happening over a number of years and to some of the administrative and constitutional changes the Tibetans were forced to give their 'assent'. The rest was done at the sweet will of the over-lords.

Resistance to such [a] state of affairs was natural. Soon it took the form of a national resistance movement.

[The] Marxism of Karl Marx was meant to be an objective science of society. But present-day communism is nothing if not a complete travesty of objectivity. Had it not been so, all the wild charges could never have been made against India and Indians. Had it not been so again, the Tibetan upsurge could not have been represented by the Chinese as only a minor disturbance caused by a handful of reactionary Lamas and landlords. It is not that communists do not know the truth. It is only that communism cannot bear the truth. Truth is communism's deadly enemy.

There is no doubt that the vested interests are also with the resistance, but its character is national rather than class. The Tibetans are fighting to win their national freedom and not to defend the feudal rights of a few nobles and monasteries. The leaders of the movement are not feudal reactionaries, but the most progressive elements in Tibetan society, who stand for reform and change.

The true history of the Tibetan national movement has yet to be told. There are Tibetans now in India who can give the world an authentic account. But one does not know when they will consider the opportune moment to have arrived to tell their story. In spite of all that has happened they perhaps feel that a settlement with the Chinese might still be possible. One admires the faith of these brave religious people and prays that their faith may be vindicated. One necessary condition for that seems to be unambiguous expression and assertion of world opinion on the side of truth and justice.

There is a point of view that is not so much expressed publicly as privately canvassed. It is said that even if the Chinese are behaving a little roughly in Tibet, why be so squeamish about it? Are they not forcibly rescuing the Tibetan masses from medieval backwardness and forcing them forward towards progress and civilization?

It is strange that as soon as some people put themselves outside their own country, they become screaming imperialists. If the right is conceded to nations to thrust progress forcibly down the throats of other nations, why were not the British welcomed as torchbearers of progress in India? But the defenders of the Chinese civilizers of Tibet will be the first to disown any such sacrilegious thought. They might, however, be thrown into real confusion if the Russians or the Chinese were to take it into their heads to march upon India to save her from 'foreign imperialists' and lead her to progress!

Secondly, the question may be asked what is progress. To some, industrialization, rising production statistics, communes, Sputniks, . . . might mean progress. There is another view that regards progress in terms of humanity—the growth of human freedom, the decline of selfishness and cruelty, the spread of tolerance and cooperation, and so on. For me Stalin was no improvement on the Czar and all the Sputniks of Russia leave me cold when I know that a sensitive and honest writer, Pasternak, the first literary genius in Russia since Gorki, is condemned raucously by so-called men of letters who have not even read the offending work. From the point of view of the *progress of man,* as distinct from the *progress of things,* Russia appears to me to be living in the Dark Ages.

It was hoped that China's ancient civilization would prevent that great country from being plunged into the same darkness, but Tibet has shown that the sun of humanity is as much under eclipse in Peking as it is in Moscow.

Apart from the progress of things, importance is attached to change of institutions. Destruction of temporal and spiritual feudalism might be considered to be an advance, but when that is replaced by a still more severe feudalism of Party and Bureaucracy, I for one am not prepared to call it an advance, far less a revolution. The yoke of the native mediaevalism was surely going to be put down sooner or later. But who can tell when the foreign yoke of communist mediaevalism will be overthrown? Who can tell when Latvia, Estonia and Lithuania will be free? And Hungary and the rest of them?

The question that I wish to consider finally is one that is on everyone's lips now; how can Tibet be saved? He would be a bold person who would venture to suggest a definite answer? A few considerations may, however, be advanced.

There is one thing of which I am absolutely clear: the need to create a powerful world opinion on this question. The Tibet situation should be presented to the world in all its naked reality. No attempt should be made for reasons of diplomacy to play down, cover up, belittle or misrepresent what is happening in Tibet. Diplomacy has a vast deal to answer for in history, and I do fervently hope that diplomacy, like the cold war, is kept out of the issue. The broad facts of the Tibet situation are clear. Those facts must be broadcast, and on their basis a strong and united world opinion must be created *against Chinese aggression and for Tibetan independence.*

Let no one cry 'cold war' at this. This is not a part of Bloc politics. This is a fight for the Rights of Man. Did anyone think that the world-wide condemnation of the Anglo-French attack on Egypt was a part of the cold war?

The Government of India is committed to the formula of Tibetan Autonomy under Chinese suzerainty. That formula is in ruins. . . . But nevertheless this whole question will have to be re-considered sooner rather than later. What happens when the autonomy of a country (or a region for that matter) is destroyed? What happens when that autonomy is not restored? What happens, in short, when aggression takes place and succeeds? It would not do to evade these questions. Till these questions are answered, there is no hope of the Government of India discovering the next step. Paralysis of action in a fast-developing situation may be dangerous. . . .

It will be recalled that when the Chinese aggression began in 1950, the Tibetan Government had moved the United Nations. The El Salvador delegate had formally called on the UN to condemn China for her 'unprovoked aggression' against Tibet, and had proposed the creation of a special committee to study what measures could be taken by the General Assembly to assist Tibet. The matter went to the Assembly's Steering Committee which, on the strength of the assurances of India's representative, decided to shelve the Tibetan complaint indefinitely.

The full facts of that affair and of our part in it have not been made public and I cannot say where the matter stands now according to the workings of the United Nations. Nevertheless, it seems to be utterly wrong that such an important event as the suppression of the freedom of a nation should take place and the world organization should not even take notice of it. It is not that the mere raising of an issue in the United Nations means that a solution will be found. We have some experience of the working of that august body ourselves. But, after all is said and done, the UN is the only organization the human family has that gives some guarantee that the world will not be converted into a jungle where the strong will eat up the weak. I have no doubt there will be many constitutional barriers and such things as vetoes in the way of the Tibet issue entering the portals of the UN. But if rules and procedures and technicalities stand in the way of international justice, it is not the latter but the former that should suffer. In whichever form the Tibet question is presented to the UN, I have no doubt that the Afro-Asian bloc must present a common front. This is the least that the countries of Asia and Africa must do to defend the right of small nations to freedom and also to assure against the danger to their own freedom from both the old and new imperialism.

It is not for me to advise the Tibetans. There is one thought, however, which I cannot help expressing. Tibet, being a devoutly Bud[d]hist country, could perhaps have turned its moment of tragedy into one of profound victory—if it could have turned to the Compassionate One and met hate with love, oppression with suffering, violence with non-violence. May be, even then Tibet would have been destroyed, but not the soul of Tibet, not the Religion of the Bud[d]ha.

Then, is Tibet lost for ever? No, a thousand times no. Tibet will not die because there is no death for the human spirit. Communism will not succeed because man will not be slave for ever. Tyrannies have come and gone and Caesars and Czars and dictators. But the spirit of man goes on for ever. *Tibet will be resurrected.*

✦ ✦ ✦

A FAIR DEAL FOR KASHMIR

Consistent with his concern for small minorities at the edge of large nation-states, Jayaprakash Narayan believed that India had to be more respectful of the rights of the residents of the disputed Kashmir Valley.

What follows is from a press statement on the question, issued by Narayan in Calcutta in December 1964.[3]

◆ ◆ ◆

The question we must squarely face is whether constitutional integration of Kashmir with India is more important in the national interest than friendship with Pakistan and justice to the people of the Valley of Srinagar. Legal technicalities will not provide the answer. What is needed is a mature and realistic reckoning. As far as I can see, the disadvantages of the present policy far outweigh the advantages.

Let me take up first the issue of justice to the people of the Valley. There has been no credible proof yet that they have freely accepted the legal fact of accession. Constitutional integration has little meaning in the absence of emotional integration. In this age and time, it is impossible to hold down by force any sizeable population permanently. If we continue to do it, we cannot look the world straight in the face and talk of democracy and justice and peace. Nor, on account of the historical circumstances, can we take shelter behind the internationally recognized limitations of the right to self-determination. Perhaps the most harmful consequences of the policy of forcible integration would be the death-knell of Indian secularism and enthronement of aggressive Hindu communalism. That communalism is bound in the end to turn upon the Hindu community itself and destroy it.

As for friendship with Pakistan, let us calculatedly determine how dearly we need that friendship. No country can afford to buy friendship at any cost. So let there be a reckoning of gains and losses. First of all, let us be mature enough to understand that if we persist in our present Kashmir policy, there can be no friendship with Pakistan. The leaders of that country have not left us in any doubt on that score. If we disbelieve them, we shall have only ourselves to blame.

Here is the pricing of Indo-Pak friendship as it appears to me. First, if Pakistan turns hostile, as I fear it would if we persist in the policy of full constitutional integration, the defence of the country would become a hundred-fold more difficult. Certain parts of it, such as Assam, NEFA and Nagaland would

3. Originally from the Jayaprakash Narayan Papers at the Nehru Memorial Museum and Library, New Delhi, here reproduced from Balraj Puri, ed., *JP on Jammu and Kashmir* (New Delhi: Gyan Publishing House, 2005), pp. 61–65.

be next to impossible to defend. Indo-Pak amity on the other hand would automatically result in large scale dis-engagement, thus strengthening considerably our defence capability. Our communications too would be automatically strengthened tenfold. As far as the defence of Ladakh, I am sure any amicable settlement of the Kashmir issue would make a provision for it.

Second, both history and geography destined the subcontinent of India to play a key role in South and South-East Asia. But as long as India and Pakistan remain at loggerheads, India's, as also Pakistan's capacity to manoeuver in this area—remains drastically restricted. No initiative taken by India can have the same value and attraction for the countries of this region unless India and Pakistan moved jointly. At present, they cancel out each other, creating a power vacuum that no one but China can fill efficiently.

Third, what is true of the South-East Asia region is very largely true of the world. India's posture on the world stage is very considerably determined by her obsession with Kashmir and her consequent relations with Pakistan. In the Afro-Asia world, this quarrel between the two big Asian countries has cost both heavily in prestige and influence and diplomatic effectiveness.

Fourth, there is the vast economic harm the quarrel is causing both countries. It is beyond doubt that the development of each would have been much faster had there been cooperation between them in the economic field.

The last and in some way the most disastrous consequence of the quarrel is its human and moral cost and the alienation of peoples that it threatens to bring about. If the quarrel continues, Muslims in India and Hindus in Pakistan would continue to live under the shadow of suspicion and suffer severe spiritual unrest. The danger of communal rioting would be ever present. These conditions would be sure to cause mass human degradation on both sides. The political division of the sub-continent cannot hide the fact that the peoples of India and Pakistan are really one people. This is not the first time that India has been divided politically. But there had always been a feeling of oneness and identity among the people divided between kingdoms and republics. Today, the Bengalis of the West and East are one people, irrespective of region; so are the Punjabis. In like manner, the Bengalis and Punjabis and Sindhis and Pathans and Jats and Rajputs and others of both countries make up one single Indian people, who are distinct from all other peoples of the world. States are passing shows, but the people are eternal. Therefore, I would consider this alienation of the people of India and Pakistan from one another to be the most disastrous consequence of the present quarrel.

This briefly is the balance-sheet as I see it. Let logic and reason rather than childish emotion guide the debate and the ultimate decision.

I am aware that settlement of the Kashmir issue would not in itself mean establishment of firm Indo-Pak friendship, but it would certainly remove the greatest obstacle on the way and create the necessary psychological conditions. I am also aware that friendship is not one-sided. But I am convinced that friendship is as precious for Pakistan as for India and they will be found to be as keen for it as we persuade ourselves to be.

A last word to the leaders of the government. At this critical moment in the country's life, it is their duty to lead and not to be led. The crippling fear of public opinion and party rank and file is only a reflection of the leadership's own weakness and division. It is for the leaders to shape public opinion and educate the back-benchers. If they fail in this, they will do disservice to the country in this hour of decision.

✦ ✦ ✦

THE QUESTION OF NAGALAND

In 1964–1965 Jayaprakash Narayan was part of a three-member peace mission to the troubled state of Nagaland, in the north-east of India. A large section of the Nagas were unreconciled to being part of the Indian Union; they wanted a sovereign nation of their own. Through the 1950s a bloody war raged between the Indian Army and the Naga insurgents. In 1964 the Baptist Church (to which most Nagas owed allegiance) was instrumental in bringing about a cease-fire. Talks between the Government of India and the rebels commenced. The peace mission of which Narayan was part was also the church's initiative. On 30 January 1965— the anniversary of Mahatma Gandhi's assassination—Narayan delivered a lecture in his home town, Patna, on the conflict in Nagaland. This was later expanded and published as a booklet in Hindi, from which the following excerpts are taken.[4]

4. Jayaprakash Narayan, *Nagaland ka Saval* (The Question of Nagaland) (Varanasi: Sarva Seva Sangh Prakashan, 1965), pp. 11–14, 22–24, 28–31. Translated from the Hindi by Ramachandra Guha.

First, Narayan explains why the Nagas have never been part of the Indian cultural mainstream.

✦   ✦   ✦

Travel to the remotest corners of India, and you will find things that are linked to our epics and scriptures. The Pandavas are said to have taken refuge in so many places one visits. Or that Bhim, Arjun, or Ramchandra came there. So many habitations are named after our sages and saints. . . . When we speak of the unity of India, we do not really mean its political unity. China may be defined by a certain political unity, but India is marked on the other hand by a cultural unity. In the past, what we now know as India was never under a single state or political unit. This was not the case in the time of the Mauryas or of the Guptas. . . .

However, Nagaland was never part of this broader Indian culture. Call it a misfortune or an 'accident of history'! In NEFA we find some Buddhist communities. . . . In Manipur[5] the followers of [the Vaishnana saint] Chaitanya Mahaprabhu settled and made the people Vaishnavites. They use the Bengali script there. . . . Among them there are Brahmins, Kshatriyas and other castes.

But only Nagaland has stayed aloof from Indian culture and civilization. . . . As a consequence, the Nagas do not really feel Indian. Even those Nagas who live in India and participate in Indian politics, do not have the sentiment of being Indian. One Naga leader, who is a Member of Parliament, once told me: 'No Naga considers himself an Indian'. . . . However, this is not a sentiment that we should fear, or dismiss as anti-patriotic. The truth is that the people of India have never ventured into these areas. The British did not permit us to go there. At the risk of our lives we could have gone there, but we didn't. We did not go to Nagaland to promote our religions, or our culture, or indeed to do social service. It was in about the year 1870 that the British gradually established their rule over the Nagas. But even as late as 1947 there were parts of the Naga Hills that were under no administration at all. Even the British had not made their presence felt there. On the one hand it was in a corner of the sub-continent and on the other it was lonely and re-

---

5. The North-east Frontier Agency (NEFA) and Manipur were both territories of the Indian Union in close proximity to Nagaland.

mote, a wilderness. This may be the reason why the people of India never reached Nagaland.

I am acquainting you with these facts so that you may understand why this movement began in Nagaland saying we are different from India. The Nagas say that they are not hostile to India, merely different—and hence they demand a separate nation. Now many people are suspicious of the Christian faith. They think that Christian preachers may have spread this sentiment of separatism among the Nagas. But this is not so. They were of a different culture and ethnicity; although the British could have tried to bring them slowly into India. The British did not allow Hindus to enter this territory, but they allowed the Christian missionaries. Some were Welsh Baptists, others American Baptists. I am of the view that if Roman Catholics or priests from the Church of England had gone to Nagaland, perhaps the sentiment of separation may have diminished. The missionaries who went there did not intensify this feeling, nor did they reduce it—that was not their focus anyway. . . .

✦   ✦   ✦

Second, Narayan explains why the Nagas can live freely and honourably under the Indian Constitution.

✦   ✦   ✦

. . . From the time that talks commenced with leaders of the Naga 'underground' I have been urging them to remain within the Union of India. . . . I kept on telling the Nagas that there is no need for you to demand a separate nation, since you can be fully free within India. There is a great difference between your situation under British colonial rule and your status as a part of independent and democratic India. Then you were subjugated, indeed all of India was subjugated. Now you are free, just as all of India is free. Now every citizen of India is free and equal. Which alien power is now ruling over Assam? Who is ruling over Bengal? Or over Bihar? Is it India? India is constituted by joining all these provinces together. These states have collectively created a Central Government and allocated it certain rights. If these states were to now say that we want a particular right back the Centre will have to return it. After all, it is the representatives of these states who sit in the Parliament in Delhi. So if they choose to decide that certain rights must be with them, then they can take them back. It is the Members of Parliament from the states who decide which rights shall be with the Centre, and which will not. In any case, this giving up of certain rights to the Centre is not done to permit India to subjugate the provinces, but rather, to safeguard the Union of India.

Take the army. That there should be a separate army for Bihar, and another one for Bengal, this will not be appropriate. If there is a dispute between Bihar and Bengal—say with regard to whether a particular district belongs to one or the other—then if there were separate armies for each state they would go to war. It is to prevent this that we have a single army. This would have soldiers from all the states, Bihar, Bengal, Assam. Issues such as defence and foreign affairs must be the responsibility of the Centre. That Bihar forge[s] a relationship with America and that Bengal do[es] so with another country, this should not happen. This is why the relations with other countries are best dealt with by the Centre. In the same manner, the country must have a single currency. If Bihar had its own currency, and Bengal its own too, imagine what confusion would arise. However, all the other subjects, such as irrigation, education, etc., must be within the control of the states. The situation today is such that without assistance from the Centre the states are not able to function. For schools, etc., the Centre has to give them money. If however they think they have the capacity to handle them, then the states can take full responsibility for these subjects.

This is what we told the Nagas. You have your own state of Nagaland now, we said; why are you still underground? You can choose your own Chief Minister now. You are not longer subjugated but free to manage your own affairs. Why you still want an independent state we cannot understand. We also told them that were Nagaland to be a separate nation, there would be real fears about its freedom. Burma is next door, China is not far away either. [East] Pakistan is also only two hundred miles away. These countries can all put pressure on you. Whether an independent Nagaland will be secure, we cannot say. In this situation, why think of being an independent nation, separate from India? You are already free, really free. Just as every part of India is independent, you are too. Are the Indians suppressing you in the way the British did? That is not the case. . . .

✦   ✦   ✦

Finally, Narayan explains why the rest of India has much to learn from the independence and community spirit of the Nagas.

✦ ✦ ✦

. . . Gandhi used often to talk of village self-rule. If you want to see village self-rule in practice go to Nagaland. The way that villages run their affairs, the strength they display, is truly admirable. Kohima town is the capital of Nagaland state. This town has no room to expand beyond its present borders. The Government of Nagaland thus wants the village council of Kohima to give it land [to build homes and offices]. They say that the Government cannot take over the land without the consent of the village council. But what is the situation in other states? There, to make roads, airports, etc., the government can uproot village after village without taking anyone's permission. But this is simply not conceivable in Nagaland. . . .

People here [in the Indian heartland] think of Nagas as uncivilized.[6] But if one travels there one sees how advanced they are. . . . Let me give you an example. Near the town of Mokokchung is a village named Ugma, which is perhaps the largest village in Nagaland. About four thousand people are resident here. There is a very big church there. This is bigger than any church found in Assam or elsewhere in this region. It has a seating capacity of five thousand. You will be astonished to learn that the church was built entirely by the voluntary labour of villagers. They used no material nor any expertise from outside. You may not believe this, but they did not even need an engineer from outside to help them construct this church. The people of the village built it themselves. And the church is so beautiful! Not just this church, even high schools were built by the villagers themselves. And these schools are very pretty too. Wood and bamboo are freely available here. . . . But the most remarkable thing is their spirit of service. A Naga even if he has a B. A. or M. A. degree, does not consider physical labour to be beneath his dignity. The deficiencies that one finds in educated people elsewhere in India are absent here. If a boy comes home on holiday, he would happily help his parents in the fields or in housework. What we [Gandhians] try to teach under the rubric of 'basic education' is already part of the teaching here. . . . The greatest quality of the Nagas is the dignity of labour in daily life, which we can learn from.

✦ ✦ ✦

6. The word Narayan uses is 'jangli', literally of the jungle, but connoting backward, primitive, even barbarian—here glossed as 'uncivilised'.

19

THE GANDHIAN LIBERAL

C. RAJAGOPALACHARI

THIS CHAPTER, LIKE THE TWO preceding it, is about someone who was once Jawaharlal Nehru's friend and party colleague but later became a bitter political opponent. This man was considerably older than Lohia and Jayaprakash Narayan. Unlike them, he enjoyed high office both before and after Independence. His seniority and distinction lent even greater substance to the criticisms he was to make of the prime minister and the Congress party.

This veteran Congressman-turned-anti-Congressman was Chakravarthi Rajagopalachari. He was born in 1878, son of a village headman in the Tamil country. He was sent to school in Bangalore, and took his first degree in that city's Central College. He then proceeded to qualify as a lawyer in Madras, where, still a student, he was moved and inspired by Bal Gangadhar Tilak's arrest in 1898.

After taking his law degree Rajagopalachari moved to the town of Salem to practice. He attended the 1906 Congress in Calcutta and was elected to the Salem Municipal Council five years later (he eventually became Chairman of the Council). He followed Gandhi's struggles in South Africa with keen interest and collected and sent Rs 1,500 (then not an insignificant sum of money) for his movement.

In 1919 Rajagopalachari moved to the Presidency capital, Madras, which provided a bigger stage for the law and for public service. The same year, he met Gandhi and at once became his devoted disciple and admirer. The Mahatma, in turn, trusted and respected his integrity and his acumen. Rajagopalachari chose to only wear home-spun cloth and gave up his law practice to devote himself full-time to the nationalist cause.

By now widely known by the diminutive 'Rajaji', Rajagopalachari went to jail in the *satyagrahas* of the 1920s and 1930s. However, what brought him even closer to Gandhi was his interest in abolishing Untouchability and promoting Hindu-Muslim harmony. He was more committed to these programmes than many other followers of Gandhi, who were interested in the attainment of political freedom alone.

In 1937, when Congress came to power in Madras, Rajaji was unanimously elected prime minister. He ran a government that was efficient but also controversial, notably for its promotion of Hindi. In October 1939, he resigned along with other Congress ministers/ministries in protest against the Viceroy's refusal to consult Indian opinion in the matter of World War II. Then, in a daring break with his party—and mentor—he opposed the Quit India movement of 1942, asking that Congress instead work harder to find common ground with the British. He became even more estranged from his old comrades when he advocated a rapprochment with the Muslim League.

Rajagopalachari had resigned from the Congress in 1942. Readmitted in 1945, he served as the first Indian Governor of West Bengal and then as the first (and last) Indian Governor General. Afterwards, he joined the Union Cabinet, before returning to Madras as chief minister. In 1954 he was forced to resign from the post and went into retirement.

When he demitted office, Rajaji was in his mid-seventies. He had been continuously in public life for close to four decades. Part of him now simply wanted to read and write. He was an autodidact, with an extraordinarily wide range of interests and reading. His biographer, Rajmohan Gandhi, tells us that when he went to jail in 1921 he took with him editions of the Mahabharata in Tamil and English, the Bible, a volume of Shakespeare, Defoe's *Robinson Crusoe,* a book on Socrates, and a copy of the ancient classic of Tamil literature and philosophy, the *Kural.* Thirty-five years later, when an Indian journalist went to see him in his modest Madras home, he found, stacked near the old man's bed, the collected speeches of Edmund Burke, G. K. Chesterton's Father Brown stories, a book by the American cultural critic Lewis Mumford, a Sanskrit edition of Valmiki's Ramayana, and some works in Tamil.

Rajaji was an accomplished writer himself. He had written pioneering short stories in Tamil and, in the 1940s, had published an abridged version of the Mahabharata. Now, in retirement, he wrote a version of the Ramayana, which like its predecessor was a best-seller in many languages.

However, there was a part of Rajaji that could not keep out of politics altogether. He had changed his mind about Hindi, which he now did not want imposed on the South. He was concerned about the global nuclear arms race. Above all, he was worried about the lack of opposition to the Congress party. In 1959, aged eighty, he started the Swatantra (Freedom) Party. He undertook this with some reluctance, for, as he told a younger colleague, he was 'too old, too long a Congressman and too close to Nehru personally to consider an active re-entry into politics'.

Under Rajaji's leadership, the Swatantra had mixed electoral success—winning twenty-two seats in the general elections of 1962, forty-four in 1967, and a mere eight in 1971. It served in coalition governments in some states. However, its chief contribution to Indian democracy was intellectual and ideological, through its searching criticisms of the economic and foreign policies of the ruling party. It achieved a sort of posthumous success when key elements of its credo—outlined in the excerpts that follow—were, much later, adopted by the Congress party itself.

A colonial governor once called Rajagopalachari the 'wisest man in India'. The sentiment was endorsed by Gandhi, who described him as the 'keeper of my conscience'. Rajaji had a sharp analytical mind and wrote English (and, of course, Tamil) extremely well. His writings were often precocious, as for example his warning in 1942 that Quit India would alienate the Congress from both the British and the Muslims. For this book, however, we have used his later writings, from the 1950s and 1960s, which speak more directly to the problems of Indian democracy today.

C. Rajagopalachari died on 25 December 1972.

OUR DEMOCRACY

In 1957 the Congress comprehensively won the second general election. It was also returned to power in all states except Kerala, where the Communist Party of India came to power. Despite being a long-time member of the Congress C. Rajagopalachari was deeply worried about the consequences of this dominance for the health of Indian democracy. Looking to the older and more stable democracies in the West, he argued in an essay of August 1957, reproduced below, that a strong two-party system was also needed in India. Note that this call for two all-India parties is consistent with his view of the rise of regional parties in the states.[1]

✦   ✦   ✦

The successful working of parliamentary democracy depends on two factors; first on a broad measure of agreement among all classes of citizens about the objectives of government; secondly, on the existence of a two-party system, in which each of the big political groups possesses effective and continuous leadership and is strong enough to take over the responsibilities of government when the majority of the country's voters wish it. If political opinion does not succeed in crystallizing into two fairly evenly balanced groups, the semblance of democracy may survive but real parliamentary democracy will not be there. When one party remains always in power, and dissent is dissipated among unorganized individuals and relatively insignificant groups which do not and cannot coalesce, government will inevitably become totalitarian.

A strong Opposition is essential for the health of democratic government. In a democracy based on universal suffrage, government of the majority without an effective Opposition is like driving a donkey on whose back you put the whole load in one bundle. The two-party system steadies movement by putting a fairly equal load into each pannier. In the human body also, two

1. Originally published in *Swarajya*, 17 August 1957, and reproduced in C. Rajagopalachari, *Satyam Eva Jayate: A Collection of Articles Contributed to Swarajya and Other Journals from 1956 to 1961*, 4 vols. (Madras: Bharathan Publications, 1961), vol. 1, pp. 70–76.

eyes and two ears aid a person to place the objects seen and heard. A single-party democracy soon loses its sense of proportion. It sees, but cannot place things in perspective or apprehend all sides of a question. This is the position in India today.

The domination by the Congress Party of the political scene is a product of history rather than of electoral success. Electoral successes are the result of this domination, not its cause. In order to justify the leadership that has resulted from history, the Congress Party has swung well to the Left. . . . As a result the Right elements are depressed and disorganized, leaving the Congress Party in irremovable power. Irremovability, in fact, makes parliamentary democracy non-existent. In such circumstances it is inevitable that the party should become more important than Parliament. Differences of opinion may exhibit themselves within the party. If the discipline and authority of the party executive does not altogether choke 'self-criticism', a two-party pattern may develop within the party itself. The leader will take decisions in accordance with majority opinion in the party. This may be deemed to be a partial alleviation of totalitarianism, but even this may not happen if the leader be an overwhelming force by himself, in which case the party may not be able to divide itself even within closed doors. The mechanics of unadulterated dictatorship would then operate unhindered.

What is wanted to save parliamentary democracy is an Opposition that will operate not privately and behind the closed doors of the party meeting, but openly and through the electorate. . . . Since, as I have said, the Congress Party has swung to the Left, what is wanted for the body politic is not an ultra or outer-Left, but a strong and articulate Right. The people of India, however docile they may ordinarily appear, are not just clay. Life, not being a mechanical system of forces but full of complex sentiments and feelings, the creaks and jolts caused by change are painful realities that have to be borne by living people in all grades of society, whose patterns of life are the product of long history. The distress is not dissipated into the stratosphere, but strikes at the living, sensitive nerves of men, women and children.

The pain of change is a simple-looking phrase that sums up all that follows from over-taxation, disemployment, high prices, exploitation by the newly-favoured classes and groups, unbalanced family budgets, and the hysteria resulting from all these things in themselves, and from the ordinary individual's sense of his own impotence in [the] face of them. Those who suffer these impacts would welcome a parliamentary party that would compel attention to these creaks and jolts and disturbances in life, and which would meet the Left on level terms and, by testing and measuring both proposed legislation and day-to-day administration, would challenge the wisdom of the governing party and compel modification when those in power act in a way which would produce more pain than profit to the community. This is the function of the Right, and there is a widespread demand for such a party. . . .

Although there is today abundant material for a powerful Opposition, hypnotic fear and the pressure of individual interests operate to prevent the gathering together of the forces. Day-to-day life cannot be carried on without appeals for favours of all kinds from the government in power, and any effort in the direction of forming an Opposition party must involve sacrifice and considerable risk on the part of those who would make such a venture. Sacrifice comes naturally with revolutions but conservative wisdom does not excite a similar emotion. Reason generates fear, and men of experience are inclined to political caution in the personal sense. Distress is accepted with fatalism, not with the spirit of sacrifice which is determined not to allow similar distresses to be inflicted on others. Unless the conservatives realize their duty, throw off their dejection, overcome their fears and unite to build a worthy Opposition, parliamentary democracy in India has a dismal future. Parties which are to the left of the Congress can never hope to function as more than prodding ginger-groups, since it is quite unrealistic for them to imagine themselves as alternatives to a government which is itself prepared to go as far to the left as it is possible to do and which has installed itself on the crest of historic success.

There is another factor that must be taken into account in India. The centrifugal force of regional interest cuts across all political issues. In a country of this size, with all the differing conditions prevailing in the various States, regional interests and issues arising from them in the effort to build welfare overshadow other matters. This creates an additional and great obstacle to two-party polarization in politics. Each regional interest is a solid reality, and this fact tends to impose on Parliament a chequered pattern which in Westminster is only faintly perceptible in Scottish and Welsh nationalism.

The solution for this problem is not to keep blowing scorn at regional feelings, but to concede greater autonomy to the States, so as to minimize regional thinking and eliminate the pressure of regional interests at the Centre, and to make the Centre an instrument for the broadest policies and not, as now, one for dealing with every tank bund, school, hospital and social service club. This statement about the Centre may seem exaggerated, but it is not. During the last few years the tendency to centralize has grown to proportions which are both ridiculous and alarming. . . .

The main remedy lies not in the remodeling of the Council of State, but in a much greater autonomy of the States themselves. The legislatures of the States and the administration of their governments should be run on the parliamentary model, while the Centre gradually crystallizes into a true federal authority. Federal powers, on issues other than foreign affairs and defence, should shrink to the barest minimum, while the powers exercised by the States should expand very greatly.

During the period of transition to greater regional autonomy, politics in the States may take a curious course. Conflict of opinion will naturally develop around the issue of division of powers between the States and the Union. The Congress Party in all the States during this period is bound to be a Unionist or Centrist party, the Opposition being a party pledged to conserve and increase local autonomy. Until a balance is reached, centrists would try to create emotion around slogans of national unity, while provincialists would fight zealously for the interests of the region. These healthy struggles would cut across and minimize caste and sub-caste politics, which in itself would be a great gain for efficiency and integrity in administration. The growth of a vigorous localist party in each State, without distinctions arising from caste feeling, will save provincial governments from deterioration on account of unchecked power in the hands of a majority.

Whatever may be the political structure, the people want fair and impartial, as well as efficient administration. In an environment dominated by family and communal loyalties and attachments, parochial authority quickly causes deterioration among officials. All-round progress and the elimination of unhealthy practices would be largely secured if, while the States are given larger powers, the personnel of administration all over India—Federal as well as State—are kept under the strict and independent guardianship of an all-India body, consisting of very senior officials, whose concern would be to maintain professional quality in the various services, and to protect the officials against political pressures and victimization. This should not interfere with greater devolution of authority to the States. The professional aspect of administration is different from the execution of policy. The defence forces, the police, and the administrative services should be true to their own standards of efficiency and character and be above party politics. They should carry out government policies irrespective of whatever party may be in power. Their discipline must therefore be self-sustained. Efficiency, independence and integrity in officials are necessary both for Federal and State affairs, and the more the services are released from political pressure and temptations to discriminate unfairly on account of political or communal influences, the better it will be for all concerned; for government as well as Opposition, and certainly for the people governed. An efficient administrative machine is absolutely necessary if democracy is to result in that general happiness which is our aim.

✦   ✦   ✦

WANTED: INDEPENDENT THINKING

In this next excerpt, from an article published a few months later, Rajagopalachari speaks of how the overwhelming political dominance of the Congress had led to the decline of independent thinking within the party and in the citizenry at large.[2]

✦   ✦   ✦

The political organization that successfully fought the British power in India was, at the close of that struggle, put in power by the latter. The British Parliament not only acknowledged the independence of India but transferred the reins of executive authority to the Congress Party to start with. This party continues to govern the affairs of the country after ten years of that event. It is well known or, to use the safer journalistic phrase, it cannot be denied that there is considerable searching of heart at the present moment among the leaders of the Indian National Congress. All is not well, it is felt, but no remedy has been found that meets the situation and consequently the customary

2. Originally published in *Swarajya*, 10 May 1958, and reproduced in Rajagopalachari, *Satyam Eva Jayate*, vol. 1, pp. 149–153.

attitude in similar situations in the case of individual sickness is adopted, to say that there is nothing very serious to worry about.

It is, for anyone,—and much more so for one who has spent the best part of his life-time serving the organization and who owes many honours and kindnesses to it—an undertaking of some degree of delicacy to examine into the cause of the present discontent about the Congress. If he avoids vagueness and visionary language and touches the true roots of the malady, he may 'come near to persons of weight and consequence who will rather be exasperated at the discovery of their errors than thankful for the occasion of correcting them. But in all exertions of duty something is to be hazarded'. I have found the words in the writings of one of the greatest political philosophers of modern times, and in that mood I venture to criticize.

As a result of tacit submission on the part of the people of emancipated India, a few good persons at the top, enjoying prestige and power, are acting like guardians of docile children rather than as leaders in a parliamentary democracy. Mutual encouragement has led to this condition of affairs. Men in a state amounting to tutelage have no chance to develop towards maturity. This was Milton's emphatic opinion and it is as true today as in the days of Cromwell and as true in one country as in another. Although men are 'fallen', to use the poet's expression, they retain enough of the original gift of God to grow towards freedom. But a chance must be given to them to discover the precious gift that lies hidden within themselves. The sort of tutelage that now prevails gives no such chance.

No theory of civil life, no 'ism' will work satisfactorily unless the citizens in the democracy are willing to undertake the responsibility of thinking and judging for themselves. . . . Instead of independent thinking and free judgment, the manners of parrots have been growing among men, even among those rightly credited with intellectual capacity of a high order. They repeat the words uttered by the established guardians without paying thought to the meaning and the implications. I am not objecting to any particular opinion but to the parrot culture that has seized the country.

For instance, and only for an instance, there is more than one road to national welfare. The Welfare State was the first formula adopted by the leaders; it was soon followed by the 'socialistic pattern' and then came the socialist State. Did people who successively re-uttered these phrases follow the various meanings of the various phrases? Has there been any known public or even private discussion of the merits of the various ideals connoted by these terms? Do men and women who repeat the word 'socialism', as a name for what is claimed to be the straight way leading to welfare, remember what Gandhiji said about it—Gandhiji whom they profess not only to admire but also to follow in all things? Do people, who now accept national socialism, do so after having considered and rejected the doctrine of trusteeship which Gandhiji told his disciples was his way and was preferable to the egalitarianism of the socialists and the interference by law with ownership of property, and its traditional incidents and obligations, which socialism meant? Have men thought about the matter and all its consequences including the concentration of all economic power and influence in those who, for the time being, wield authority? Have they even thought about whether the management of things by men is likely to be carried out better when they have a proportionate interest in the good stewardship and in its result, or when they do it on salaries and on behalf of the State? Or has socialism been adopted only as parrots learn to speak?

This is only an instance. What I plead for is a climate of independent thinking among citizens. It is no good imagining it is there when we see no sign or symptom of it. Without this essential accompaniment, self-government through democracy will prove itself to be a house of cards.

The reason for a gradual collapse of independent thinking is the confusion in the people's minds between a political struggle against foreign domination and its discipline, and day-to-day government: between revolution and administration. The figures of speech employed in appeals and manifestoes, oral and written, encourage this confusion between battle and government and between the respective disciplines required for them. The long reign of popular favourites, without any significant opposition, is probably the main cause for the collapse of independent thinking. 'You have not gone far enough', 'you do not mean what you say'—these are the only criticisms that some people venture to offer. No one dares to say 'your policy is wrong and must be re-examined'. The opposition is at best a charge of inefficiency in carrying out policy or a suspicion of insincerity. There is no attack on the policy itself.

Democratic civil life calls for independent thinking among the citizens— among the governed as among the governors. Criticism and reply, and counter-reply make for health in the air. Diseases of corruption and intrigue are by a process of natural hygiene driven out in such an atmosphere. Burke said he liked 'clamour'. 'I am not of the opinion,' he said, 'of those gentlemen who are against disturbing the public repose. The fire-bell at midnight might disturb your sleep, but it keeps you from being burned in your bed.'

If subservience and slavish adulation take the place of independent thinking and criticism is never resorted to but with fear and trepidation, the atmosphere quickly breeds the political diseases peculiar to democracy. If we have not the free and critical atmosphere of a well-balanced democracy, a Welfare State is most favourable soil for the growth of the weeds of careerism, intrigue and various types of degrees of dishonesty. An Opposition is the natural preventive for such poisonous weeds. An Opposition is therefore the urgent remedy indicated by the symptoms—not mere psychotherapy. 'You are all right. Indeed you are better than you were. Don't believe you are sick. You are *not* sick!'—this cannot restore a fractured leg. We need an Opposition that thinks differently and does not just want more of the same, a group of vigorously thinking citizens which aims at the general welfare, and not one that in order to get more votes from the so-called have-nots, offers more to them than the party in power has given, an Opposition that appeals to reason and acts on the firm faith that India can be governed well as a democratic Republic, and that the have-nots will not reject sound reason.

It is not the quality of true faith in democracy to fear that truth will not succeed with the electors. What will lead to permanent welfare the voters will accept, if not at once, at least in course of time. We must have the faith that they will see through the corrupt offers of immediate gains at the cost of injury to the general welfare. On such faith an Opposition should come into being that will set a proper balance to the authority of the party in power and put our free Commonwealth on its two feet.

Such an Opposition, even if it should not succeed in ousting a powerful majority from its seat, may at least see that its power is not absolute power, which corrupts absolutely, but something controlled, so that the evils that flow from power may be kept within limits.

Some people frightened by the hopeless prospect of bidding against a socialist Government for the favour of the have-nots believe that the only course open is to wait for the fading away of the Congress by reason of its own weakness and diseases and then to form a new political party on right lines. This cannot be done. No party can issue out of chaos except one backed by physical force and terrorism. If we desire a parliamentary party to come into being for steadying the machinery of government, it must be accomplished when the government is running under Congress rule. It would be fatal to wait for its disintegration which will result only in rule by force.

✦   ✦   ✦

THE CASE FOR THE SWATANTRA PARTY

Finally, Rajagopalachari decided to take the initiative himself in fostering an alternate political and ideological alternative to the Congress Party. This was the Swatantra (Freedom) Party, whose first manifesto, drafted by its octogenarian founder, is excerpted below.[3]

✦   ✦   ✦

...The Swatantra Party stand[s] for minimum government and minimum State interference, for minimum expenditure in administration and for minimum taxation, for minimum interference in the private and professional affairs of citizens and for minimum regulation in industry and trade. As against this are the declared policies, intentions and tendencies of the Congress Party in favour of what has been called "socialism" which is State control of everything. The thesis of the Congress Party is that welfare and social justice can be secured only by increasing State control, as against the antithesis that prosperity, welfare and justice can be more effectively achieved by minimizing State interference and enlarging individual incentive and fair competition. The Swatantra Party stands for the latter proposition and all that follows from it under modern conditions.

The Swatantra Party does not deny the need for regulation, but holds that regulation must be limited to requirement and not expanded to the point of killing individual incentive. Aggregate wealth and production depend on individual incentive and production. State management and State investment involve maximum waste and maximum expenditure as against the frugal

---

3. This is from a manifesto issued in August 1959, written by C. Rajagoplachari and printed in different newspapers and magazines in India.

conditions accompanying all individual enterprise and decentralized effort. Responsibility is reduced if the individual disappears and multiple ownership and delegated authority take over the management.

The Congress Party has so far run without a true Opposition. It has run with accelerators and no brakes. It has put into effect policies and plans that have increased administrative expenditure and caused inflation. Prices have gone up all round and taxation has reached the breaking point. The waste associated with State management is brought to light on every occasion when a window is opened. Widespread dissatisfaction over these things is undeniable and there is no need to give details.

The basic need for prosperity is adequate food production. It is admitted on all hands that attempts at egalitarian distribution of wealth would be utterly foolish before the deficit in food production is set right and much more production all round is assured. Egalitarian distribution of distress and poverty is not what anybody wants.

The Congress Party has unfortunately resolved to tinker with the basic machinery of food production on the assumption that the fault lies there. It has resolved, on the one hand, on fragmentation and, on the other, on destroying individual incentive and handing over farm production to multiple ownership without individual incentive. This is the meaning and the effect of the proposals for putting [a] ceiling on the extent of individual ownership of land and placing the expropriated excess under what is called co-operative management, which in effect means delegated authority to paid officials.[4] . . .

The Swatantra Party has been born out of this conflict between reality on the one hand and inexperienced ambition on the other. The Swatantra Party stands for non-interference with the ownership of land, and against any policy that extinguishes individual incentive in that field and seeks to substitute official management for owner-management. . . .

Going into the affairs of the political party which the Indian National Congress has converted itself into, there has been a great deterioration in what matters most, namely, the moral quality of the elements composing the party. Careerism has taken the place of character, and material desires that of pa-

---

4. The Congress Party was then thinking of promoting collective or co-operative farming on the model of the socialist countries.

triotism. The public reputation and presumption of highmindedness which every Congressman as such enjoyed when we fought the foreign regime [are] no longer there. A general feeling of aversion has taken the place of the universal respect and affection which were once the privilege of the Congressman. This along with the prevailing feeling of uncertainty in all matters where the ruling party exercises authority—and that is a wide field—makes the organization of a new party necessary to restore confidence and interest in public life.

It is not possible to improve the Congress from inside. People have tried it. But vested interests prevent this, and here the phrase has its real derogatory meaning. All the men who control the decisions of the Congress as to its composition or organization are against any changes that will alter its present deteriorated character, for they are interested in its continuing as an instrument for their own individual advantage. An external attack may however change the situation. Reform may set in as a defence.

The Swatantra Party believes that social justice and welfare can be reached more certainly and properly in other ways than through the techniques of so-called socialism with all its accompaniments of injustice, expropriation and repudiation of obligations. . . . It is not good for the nation to allow the State, which be it remembered must always be in the grip of some political party with its own motives and interests, to run all the beneficent activities of the nation as its exclusive monopoly, at the same time taxing the people for all the wasteful cost of that monopolized charity.

The party believes that all the educational activities of the Government, direct and indirect, should be such as to emphasise the moral obligation of those who possess wealth to hold it in trust for society, and a doctrine of life based on that moral obligation as distinguished from seeking to establish a socialistic structure based on legislative sanctions, involving expropriation and loss of incentive for the individual to work and increasing dependence on the State and its officials in every walk of life. The party is opposed to all those policies and forecasts of future Governmental action which have created an all-pervading and deep sense of uncertainty drying up all interest in land and factory alike.

The party recognizes the paramount need for increasing food production and believes that it is best attained through the continuance of the self-employed peasant-proprietor who stands for initiative and freedom and is interested in obtaining the highest yields from the land. The party believes in an intensive programme of agricultural improvement without disturbing the harmony of rural life amongst the elements that compose it, and by promoting the material and psychological inducement for modern production. The party seeks to introduce a more intensive programme than is now being followed in respect of the supply of material, implements and credit to the farmer without any discrimination among individuals and without in any way interfering with the cultivator's rights of ownership, management and cultivation of the land. The party is opposed to cultivation through organizations which are a loose kind of multiple ownership, certain to sap the incentive of the farmer, reduce farm output and end in a collective economy and bureaucratic management.

The party stands for raising the level of life of the farmer by taking steps to maintain a reasonable and fair price for his produce. In Industry, the party stands for the increase of incentives for higher production and expansion which are promoted by competitive enterprise, with adequate safeguards against excessive and unreasonable prices, profits and dividends where the competition itself does not secure these ends. The party would restrict State enterprise to heavy industries to supplement private enterprise in that field, national services such as the railways and the starting of pioneer industries where private initiative is lacking. The party wants taxation to be kept at such a level that it does not interfere with reasonable living standards for the people, both rural and urban, and which, while being necessary and sufficient for carrying on administration and such social services as must be undertaken, is yet not so high and exacting or so ubiquitous as to prevent capital formation and investment by individuals; it is opposed to hasty and lopsided development based on heavy taxation, deficit financing and foreign loans out of all proportion to economic repayment-capacity, leading to excessive inflation. . . .

The philosophy of the Swatantra Party has thus been set out in concrete shape. It stands for the individual to retain his identity and his motives for honest endeavour and for his serving the community with a willing heart and not out of compulsion. . . . Those who are materially prosperous should consider themselves bound to help the less fortunate. People should cease deceiving one another and begin honestly to help those who come to them. If we have no faith in our people, if we do not trust one another, democracy will be a poor make-believe and will break down with anarchy into rule by force. So-cial Co-operation has always been our Dharma. The State should recede into comparative insignificance and Dharma should be restored to its original po-sition as sovereign over men, women and government.

+ + +

REFORMING THE SYSTEM OF ELECTIONS IN INDIA

In 1962, after the Congress had won its third successive general elec-tion, Rajagopalachari argued that the electoral system in India was bi-ased towards the ruling party. Further, it was subject to the influence of big business and not transparent. In our next excerpt, he outlined how elections in India could be made more efficient and transparent. This is the last of four essays by Rajagopalachari which—in the view of this editor—collectively demonstrate that no one, before or since, has thought through the problems of Indian democracy with such acuity and insight.[5]

+ + +

Reform of electoral procedure has been talked about and [it] seems as if the Congress Government is satisfied that all that is needed has been done. The Congress Party does not seem to object to elections being, by and large, a private enterprise, as it has capital enough to run them as such. Why should the Government not arrange to give to every voter his or her identification card and serial number? This would substantially reduce the expense for the candidate. It is the expensiveness of the election campaigns and the monop-oly of funds that it commands that chiefly contribute to the Congress Party's success. Nothing is being done towards reducing the expenses of candidates or of parties, which is the same thing. . . .

5. Reproduced from *Dear Reader: Weekly Colloquy of C. Rajagopalachari with the Readers of* Swarajya, *1961–1972* (Coimbatore: Bharatiya Vidya Bhavan, 1993), pp. 54–66.

The Indian electorate suffers from well-known defects from which Western democracies are relatively free. The Indian voters are in great measure poor and vulnerable to bribery: even a day's expense for food serves to buy a large number of the poor voters. They are in a great measure ignorant and do not know, for instance, why prices rise. They are ignorant of the connection between Government policies and their consequences in a nation's life. They are moved by caste and community affiliations. They like to vote for the party likely to succeed, irrespective of policies or merits.

It is therefore highly unsatisfactory that the press should day in and day out publish during the critical fortnight captions forecasting success for the Congress Party. The freedom of the press is sacred and I am as much a defender of it as Milton or John Stuart Mill. But this is definitely rigging the contest in favour of the ruling party. Among the many difficulties mentioned above, this is an additional handicap for opposition parties for which the press is responsible, possibly without intending it. . . .

There is no way of salvaging democracy in India unless the former Election Commissioner[6] with his great experience works out a very inexpensive election procedure putting a maximum share of the cost on the State and saving the expense for candidates. We must choose between evils and cannot hope to have everything good. I would put the burden of distributing identification slips on the Government. I would also like mobile arrangements for collecting votes at the voters' residences.

We can even think of two stages in the General Elections, the first stage being the election of a front-rank leader to lead the Government of India, and the second stage being the election of all MPs after the public knows the result of the first stage. This may be treated as a compromise between the American and the British system. We are not in the same situation as we were in the first decade of Independence when we had quite a few 'old guard' men available who were known and respected all over India. . . .

At long last the Election Commission has expressed the desire to work out a plan by which every voter casts his vote at his doorstep. This has been my cry all these years. I hope the plan will not be given up on account of seeming difficulties and objections, but will be worked out properly. It will reduce cor-

6. This is Sukumar Sen, the mathematician-turned-civil servant who had successfully supervised India's first two general elections.

ruption as well as intimidation. It will reduce the expense of elections and make it possible for candidates to stand without depending on money to be obtained from others. It is a bold step that is involved. I hope the Election Commission will not retreat but press on with this far-reaching reform.

The one man Election Commission, we are told, is thinking of having mobile polling booths in 'risky' areas and places where violence and intimidation are rife. Those who know how much money is spent by parties and candidates in elections and how it is spent, would tell the Election Commission that corruption would be much minimized and honesty would have a chance if house-to-house taking of votes in mobile booths could be introduced everywhere. The Government should spend more and the actual expenses of parties and candidates should be considerably reduced.

It appears from what has been reported in the press that the Election Commissioner objects to candidates writing, typing or rubber-stamping their names on the identity slips they give to the voters. This is a just objection that the Election Commissioner has taken. If electioneering misdemeanours are to be reduced to the minimum, the State should recognize and fulfil its duty to acquaint each voter of his right to vote, and give him a card showing his name and number in the roll, and not leave it to the candidates to do this work. It is this that gives the opportunity for misdemeanours. The Commissioner's objection confirms the validity of my long standing proposal that the Government should give cards of identification to voters and also collect the votes on the appointed days in mobile polling-booths so as to keep candidates' conveyances out of the field.

The duplication of expenses incurred in telling the voter that he has a vote and persuading him to go to the booth to lodge his vote ought to be avoided and the State as a whole should incur the trouble and the expense. The candidates should be left to earn their preferences by their merits and their campaigning and not by reason of having taken the trouble to acquaint the voter of his right and by reason of making it easy for him to go to the polling-booth. Our voters are simple-minded and they feel it their moral duty to oblige those that take some trouble on their behalf during the polling week. This leads to making the election a mere bargain.

The reform I have proposed and which I have kept insisting upon should be made the rule as early as possible. Mobile booths to collect votes may appear to be a rather expensive scheme. . . . The total national expenditure on the elections would be less, more burden falling on the Government, and much less on the candidates, which is just the right thing if we desire to give an equal chance to all the candidates, rich or poor. Let us nationalize the elections before we nationalize business concerns which will suffer and not improve by nationalization. . . .

Pothan Joseph, writing in the *Sunday Standard,* winds up a most readable review of Mr. Nehru's campaign-language thus:

'The standard of 1962 oratory did not contribute to a glorious chapter of sober education for the 210 million adults in the voters' lists'.

What is to be deplored most in the recent elections, however, is not the language but the terrible rise in election expenditure and the manner in which money flowed for the purchase of the votes of the poor and illiterate. Money running so alarmingly ahead of education, leads one to ask what hope or way out is there for democracy. The hunger for good government thus foiled inevitably leads to some form of violent escape which spells disaster for democracy.

It should be made a binding rule that no Minister responsible for Industries, either at the Centre or in the States, should undertake collection of funds for the ruling party for the coming general elections. Otherwise it is open large-scale corruption, whatever may be the camouflages set up. It is not enough that this convention is publicly accepted if indirect arrangements are put into motion contrary to the principle. . . .

All kinds of collection of money are going on, called 'voluntary' donations for unofficial funds in which the Congress Party is interested, and in which officials of the status of collectors of districts and ministers of States are asked to take a direct part and considerable interest. The other day a collector gave ten lakhs of rupees as the 'quota' for his district for the Nehru Fund. . . .

We cannot save democracy for India unless we make elections less expensive than they are today. The officially ordained ceiling does not tell us the real story. The expense to be incurred whether by the candidate or the party is far too great and we must investigate and see what we can do to make it possible for a decent man of moderate means to get elected. I have been advocating mobile polling booths and placing the responsibility on the administration of giving to every voter his identity card with his or her name and number in the electoral list. At present all this work is of the nature of private enterprise run by candidates. If what I have been suggesting is not satisfactory, some other means must be found. But that elections should be made much less expensive is an imperative necessity.

The elections cost candidates fabulous sums of money—not particularly on account of bribing, but by reason of necessary expenditure on men to be engaged in the various transactions involved in the process of direct elections based on adult suffrage. The whole structure must break down under the weight of this expense, when the subservience of industry to politics is got rid of, as it must be, one day. Shareholders' money is now being misused by the managing agencies for political purposes as a result of government being a Permit-Licence Raj; but this cannot go on for long. One day or other, a ban will have to be placed on contributions by company managements of shareholders' money to political parties for distribution among their candidates for electioneering expenses. Then this expensive structure must break down. . . .

All changes involve trouble in the beginning. Even very desirable reforms involve trouble. Conservative officials not wishing to incur these troubles may present impediments and objections. But unless these are over-ruled and mobile booths go round and collect votes, elections will be too expensive for our country, its people and the candidates. Money will rule and not opinions.

Any amount of talk may go on a beguiled people. But until the election procedure is altered radically so as to throw the great burden of identification and getting the voters to cast their votes on the Government without making it an expensive handicap for poor candidates and poor parties, practically deeming elections to be a private enterprise, there can be no real socialism. Expropriation and curbing and discouraging free production do not make socialism but make poverty. Envy is not socialism. What is at the basis of all present-day errors in the art of government is that reform is based on conflict and envy and not on good sense.

+ + +

FREEING THE ECONOMY

The economic policies of Jawaharlal Nehru, and of the Government of India, assigned a key role to the states. Rajagopalachari thought these policies constituted a 'license-permit-quota Raj' that stifled entrepreneurship and private initiative. His own economic ideas are succinctly summarised in our next excerpt from this writing.[7]

✦   ✦   ✦

It is remarkable that in this scientific and rationalistic age, centralized economic planning by the State has been raised to the pedestal of a holy cult. The dominant theme in India for some years past has been the economic uplift of the masses, and centralized all-out planning has been resorted to as the means of promoting that object. And this, in spite of reiterated lip-service to decentralization. The major fault of centralized, comprehensive planning is that it imposes a monolithic burden on a people composed of diverse elements at all levels and in all occupations. The achievements that it might show in a few selected areas are bought at the cost of the freedom and enterprise of the individual. The individual and his creative ability are smothered by a proliferating bureaucracy and innumerable rules and regulations. . . .

Planning has proceeded in our country on the assumption that people do not know what is good for them and, therefore, they must be told what to do. It has proceeded on the basis that a few bright persons are omniscient and are capable of directing the destinies of the nation in an infallible manner. We have had many warnings to teach us humility. The Bhakra dam, which was described as the new and real temple for India, can be aptly described as the projection of our folly in thinking that big names are the best things. It must come as a revelation to all of us that, apart from crores of rupees sunk into this mammoth project, the danger of anything going wrong with the dam would be an inundation of indescribable magnitude. The bigger a man builds, the smaller becomes his control over the things he builds. What I deplore is not the building of this particular dam but the megalomania for big projects. These projects have a political corollary—the centralization of all authority, to the detriment of the future of the nation. Until and unless we develop to a stage when the requisite administrative set-up, technical skill and, above all, conscience are all geared to the needs of such projects, it is foolhardy to venture on them. . . .

What we need is not just big projects, but useful and fruitful projects. There is nothing inherently wrong with bigness, just as there is nothing inher-

---

7. Article written in December 1959 and reproduced in Rajagopalachari, *Satyam Eva Jayate*, vol. 1, pp. 474–481.

ently good in bigness. Big dams are good, but more essential are thousands of small projects which could be and would be executed by the enthusiasm of the local people because they directly and immediately improve their lives. So also in the setting up of industries, there should be encouragement to industries producing consumer goods, which give content and meaning to the phrase 'standard of living' and which can be produced in small and medium scale industries. Private enterprise should be fostered by every means available and not treated as a dangerous enemy. Industrial enterprise would then spread at various levels in the countryside and reduce the tensions that attach to centralized industrialism.

The federal structure of India is not only not used but is sought to be sabotaged. For instance, although industries are today listed by the Constitution under the State Schedule (excepting strategic industries), those who wish to start industries must all rush to New Delhi for permits and comply with or otherwise negotiate a host of regulations. As a consequence, unemployment stands unchanged. It will be argued that there should be co-ordination and uniformity. But economic development takes place faster when diversity is permitted and the fullest use is made of local, physical and social conditions by those who know them.

One of the most neglected aspects of planning in this country is the gearing up of the administrative machinery and the simplification of procedures. It is no use directing appeals of patriotism to clerks whose personal lives cannot permit room for any thought beyond their day-to-day household troubles. Unless conditions are radically changed to provide incentives, to remove inefficiency and to fix responsibility, economic development in this country will be hampered by the very administrative machinery which is supposed to help it.

The role of the Government should be that of a catalyst in stimulating economic development while individual initiative and enterprise are given the fullest play. The Government can do a great deal by way of providing a network of highways and village roads, in improving waterways and developing small harbours, improving communication and transit facilities, which would all serve to boost the economy. Many important things have been neglected because the Government has forgotten them in its obsession with a 'command economy'. Wise planning means Government help to foster private enterprise and self-help among individuals. Otherwise, there can be no real progress.

✦   ✦   ✦

ASSISTING THE BACKWARD

The Indian Constitution had mandated affirmative action for the former Untouchables and 'tribals'. A percentage of seats in Parliament
and state assemblies, and in government jobs, were reserved for them.
There were continuing pressures to expand these programmes to include other economically backward classes. In our next excerpt, Rajagopalachari argues that all such schemes should be based on economic
criteria alone.[8]

✦   ✦   ✦

There is a problem in our public affairs which is almost interminable—that of
the community as a whole acting through the State helping the backward elements to rise to a better life in material terms and to a higher level of culture.
We seek to do away with all caste divisions but all statutory and other concessions given for the uplift of the backward elements, are prescribed on the
basis of caste, although castes and sub-castes are branded as wicked and
stand abolished in the national ideology. Caste was and still continues to be
deemed as the best means of identifying the beneficiaries and distributing
the concessions. It has, however, been increasingly felt that this is a basically
erroneous procedure, being in conflict with the no-caste ideology of the nation. It is seen more and more clearly that it creates a vested interest in backwardness and in belonging to a particular caste. It is easily exploited to the
advantage of a few individuals 'belonging' to a 'backward' caste, these beneficiaries themselves being in no sense backward. Not only does the community remain backward, notwithstanding the concessions and assistance given
by the State, but the benefiting individuals insist on classifying the community
as backward and [are] therefore interested in keeping it as backward. This is in
increasing measure recognized by the general body of even those castes. They
themselves have often protested against exploitation by favoured individuals
of the assistance given to the community or sub-community concerned.

The question, therefore, must soon be tackled boldly whether the caste-
wise approach should not be given up and a secular economical test substi-

8. Originally published in *Swarajya*, 8 October 1960, and reproduced in Rajagopalachari, *Satyam Eva Jayate*, vol. 1, pp. 643–645.

tuted for all the State assistance and concessions to be given for the uplift of the backward. A definition based on economic condition would prevent exploitation and be capable of more general application, so as to avoid the charge that these uplift concessions are fundamentally discriminatory, and by such discrimination creating new classes of under-privileged people, while not helping the old backward classes. The whole question should be examined in the dry light of justice and reasonableness, and a formula arrived at which would decide who needs help and what concessions should be given to him to do him justice. The formula must necessarily be in individual economic terms and not one based on locality or community. Locality and community combined may be a convenient basis for *enquiry,* but should not itself be the final grounds for *classification.*

The terms privileged and under-privileged are sometimes used in connection with the need for State assistance. Privilege—or the opposite of it, disability—applies to a condition determined by worldly possessions or caste conventions conferring material advantages or imposing disabilities. There is in India no question now of any legal status associated with caste. If any advantage or disability existed once upon a time, based on caste, it no longer exists. What exists is poverty in varying degrees. This is a condition demanding attention wherever it exists, that is to say, whatever caste the individual belong[s] to. Otherwise, if the individual should be benefited by a subsidy or a concession on account of his caste, it becomes a new privilege which it is not good policy to create or perpetuate. There should be no slackening or reduction of assistance to individuals deserving it. But it should not be done by reference to the caste to which the individual belongs.

At the base of any programme of helping the backward, education must play the largest part. Boys and girls falling within the economic definition arrived at must be given education in schools organized for them, wherein all the facilities decided upon may be given to all the pupils without reference to castes or sub-castes for the purpose of giving such help, and without perpetuating a classification which we want to be forgotten. It would thus be all reduced to financial terms and be part of general financial policy instead of a kind of communal discrimination for purposes of uplift. We will have to allot funds for institutions in which there would be no charge for tuition or board for poor and deserving pupils. The present scheme of concessions has gone so far to perpetuate caste that Christians and Muslims classify themselves under their Indian caste names of origin, although when adopting these faiths the intention was to wipe out all forms of untouchability or isolation, and to forget it. The very agents who brought about the conversion to Islam or Christianity plead for recognition of their 'Harijan' status in order to obtain the government concessions for their protégés. . . .

A simple economic basis unconnected with caste should be substituted for the caste basis on which the concessions are now given. It would stop the competition for backwardness and the increasing jealousies between community and community arising out of the grant of these concessions to some and refusal to others, although the individuals concerned are equally in need of them.

+ + +

WHY WE NEED ENGLISH

Where Rammanohar Lohia had opposed the use of English as an official language in India, Rajagopalachari supported it. This was in part the product of a north/south divide—for southern politicians felt that English was more acceptable as compared to the northern language some wanted it to be substituted by, Hindi. In the next excerpt, Rajaji makes the case for English in his characteristically economical and direct prose.[9]

+ + +

All the reasons that have been advanced to retain English as the official language of the Union and not to seek to replace it by Hindi—and they are substantial reasons—have been left unanswered, but two arguments are repeatedly advanced by the Hindi protagonists. One is that English is a language of foreign origin and not one of the Indian languages, and therefore it would be derogatory to national prestige to allow it to continue as the medium of official work in India.

9. Originally published under the title 'Panch-Maaya' [Five Illusions] in *Swarajya*, 15 February 1958, and reproduced in Rajagopalachari, *Satyam Eva Jayate*, vol. 1, pp. 135–139.

Our national prestige has not suffered during these ten years after Independence and it is not going to be adversely affected if we make no change but go on indefinitely with English. Those whose mother-tongue is Hindi and who expected it to be made the official language not only in their own State governments but also at the Union level, may feel disappointed and even angry that they have had to yield to the protests of non-Hindi people, but this, far from lowering, will enhance the prestige of Indian democracy and strengthen confidence in India herself.

English no doubt entered India as the language of the foreign people whom we allowed to take possession of India. But the secret of its strong entrenchment where it was placed, even though it was foreign soil, is that it has been to us the gateway of all modern knowledge and modern progress. It is erroneous to suppose that it has struck root in India by reason of official patronage. That we stuck to it even after Independence was not due to any pressure from abroad or force of habit only. It was due to our appreciation of its utility in more than one respect. All our hopes in the material plane are centred on the advancement of modern knowledge, and the English language cannot but be associated intimately with those hopes. It is the vast new knowledge that it brought, and has yet to bring, that is the secret of the widespread attachment in India to the English language. The claims of mere patriotic sentiment must recognize and yield to this.

The other argument advanced for doing away with English in favour of Hindi is a doctrinal one. In a democracy, it is argued, there should be identity of medium between government and the people. The language of the people must be the official language, otherwise it would be a failure of democratic integration. I do not deny the force of this argument. But I claim that the doctrine of identity of language between government and the people is fulfilled if every one of the States in the Union functions in the language of the area. There are over a dozen languages in India and millions are the votaries of each one of them, and they are located in the territories of each linguistic State. If each State functions in the regional language, the doctrine of identity of medium is completely fulfilled. The whole is the sum of its parts, and nothing remains to be done to fulfill the demands of this doctrine. On the other hand, if Hindi is made the language of the Union Government, there will be no identity between that and the language of the people of Bengal or Madras or any other non-Hindi State. It is not, be it remembered, a matter of consent or protest but a question of identity of language and we can devise no trick by which we can discover a language for the Union Government which will not leave tens of millions and vast tracts outside its vogue. The argument that Hindi will help us to fulfill the doctrine of identity of language between the people and government is based on a delusion, either that consent makes up for a deficiency, or that two-fifths is enough fulfillment. It boils down, if we get rid of the fallacies, to a simple preference for an Indian to a foreign language, even though in either case the doctrine of democratic identity with the people's language is not really satisfied. Once again therefore we go back to the sentimental argument against English.

But let us see whether and how far the same doctrine of identity between government and the people is fulfilled in the case of the English language. All the educated people of India in all the States, all the officials of the Union and State governments all over India, have a very fair acquaintance with and command over the use of English, whereas the same is not the case by any means with Hindi or any variant of it. So then it will be seen that, although there are a dozen languages spoken in India, the educated section in any part of India commands a knowledge of English and no other single language has this vogue.

And this will continue to be so, because it is admitted on all hands that a sound knowledge of English is an essential part and will continue to be an essential part of education in India in all the States, whereas a knowledge of Hindi is still only a desideratum in most part[s] of India, and is still a controversial item in certain educational circles. The fact of the matter is that interest in language goes hand in hand with the modern knowledge it brings. The substance of knowledge, for which English books serve as medium, is the motive power behind the attention to that language. What modern knowledge now or in the future will Hindi bring? Can we be really dependent on translated material, translated not by men eminent in the science or the technology of which the book is an exposition but by mere translators of words? The fact of the matter is that new knowledge brings its own language, the language of the men who have made and are making that science or other branch of modern knowledge. Anything else is second-hand and we have no time, neither we nor the young people in schools and colleges, to waste on prestige when progress depends on knowledge.

Then there is a third fallacy. We have to discard the *maaya* [illusion] that Hindi is rich enough and good enough for all our purposes. Government is not an easy or simple affair in the present days. The semi-educated may fancy that his mother-tongue is as good as English and can serve every purpose. The educated may fancy that with a little exertion all deficiencies may be supplied. But language is not a mere collection of symbols made and brought together anyhow and we cannot but go terribly wrong if we think we can make Hindi as rich as English straightaway.

It is a delusion again that Hindi, such as it is, is easy to learn for all the people of India. It is by no means easy for the millions whose languages are not of the same stock. There are fundamental differences that make it difficult. Yet, I know that most Hindi protagonists who have no knowledge whatsoever of the Southern languages honestly believe that it is only laziness or cussedness that prevents Hindi being learnt. Everyone believes that his mother-tongue is the easiest of all languages and those who object to learn it are just unwilling people. The claim made on behalf of Hindi has a subtle illusion behind it. Those who speak Hindi and who find it spoken all round them, believe that it will one day become the mother-tongue of all the peoples of India. I need hardly point out that this fourth delusion is a dangerous and vain notion. The other languages of India will not die, leaving place for Hindi to become the mother-tongue of the people now speaking Tamil, Kannada or Bengali. It is not like the case of a few settler-families adopting the language of the place and forgetting their own mother-tongue. The mass and the distribution of the people speaking languages other than Hindi render any such hope an unthinkable proposition.

Fifthly and lastly, there is the greatest fallacy of all, the notion that unity is brought about by the adoption of Hindi as the official language of the Union. What is brought about is protest, dissatisfaction and discord, not unity. Hostility can be overcome by political dodging or pressure but that way heart-rankling is produced, not unity. Where the principle of justice is materially ignored, we cause a wound which will not heal easily. He who points this out is not the offender, but he who inflicts the wound.

I appeal to my brethren and friends in the North to abstain from this plan and to join with me in asking that Part XVII of the Constitution be suspended[10] as an erroneous step taken when thought was not ripe. It would be a gesture

10. This mandated that from 26 January 1965—fifteen years after the passing of the Constitution—only Hindi would be used in all communications between the Centre and the States. Till then, English was also to be allowed. In the event, owing to protests from the South, this 'grace period' for English was extended indefinitely.

of great value for the unity and emotional integration of India. Let no one imagine that I have lost my love for India or my concern for all its parts. Indeed it is greater than ever, and it is that which now makes me talk and write in this unpleasant way. The Hindi speaking people injure themselves in the long run by pressing that their mother-tongue should be accepted as the Union official language by those who do not speak it. I beg of them to concentrate on their work at State-level and declare the match drawn at the Union level and leave the *status quo* intact with no threats hanging over the heads of people. Let English continue.

'This stone which the builders refused is become the head stone of the corner'. So the Psalmist sang. The builders had rejected it as being of curious shape, not rectangle and none of its sides square or oblong. But it became the key-stone of the arch and its strange shape was its merit. Not some one of our own languages but this strange one will keep the arch firm and all the languages together. It is the Lord's doing and marvellous in our eyes! So be it.

✦   ✦   ✦

THE INDIA WE WANT

Our last excerpt from Rajagopalachari is from an essay he wrote in October 1961, after his old friend-turned-political adversary, Jawaharlal Nehru, had visited Madras and made some critical remarks about him at a public meeting. Nehru had referred to Rajaji as being 'continually angry'.[11]

✦   ✦   ✦

Nehru came to Madras with all the paraphernalia of the Prime Minister of India and attempted in his speech to answer my oft-repeated charges; he made counter-charges against me of speaking in anger and in the confusion of mind caused by unaccountable anger. I am grateful for the respect he continues to have for me. He wants me to say precisely what I want and paint the

11. Reproduced from Vuppuluri Kalidas, ed., *Rajaji Reader: Selections from Writings of C. Rajagopalachari* (Madras: Vyasa Publications, 1980), pp. 130–132.

picture of India as I desire it to be. The Swatantra manifesto answers this challenge and not even adverse newspapers have found it wanting in definiteness
or clarity. But [as] Nehru has had no time to read it, here is my picture.

I want an India clear of the atmosphere of fear in which it is now enveloped, where honest men engage in the difficult tasks of production or trade
can carry on their occupation without fear of ruin at the hands of officials,
ministers and party bosses.

I want an India where talent and energy can find scope for play without
having to cringe and obtain special individual permission from officials and
ministers, and where their efforts will be judged by the open market in India
and abroad.

I want the dense permit-licence fog not to sit on us. I want Statism to go
and Government reduced to its proper functions.

I want the inefficiency of public management to go where the competitive
economy of private management can look after affairs.

I want the corruptions of this permit-licence raj to go.

I want the officials appointed to administer laws and policies to be free
from the pressures of the bosses of the ruling party, and gradually restored
back to the standards of fearless honesty which they once maintained.

Nehru says he has not been approached by any permit-seeker. True. But he
has an army of 150 ministers under him and numerous professional Congressmen busy in this new occupation of assisting men to get quotas and permits.

I want real equal opportunities for all and no private monopolies created
by the permit-licence raj.

I want an India where the peasants are not intimidated or beguiled into
giving up their lands ... to build castles in the air through co-operative
farming.

I want security for all owners of property, land or other forms of acquisitions, without a Sword of Damocles hanging over them threatening expropriation without payment of just and full compensation as fixed by judicial authorities on correct principles and not according to the dictation of political
legislation.

I want the fundamental rights to be restored to their original shape and
kept intact.

I want an India where heavy direct and indirect taxes do not prevent the
building-up of private capital, discouraging enterprise and effort.

I want an India where the budget of the Centre does not cause inflation and soaring prices.

I want an India where the State does not tax for capital investment, making the present generation's life miserable.

I want the money power of big business to be isolated from politics. Democracy is hard to be worked and it should not be ruined by money power and rendered into a simulacrum by expensive elections and big business supporting the ruling party with funds in return for privileges or in fear of the State's regulatory powers. . . .

I want the spirit of compassion and benevolence to have free play and not [be] stifled by State schemes of monopolizing all welfare by over-taxation and over-centralization.

I want the State to know its limitations and function in humility and the citizens to realize spirituality through the traditional channels inherited by them in that regard.

I want a strong party to be in real opposition to the ruling party—whichever party it may be—so that the wheels of democracy may run on the straight road.

I want India to regain her moral stature abroad and I do not want our people to be bamboozled into thinking that we have not lost what moral authority we commanded during Gandhiji's days.

✦ ✦ ✦

20

THE DEFENDER OF THE TRIBALS

VERRIER ELWIN

IN ABOUT 1900, GOPAL KRISHNA GOKHALE wrote that 'the India of the future could not now be only a Hindu India or a Muhammedan India; it must be compounded of all elements which existed in India— Hindu, Muhammedan, Parsee, Christian, aye, and the Englishman who adopted India as his country'. In adding that last caveat Gokhale may have had in mind the founder of the Indian National Congress, Allan Octavian Hume, as well as the Irishwoman who had recently made her home in India, Annie Besant. At any rate, the remark was prescient as well as generous, opening the way for other British men and women to exchange their nationality for that of a country which had once been under their subjection.

A remarkable Englishman-turned-Indian was Verrier Elwin, the Oxford scholar who became the foremost scholar of, and spokesman for, India's tribal peoples. Born in 1902, the son of a colonial Bishop, Elwin was reared in a fiercely evangelical family. It was to escape this background that he came to India in 1927, a freshly ordained priest, with first-class degrees in English and Theology under his belt. He joined the Christa Seva Sangh (CSS), an organisation that sought to root

Christianity in Indian soil, and whose members wore home-spun cloth, ate vegetarian food, and incorporated Indian motifs into their liturgy.

The CSS was based in Puné. Elwin thus became acquainted with that city's reformist and liberal traditions. He also befriended Kamaladevi Chattopadhyay, who was living in Puné in the late 1920s. But his most consequential contact was with Gandhi, who often visited Puné, and whose own *ashram* in Ahmedabad was but a night's train journey away. Elwin was deeply attracted to Gandhi, whom he saw as the finest modern interpreter of the message of Christ himself.

In 1931 Elwin left the CSS to engage more directly with the lives of the Indian poor. He first thought of making his home in an Untouchable quarter of Bombay, but eventually decided to work with the tribal people of central India. With a CSS friend, Shamrao Hivale, he moved to a village in the upper Narmada Valley, where he sought to bring modern education and health care to the Gond tribals. Seeking to uplift the tribals, he was converted by them instead, enchanted by their love of music and dance, and their liberated attitude to sex and marriage. At the same time, he was greatly exercised by their economic plight, the loss of their land to moneylenders, and the loss of their forests to the state.

In 1936 Elwin was delicensed by the Church of England for his refusal to take the Gospel to the tribes. Four years later he married a Gond girl, deepening his identification with her people. (The marriage broke up after a decade, whereupon Elwin married another tribal.) Meanwhile, he had begun publishing essays and books on different aspects of tribal life and culture. Some of his works were descriptive and ethnographic—others, analytical and polemical. He had gone to the Gond country as a social worker, but now, as he told a friend, 'the pen is the chief weapon with which I fight for my poor'.

As we have seen, Gandhi paid close attention to the problems of women, Muslims, and Untouchables. However, despite being some 8% of India's population, the tribals had been ignored by the national movement. Nor had other political thinkers and activists focused on them. Once, when charged with the question of why he didn't take up tribal questions, B. R. Ambedkar answered: 'I have never claimed to be a universal leader of suffering humanity. The problem of Untouchables is quite enough for my suffering strength'. This was reasonable, but it still left a large and vulnerable section unrepresented in public discourse. This was the gap that Verrier Elwin sought to fill.

Through the 1940s, Elwin published a series of major books on individual tribes. He also wrote many articles in newspapers and magazines on policy matters. The range and sheer bulk of his work was matched by a manifest sympathy with his subjects, with the findings of his research communicated with a grace uncharacteristic of academic writing.

After Independence, Elwin became a citizen of the Indian Republic. In 1954 Jawaharlal Nehru appointed him Adviser on Tribal Affairs to the administration of the North-east Frontier Agency (NEFA). This was a large territory at the trijunction of India with China and Burma, inhabited by very many different tribes who were largely unknown to the administration. Elwin was charged with designing policies to facilitate and smoothen their cultural integration with the rest of India.

Elwin spent ten years in the north-east, travelling to all parts of NEFA, and also spending extended periods of time in Assam and Nagaland. As before, he wrote about tribal art and folklore, but also about land and forest policies. He died in 1964, an esteemed if also somewhat controversial public figure in his adopted homeland.

Verrier Elwin is represented in this book because of the quality of his thought (and prose) and because he focused attention on the problems of the two large concentrations of tribals in the country. These reside in the forested hills of central India and the north-east, respectively. The former is now the epicentre of a Maoist rebellion; the latter, home to apparently intractable insurgencies. Intrinsic worth, as well as contemporary relevance, thus justify the choice of Elwin as a maker of modern India.

FREEDOM FOR THE TRIBALS

In the early 1940s the word 'freedom' was ubiquitous. Gandhi talked of freedom for Indians; Jinnah of freedom for the Muslims. The British prime minister, Winston Churchill, argued that the war then under way was a battle of freedom versus tyranny. The American president, Franklin Delano Roosevelt, spoke of fighting for four freedoms—the freedom of expression, the freedom of worship, the freedom from want, and the freedom from fear. In the following excerpt, Verrier Elwin invokes the politicians' rhetoric to ask for freedom for India's long neglected tribal people.[1]

✦ ✦ ✦

Let us make a brief summary of the things that have broken the nerve and depressed the spirit of the once happy and free tribesmen. First and foremost is the loss of land. The indolent and pleasure-loving temperament of the tribesmen has always rendered them an easy prey to the educated cunning and intelligence of the men of the plains. It is a deplorable fact that it has been actually proposed as a measure of social uplift to bring the hillmen down to the plains and thus expose them to these adventurers. Those more or less nomadic tribes who had lived by shifting cultivation lost all rights over the forests where they once freely roamed, and many of them today are landless coolies.

The establishment of Forest Departments to protect the forest, in many respects inevitable, proved another serious blow to tribesmen who lived by axe-cultivation, digging for roots and hunting. . . .

The disappearance of the ritual hunt, which in many tribes preceded their major festivals, the cancellation of fishing rights and the suppression of the home distillery suggested to the aboriginals that civilization was hostile to their most cherished traditions. Liquor, for example, is a necessary ingredient in all forms of aboriginal worship and social ceremonies. The Congress has here shown a liberal spirit and has declared that it will not apply the prohibition laws to the tribesmen. But, as usual, puritan reformers are trying to force their hand. Everyone will wish to see habits of temperance extended, but to prohibit liquor-drinking altogether will be to deprive the hillmen of a valuable tonic and stimulant and will drive them to the far more injurious use of opium and other drugs.

The effect of literary education on people who can never afford a book to read or a piece of paper to write on has generally been deplorable. Primary education in the tribal areas is in the hands of the District Councils, bodies com-

1. From Verrier Elwin, *The Aboriginals*, 2nd ed. (Bombay: Oxford University Press, 1944), pp. 14–19, 29–32.

posed of landlords, lawyers and business men who have often risen to power by exploiting the aboriginals and whose interests are directly opposed to theirs. Schools, totally divorced from the life of the people, staffed by the most inferior type of teacher, which teach the tribesmen to despise their own culture, to abandon their natural and simple dress, dancing and other recreations, are opened in the remotest areas and there is a desire on the part of some politicians—although Mahatma Gandhi and the Congress have condemned this type of education in the most emphatic terms—to introduce it on a compulsory basis wherever they can. The opening of workshops in which carpentry, agriculture and any other means of teaching the people to make useful and beautiful things would, of course, be invaluable. But the miserable little schools for introducing an unwanted literacy are worse than useless. The trouble is that the present unregulated system of education, far from preserving or developing aboriginal culture, destroys it. The schools are generally situated in centres of the non-aboriginal population and the jungle child grows up among those who regard him and his way of life with scorn. Even where this is not so, the teachers are usually urban-minded, regard themselves and their civilization as infinitely superior to the 'savages' among whom they have to live, and either ignore or condemn their institutions. Hindu, Muslim and Christian, but not aboriginal, festivals are marked by holidays. The children learn to chant in a nasal sing-song and pray to alien gods, but never to the old gods of the soil to whose worship their parents are deeply attached. They study in what is to them a foreign language. They read the lives of Indian Liberal leaders or English Viceroys, but hear nothing of their own cult-heroes or leaders. How many Gond schoolboys could recite the beautiful legend of Lingo, the mythical founder of their tribe, or say how many Gond Rajas there were in India? The aesthetic effect of education is disastrous. How beautiful is a Muria or Uraon boy fresh from the forest, with his long curly locks, his bright necklaces, the feathers and flowers in his hair! But the schoolmaster plucks the feathers from his hair, shaves his elfin locks, derides his ornaments; a small round cap replaces the becoming turban, and soon filthy khaki shorts and a dirty little coat cover 'the eternally dressed nakedness of the brown skin'. . . .

India is all too full of people like Mr. Pumblechook[2] who, it will be remembered, could not see a small boy without trying to benefit him by setting him

2. A character in Charles Dickens's novel *Great Expectations*.

problems in mental arithmetic. The Pumblechooks of India try very hard to make the aboriginal good: they only succeed in making him dull. It is hard to convince the missionary and reformer of whatever religion that the romance and gaiety of tribal life is necessary for its preservation. But it is true. 'The tribe that dances does not die.'

But are we to regret the rapid decay of customs and superstitions that can have no place in a modern world? Certainly not, if those superstitions and customs are replaced by something better. Unfortunately the almost inevitable result of unregulated cultural change is not real improvement, but decay. Moreover, in spite of certain admitted evils in aboriginal life (and it should be remembered that these evils are not worse than those which may be found in other parts of India and of the world) there are many elements that are well worth preservation; elements in which the tribesmen may not indeed be superior to the finest flower of Oriental or European civilization, but in which they have a great deal to teach their supposedly more civilized neighbours.

The aboriginals have to a very high degree developed the art of recreation, an art which is lamentably absent from the ordinary Indian village. We may note the magnificent dances of the Nagas and of the Bison-horn Marias, the mimetic ballet of the Juangs, the haunting music of the Baiga Karma. Throughout tribal India there are songs of rare beauty and deep simplicity. Children's games are highly developed among certain tribes; for example, over fifty, some of them most exciting and amusing, have been recorded among the Maria.

The tendance of the dead, devotion to the soil, the power to stage a magnificent and colourful tribal festival, the discipline of tribal law, are things which modern village religion should not willingly let die. In the spirit of economic fellowship and the tradition of communal living, some primitive villages are a hundred years ahead of the modern world. This communal life of the wilder people, in which almost everything is shared and in which the joy or sorrow of one is the joy and sorrow of the whole community, is a beautiful thing to witness, and it too perishes immediately before the chill breath of education and advancement. Equally perishable are the aboriginal virtues of simplicity and honesty, frankness and humour.

The unspoilt aboriginal is notable for the purity of his taste, and the beauty of such simple artistic creations as the materials available to him make possible. He is an expert in the art of personal ornamentation, in the decoration of his house (when he has a house), in the carving of masks, combs, snuff-

boxes, in the use of cowries and beads. It is a tragedy that weaving is generally taboo to him; similarly pottery in which he might express himself is the
monopoly of a minor Hindu caste. But still more tragic is the way in which
the aboriginal's instinct for beautiful and artistic creation disappears directly
he is educated.

Domestic fidelity is another virtue in which the real primitives might stand
as an object-lesson to the whole world. When I recently conducted a survey of
domestic life among the Murias of Bastar State, I found that out of 2,000 marriages examined all but 43 husbands were living with their own original wives.
Adultery was almost unknown, and divorce exceptional. . . . In most tribal
societies woman holds a high and honourable place. She goes proudly free
about the countryside. In field and forest she labours in happy companion-
ship with her husband. She is not subjected to early child-bearing: she is
married when she is mature, and if marriage is a failure (which it seldom is)
she has the right of divorce. The lamentable restrictions of widowhood do not
await her: should her husband die, she is allowed, even enjoined, to remarry;
and in many tribes she may inherit property. Her free and open life fills her
mind with poetry and sharpens her tongue with wit. As a companion, she is
humorous and interesting; as a wife, devoted; as a mother, heroic in the service of her children. Her brave, laborious, faithful life is an inspiration. . . .

That aboriginal life is marked by crude superstitions and other evils no one
will deny. For example, some of the Nagas enjoy (along with the most advanced
nations of Europe) the custom of head-hunting and the practice of human sacrifice. The only difference is that the poor aboriginal sacrifices only one or two
human beings in the name of his gods, while the great nations offer up millions
in the name of empire and enlightenment. The belief in witchcraft also sometimes leads the aboriginals (like their educated neighbours) into excess, and
they have many superstitions which like the superstitions of advanced Indian
society and the capitals of Europe are to be regretted and if possible cured. But
after ten years of life in closest and most realistic contact with the aboriginals,
I can say that though I have found 'evils' I have found none that do not exist in
a more virulent form in 'civilized' society. The idea that there is something inherently vicious in primitive life must be abandoned. . . .

My own plan for the aboriginals has no claim to scientific authority. It is a
simple practical scheme that has been impressed upon me by the actual realities of life during twelve years in a Gond village. It is based on my division of

the aboriginals into different classes. The twenty million, who are already in contact with some sort of 'civilization' and are likely in the next few decades to be overwhelmed by it, do not ultimately present a problem very different from that of other peasants throughout India. The aboriginal problem cannot be considered apart from the general village problem. The great majority of Indian villagers are still illiterate; they are still attached to antiquated and economically injurious social, religious and agricultural habits; they have little medical assistance, meager educational facilities, bad communications; they are exploited and oppressed just as the aboriginals are. Wiser heads than mine will plan and great political and economic movements will determine the fate of these multitudes. The twenty million semi-civilized aboriginals will have to take their chance with the rest of the population. It is evident that there is little possibility of protecting them, although locally it may often be possible to ameliorate their lot by special treatment. . . . The twenty million aboriginals need what all village India needs—freedom, prosperity, peace, good education, medicine, a new system of agriculture and a fair deal under industrialization.

It is the remaining five millions who present a problem that may well tax our brains and patience. The difficulty here is that not only are there no workers available to solve the problem, but that many people in India refuse to admit that any problem exists. They are ignorant of or have forgotten the appalling consequences of a too rapid acculturation in other parts of the world. They have a pathetic faith in the 'march of progress' to solve every human problem. There is a great deal of glib talk in the cities about 'uplift' and the most ready with their opinions are those who have never seen the aboriginals and who themselves have never moved a finger to help them.

It is little use to say that we should give the blessings of civilization to the remotest aboriginals when we cannot give it to the workers in our great cities or to the peasants in accessible areas in the plains.

I suggest, therefore, that until the social sciences have come to more definite conclusions about the safeguards necessary for primitive people advancing into civilized life, until there are properly trained workers and teachers of integrity and enterprise, until there is sufficient money to do the job of civilizing properly, the five million wilder aboriginals should be left alone and should be given the strictest protection that our Governments can afford. This is, I admit, a desperate measure and one that is easily misunderstood and still more easily misrepresented. It is a purely practical measure. It is based on no philosophic principle. Least of all does it suggest that the aboriginals are to be kept for ever primitive. I only urge that unless we can civilize them properly it is better not to interfere with the small minority of the most primitive hillmen at all. Casual benefits only destroy and degrade; it needs a lifetime of love and toil to achieve permanent advance.

This view is hotly contested by people who know nothing of the realities of the problem. I have heard very little criticism from those who have actually lived among and studied these aboriginals. The man in the city cannot believe that they can be happy without the radio and the cinema, that they can have a good physique without penicillin, that they can be honourable and decent without going to church, that they have a life that is good, peaceful and free. They feel that the very suggestion is a sort of criticism of their own advancement. I do not suggest that the primitive hillman is better than the finest flower of modern culture, but my experience, which is now extensive, is that these tribes in the freedom and glory of their mountains are infinitely better and better off than the semi-civilized and decadent clerks or coolies which is all that we seem able to produce by our present methods of uplift and reform.

For the great majority of the aboriginals, however, we should press forward with the best schemes of rural reconstruction and education that our wisest brains can devise. For the small minority, who in any case can scarcely be reached, there should be a temporary scheme of protection and isolation. Even for this minority, protection does not mean that nothing is to be done. For them, as for the other aboriginals, there is much that all men and women of goodwill may do immediately.

We may fight for the three freedoms—freedom from fear, freedom from want, freedom from interference. We may see that the aboriginals get a square deal economically. We may see that they are freed from cheats and impostors, from oppressive landlords and moneylenders, from corrupt and rapacious officials. We may see that they get medical aid from doctors with some sense of professional integrity. If there must be schools, we may see that these teach useful crafts like carpentry and agriculture, and not a useless literacy. We may work to raise the prestige and the honour of the aboriginals in the eyes of their neighbours. We may guard them against adventurers who would rob them of their songs, their dances, their festivals, their laughter.

The essential thing is not to 'uplift' them into a social and economic sphere to which they cannot adapt themselves, but to restore to them the liberties of their own countryside.

But whatever is done, and I would be the last to lay down a general programme, it must be done with caution and above all with love and reverence. The aboriginals are the real swadeshi [indigenous] products of India, in whose presence everyone is foreign. These are the ancient people with moral claims and rights thousands of years old. They were here first: they should come first in our regard.

✦   ✦   ✦

NEITHER ISOLATION NOR ASSIMILATION

As Elwin grew older his tone grew less polemical and more even-tempered. This is manifest in this excerpt from a book of 1959, where he revisits the tribal question. That he was now a government official rather than a freelance radical may also explain the more measured style. The defence of tribal culture and tribal rights is undertaken more gently, but with no less conviction.[3]

✦   ✦   ✦

Is there not a case for the view that by and large the tribal people will probably be happier if they are left alone, or at least very largely alone, in the grandeur and freedom of their hills? They lack many of the amenities of life, but on the other hand they are free: no one interferes with them; they are able to live according to their own religion and traditions. Voltaire's Candide, after exploring all the civilization of his contemporary world, came to the final conclusion that there was no greater happiness than in cultivating one's own garden. Why not let them do so?

On the other hand, it is argued, would it not be better to 'civilize' them as rapidly as possible? Their life is nasty, brutish and short; their art is crude,

3. From Verrier Elwin, *A Philosophy for NEFA,* 2nd ed. (Shillong: Adviser to the Governor of Assam, 1959), pp. 44–60.

their religion a medley of superstitions; they are dirty and diseased. The early explorers and administrators tumbled over one another in their use of uncomplimentary adjectives to describe the people of NEFA.[4] The Singphos are described as 'a rude treacherous people', the Khamptis as 'a discontented, restless, intriguing tribe', the Nagas as 'a very uncivilized race with dark complexions and hideously wild and ugly visages'; the Abors are 'as void of delicacy as they are of cleanliness'. . . .

Few of us today would adopt either of these views in their entirety, certainly not if they are expressed in so crude a form. Yet the two policies have both been advocated, and followed, in India during the past fifty years.

The British Government inclined, on the whole, to leave the tribesmen alone, partly because the task of administration, especially in the wild border areas, was difficult and unrewarding, partly from a desire to quarantine the tribes from possible political infection, and partly because a number of officers sincerely held the view that the people were better and happier as they were. . . .

Let us briefly consider what is wrong with the policy of isolation.

It is exposed to at least three important criticisms. In the first place it has rarely been implemented in practice. There are some twenty million tribal people in India, and before Independence little was done for them. At the same time, they were not in actual fact left alone. As I have said, they were exploited by landlords and zamindars, robbed by money-lenders, cheated by merchants, and their culture was largely destroyed by foreign missionaries.

Secondly, the belief in the happy care-free Noble Savage is a myth, except perhaps in the South Seas long ago. In NEFA at least the people had not enough food; they suffered from abominable diseases; they died young; they were heavily burdened with anxiety; their life was distracted by war, kidnapping, slavery and cruel punishments. They were not even free: weaker tribes had to pay tribute to the strong; rich and powerful Chiefs grew richer on the labour of hundreds of serfs; freedom of movement was severely restricted by inter-village conflict.

And thirdly, while isolation was possible in the last century, it is impossible today. Modern industry is transforming the whole world; the humanitarian

---

4. The North-East Frontier Agency, to whose administration Elwin served as an adviser.

ideals of a welfare state no longer permit the neglect of any section of the population; political necessities forbid the existence of any administrative vacuum on the international frontier; tribal leaders themselves demand greater opportunities. And no one (least of all the scientist) wants to keep the tribal people as museum specimens for the benefit of science. . . .

In sharp contrast to the first policy is a second one of assimilation or de-tribalization. This has now become popular and Christian missionaries, social reformers and village uplifters are following it, sometimes on a large and enthusiastic scale. For this too there is something to be said. The Christian missionaries have produced a number of educated tribesmen who are proving of great value to the country, and not least to the NEFA administration. Assimilation into Hindu society has sometimes led to a better way of living and to economic advance.

In general, the supporters of this policy take a rather poor view of tribal life: 'animism' should be replaced by the purer ideals of Christianity or Hinduism; the social organization, the 'vices', the 'superstitions' should go; tribal dress is a mark of inferiority and should be replaced by shorts and shirts, blouses and frocks. You cannot make an omelette without breaking eggs, and the continued existence of the tribes as tribes is regarded as of less importance than the march of civilization.

Detribalization is a possible solution of the future of India's tribesmen. It is simple and easy, and it sometimes works. It has, however, serious disadvantages. Its type of progress is by a break with the past, not by an evolution from it. It tends to make the tribesman ashamed of his own culture and religion and so creates that inferiority complex which is a political as well as a social danger. Although it favours a few gifted individuals, who are able to assimilate the new way of life, it generally deprives the mass of the people of their standards and values without putting anything comparable in their place. All over the world it has been noted that the break-up of tribal society leads to a loss of the tribal virtues and a rapid acquisition of the vices of civilization.

The weakening of tribal solidarity and of the folk-legal sanctions deprives the younger generation of their moorings and sets them adrift in an unfamiliar world. All too often, the arts and crafts, the music and dancing, the former self-reliance and independence, the corporate discipline disappear. At the same time, throughout tribal India there is a tendency towards the transformation of tribes into castes, and these 'castes' are usually at the bottom of the social scale. In areas where free commercial penetration has been permitted, there has been much economic exploitation, inevitable among a people who but yesterday learnt the use of money and who are simple and trusting. . . .

Is there any way out of this dilemma? We are agreed that the people of NEFA cannot be left in their age-long isolation. We are equally agreed that we can leave no political vacuum along the frontier; that we must bring to an end the destructive practices of inter-tribal war and head-hunting and the morally repugnant practices of slavery, kidnapping of children, cruel methods of sacrificing animals and opium-addiction, none of which are fundamental to tribal culture. We wish to see that the people are well-fed, that they are healthy and enjoy a longer span of life, that fewer babies die, that they have better houses, a higher yield for their labour in the fields, improved techniques for their home-industries. We would like them to be able to move freely about their own hills and have easy access to the greater India of which at present they know little. We want to bring them into contact with the best people and the finest products of modern India.

Above all, we hope to see as the result of our efforts a spirit of love and loyalty for India, without a trace of suspicion that Government has come into the tribal areas to colonize or exploit, a full integration of mind and heart with the great society of which the tribal people form a part, and to whose infinite variety they may make a unique contribution.

And at the same time, we want to avoid the dangers of assimilation and detribalization which have degraded tribal communities in other parts of the world. . . .

This attempt to steer a middle path between the two older ways of approach is hard and delicate: it demands imagination, sincerity and constant care. The assimilation or detribalization policy, which held, as we have seen, that there is not very much to be said for tribal life; that if it disappears, it will not matter greatly; that the 'backward' must be brought forward and the low 'uplifted', is simple and straightforward; it is logical and it brings certain benefits—at a price. So did the old British policy of leaving well alone, though at a different price. . . .

Today we can see the tribal peoples without sentiment, but equally without prejudice. Isolation in the modern world is impossible; it would not be desirable even if it was possible. The old controversy about zoos and museums has long been dead. We do not want to preserve tribal culture in its colour and beauty to interest the scientists or attract the tourists. To try to preserve and develop the best elements in tribal art, religion and culture is something very different from wishing to keep the people in a zoo.

We do not want to preserve the tribesmen as museum specimens, but equally we do not want to turn them into clowns in a circus. We do not want to stop the clock of progress, but we do want to see that it keeps the right time. We do not accept the myth of the Noble Savage; but we do not want to create a class of Ignoble Serfs.

We see now that the tribal people will be of the greatest service to India if they are able to bring their own peculiar treasures into the common life, not by becoming second-rate copies of ourselves. Their moral virtues, their self-reliance, their courage, their artistic gifts, their cheerfulness are things we need. They also need the comradeship, the technical knowledge, the wider world-view of the plains. The great problem is how to develop the synthesis, how to bring the blessings and advantages of modern medicine, agriculture and education to them, without destroying the rare and precious values of tribal life.

We can solve this problem if we do not try to go too fast: if we allow the people a breathing-space in which to adjust themselves to the new world: if we do not overwhelm them with too many officials; if we aim at fundamentals and eliminate everything that is not vitally necessary; if we go to them in genuine love and true simplicity. . . .

✦   ✦   ✦

PART FIVE

A TRADITION RE-AFFIRMED

INTRODUCTION TO PART V

WHEN JAWAHARLAL NEHRU DIED in May 1964 he was the subject of a short but peculiarly affecting obituary penned by C. Rajagopalachari. This is what Rajaji wrote on the passing of his old colleague-turned-adversary:

> Eleven years younger than me, eleven times more important to the nation, eleven hundred times more beloved of the nation, Sri Nehru has suddenly departed from our midst and I remain alive to hear the sad news from Delhi—and bear the shock. . . .
>
> The old guard-room is completely empty now. . . . I have been fighting Sri Nehru all these ten years over what I consider faults in public policies. But I knew all along that he alone could get them corrected. No one else would dare do it, and he is gone, leaving me weaker than before in my fight. But fighting apart, a beloved friend is gone, the most civilized person among us all. Not many among us are civilized yet.
>
> God save our people.

Gandhi died within months of the birth of the nation. By the time Nehru passed on, India was moderately well established. But the future looked uncertain. The defeat at the hands of the Chinese in the war of 1962 had led to a serious loss of national morale. Despite his weaknesses and mistakes, and his ill-health during his last years, Nehru towered above his contemporaries. It was hard to see who, if anyone, could re-place him.

In the event, Nehru was succeeded as prime minister by Lal Bahadur Shastri, a greatly under-rated figure who has perhaps not got his due from historians (still less from the general public). Shastri set in motion reforms that would in time greatly augment agricultural productivity, and led the nation well when it was attacked by Pakistan in 1965. How-ever, he died soon afterwards. His successor was the then very inexpe-rienced and vulnerable daughter of Nehru, Indira Gandhi.

The 1960s were a time of great fear and insecurity in India. The wars with China and Pakistan had stunned a nation weaned on the Gandhian ideals of brotherhood and non-violence. Famine stalked the land. With Nehru's passing, the forces of militant Hinduism sensed an opportu-nity to regroup. There were fresh insurgencies in the north-east and the rise of a Maoist movement in the heart of the country. It is against this backdrop of conflict and instability that our last maker of modern India wrote the essays which are excerpted in this part of the book.

These essays dealt with a topic that had remained current and urgent since the late nineteenth century—namely, the present and future of Hindu-Muslim relations. The first biographer of Syed Ahmad Khan, writing when his subject was still alive, remarked that 'had it not been for his great efforts, the Mohammedan would have been far further be-hind the Hindu community as regards education than it now is; and if the movement increases with the rapidity which has hitherto character-ized it, the Mohammedans will soon be abreast of the Hindus'.

The hopes were illusory. In the next century, Hindus continued to be more alert to the opportunities provided by modern education. They took in greater numbers, and in higher proportions, to the English lan-guage, to the study of science and engineering, and to professions such as medicine and the law. This discrepancy was at the root of the popu-lar movement for the creation of Pakistan. Educated Muslims across India supported Jinnah and the Muslim League in good part because they hoped that in Pakistan they would not have to face competition from Hindu lawyers, doctors, teachers, civil servants, and businessmen.

The creation of Pakistan led to a large migration of Muslim profes-sionals to the new nation from other parts of India—from the United

Provinces and Bihar especially, but also from the Bombay Presidency. The Muslims who could not or would not migrate were peasants, workers, and artisans, who were poor and illiterate. Bereft of an intellectual and modern leadership (the potential members of which were now in Pakistan), they became captive to the interests of a conservative and backward-looking clergy.

The debate on how to deal with the very large Muslim minority that remained in India was chiefly conducted between the followers of Jawaharlal Nehru and M. S. Golwalkar, respectively. The former insisted that despite the provocations of Pakistan, minorities were equal citizens of the Republic of India. However, Nehru was himself too preoccupied with other matters to actively promote the modernisation of Indian Muslims. The Congress was content to leave the Muslims in the hands of the clergy, so long as they guaranteed that, at election time, their flock would cast their votes in favour of candidates of the ruling party. On the other hand, Golwalkar and the Rashtriya Swayamsewak Sangh saw Indian Muslims as second-class citizens at best and as traitors at worst. Muslims were continually being asked by the RSS to prove their loyalty to India and to the allegedly Hindu essence of the nation.

The sole maker represented in Part V of this book staked out a position rather different than that of the Congress and the RSS. Born and raised as a Muslim, he was a moderniser from within the community. His ideas were powerful as well as prescient—for example, he anticipated the rise of Hindu fundamentalism following the failure of a robust and credible movement of modernism among Muslims. His arguments are relevant to Indians of all faiths, for he worked and hoped for 'the emergence and sustained growth of . . . a class of modern, secular, dynamic liberals' whose members would be unencumbered by public allegiance to any religion or community. Nor is his work of interest only to India and Indians. In a post-9/11 world, his writings can, I think, be read with profit in all countries and continents where members of different religions seek to live peaceably together, and whose leaders— we may hope—wish to make belief in a personal God compatible with a collective and public commitment to democracy and modernity.

21

THE LAST MODERNIST

HAMID DALWAI

OUR LAST MAKER OF MODERN INDIA was, like his fellow Maharashtrian Tarabai Shinde, little known in his lifetime, and has been largely
forgotten since. Like Tarabai again, the details of his personal biography
are obscure. The parallels continue—for what we do know of his life and
work is largely owed to the devoted labours of his editor and translator.

Hamid Dalwai was born in 1932 on the same Konkan coast where
Gokhale and Tilak first saw the light of day. There the similarities end;
whereas the other two were middle-class Brahmins, Dalwai was born
into a working-class Muslim household. We know nothing of his formal education. He does not appear to have attended college. In his early
teens he joined a nationalist youth organisation, the Rashtra Seva Dal,
the only Muslim in his village to do so. In his twenties Dalwai moved to
Bombay, and became active in socialist politics. He also began publishing short stories in Marathi.

From the time he came to Bombay, Dalwai's main interest, and perhaps obsession, was with changing the attitudes of Indian Muslims towards democracy and modernism. To this end, he left the Socialist Party
and devoted himself full-time to social reform. In 1970 he founded the

Muslim Satyashodak Samaj, the name deliberately echoing that of the organisation that Jotirao Phule had established a century before. This newer organisation focused on the enhancement of the rights of Muslim women. Among its campaigns was the attempt to abolish, by law and in custom, the practice of triple *talaq*, whereby the husband could divorce his wife by uttering a single word three times.

Hamid Dalwai also advocated a common civil code for all Indian citizens. More broadly, he wished to erase communal markers and distinctions in public life, in pursuance of a common citizenship for all Indians in a genuinely secular and democratic nation.

In the 1950s, Dalwai befriended Dilip Chitre, a talented Marathi writer and poet. In later years, Chitre set aside his own work to translate and publicise the work of his friend. In introducing a translation of Dalwai's essays, published in 1970, Chitre wrote that 'in addition to being a Yavan [foreigner] to Hindus, he has achieved the distinction of becoming a kafir [infidel] to Muslims'. Dalwai challenged the sanctity of the Koran; in particular, he felt that it had no relevance to social or political life. This was consistent with his attitude to religion in general, which he considered a personal matter, to be negotiated between an individual and his god—or gods—with no relevance to the worlds of the law, economics, or social relations.

Dalwai died in 1977, aged forty-four, of kidney failure. In an essay published in 2002, Dilip Chitre linked his friend to a tradition of radical social reform inaugurated in Maharashtra by Phule and carried on by B. R. Ambedkar. Whereas his predecessors had campaigned against the caste system, Dalwai's target was orthodox Islam. 'Both Brahminical Hinduism and fanatical Islam', wrote Chitre, 'are iniquitous social ideologies that implicitly encourage intraspecific aggression in the name of spiritual uplift. As categories, "dharma" and "adharma" are identical to "dar-ul-Islam" and "dar-ul-Harb"'.

In terms of regional identity, Dalwai was linked to Maharashtrian reformers such as Phule, Gokhale, and Ambedkar. In terms of religious affiliation, one can think of him as a latter-day Syed Ahmad Khan. However, Dalwai hoped not merely to make Muslims abreast of Hindus in terms of access to modern education but to liberate them from the tyranny of faith altogether. The historian Faisal Devji has called Syed

Ahmad an advocate of an 'apologetic modernity'. There was nothing apologetic about Hamid Dalwai, whose modernism was militant and uncompromising.

Dalwai's task may have been harder than Syed Ahmad's. Tragically, he lived a much shorter life. In a later essay (published in 2007), Chitre, with characteristic generosity and self-awareness, contrasts his friend's social commitment to his own focus on writing and painting for the pure pleasure of it. 'I would not', says Chitre, 'make the kind of sacrifice Hamid made devoting his life to changing the hardened mind-sets of obscurantist *mullahs,* populist communal politicians, husbands who treated their wives in the worst possible male chauvinist tyrannical fashion, and women suffering slavery before a *purdah* they dared not lift'. This is true, after a fashion, but we should not discount either the sacrifice Chitre made in setting aside his own creations to translate, for a wider and continuing audience, his friend's writings and speeches in Marathi, excerpted below in their English renditions.

THE BURDEN OF HISTORY

Our first excerpt from the writings of Hamid Dalwai identifies the obstacles to the creation of a Muslim liberalism and explains how they may be overcome.[1]

✦   ✦   ✦

It is an old habit of Indian Muslims to blame Hindus for their woes. However, the Indian Muslim intelligentsia has never really been critically introspective. It has not sought to relate its problems to its own attitudes. It has not developed a self-searching, self-critical attitude. Compared to the Hindus, the Indian Muslims accepted Western education rather late. As a consequence, the Muslims remained comparatively backward in several fields. The real cause of Muslim backwardness is found in the Muslim opposition to educational reform during the early days of British rule in India. Behind this view was a peculiar sense of resentment. Muslims in India believed that the British snatched

1. From Hamid Dalwai, *Muslim Politics in India* (Bombay: Nachiketa Publications, 1968), pp. 32–40. The translator of these and later excerpts from this book is Dilip Chitre.

away from their predecessors what was a Muslim empire. When Sir Syed Ahmed Khan urged Muslims to accept modern Western education the *ulema* of Deoband came out with the *fatwa* that Sir Syed was a *kafir*.[2] How can one blame the Hindus for this?

Muslims remained backward because they were religion-bound revivalists who refused to modernize themselves. Sir Syed Ahmed Khan in this light appears as a great visionary who heralded the Indian Muslim renaissance. It was due to his great efforts that the rigidly religious mind of Indian Muslims began to show the first signs of a thaw. Educated Muslims began to redefine life in terms of the modern age. They gave up the grand dream of converting India to Islam. This was the beginning of a great upheaval among educated Indian Muslims. A process of transformation had begun. It was this process that should have brought Muslims close to Hindus and broadened their view of man and society. The trend of this process was toward a view according to which Hindus and Muslims would have been looked upon as equals.

This process was, however, ironically reversed because modern Indian Muslims proved unequal to the task. Their modernity proved limited and they lacked the broad vision that could have ensured the complete success of the Aligarh renaissance. Ironically, this very process separated the Muslims from the Hindus instead of bringing them closer together. The old Muslim habit of blaming the Hindus for their problems reappeared and was set more firmly than ever. Although Sir Syed Ahmed Khan was free from the vice of religio[us] fanaticism, he lacked the virtue of being free from the atavistic vanity of an inheritor of the Moghul past. In this very period, when it was possible for a national consciousness to emerge, Sir Syed Ahmed Khan himself succumbed to the egoistic conception that Muslims were the conquerors of India. It has he who was the father of separatist Muslim nationalism, and not Jinnah as it is erroneously supposed. Jinnah is only a later version of Sir Syed, revised and enlarged. Thus the aberrant modern Muslim himself was responsible first for a separatist Muslim nationalism and later for the creation of Pakistan. The foundation of Muslim nationalism is the postulate that Hindu and Muslim societies are autonomous and parallel social structures. . . .

It is only once in a while that an individual or a society gets an opportunity to make or mar its own future. The Muslims lost their rare chance of embracing

---

2. Deoband was an orthodox Muslim seminary in northern India, whose *ulema* or clergy had declared that Khan was a heretic or *kafir*.

modernity simultaneously with the Hindus when they yielded to the pressure exerted on them by the *ulema* of Deoband and rejected English education. History gave them another chance a little later—the opportunity to strengthen Indian nationalism by joining forces with the Hindus. But they let go even this opportunity by succumbing to the erroneous notion that Hindu and Muslim societies were autonomous and parallel social structures. They paid scant heed even to geographical realities and refused to consider where they lived and would live in the future. The problems faced by Indian Muslims today can be traced back to these two lost opportunities. If a chance that comes only once in a century is wasted, it takes another century to make up for the loss. . . .

It is a tragic fact that there does not yet exist a class of critically introspective young Muslims in India. A society which puts the blame on the Hindus for its own communalism can hardly be called introspective. If Hindu communalism is responsible for Muslim communalism, by the same logic it would follow that Muslim communalism is equally responsible for Hindu communalism. The truth of the matter is that the Muslim intelligentsia has not yet given up its postulate of parallel society. It has still not learnt to separate religion from politics. Their idea of religious freedom is merely that the structure of the Muslim society in India should remain unaltered. Basically, they are still 'Muslim nationalists'. They have not accepted the modern concept of nationalism, and hence their attempts to preserve Muslim nationalist trends in the present structure of the Indian polity. . . .

Will the younger generation of Indian Muslims face this challenge? This is their third, and perhaps last, chance to liberate and modernize themselves. If they avail themselves of it, they can still make up for the loss the Muslim community has suffered by wasting the two previous opportunities to create a tradition of modern, enlightened liberalism. The only effective answer to the problems of Indian Muslims would involve on their part a total rejection of the prejudices of history. Only when they rid themselves of the misconceptions that history and tradition produce can they arrive at the conception of a free, modern mind committed only to fundamental human values. . . .

The idea of a common Indian nationality requires that Muslim society be integrated in the fabric of a secular Indian society. The only way in which this can be achieved is by first creating a small class of modern, liberal and secular Muslims. This is precisely what people like me are attempting to do. Personally, I believe that no religion can provide the foundation for an ideal society. It follows that neither Islam nor Hinduism can be the basis of an ideal social order. Several people ask me where precisely I differ from communal Hindus. It should be fairly obvious now where I differ from them and how radical the differences are. However, I agree with them on certain points and it would be worthwhile to demarcate clearly the area of agreement between us. I agree with them that Muslim communalism is a strong force in this country at present. I also agree with them that in this nation minorities have a claim to equal rights and equal opportunities but they should not have a claim to special status or privileges. I also agree with them that Kashmir is a part of India and that every Pakistani aggression on Indian soil must be answered by a strong counter-attack. . . .

However, I consider suicidal the Hindu communalist attempt to answer Muslim communalism by obscurantist Hindu revivalism. Muslim communalism will be defeated only when the Hindu achieves a greater degree of social progress and modernizes himself. By making the Hindus more obscurantist—by making them more puritan and orthodox—Muslim communalism can never be eliminated. The movement for a ban on cow-slaughter provides an apt example.[3] I oppose the ban on agro-economic grounds. But I oppose it even more strongly on non-economic grounds, because if the Hindu belief in the sacredness of the cow is encouraged, it would prevent the Hindus from modernizing themselves and from achieving a greater degree of social progress. The Hindus have slid backward only because of their religious obscurantism. Mahmud Ghazanvi[4] could defeat Hindu armies simply by using herds of cows as a shield for his own army! One hopes that such history will not be repeated in modern times. Hindus must discard all those religious beliefs which hindered their progress and deprived them of their freedom. . . . I attack all aspects of mediaeval religious obscurantism whether it [sic] is Muslim or Hindu. And hence I am opposed to the movement for a ban on cow-slaughter. Eighty-five per cent of the population of this country is Hindu and therefore the progress of this nation depends on the Hindus becoming dynamic, modern and advanced.

3. In the 1960s the Rashtriya Swayamsewak Sangh had organized a movement asking for a ban on the killing of cows on the grounds that the animal was sacred to Hindus.

4. Mahmud of Ghazni was an Afghan chief and military adventurer whose forces had several times invaded the Indian sub-continent in the eleventh century.

And I want this nation to be advanced, powerful and prosperous because my individual future is inextricably tied up with it. I would go even further and tell the communalist Hindus that they cannot free Muslims from the shackles of their own obscurantist beliefs if the Hindus themselves remain religion-bound. To modernize Indian Muslims, Hindus must first strengthen the forces of modernization among themselves. . . .

History, which has bred prejudices and animosity, is a hindrance to all of us. All of us have to come out of the grip of our prejudices which originate in our past. Hindu communalists must also break away from the grip of their prejudices. It is not the fault of the young Brahmins of today that their ancestors gave inhuman treatment to the untouchables, and today's Indian Muslim is not responsible for the oppression to which Mahmud Ghazanvi or Aurangzeb subjected the Hindus. Fortunately, there is a class of Hindus today which bears the burden of its ancestors' sins and conscientiously tries to undo the damage by embracing social equality as a fundamental value. Similarly, there has to emerge a class of Muslims which would accept the sins of Aurangzeb and, to undo the damage, would therefore embrace the concept of secular citizenship. The emergence and sustained growth of such a class of modern, secular, dynamic liberals is the only effective answer to the Hindu-Muslim communal problem. . . .

✦   ✦   ✦

THE CHALLENGE OF SECULARISM

The second excerpt from Hamid Dalwai makes a strong case for the separation of faith from state in modern India.[5]

✦   ✦   ✦

Secularism implies a dissociation of religious considerations from political and social life. The modern view of man and society includes a secular attitude to all political and social activities. It does not insist on abolishing religion altogether but regards religion as a matter of personal faith. The ethical values on which modern secular society is based are secular ethical values

5. From Dalwai, *Muslim Politics in India*, pp. 85–90.

which are rationally derived. Religions may or may not contain a notion of fundamental human rights as we understand them today. As modern men, we do not rely on religion for deriving our concept of social conscience. Our social conscience is inherent in the democratic system of government we have accepted. The democratic ethic is liberal and is therefore heterodox. It is thus necessary for a democracy to be secular, that is, totally dissociated from religion, to be a democracy at all. All communities and individuals in a democratic society have to conform to the basic liberal democratic ethic.

In many instances, we witness an inevitable conflict between human rights and religion-based social attitudes. In such a situation, the only choice we have as modern democrats is to eliminate the obstacles to democracy created by certain religious attitudes. The very fact that in India we call Muslims a minority and Hindus the majority implies a non-secular attitude. Yet all political parties seem to regard this as a proper division. A secular distinction between people would be in the nature of a class distinction. For instance, a leader of the working class is a secular leader; a leader of Hindus or Muslims is not.

Secularism in India, although embodied in the Constitution, is as yet only an aspiration. It has not yet permeated our social life. It is even in danger today. Within the Hindu majority, there is a strong obscurantist revivalist movement against which we find a very small class of liberals engaged in [a] fight. Among Indian Muslims there is no such liberal minority leading the movement towards democratic liberalism. Unless Indian liberals, however small they are as a minority, are drawn from all communities and join forces on a secular basis, even the Hindu liberal minority will eventually lose its battle with communalist and revivalist Hindus. If Muslims are to be integrated in the fabric of a secular and integrated Indian society, a necessary precondition is to have a class of Muslim liberals who would continuously assail communalist dogmas and tendencies. Such Muslim liberals, along with Hindu liberals and other[s], would comprise a class of modern Indian liberals.

Liberal intellectuals emerge in any society only through a long and complex social, cultural, political, and historical process. Today Hindus have an influential liberal elite only because Hinduism is historically heterodox and can accommodate dissent. The modern Indian liberal tradition starts from Raja Rammohan Roy, who was a product of Hindu society. It leads through such secular (as against Hindu) liberals as Nehru to the present time.

The target of Hindu liberals has been Hindu orthodoxy. And due to their continuous critical evaluation and leadership in social reform, Hindu society as a whole has been benefited to a certain extent. I do not wish to suggest here that Hindu society has accepted the liberal democratic ethic and has modernized itself to any satisfactory extent; it has not. But this continuing liberal tradition places the Hindu community in a culturally better position than that of Muslims in India.

Why do Muslims in India lack a liberal elite? The answer has many facets. But one thing is certain. The explanation of Muslim backwardness is to be found in the very make-up of the Muslim mind.

Indian Muslims believe that they are a perfect society and are superior to all other communities in India. One of the grounds for this belief is the assumption that the Islamic faith embodies the vision of a perfect society and, therefore, being a perfect Muslim implies not having to make any further progress. This is an unacceptable claim by modern criteria. . . .

The second reason for this belief is the fact that Indian Muslims resent being a minority and still dream of spreading their faith throughout India or at least of ruling India. They suffer from delusions of grandeur and also from a persecution mania. . . . Muslims have always believed that they are a state within a state and a society within a society. Their ideas of representation are based on this claim and therefore they run contrary to the concept of a democratic society itself. Today they believe in a parallel co-existence with the majority with complete autonomy as a community. This explains their resistance to a change in their personal law. But, going even further, Indian Muslims oppose family planning because they are obsessed with the idea of increasing their numbers to be effective in power politics. . . .

The only leadership Indian Muslims have is basically communalist. An exceptional Muslim like M. C. Chagla[6] has no place in Indian Muslim society. Nor will individual modern liberals suffice. Indian Muslims today need an *avant garde* liberal elite to lead them. This elite must identify itself with other modern liberals in India and must collaborate with it against Muslim as well as Hindu communalism. Unless a Muslim liberal intellectual class emerges, Indian Muslims will continue to cling to obscurantist medievalism, communalism, and will eventually perish both socially and culturally. A worse possibility is that of Hindu revivalism destroying even Hindu liberalism, for the lat-

---

6. M. C. Chagla was a distinguished jurist and public servant who had served as Chief Justice of the Bombay High Court, as India's Ambassador to the United States, and as a senior cabinet minister in the Government of India.

ter can succeed only with the support of Muslim liberals who would modernize Muslims and try to impress upon them secular democratic ideals. . . .

There are some Muslims who are members of the Indian elite but who are afraid of their own community's reaction to modern attitudes. These uncommitted and hypocritical liberals are not only of no use, but are also a hindrance to the progress of Indian Muslims. They are either moral cowards or are apathetic to a great social problem which is also a problem of democracy in India. They must make a choice now. If they do not provide liberal intellectual leadership to Indian Muslims, the younger generation has to commit itself and carry out this task.

It is often argued that Muslim communalism is only a reaction to Hindu communalism. This is not true. The real conflict in India today is between all types of obscurantism, dogmatism, revivalism, and traditionalism on one side and modern liberalism on the other. Indian politicians being short-sighted and opportunistic, communalism and orthodoxy is [sic] always appeased and seldom, if ever, opposed. This is why we need an agreement among all liberal intellectuals to create a non-political movement against all forms of communalism. If this is not done, democracy and liberalism will inevitably collapse in India. The stakes are high. It is a pity that few people realize the gravity of the situation. It is even more unfortunate that they are hardly informed about the true nature of the problem.

✦ ✦ ✦

FOR A UNITED FRONT OF LIBERALS

In this last excerpt from Dalwai he calls for Hindus and Muslim liberals to come together on a common platform to create a secular and modern India.[7]

✦ ✦ ✦

. . . I believe that if the Hindu were sufficiently dynamic, the Hindu-Muslim problem would be solved. For if the Hindus were dynamic, they would subject the Indian Muslims to several shocks which history has spared them. Muslims

7. From Dalwai, *Muslim Politics in India,* pp. 94–100.

would be left with the one stark alternative to perish if they did not wish to change. And any society prefers change to extinction. Hindus can accept the challenge of Muslim politics in India only by developing dynamism and a balance of mind. But to develop such dynamism Hindu orthodoxy itself has to be liquidated. The caste system has to be eliminated. The Hindus must embrace modernism. They must create a society based on fundamental human values and the concept of true social equality. Unfortunately, the Hindu mind lacks balance. Even those Hindus who have accepted modernity, justice and brotherhood as their guiding principles sometimes support Muslim communalism. Some avoid speaking against it and some even indirectly encourage it. Those Hindus who ought to be combating communalism today seem, instead, to be trying to put the clock back. They are supporting obscurantism, revivalism, the caste system and the cult of the cow. This is a process which would drain Hindu society of whatever little dynamism it may still have. There have to be enough Hindus trying to modernize the Hindu society and, at the same time, opposing the irrational politics of Muslim communalism. I hope this would happen. For that would precisely be the process by which the Hindu-Muslim problem can be eliminated. Muslim communalism today makes the most of the rift between liberal Hindus and communalist Hindus. It is ironical that Muslim communalists gain the support of Hindus, both liberal and communalist. The Muslim communalist demand for making Urdu a second official language in Uttar Pradesh and Bihar has been supported by the so-called modernist Hindus under the impressive label of secularism. The 'secularism' of such Hindus encourages the anti-secularism of the Muslims. These so-called secularist Hindus are opposed to the creation of a common personal law because it might displease the Muslims. . . .

Consider, next, the orthodox Hindu. He stages an agitation against the proposed removal of the word 'Hindu' from Banares University, and secures the support of the Muslim League. He would start an agitation for a ban on cow-slaughter and Muslim communalists would support even that. For when they support him on such issues, both of them can establish a united front against Mr Chagla, and then the Muslim communalist would also be left free to stage nation-wide agitations for a re-display of the Prophet's lost hair. He can bully critics of the Prophet. In short, he will always turn Hindu revivalism to his own benefit. It must be remembered that the obscurantism of one community helps to strengthen the obscurantism of other communities. If Hindu obscurantism is attacked and eliminated, it would also be a strong blow to Muslim obscurantism.

Who then is really fighting Muslim communalism? The answer is, a handful of modern Muslims. Mr Chagla in fact leads the modern liberal Muslims. And all of us know Mr Chagla's situation now. He is opposed by the Muslims and unsupported by the Hindus.

There is no doubt that the picture I have painted of Indian Muslims is terrible. But it is true. One would be deceiving oneself if one tried to believe it was otherwise.

This, however, is what we observe on the surface. On the surface, Muslim society appears to be mediaeval in its make-up. Yet, somewhere deep down, a change is taking place in this society. There is nothing dramatic about this change. It is largely imperceptible and indeed very slow. It is a process which began quite a few years ago. It has still to cover many stages before it reaches its completion. Sir Syed Ahmed Khan represents the first phase in the modernization of Indian Muslims. He wanted to modernize the Muslims although he was still opposed to the Hindus. Jinnah and Iqbal represent the second phase. In the beginning [when] they began to talk in the name of Islam . . . , neither Jinnah nor Iqbal was anti-Hindu. However, Islamism ultimately led to anti-Hinduism. This is where the process of Muslim modernization was arrested. The Hindus, on the other hand, had progressed much further. . . .

However, a new generation of Muslims is emerging in India today. One can see the first glimmers of a genuine modern humanism in them. In the vast mass of a mediaeval Muslim society one witnesses a few young Muslims who have a modern, humanistic and rational attitude. They are still scattered and isolated like islands in a vast ocean. Their modernity is reflected in what they speak and write. It is seen in their actions.

It may be useful to cite a few examples. Some educated Indian Muslims show the signs of a newly emerging attitude of unbiased detachment. For instance, Professor Mohammad Yasin's book, *Social History of Islamic India*, Professor Athar Rizvi's work analyzing Muslim revivalism in the 16th and 17th centuries, and Professor M. Mujeeb's book *Indian Muslims*, reveal a new attitude of critical detachment. This kind of modern attitude is also shared by Professor Mohammad Habib [of Aligarh Muslim University] and the Head of the Department of Political Science at Osmania University, Dr Rashiduddin Khan. During my recent visit to Aligarh I had a chance to meet and talk to some men and women students as well as some of the teaching staff. Even among them I found the hopeful signs of a critically introspective attitude. In many cities in Northern India not only is the *purdah* fast disappearing but there is also a rapid spread of education among Muslim women. Many of these have married men of other faiths. It is significant to note that these men of other religions who married Muslim women were not urged to become Muslims. All these trends indicate the emergence of modernity among Indian Muslims.

Are we going to welcome these new trends? Are we going to encourage them and let them flourish? This is what we have to decide now. We have to check Pakistani expansionism and protect our borders. We have to adopt a clear and decisive long-range policy towards Pakistan. We have to support Muslim modernism in India. We have to insist on a common personal law for all citizens of India. All marriages in India must be registered under a common Civil Code. Religious conversion should not be allowed, except when the intending convert is adult and the conversion takes place before a magistrate. Children born of inter-religious marriages should be free to practice any religion but only after they reach legal adulthood. If either a [Muslim] dargah[8] or a [Hindu] temple obstructs the passage of traffic on a thoroughfare, it ought to be removed. Government should have control over the income of all religious property. This income should be spent on education and public welfare alone. It should not be obligatory to mention one's religion and caste (even today, the admission form used in schools compels students to state their religion). . . .

For all this to happen, the present division among the Hindus should cease to exist. Those Hindus who want to counter Muslim communalism unfortunately try to strengthen Hindu revivalism. And those Hindus who want to lead the Hindus and ultimately the whole of this nation on the way of modernity are unfortunately supporting Muslim communalists. This has to change. I am on the side of all Hindus who oppose Muslim communalism; but when the same Hindus help Hindu revivalism, I am opposed to them. I support all those who want to modernize the Hindus; but when they adopt a policy of not opposing Muslim communalism, I oppose them. If the Hindus develop a proper balance of mind, I believe the present tensions would soon begin to resolve. . . .

✦   ✦   ✦

8. A dargah is a shrine built to honour a Muslim religious figure.

EPILOGUE

India in the World

I

AS THE PRECEDING PAGES DEMONSTRATE, the Indian political tradition has been continuous as well as cumulative. To be sure, the continuities may have been emphasised by the way in which this book has been structured. But the tradition itself is by no means the product of an editor's artifice. The ways in which thinkers who come later refer to those who came before, the ways in which they challenge or contest those who are their contemporaries—these patterns make it clear that what we have here is not a random collection of interesting individuals but a connected political *tradition*.

The essentially disputatious nature of this tradition is manifest throughout this book. Even though I have termed him the 'first liberal', Rammohan Roy was not writing on a clean slate. In advocating a free press and greater rights for women, Rammohan Roy was articulating ideas which challenged both the dominant mores of Indian (or specifically Hindu) society, as well as the policies promoted by the British in India. The thinkers profiled in Part II were more directly arguing amongst themselves. Tilak and Gokhale were major leaders of the Indian National Congress but disagreed about the direction that their party should follow. Neither Phule nor Shinde were members of the Congress, yet both shared a home town (Puné), a language and culture (Marathi and Maharashtrian), and a political situation (subjecthood within the British Empire) with Tilak and Gokhale. The emphasis of one on the rights of the lower castes and of the other on the status of women was, directly or indirectly, a refutation of the credo that Gokhale and Tilak (albeit in different ways and with different emphases) advanced with regard to greater representation for Indians as a whole. As for Syed Ahmad Khan, he stood outside the ambit of the Congress and of Hindu society; in opposing the former, he wished at the same time to make his fellow Muslims as sensible of the need for modern education as the latter.

Part III features a different set of protagonists and a more intense set of arguments. These centre around the figure of Mahatma Gandhi. As we have seen, Gandhi took elements from both Tilak and Gokhale, but not mechanically. Rather, he adapted, re-invented, refined, synthesised, and transcended their legacy in forging a political programme he thought more appropriate to the times. Gandhi's ideas, in turn, were expanded by Kamaladevi Chattopadhyay, contested by Rabindranath Tagore, challenged by E. V. Ramaswami, and rejected by B. R. Ambedkar and Mohammad Ali Jinnah. Sometimes, these thinkers hark back to earlier and still revered members of the tradition—as in Tagore's invocation of Rammohan Roy. Frequently, they address themselves directly to Gandhi, who is their often-named and sometimes unnamed interlocutor or disputant. Nor does the debate stop there; for Gandhi, in reaction to his critics, re-formulates his ideas to make them more consistent or more appealing to his diverse audiences.

Moving to Part IV, it is evident that Nehru locates himself in the tradition of Congress nationalism that Gandhi best embodied and whose other exemplars included Tilak, Gokhale, and Tagore. To be sure, like Gandhi again, some ideas are all his own (those on foreign policy, for example). Yet other ideas (for example, on Hindu-Muslim harmony), while deriving from Gandhi, are re-stated in ways that challenge Jinnah's claim that the Congress cannot be fair to Muslims, or M. S. Golwalkar's claim that only Hindus can be reliable citizens of independent India.

Golwalkar himself can only be understood as being, in key respects, the 'Other' of Nehru—opposing or inverting not just his attitude to Indian Muslims but his economic and foreign policies for independent India as well. The other thinker-activists in this section had more complicated—and, dare one say, more interesting—political genealogies. Lohia, Rajagopalachari, and Narayan had all been deeply influenced by Gandhi. Like Nehru, they considered themselves followers or disciples of the Mahatma. However, they read the message of the Master in ways congenial to their own orientations and political practice. Like Gandhi, Lohia was sceptical of the uses of English; like Gandhi, Rajagopalachari was sceptical of the professedly benign intentions of the modern state; and, like Gandhi again, Narayan was sceptical of the efficacy of parliamentary democracy. At the same time, these thinkers were also innovators. Lohia with regard to caste, Rajagopalachari with regard to the economy, and Narayan with regard to the people of India's borderlands—all offered perspectives different from and in many ways opposed to that of Nehru.

As for Verrier Elwin, he too knew and admired Gandhi. Yet he believed that the national movement had neglected the problem of the tribals, in contrast to the problems of women and those of lower castes, which they had seriously reflected upon. In his writings before and after Independence, Elwin sought to make politicians and policy makers more sensitive to the rights and claims of the tribals of central and north-eastern India.

Our last exemplar, Hamid Dalwai, was deeply aware of this long lineage of debate and disputation. In his writings he refers to Rammohan Roy, Syed Ahmad Khan, Mohandas K. Gandhi, M. A. Jinnah, Jotiraro Phule, and Jawaharlal Nehru; sometimes appreciatively, at other times critically. He places himself in this tradition explicitly by naming his organisation the Muslim Satyashodak Samaj as well as implicitly by calling for a Muslim Nehru (who might indeed have been himself).

II

This book represents the public face of the Indian political tradition. But there was also a *private* face. Consider, for example, this fascinating exchange between two 'makers of modern India' at the time of the country's second General Elections in 1957. While the campaigning was on, the prime minister, Jawaharlal Nehru, received an extraordinary letter from a comrade turned political adversary. This was Jayaprakash

Narayan, who by now had abandoned politics for social work, but who nonetheless made speeches on behalf of the Opposition candidates in the elections. In his letter, Narayan suggested that the prime minister function as a 'national rather than a party leader'; that, even while he ran the Government, he should 'encourage the growth of an Opposition' so as to 'soundly lay the foundations of parliamentary democracy' in India.

During the elections, Narayan had tried, and failed, to get Opposition parties to avoid three-cornered contests in individual constituencies, since from a division of the vote only the Congress would benefit. 'In doing so', Narayan told Nehru, he was

> not guided by dislike of or hostility to the Congress as you have repeatedly been suggesting but merely by certain dispassionate political principles. According to parliamentary democracy theory it is not necessary for the opposition to be better than the ruling party. Equally bad parties in opposition are a check on one another and keep the democratic machine on the track. . . . As a Socialist my sympathies are all with the British Labour Party, but I concede that when Labour is in power the Conservatives perform a valuable democratic function without which the Labour government might become a menace to the people. So, I realise that if my advice had been followed by the opposition parties, it would have led to some undesirable parties gaining somewhat in strength. I was prepared, however, to take that risk on the ground[s] (a) that between the two evils of absoluteness of power and a little increase in the strength of certain undesirable parties, the former was the greater evil and (b) that there would be five years after the election in which a sound opposition party could be created.

In one of his speeches, Nehru had apparently chastised Narayan for 'playing hide-and-seek' between the pillars of politics and social service. The younger man, he said, 'claim[ed] to have given up politics' but 'continue[d] to dabble in it'. Narayan replied that he did 'not see why only active party and power politicians should express political opinions and no others. Politics would then be reduced to a sordid party game with which the citizen would have no concern'. There was a particular responsibility for Gandhian 'constructive workers' to speak out. These workers, insisted Narayan, would

> betray their ideals if they did not boldly play a corrective role, offering friendly, constructive, non-partisan advice and criticism and, if need be, even opposition in the form of non-cooperation and the like. Nor can eschewing of party politics mean indifference to the manner and outcome of elections. True, those who have eschewed party politics are not expected to take any partisan stand, but they may, with complete consistency, raise general political and ideological issues for the guidance of the electorate, the parties and the candidates.

Narayan ended his letter on a somewhat despairing note. Whatever the outcome of the elections, he remarked, 'the verdict is inescapable that the present political system has proved a failure. Therefore, the need after the elections is for the leaders of the country to get together in order to find out if there is a better alternative. I think there is and, in the larger interest of the country, we must seek it out. It is here that your leadership is most needed, because without you this cannot be done'.

Narayan's letter extended over six typed pages; Nehru's reply was even longer. He had 'quite failed to understand' what Narayan meant 'by my becoming a national leader, rather than a party leader'. 'What does a national leader do?' asked Nehru:

> If it is meant that he should collect a number of important people from different parties and form a government, surely this can only be done if there is some dominant common purpose. Without such a purpose, no government can function. Sometimes, such national governments are formed in wartime, when the only dominant purpose is winning the war and everything is subordinated to it. Even so, they have not been much of a success in parliamentary democracies. Apart from a war, however, we have to deal with political and economic problems, national and international. There must be some common outlook

and unity of purpose in dealing with these problems. Otherwise, there would be no movement at all and just an internal tug of war.

Nehru argued that by being a 'party leader' he had not sacrificed any policy that he may have followed had he been a 'national' leader. The economic and foreign policies of his administration were, he believed, in the best interests of the nation. They were not merely a reflection of the Congress Party's prejudices or preferences. If the Government that Nehru led had made any compromises, this was 'not because of the party, but because of the facts that encompassed us. We have to function as a Government dealing with these facts and not with theoretical propositions'.

Nehru then turned to the question of a robust opposition to the Congress. 'So far as I understand parliamentary democracy', he said,

> it means that every opportunity should be given for an opposition to function, to express its views by word or writing, to contest elections in fair conditions, and to try to convert the people to its views. The moment an opposition is given some kind of a protected position, it becomes rather a bogus opposition and cannot even carry weight with the people. I am not aware of any pattern of parliamentary democracy in which it has ever been suggested that the opposition should be encouraged, except in the ways I have mentioned above.

Nehru disagreed with the view that the opposition in the legislatures was not adequate. Of the 500 or so members of the Lok Sabha, about 150 were members of opposition parties. They were 'virile and active', but being in a minority were generally voted down. 'Presumably, you would like larger numbers in the opposition', said Nehru to Narayan, adding: 'Even if there were larger numbers, it would be voted down. And how am I to produce the larger numbers?'

Narayan had asked Nehru to look beyond the confines of the party system, a challenge the older man threw back at him. Apart from the opposition parties in the legislatures, he pointed out, in India there are all kinds of disruptive and reactionary forces. There is also the inertia of ages. And it is very easy for the inert mass to be roused by some religious or caste or linguistic or provincial or like cry, and thus to come in the way of all progress. That is the real opposition in the country, and it is a tremendously strong one. And that is what you seem to ignore completely. We have constantly to battle against it.

Nehru ended with a qualified defence of parliamentary democracy. It was, he admitted, 'full of faults', but had been adopted in India because 'in the balance, it was better than the other possible courses'.[1] He did not agree with Narayan that it was a failure. Like any other system of governance, parliamentary democracy depended on the quality of the human beings who staffed it. 'I do not think that the present system is a failure', said Nehru to Narayan, 'though it may fail in the future for all I know. If it fails, it will not fail because the system in theory is bad, but because we could not live up to it. Anyhow what is the alternative you suggest?'[2]

There are, I think, at least four reasons why this exchange of personal letters between Jayaprakash Narayan and Jawaharlal Nehru is important. First, for its intrinsic interest, for the passion and intelligence with which each person articulated his view of what democracy meant. The ideas of both men emerged from many years of political engagement, but also from wide reading and the enlargement of one's vision that comes from travel to other countries. Their intelligence is complemented and reinforced by their sincerity. These were busy men, leading very full lives, who were so engaged with the political system of their country that they devoted many hours to debating it in private.

1. This recalls Winston Churchill's remark that parliamentary democracy was the worst form of government, 'except for all the others'. The echo was probably unconscious.

2. Jayaprakash Narayan to Jawaharlal Nehru, 7 March 1957; Nehru to Narayan, 3 April 1957, both in Brahmanand Papers, Nehru Memorial Museum and Library, New Delhi.

Second, the exchange was part of an ongoing conversation that was intellectually as well as politically productive. At the time of the first general elections, for example, the two men had argued about the extent to which the Congress party as a whole reflected the socialist ideals of the prime minister. The arguments provoked by the polls of 1957 were to continue. Nehru challenged Narayan to come up with an alternative to the parliamentary system; two years later, Narayan wrote his *Plea for the Reconstruction of the Indian Polity,* excerpts from which are contained in this book. That public pamphlet would most likely not have been written had those private letters not been exchanged.[3]

There must surely be few other illustrations from history of such an exchange between the most powerful politician in a country and its most respected social worker. In a more general sense, however, the Nehru-Narayan debates were representative of the ways in which political argument operated in modern India. The books and articles excerpted in these pages were all written as contributions to an ongoing debate on how to win or exercise political power and how to reform or reshape society. Although they contained sometimes strikingly original ideas, these were not academic treatises but political interventions. Crucially, these interventions were on behalf of a particular policy or programme, this presumed to be superior to some other policy or programme.

The last reason for us to flag the Nehru-Narayan exchange is that while, from the perspective of its time, it was representative, from the perspective of our times it has a whiff of the archival and the archaic. Such debates do not take place anymore, at least not among full-time politicians. The tradition that this book has showcased is dead. No politician now alive can think or write in an original or even interesting fashion about the direction Indian society and politics is or should be taking. The discussion of what Narayan, in his letter to Nehru, had

3. In the 1990s, after Nehru and Narayan had both died, the Congress Government of the day passed legislation mandating the creation of village councils in all States of the Union. Those responsible for what was now the seventy-third Amendment to the Indian Constitution did not appear to recognise that this was in continuation of the efforts of a long-time opponent of the Congress party.

called 'dispassionate political principles' has now been left, as in other democracies, to the scholars.[4]

III

The historian Gertrude Himmelfarb has provocatively and (to my mind) persuasively argued that there was a British 'Enlightenment' that is as worthy of study and celebration as its better known American and French counterparts. Each tradition had different orientations and emphases. Whereas the French Enlightenment emphasised scepticism and reason, and the American Enlightenment exalted liberty and freedom, the British Enlightenment put the spotlight on 'social virtues' such as benevolence, compassion, and tolerance. Thus, 'at a critical moment in history, these three Enlightenments represented alternative approaches to modernity, alternative habits of mind, of consciousness and sensibility'.[5]

Himmelfarb is writing of the eighteenth and nineteenth centuries, but now, at our own critical moment in history, it may be apposite to

4. As in, among other works, André Béteille, *Society and Politics in India* (London: Athlone Press, 1987); Béteille, *Chronicles of Our Times* (New Delhi: Penguin India, 2000); Sunil Khilnani, *The Idea of India* (New Delhi: Penguin India, 1997); Niraja Gopal Jayal, ed., *Democracy in India* (New Delhi: Oxford University Press, 2000); Pratap Bhanu Mehta, *The Burden of Democracy* (New Delhi: Penguin India, 2004); Partha Chatterjee, *The Politics of the Governed: Reflections on Popular Politics in Most of the World* (New Delhi: Permanent Black, 2004); Niraja Gopal Jayal and Pratap Bhanu Mehta, eds., *The Oxford Companion to Indian Politics* (New Delhi: Oxford University Press, 2010). Apart from books, these debates are also conducted in essays in serious journals of opinion, such as the *Economic and Political Weekly*, published out of Mumbai, and the monthly *Seminar*, published in New Delhi.

5. Gertrude Himelfarb, *The Roads to Modernity: The British, French and American Enlightenments* (2004; reprint, London: Vintage Books, 2008). Some writers have spoken of a specific 'Scottish' Englightenment as distinct from a more general 'British' one. Himmelfarb, however, collapses the two, on the grounds that philosophers such as Hume and Smith 'chose to identify themselves as North Britons rather than as Scots' (ibid., pp. 12–13).

add a fourth national experience to the list. I am myself uncomfortable with the word 'Enlightenment'. Let us simply say that the Indian political tradition is as relevant to the dilemmas of the early twenty-first century as any other. This relevance is in part a product of the distinctiveness of the individual thinkers profiled here, but in greater part it is a product of the distinctiveness of the trajectories of Indian nationhood. For India was the first country to win its freedom by non-violent means, the first democracy to be successful and sustainable in Asia and Africa, the only nation to have as many as seventeen different languages and scripts on its currency notes.

In this age of globalisation, these multiple histories of modern India must surely have a resonance in other parts of the world—in Africa and in Europe, in North America and in Latin America, where people of different faiths have likewise to learn to live with one another, where the desire to uplift and emancipate the poor by state action likewise conflicts with the freedom and dignity of the individual, where nation-states have likewise to choose between privileging a single 'national' culture or permitting a hundred flowers to bloom.

'It is sinful', writes Himmelfarb, 'to try to paraphrase Smith, Burke, Tocqueville, the American Founders, and others who expressed so trenchantly and elegantly what could only be trivialised and vulgarised by summary or restatement'.[6] She thus quotes their works extensively in her book. I have followed this principle even more faithfully—or dogmatically—by fashioning this book as an editor-driven anthology rather than an integrated narrative appearing in the name of a single author.

Perhaps this greater reliance on their own words may help further the case that many of these thinkers should have a wider, or trans-Indian, relevance. In the past, it was not just Frenchmen who read Voltaire, or merely Englishmen who admired John Stuart Mill, or only Americans who were inspired by Tom Paine or Thomas Jefferson. Likewise, as democracy seeks to establish itself (with so many false starts!) in the countries of Asia and Africa, it may turn out that the ideas of Gandhi and Nehru and Ambedkar are as, or perhaps even more, important to these strivings than the ideas of the great Western thinkers

6. Ibid., p. xvi.

of the eighteenth and nineteenth centuries. And as the countries of Europe and America become more diverse owing to the immigration of followers of faiths and speakers of languages earlier considered alien or foreign, these older nations may yet benefit from a sideways look at the historical experience of the most heterogeneous society in the world. The Indian experience is highly pertinent, as well, to the countries of Latin America, whose democratic traditions are longer than in Africa but more regularly interrupted than in North America or Western Europe. Most Latin American countries seek also to harmonise democracy with cultural pluralism, a process in which the ideas of these makers of modern India may not be entirely irrelevant.

The fragile democracies of Asia and Africa, the mature democracies of Europe and North America, the 'in-between' democracies of Latin America—to this list of nations to which these dead Indian thinkers speak, let me add one more: Communist China. From Rammohan Roy's worries about the damage to society caused by the state's suppression of the free flow of information, to Tagore's prophetic warnings about militaristic nationalism, to Ambedkar's defence of democracy, via Gandhi's plea for inter-faith dialogue and his faith in non-violent resistance—this anthology has, I think, materials aplenty for the Chinese to study, be they politicians in power or intellectuals in dissent.

One of modern India's potential contributions to the world is its linguistic diversity, which is both mandated by law and affirmed by social practice. It was once believed that a single shared language was constitutive of national identity. Writing in the 1950s, D. W. Brogan remarked that 'it is not accidental that nearly all modern nationalist revivals have begun by defending the claims of a linguistic culture'. In nineteenth-century Europe, for example, 'it was in the submerged nations, in partitioned Poland, in Bohemia, in Finland that the linguistic revival became the embodiment of the national spirit'. Moreover, 'states which were not linguistically united faced a real, political problem. For . . . there were obvious administrative advantages in linguistic unity and obvious political advantages in securing the kind of spiritual unity that linguistic unity makes possible'.[7]

7. D. W. Brogan, *The Price of Revolution* (London: Hamish Hamilton, 1951), pp. 111–113.

Two influential South Asian politicians drew the same lesson from European history. These were Mohammad Ali Jinnah of Pakistan and S. W. R. D. Bandaranaike of Ceylon (later Sri Lanka). Each tried to impose a single language on the citizens of their nation. In contrast, the leaders of independent India permitted different languages and scripts to flourish, allowing people to be educated and governed in the language of their choice and their region. In Pakistan, the bid to impose Urdu on the Bengali-speakers of the east led to the secession of that part of the nation, which emerged in 1971 as the sovereign state of Bangladesh. In Sri Lanka, the suppression of Tamil and the promotion of Sinhala provoked a civil war that lasted thirty years and cost more than a hundred thousand lives. In India, on the other hand, the protection and promotion of different languages has deepened the sense of national unity.[8]

The Indian solution to linguistic diversity was innovated rather than theorised. E. V. Ramaswami and C. Rajagopalachari did write at some length about the dangers of a single national language. Gandhi spoke in favour of linguistic provinces on several occasions. However, the politicians and administrators who redrew the provincial map of India in the 1950s to create linguistic states did not write about it at all. Likewise, the decision not to impose Hindi on South India in the 1960s was taken in response to a massive popular movement opposing it, not as a consequence of words on the page.

Sixty years of Indian history have decisively refuted the European idea—or conceit—that a nation must be defined by a single language alone. Its experience in this regard is very relevant indeed. It has already had a salutary effect on South Africa, which after the demise of apartheid officially constituted itself as a multi-lingual nation-state. It may still promote a more sympathetic attitude to minority languages in nations whose laws and customs privilege one language alone.

Admittedly, there has in recent years been a belated recognition of the Indian experiment. As other ex-colonial nations have succumbed to military dictators or one-party rule, the fact that this poor, large, and diverse nation has a robust multi-party system based on free and fair

8. See Ramachandra Guha, *India after Gandhi: The History of the World's Largest Democracy* (New York: Ecco Press, 2007), chapter 9 and epilogue.

elections has come increasingly to the attention of the world. (The end of the Cold War has helped here, for while that conflict lasted, India's refusal to entirely side with the Western bloc was deemed more important than its democratic traditions.) While the freedom of expression and the freedom to choose one's leaders in India is now widely appreciated, how India survives as a single nation despite its staggering diversity is as yet imperfectly understood. For more than scholarly reasons, the institutional and ideational origins of Indian democracy and nationhood need more careful attention than they have perhaps received in the past.

To be sure, the learnings must be reciprocal. In the past, the Indian political tradition innovatively adapted Western ideals and values. Rammohun Roy read, with interest and profit, the works of Rousseau and Bentham. Gokhale was a liberal in the best British tradition—he even rendered into Marathi a book on compromise by John Morley, the follower and biographer of Gladstone. Tagore travelled across Asia and Latin America as well as Europe and America. In these travels he spoke, but he also listened and learnt. Gandhi was deeply influenced by Western thinkers such as Tolstoy and Ruskin. Ambedkar was influenced by the pragmatism of John Dewey, who was one of his teachers at Columbia University. Nehru, Kamaladevi, Narayan, and Lohia were all influenced (albeit in different ways) by European socialism.

In the present, too, India has much to learn from the world. Despite its absolutism, the Chinese state has been far more focused on creating equality of opportunity through the provision of decent education and health care. Western political parties, unlike their Indian counterparts, are not run as family firms. Also in the West, public institutions such as government bureaucracy and the judiciary function with greater efficiency and honesty.

In a book on the democratic traditions of his country, Ronald Dworkin remarks that 'Americans of goodwill, intelligence, and ambition have given the world, over the last two centuries, much of what is best in it now'. He continues:

> We gave the world the idea of a constitution protecting the right of minorities, including religious dissenters and atheists,

a constitution that has been the envy of other nations and is now increasingly, at least indirectly, an inspiration for them. We gave the world a lesson in national generosity after the Second World War, and we gave it leadership then in its new enthusiasm for international organization and international law. We gave it the idea, striking in mid-twentieth century Europe, that social justice is not the preserve of socialism; we gave it the idea of an egalitarian capitalism and, in the New Deal, a serious if limited step towards their achievement.[9]

The United States has given the world some noble social and political ideals. So have France, the United Kingdom, and perhaps also India. In Dworkin-esque mode I could thus write that 'India can give the world the idea of a state and constitution that protects far greater religious *and* linguistic diversity than is found in any other nation. We have shown other young nations how to nurture multi-party democracy based on universal adult franchise, mass poverty and illiteracy notwithstanding. But even older nations may learn from our model of nationalism, which is inclusive within and outside its borders, and open to ideas and influences from even the powers that once colonised it. We have demonstrated that nationalism can be made consistent with internationalism; without ever having waged war on another nation, we have contributed to peace-keeping efforts in other countries and continents and lent moral and material support to such causes as the anti-apartheid movement in South Africa. Finally, despite our own past history of hierarchy and inegalitarianism, we have designed and implemented the most far-reaching programmes of affirmative action on behalf of the discriminated and underprivileged'.

I V

To make the Indian experience more central to global debates is one aim of this book. Another, and perhaps greater, aim is to make Indians

9. Ronald Dworkin, *Is Democracy Possible Here? Principles for a New Political Debate* (Princeton, N.J.: Princeton University Press, 2006), pp. 163–164.

more aware of the richness and relevance of their modern political tradition. Unfortunately, the works presented in these pages remain far less known than we might suppose. One reason is the bias within the literature towards economic, political, and social history. Thus many scholars, Indian as well as foreign, have written insightfully and at great length about the impact of colonial rule on the indigenous economy; about the various competing strands of Indian nationalism and how they jockeyed for position during the last phase of British rule; and about the culture and social life of peasants, tribals, women, and other subaltern groups.

Within the vast and still proliferating literature, however, the history of ideas remains a poorly tilled field.[10] Thus, with the exception of Gandhi—whose ideas have indeed been carefully and systematically studied by scholars—there are few serious books on the thought (as opposed to life) of the individuals featured in this book.[11] Astonishingly, this is true even of some hugely influential individuals such as Tagore, Nehru, and Ambedkar. We have studies of their lives, their political careers, and—in Tagore's case—of their creative writings, yet no scholar has written about their political or social ideas with any rigour or depth.

A second impediment to a deeper understanding of the Indian political tradition is sectarianism and partisanship. Rabindranath Tagore, for example, is treated as a Bengali poet; B. R. Ambedkar as a Dalit icon alone; Jawaharlal Nehru as the property of the Congress party. This capturing of individuals by the sect to which they originally belonged has obscured their wider relevance to intellectual and political life in India as a whole. The appropriation is at once defensive and aggressive,

10. As illustrated by the text and bibliography of an excellent survey of the historiography of modern India, Sekhar Bandopadhyay's *From Plassey to Politics* (Hyderabad: Orient Longman, 2004). The few books that do exist are written by political scientists rather than historians; they are in the nature of general surveys rather than works based on primary research. See, for example, A. Appadorai, *Indian Political Thinking in the Twentieth Century from Naoroji to Nehru* (Bombay: Oxford University Press, 1972); K. P. Karunakaran, *Indian Politics from Dadabhai Naoroji to Gandhi: A Study of the Political Ideas of Modern India* (New Delhi: Gitanjali Prakashan, 1975); and, most recently, V. R. Mehta and Thomas Pantham, editors, *Political Ideas in Modern India: Thematic Explorations* (New Delhi: Sage, 2006).

11. The relevant works are cited in the 'Guide to Further Reading' that follows.

seeking to claim individuals exclusively for a particular sect while proclaiming their superiority over individuals privileged by another sect.

This (to my mind) lamentable tendency is manifest most obviously in the sharp opposition of Ambedkar to Gandhi by their latter-day admirers. They ask that we follow one man completely while rejecting the other man in toto. To a lesser degree, this competitive partisanship vitiates the understanding and appreciation of other remarkable Indians as well. Thus, in current debates on the economy, free-market advocates uphold Rajagopalachari and villify Nehru, whereas those in favour of more state intervention tend to do exactly the reverse. These rhetorical invocations are often based on a casual and superficial understanding of the thinkers themselves. They make it hard, if not impossible, for anyone to follow a catholic approach—to study and appreciate *both* Gandhi and Ambedkar, or *both* Nehru and Rajagopalachari, on the basis that these legacies may be equally relevant or significant, albeit in different and arguably complementary ways.

The third reason why even well-educated Indians remain unacquainted with these thinkers is the widespread nostalgia for the very distant past. There is one kind of Indian who thinks that it was when the Hindu scriptures were composed that his civilisation was the most advanced in the world. This orients him towards the study of the sages and rulers of ancient times, in the belief that it may help the Hindus once more rule, or at least dominate, the world. If one believes more deeply in Hindu ideals, if one more vigorously affirms one's love for the deities of the Hindu pantheon, the argument runs, then one is certain to (once more) conquer the world.[12]

---

12. M. S. Golwalkar thus asks each Hindu to remind himself that 'for generations, my great forefathers have striven to make this the greatest and noblest nation—an ideal nation of ideal men—on the face of this earth.' He further asks them to take 'pride in our glorious national past, in our unique cultural heritage and aspiration to see our Bharat Mata reseated in her pristine glory and honour in the comity of nations, . . .' and to 'pray to the Almighty . . . [to] guide our leaders in this dark hour and inspire them with the right understanding and instil in them courage to tread along the right path for a glorious revival of our Great People'. M. S. Golwalkar, *Bunch of Thoughts* (Bangalore: Vikrama Prakashan, 1966), pp. 290, 325, 437.

Liberal and secular Indians who are uncomfortable with this kind of Hindu irredentism instead seek inspiration in ancient rulers and institutions that owed nothing to the Hindu faith. They thus claim that the Buddhist councils of the Mauryan period were the prototype of modern electoral democracy and that the syncretism of the Mughal Emperor Akbar was the basis of Indian secularism.[13]

The fantasies of the Hindu supremacists are not appealing. At the same time, the argument that modern ideas of democracy and secularism have ancient origins is hard to sustain. The Indian electoral system is clearly based on the Westminster model. Further, as the sociologist Imtiaz Ahmad has pointed out, 'the evidence of history does not support the view that secularism as embodied in the Indian Constitution is derived from ancient Indian traditions, or that there is a pre-existing place for secularism in the Indian system of values'. He notes that under Hindu kings, the 'system of justice in ancient India was founded on the principle of inequality' and that 'the religious policies of the Muslim rulers were characterised by bigotry and fanaticism'. Ahmad then significantly adds: 'Akbar no doubt gave official encouragement to the spirit of religious tolerance, but the institutional separation of religion and state was probably as foreign to his political theory as it was to those of the ancient Hindu kings. In essence, therefore, the ideal of secularism as embodied in the Indian Constitution . . . *constitutes a radical break with India's past traditions'.*[14]

In my opinion, there was little in the history and politics of the sixth or sixteenth century (not to speak of times even more remote) that could have aided Indians in interpreting and confronting the profound changes that came in the wake of colonial rule. The necessity of a free press, the equality of women, the abolition of Untouchability, the rights of equal citizenship, the ending of mass poverty—these ideals and aspirations were beyond the experience and imagination of ancient or medieval scholars and rulers. Rather, they were the product of the national

---

13. Cf. Amartya Sen, *The Argumentative Indian: Reflections on Indian History, Culture and Identity* (London: Allen Lane, 2005).

14. Imtiaz Ahmad, 'Secularism and Communalism', *Economic and Political Weekly,* Special Number, July 1969, p. 1139; emphasis added.

and democratic revolutions that took place in the nineteenth and twentieth centuries, and of the urban, industrial, and social revolutions that accompanied them.

What I termed (in the Prologue) the 'distant' tradition of argument in India remains of interest largely to scholars, whereas the 'proximate' tradition should be of interest to ordinary citizens as well. For the five revolutions that I have spoken of are ongoing and unfinished. As the economy industrialises, it produces tensions between urban producers and consumers on the one hand and farmers and rural artisans on the other. Despite sixty years of electoral democracy, the political culture of India is to a great extent marked by sycophancy and deference. Despite formal gender equality and the legal abolition of Untouchability, women continue to be oppressed and the lower castes discriminated against. Despite the official commitment to secularism, riots between Hindus and Muslims break out at periodic intervals.

As I write, the national unity of India is being challenged by secessionist movements in Kashmir and the north-east. The borderlands are disturbed; and so too are the countries in our neighbourhood. The plural, multi-party political system of India is being challenged by the rise of a Maoist insurgency that extends over a wide swathe of the country. This insurgency, which aims to construct a single-party state on the Chinese model, has its roots in the deprivation and dispossession of tribal people. The workings of Indian democracy are also undermined by the growing inefficiency and corruption of the political class, the civil service, the police, and the judiciary.

To understand these (and other) problems, we may turn to those Indians who have seriously thought through these issues in the (comparatively recent) past. Thus, of the nineteen thinkers represented in this book, perhaps sixteen speak directly to the concerns of the present.[15] Thus, for example, one might turn to Ambedkar, Lohia, Phule, Gokhale,

---

15. The three I leave out are Tilak, Jinnah, and Golwalkar—for different reasons. Tilak's radical nationalist politics lost its relevance with the achievement of Indian independence; so too Jinnah's Muslim separatism with the creation of Pakistan. As for Golwalkar, the subsequent career of Pakistan itself acts as a warning to those who might wish to merge Faith with State. A Hindu Rashtra would both be inimical to democracy and lead to even more strife between religions.

and Gandhi to continue the struggle against caste discrimination; to Syed Ahmad Khan and Hamid Dalwai to modernise Indian Islam; to Tarabai, Kamaladevi, Rammohan Roy, Nehru, and E. V. Ramaswami to further the emancipation of women; to Gokhale, Gandhi, and Nehru to sustain good relations between Hindus and India's religious minorities; to Jayaprakash Narayan to promote understanding and goodwill between the Indian State and its still disturbed borderlands; to Phule to bring dignity and a secure livelihood to the farmer; to Gandhi and Narayan to promote the decentralisation of political authority; to Verrier Elwin to protect the tribals from discrimination; to Rajagopalachari to reform the electoral system and to curb the excesses of a potentially overbearing State; to Tagore to cultivate a productive and open-minded engagement with the other nations of the world.[16] In this sense, the 'makers' of the book's title is appropriate in more than the past tense. These Indians undoubtedly made India the nation it now is, but their legacies may yet help make India a nation that more fully lives up to its (so far imperfectly realised) ideals.

H. L. Mencken once wrote that 'politics, as hopeful men practice it in the world, consists mainly of the delusion that a change in form is a change in substance'.[17] Here, as elsewhere, one admires the elegance of Mencken's prose without endorsing his cynicism of outlook. The makers of modern India did not think that their life's work was all show and rhetoric. Nor were they necessarily self-deluding in believing that they could contribute, in some measure, to the diminution of human suffering, the promotion of religious pluralism, a respect for the rights of the individual citizen. To be sure, India remains a less than united nation, a less than perfect democracy, a less than equal economy, and a less than peaceful society. For those of us who might wish to close the gap between the ideal and the reality, the materials in this book may not be the worst place to start.

16. This list, of course, is merely illustrative. Readers will, I trust, find other things that appeal to them in the work and legacy of these sixteen men and women.

17. 'On Government', in H. L. Mencken, *Prejudices: A Selection,* ed. James T. Farrell (New York: Vintage Books, 1956), p. 182.

GUIDE TO FURTHER READING

In what follows I have, where necessary and relevant, cited books recently published and quite easily available. That said, this guide is biased towards older works, for the reason that political history and biography have for some time now been out of fashion within the academy. For those who do not have access to a decent library, I should note that the out-of-print books that I recommend below are available—albeit in limited numbers—from online stores such as Amazon (www.amazon.com) and Abe Books (www.abebooks.com).

PART ONE

For overviews of British rule in India, see Penderel Moon, *The British Conquest and Dominion of India* (London: George Duckworth, 1989), which is especially strong on military and administrative matters; Tirthankar Roy, *The Economic History of India, 1857–1947*, 2nd ed. (New Delhi: Oxford University Press, 2006), a cool, judicious treatment of a complex and controversial subject; C. A. Bayly, *Indian Society and the Making of the British Empire* (Cambridge: Cambridge University Press, 1988); and John F. Riddick, *The History of British India: A Chronology* (Westport, Conn.: Praeger Publishers, 2006). On the British impact on Bengal in particular, see P. J. Marshall, *East Indian Fortunes: The British in Bengal in the Eighteenth Century* (Oxford: Clarendon Press, 1976);

Marshall, *Bengal: The British Bridgehead, Eastern India, 1740–1828* (Cambridge: Cambridge University Press, 1987); A. F. Salahuddin Ahmed, *Social Ideas and Social Change in Bengal, 1818–1835* (Leiden: E. J. Brill, 1965); and B. S. Kesavan, *History of Printing and Publishing in India: A Story of Cultural Re-awakening*, vol. 1: *South Indian Origins of Printing and Its Efflorescence in Bengal* (New Delhi: National Book Trust, 1985).

The most exhaustive biographical study of Rammohan Roy remains Sophia Dobson Collet, *The Life and Letters of Raja Rammohun Roy*, ed. Dilip Kumar Biswas and Prabhat Chandra Ganguli, 4th ed. (Calcutta: Sadharan Brahmo Samaj, 1988 [originally published in 1900]). A useful shorter work is Bruce Carlisle Robertson, *Raja Rammohan Roy: The Father of Modern India* (New Delhi: Oxford University Press, 1995). Robertson is also the editor of *The Essential Writings of Raja Rammohan Roy* (Delhi: Oxford University Press, 1999). Roy's political ideas are the subject of a recent essay by C. A. Bayly, 'Rammohan Roy and the Advent of Constitutional Liberalism in India, 1800–30', *Modern Intellectual History* 2, no. 1 (2007).

PART TWO

On the different trends in Indian politics between the founding of the Congress and the onset of World War I, see Sumit Sarkar, *Modern India, 1885–1947* (New Delhi: Macmillan, 1983); S. R. Mehrotra, *The Emergence of the Indian National Congress* (New Delhi: Vikas, 1971); Anil Seal, *The Emergence of Indian Nationalism* (Cambridge: Cambridge University Press, 1968); and Briton Martin Jr., *New India, 1885: British Official Policy and the Emergence of the Indian National Congress* (Berkeley: University of California Press, 1969). On the history of Maharashtra (home to four of the five individuals featured in this section of the book), see Ravinder Kumar, *Western India in the Nineteenth Century: A Study in the Social History of Maharashtra* (London: Routledge and Kegan Paul, 1968); D. D. Karve, ed. and trans., *The New Brahmans: Five Maharashtrian Families* (Berkeley: University of California Press, 1963); B. G. Gokhale, *The Fiery Quill: Nationalism and Literature in Maharashtra* (Mumbai: Popular Prakashan, 1998); and G. P. Deshpande, *The World of Ideas in Modern Marathi* (New Delhi: Tulika Books, 2009).

On Muslim politics and identity in the late nineteenth century, see M. Mujeeb, *The Indian Muslims* (London: George Allen and Unwin, 1967), and David Lelyveld, *Aligarh's First Generation: Muslim Solidarity in British India* (Princeton, N.J.: Princeton University Press, 1978).

Among the more valuable of the many older biographies of Syed Ahmad Khan are Altaf Husain Hali, *Hayat-i-Javed: A Biographical Account of Sir Sayyid*, trans. from the Urdu by K. H. Qadiri and David J. Matthews (Delhi: Idarah-i Adabiyat-i Delli, 1979), and G. F. I. Graham, *The Life and Work of Syed Ahmad Khan* (1885; reprint, Delhi: Idarah-i Adabiyat-i Delli, 1974). For a recent assessment of Khan's legacy, see Faisal Devji's essay 'Apologetic Modernity', *Modern Intellectual History* 2, no. 1 (2007). For a selection of Khan's own writings, see Shan Mohammad, ed., *Writings and Speeches of Syed Ahmad Khan* (Bombay: Nachiketa Publications, 1972).

Jotirao Phule is the subject of a model work of intellectual biography, Rosalind O'Hanlon's *Jotirao Phule and Low Caste Protest in Nineteenth-Century Western India* (Cambridge: Cambridge University Press, 1985). Some valuable information is contained in Dhananjay Keer, *Mahatma Jotirao Phooley: Father of Our Social Revolution* (Bombay: Popular Prakashan, 1964). In the 1960s and 1970s the Maharashtra Government issued several volumes of Phule's writings; these are now scarce, but for a more recent selection, which is carefully annotated as well as elegantly produced, see G. P. Deshpande, ed., *Selected Writings of Jotirao Phule* (New Delhi: LeftWord Books, 2002).

Gopal Krishna Gokhale is the subject of two excellent biographical studies: B. R. Nanda's *Gokhale: The Indian Moderates and the British Raj* (Princeton, N.J.: Princeton University Press, 1977), also available in an omnibus edition of the author's works published by Oxford University Press in 2004, and Govind Talwalkar's *Gopal Krishna Gokhale: His Life and Times* (New Delhi: Rupa and Co., 2006). To read Gokhale in the original, one should consult *Speeches of Gopal Krishna Gokhale*, 2nd ed. (Madras: G. A. Natesan, 1916), a thousand-page-plus volume that I own (and that has recently been republished in a four-volume edition by a Delhi publisher), or the equally substantial three-volume selection edited by D. G. Karve and D. V. Ambekar, *Speeches and Writings of Gopal Krishna Gokhale* (Bombay: Asia Publishing House, 1967).

Bal Gangadhar Tilak is a once famous but now neglected figure. Perhaps the most serviceable of the older biographies is D. V. Tahmankar, *Lokmanya Tilak: Father of Indian Unrest and Maker of Modern India* (London: John Murray, 1956). Also useful is Stanley Wolpert's *Tilak and Gokhale: Revolution and Reform in the Making of Modern India* (1961; reprint, New Delhi: Oxford University Press, 1989). For this book I have used *Bal Gangadhar Tilak: His Writings and Speeches* (Madras: Ganesh and Co., 1918), a few copies of which seem to be available from Abe Books.

For Tarabai Shinde, see Rosalind O'Hanlon, ed. and trans., *A Comparison between Women and Men: Tarabai Shinde and the Critique of Gender Relations in Colonial India* (New Delhi: Oxford University Press, 1994), which prints the translated text of Shinde's sole book, prefaced by a biographical introduction. For perspectives on the status of women in modern Maharashtra, see Meera Kosambi, *Crossing Thresholds: Feminist Essays in Social History* (Ranikhet: Permanent Black, 2007); for a broader sampling of feminist or proto-feminist literature, see Susie Tharu and K. Lalita, eds., *Women Writing in India*, 2 vols. (New Delhi: Oxford University Press, 1993).

PART THREE

For overviews of the politics of the inter-war period, see D. A. Low, *Britain and Indian Nationalism: The Imprint of Ambiguity, 1929–1942* (Cambridge: Cambridge University Press, 2002), and Sumit Sarkar, *Modern India* (cited above). Useful studies of the Congress in its regional dimensions include D. A. Low, ed., *Congress and the Raj: Facets of the Indian Struggle, 1917–47*, 2nd ed. (New Delhi: Oxford University Press, 2006); Gyanendra Pandey, *The Ascendancy of the Congress in Uttar Pradesh* (1978; reprint, London: Anthem Press, 2002); and David Hardiman, *Peasant Nationalists of Gujarat* (New Delhi: Oxford University Press, 1981). Gandhi's transformative impact on the Congress is the subject of an old but still valuable essay by Gopal Krishna, 'The Development of the Indian National Congress as a Mass Organization, 1918–1923', *Journal of Asian Studies* 25, no. 3 (1966), and of a superb and enduring collection edited by Ravinder Kumar, *Essays on Gandhian Politics*

(Oxford: Clarendon Press, 1969). On Muslim political trends in the 1930s and 1940s, see David Page, *Prelude to Partition: The Indian Muslims and the Imperial System of Control* (New Delhi: Oxford University Press, 1982), and Wilfred Cantwell Smith, *Modern Islam in India* (1946; reprint, Delhi: Usha Publications, 1985). On left-wing trends, see Gene D. Overstreet and Marshall Windmiller, *Communism in India* (Berkeley: University of California Press, 1959).

For the economic context of interwar politics, see Basudev Chatterji, *Trade, Tariffs and Empire* (New Delhi: Oxford University Press, 1990). For the social impact of colonialism, see M. N. Srinivas's *Social Change in Modern India* (Berkeley: University of California Press, 1973). Geraldine Forbes's *Women in Modern India* (Cambridge: Cambridge University Press, 1995) is an informative survey of an important but still too often neglected subject. The critical role played by the press in the development of Gandhian nationalism is dealt with in Milton Israel, *Communication and Power: Propaganda and the Press in the Indian Nationalist Struggle, 1921–1947* (Cambridge: Cambridge University Press, 1994).

On Gandhi, the most accessible and readable single one-volume life remains Louis Fischer, *The Life of Mahatma Gandhi*, first published by Harper & Row in New York in 1950 and continuously in print ever since. For the more dogged and devoted admirer, there is D. G. Tendulkar's eight-volume *Mahatma: Life of Mohandas Karamchand Gandhi*, 2nd ed. (1963; reprint, New Delhi: Publications Divisions, 1990). Among the very many thematic studies of Gandhi's ideas, I would especially recommend David Hardiman, *Gandhi: In His Time and Ours* (New York: Columbia University Press, 2004); Denis Dalton, *Mahatma Gandhi: Non-Violent Power in Action* (New York, Columbia University Press, 1996); J. T. F. Jordens, *Gandhi's Religion: A Home-Spun Shawl* (New York: St. Martin's Press, 1998); Bhikhu C. Parekh, *Colonialism, Tradition and Reform: An Analysis of Gandhi's Political Discourse* (New Delhi: Sage Publications, 1989); and Rajmohan Gandhi, *The Good Boatman: A Portrait of Gandhi* (New Delhi: Penguin India, 1995). To read Gandhi in the original, those with more time and greater interest would want to consult the print or web editions of the *Collected Works*; for those seeking a sensible shortcut, I would recommend, among the existing anthologies, either Raghavan Iyer, ed., *The Moral and Political Writings of Mahatma Gandhi*, 3 vols. (Oxford: Clarendon Press, 1987), or Gopalkrishna Gandhi, ed., *The Oxford India Gandhi: Essential Writings* (New Delhi: Oxford University Press, 2008). For those interested in specific themes, Gandhi's own publishers, Navajivan Press, have from time to time issued volumes of his writings and sayings on such topics as caste, women, non-violence, and communal harmony. These can be obtained at Gandhian bookstalls across India.

On Rabindranath Tagore, see the readable and well-researched life by Krishna Dutta and Andrew Robinson, *Rabindranath Tagore: The Myriad-Minded Man* (New York: St. Martin's Press, 1996). A representative selection of his writing is contained in Sisir Kumar Das, *The English Writings of Rabindranath Tagore*, 3 vols. (New Delhi: Sahitya Akademi, 1996). On Tagore's relationship with Gandhi, see Sabyasachi Bhattacharya, ed., *The Mahatma and the Poet: Letters and Debates between Gandhi and Tagore* (New Delhi: National Book Trust, 1997). Finally, Tagore's seminal tract, *Nationalism*, was republished in 2009 as a Penguin Modern Classic with an introduction by the present writer.

B. R. Ambedkar has been the subject of a number of reverential studies in English in recent years. However, none can match, for sheer mass of detail, the older biography by Dhananjay Keer, *Dr Ambedkar: His Life and Mission*, 3rd ed. (Bombay: Popular Prakashan, 1971, reprinted several times since). Valuable analytical studies of his thought and legacy include Eleanor Zelliot, *From Untouchable to Dalit: Essays on the Ambedkar Movement* (New Delhi: Manohar, 2001); and D. R. Nagaraj, *The Flaming Feet: A Study of the Dalit Movement in India and Other Essays*, ed. Prithvi Datta Chandra Shobhi (Ranikhet: Permanent Black, 2010). Ambedkar's collected writings were published in a now scarce multi-volume edition brought out by the Government of Maharashtra. A handy one-volume selection is available in Valerian Rodrigues, ed., *The Essential Writings of B. R. Ambedkar* (New Delhi: Oxford University Press, 2002).

The two best studies of Mohammad Ali Jinnah, albeit from contrasting perspectives, are Stanley Wolpert, *Jinnah of Pakistan* (Delhi: Oxford University Press, 1985); and Ayesha Jalal, *The Sole Spokesman: Jinnah, the Muslim League and the Demand for Pakistan* (Cambridge:

Cambridge University Press, 1985). For this book I have used an edition of Jinnah's speeches from the 1940s; a more recent effort in this direction is S. S. Pirzada, ed., *The Collected Works of Qaid-e-Azam Mohammad Ali Jinnah*, 3 vols. (Karachi: East and West Publishing Company, 1996).

There is no proper biography of E. V. Ramaswami in English. However, his ideology and legacy have been treated in, among other works, Marguerite Ross Barnett, *The Politics of Cultural Nationalism in South India* (Princeton, N.J.: Princeton University Press, 1976); Narendra Subramanian, *Ethnicity and Popular Mobilization: Political Parties, Citizens and Democracy in South India* (New Delhi: Oxford University Press, 1999); and V. Geetha and S. V. Rajadurai, *Towards a Non-Brahmin Millennium: From Iyothee Thass to Periyar* (Calcutta: Samya, 1998). A selection of his writings and speeches in translation is contained in K. Veeramani, ed., *Collected Works of Periyar E. V. R.* (Chennai: The Periyar Self-Respect Propaganda Institution, 2007).

Despite her being arguably the most remarkable Indian woman of the twentieth century (as well as the most influential apart from Indira Gandhi), the literature on Kamaladevi Chattopadhyay's life and career is surprisingly scarce. She seems to have kept no letters or papers, which is why her biographers rely so largely on anecdotes and interview material. But worth consulting nonetheless are Reena Nanda, *Kamaladevi Chattopadhyaya: A Biography* (New Delhi: Oxford University Press, 2002); and Sakuntala Narasimhan, *Kamaladevi Chattopadhyaya: The Romantic Rebel* (New Delhi: Sterling Publishers, 1999). Kamaladevi's own memoirs, written or dictated towards the end of her life and hence somewhat fragmentary, are entitled *Inner Recesses, Outer Spaces* (New Delhi: Navrang Publishers, 1986). Her late assessment of the position of women is contained in *Indian Women's Battle for Freedom* (New Delhi: Abhinav Publications, 1983).

PART FOUR

For a political and social history of India since Independence, see Ramachandra Guha, *India after Gandhi: The History of the World's Largest Democracy* (London: Macmillan, 2007). The major political trends are also analysed in the contributions to Niraja Gopal Jayal and Pratap

Bhanu Mehta, eds., *The Oxford Companion to Indian Politics* (New Delhi: Oxford University Press, 2010), and in two important books by André Béteille, *Society and Politics in India* (London: Athlone Press, 1987) and *Chronicles of our Times* (New Delhi: Penguin India, 2000). The changing dimensions of the caste system are best followed through the work over five decades of India's pre-eminent sociologist, M. N. Srinivas. See especially the essays reproduced in A. M. Shah, ed., *The Oxford India Srinivas* (New Delhi: Oxford University Press, 2009). Granville Austin has written outstanding studies of the making and working of the Indian Constitution, respectively: *The Indian Constitution: Cornerstone of a Nation* (Oxford: Oxford University Press, 1966) and *Working a Democratic Constitution: The Indian Experience* (New Delhi: Oxford University Press, 1999). Debates on economic policy are discussed in A. H. Hanson, *The Process of Planning: A Study of India's Five-Year Plans, 1950–1964* (London: Oxford University Press, 1966), and in Francine Frankel, *India's Political Economy: The Gradual Revolution,* 2nd ed. (New Delhi: Oxford University Press, 2004). On secularism and religious identity, see, for the period just after Independence, D. E. Smith, *India as a Secular State* (Princeton, N.J.: Princeton University Press, 1963) and, for later decades and debates, Rajeev Bhargava, ed., *Secularism and Its Critics* (New Delhi: Oxford University Press, 1999). For insights into the predicament of India's largest minority, consult A. G. Noorani, ed., *The Muslims of India: A Documentary Record* (New Delhi: Oxford University Press, 2003).

For the serious student of the life and legacy of Jawaharlal Nehru, the three-volume biography by Sarvepalli Gopal, published by Oxford University Press between 1975 and 1984, is indispensable. Michael Brecher's *Jawaharlal Nehru: A Political Biography* (London: Oxford University Press, 1958) remains valuable. An excellent shorter study is Walter Crocker, *Nehru: A Contemporary's Estimate,* 2nd ed. (New Delhi: Random House India, 2009). Nehru also looms large in Sunil Khilnani, *The Idea of India* (New Delhi: Penguin India, 1997), and in my own *India after Gandhi.* The three books Nehru himself wrote (all published before Indian Independence) are avaiable in Penguin Classics. Of these, the one most relevant to understanding his thought is *The Discovery of India,* written in prison and first published by The

Signet Press, Calcutta, in 1946. The serious student must go beyond these to his writings after Independence, especially the five volumes of his *Letters to Chief Ministers,* published by the Jawaharlal Nehru Memorial Fund between 1985 and 1989. A representative selection of his writings before and after Independence is contained in Sarvepalli Gopal and Uma Iyengar, eds., *The Essential Writings of Jawaharlal Nehru,* 2 vols. (New Delhi: Oxford University Press, 2002).

M. S. Golwalkar is best studied through his own words, especially his *Bunch of Thoughts* (Bangalore: Vikrama Prakashan, 1966). A fine short study of his ideas is Jyotirmaya Sharma, *Terrifying Vision: M. S. Golwalkar, the RSS and India* (New Delhi: Penguin India, 2007). For a broader analysis of the development of the Rashtriya Swayamsewak Sangh and its associated organizations, see Christophe Jaffrelot, *The Hindu Nationalist Movement and Indian Politics: 1925 to the 1990s,* 2nd ed. (New Delhi: Penguin India, 1999); B. D. Graham, *Hindu Nationalism and Indian Politics: The Origins and Development of the Bharatiya Jana Sangh* (Cambridge: Cambridge University Press, 1990); and Walter K. Andersen and Shridhar D. Damle, *The Brotherhood in Saffron: The Rashtriya Swayamsewak Sangh and Hindu Revivalism* (New Delhi: Vistaar Publications, 1987).

For Lohia, see Indumati Kelkar, *Dr. Rammanohar Lohia: His Life and Philosophy* (New Delhi: Anamika Publishers and Distributors, 2009), a reverential yet informative work. Also useful is Chitrita Chaudhuri's *Rammanohar Lohia and the Indian Socialist Thought* (Calcutta; Minerva Associates, 1993). Lohia's writings have been collected and published in thematic volumes by a group of his admirers based in Hyderabad (Rammanohar Lohia Samata Vidyalaya Nyas, 4 May 1946, Sultan Bazar, Hyderabad—500001). A one-volume selection, to be published by a more 'mainstream' press, is currently being prepared by Yogendra Yadav and Rajaram Tolpady.

Lohia's one-time comrade Jayaprakash Narayan is the subject of two biographical studies: Allan and Wendy Scarfe, *J. P.: His Biography* (New Delhi: Orient Longman, 1975), and Ajit Bhattacharjea, *Unfinished Revolution: A Political Biography of Jayaprakash Narayan* (New Delhi: Rupa and Co., 2004). Also worth consulting is Madhu Dandavate, *Jayaprakash Narayan: Struggle with Values* (New Delhi: Allied Publishers, 2002), an affectionate appreciation by a latter-day socialist politician. Narayan's writings have been brought out in seven volumes issued under the imprint of the Nehru Memorial Museum and Library and edited by Bimal Prasad. A handy one-volume selection is Jayaprakash Narayan, *Nation Building in India* (Varanasi: Navachetna Prakashan, 1975), edited by JP's long-time secretary Brahmanand.

C. Rajagopalachari is the subject of a thorough biography by Rajmohan Gandhi, *Rajaji: A Life* (New Delhi: Penguin India, 1997). An insightful recent study of his thought is Vasanti Srinivasan, *Gandhi's Conscience-Keeper: C. Rajagopalachari and Indian Politics* (Ranikhet: Permanent Black, 2009). The credo and career of the party he founded are treated in H. L. Erdman, *The Swatantra Party and Indian Conservatism* (Cambridge: Cambridge University Press, 1967). As for his own writings, those from the crucial decades of the 1950s and 1960s are contained in C. Rajagopalachari, *Satyam Eva Jayate: A Collection of Articles Contributed to* Swarajya *and Other Journals from 1956 to 1961,* 2 vols. (Madras: Bharathan Publications, 1961), and in *Dear Reader: Weekly Colloquy of C. Rajagopalachari with the Readers of* Swarajya, *1961–1972* (Coimbatore: Bharatiya Vidya Bhavan, 1993).

Verrier Elwin is the author of a charming autobiography called *The Tribal World of Verrier Elwin* (Bombay: Oxford University Press, 1964). Among his other books, I would recommend especially *The Baiga* (London: John Murray, 1939), and *A Philosophy for NEFA,* 2nd ed. (Shillong: Adviser to the Governor of Assam, 1959). Elwin's life and thought are the subject of Ramachandra Guha, *Savaging the Civilized; Verrier Elwin, His Tribals and India* (Chicago: University of Chicago Press, 1999). A selection of his writings is contained in G. N. Devy, ed., *The Oxford India Elwin* (New Delhi: Oxford University Press, 2009).

PART FIVE

The religious politics of the 1950s and 1960s are treated in Donald E. Smith, ed., *South Asian Politics and Religion* (Princeton, N.J.: Princeton University Press, 1966), and in Mushirul Hasan, *Legacy of a Divided Nation: India's Muslims since Independence* (New Delhi: Oxford University Press, 1997). Hamid Dalwai's political essays are reproduced in *Muslim Politics in India* (Bombay: Nachiketa Publications, 1968). This work has been edited and translated by Dilip Chitre, as has Dalwai's novella about small-town life in coastal Maharashtra, published in English under the title *Fuel* (New Delhi: National Book Trust, 2002).

ACKNOWLEDGEMENTS

I first broached the idea of this book to Ravi Singh of Penguin India in a Bangalore restaurant in the summer of 2008. Ravi gave the project his enthusiastic endorsement, as did Sharmila Sen of Harvard University Press when I sent her a proposal by e-mail a few months later. Between them, the quiet and understated Ravi and the sparkling Sharmila have sustained this book from start to finish.

Beyond these proximate debts lie some more distant ones. My interest in the Indian political tradition stems from two sources: time spent commenting in public on current affairs, and time spent more reclusively in the stacks and manuscript collections of the Nehru Memorial Museum and Library (NMML) in New Delhi. Despite Establishment apathy (and worse), the wonderfully gifted and committed staff of the NMML have helped and encouraged me for some three decades now—as they have many other scholars for lesser or longer periods of time. *The Makers of Modern India* is based in good measure on books and pamphlets read or first encountered in the NMML. I am also grateful to two individuals who have supplied me a steady stream of out-of-print materials—Vijay Kumar Jain of Prabhu Books, Gurgaon; and K. K. S. Murthy of the Select Bookshop, Bangalore.

In constructing this anthology and drafting its prologue and epilogue, I have had the benefit of the advice and support of Michael Adas, Rukun Advani, Rukmini Banerji, Millicent Bennett, Deepa Bhatnagar,

David Gilmour, Keshava Guha, Niraja Gopal Jayal, Sunil Khilnani, Enuga S. Reddy, and Nandini Sundar. These have been friends and counsellors. In another category, of mentors, fall the wisest man in India, André Béteille, and the Catalan polymath Joan Martinez-Alier. Professor Béteille has made me less deficient in my understanding of Indian society and politics; Professor Martinez-Alier made me more aware of political developments in other parts of the world.

I am thankful to Professors G. P. Deshpande and Rosalind O'Hanlon for permitting me to reproduce translations supervised or conducted by them (of Jotirao Phule and Tarabai Shinde, respectively); to Professor A. R. Venkatachalapathy for freshly translating some speeches by E. V. Ramaswami for this volume; and to Ravela Somayya for sending me some very scarce materials on and by Rammanohar Lohia. Veena Soans expertly rendered hundreds of pages of photocopied materials into soft copy fit to edit (and, in time, to print). Nandini Mehta sensitively edited the final manuscript; I am grateful to her for that and for her friendship and encouragement over the years.

My final debts are to my wife and children, without whose indulgence I would not have begun this book (or any other); and to my agent, Gill Coleridge, whose counsel has, as always, been critical.

INDEX